Bell

THE
GREAT
TRANSITION

A Short
History of
Twentieth-Century America

ALLYN AND BACON, INC.   BOSTON, MASSACHUSETTS

THE
GREAT
TRANSITION

GERALD D. NASH

The University of New Mexico

To My Parents

Library of Congress Catalog Card Number: 72-106237

12- 17-71

Printed in the United States of America

CONTENTS

PREFACE

The title of this volume is an index to the course of events which it seeks to describe and analyze. Between 1877 and 1970 the United States underwent one of the great transitions in its history. From 1877 to 1940 it evolved from an agrarian nation into an industrial society; and from 1941 to 1970 it changed from an industrial to a technological society. The road traveled by the American people on this journey was long and paved with obstacles. No wonder that their experience resulted in a gradual transformation of civilization in the United States. Whereas until 1890 Americans had been primarily a rural people, they became increasingly a nation of urban and suburban dwellers. Whereas they had once constituted a community of farmers, they became blue-collar or white-collar workers. Whereas they were once of relatively homogeneous ethnic, racial, and religious backgrounds, they became more heterogeneous, reflecting great ethnic, racial, religious, and cultural diversity. Whereas they had once been primarily a middle class society, they became increasingly conscious of the low income classes and the poor in their midst. And whereas they had once been occupied mainly with domestic problems, they revealed a growing concern with international relations. This book attempts to describe the course of these events and to provide an understanding of the forces that shaped America in the twentieth century.

This book is not designed to serve the same functions as a long and more elaborate treatise, for many volumes of this type are already available. Nor is this work intended to be a highly interpretive, selective account of life in the United States during the last ninety years. Other works can, and do, serve such a purpose. Rather, this book is designed as a general survey addressed to students and general readers and is intended to provide them with an introduction to a complicated subject.

ix

My primary aim has been to write a short, clear, and uncomplicated handbook that emphasizes major trends and is characterized by breadth, balance, and objectivity. Such a brief account should have at least two uses. First, because of its brevity, this book should allow instructors to introduce a larger number of paperback books, supplementary readings, or other assignments than would be possible with use of the much longer texts presently available. Second, by furnishing a general framework for twentieth-century United States history, this volume should permit its readers to concentrate in depth on such specific events or controversial issues as they may desire. Hopefully, my format will leave students and instructors more time to devote to special topics or interpretive problems.

An alternative use of this work is to provide a foundation for introductory courses that make only limited use of supplementary readings. It provides a relatively brief, but complete, survey intended to acquaint the reader with the major trends and figures responsible for shaping twentieth-century America. The organizational framework of individual chapters and their particular internal arrangement have been designed to facilitate comprehension and understanding for readers whose background in the field is relatively limited.

We study the past to understand the present and the future. So, I assume that you — the reader — might want to learn about the history of the United States in the twentieth century primarily to find out how it relates to you and your interests, and to secure guidance in developing judgments and attitudes concerning the great and small issues of your own day. And then, to be young is to dream about the future. Almost every young man or woman at some time or another wonders about his or her own immediate future, about that of family, friends, and nation, and, indeed, about the state of the world. An understanding of the American experience since 1890 cannot assure certainty for such musings, but it can provide guideposts to the resolution of many questions. To know ourselves in the future we must know what we have been in the past.

It remains for me only to express my thanks to countless colleagues who have given me counsel, criticism, and advice, and especially to my students at Stanford University, Northern Illinois University, New York University, the University of Maryland, and the University of New Mexico, who in a very real sense are responsible for the production of this work. Finally, I would like to thank my wife, who was of inestimable aid in various stages of my work and who typed portions of the manuscript.

I
THE INDUSTRIAL SOCIETY
1877-1940

1

THE NEW AMERICA

Prelude to the Twentieth Century

Around 1877 the tempo of change in the United States increased. Most Americans felt more and more that the old agrarian order they had known was rapidly disappearing and that a new industrial state was unfolding before their eyes. This new society appeared to have at least five characteristics that distinguished it from the agrarian order of the earlier nineteenth century: (1) the development of an industrial complex in the United States; (2) increasing dependence on technological change for economic growth; (3) a greater degree of heterogeneity in the social structure than previously existed; (4) an inevitable response of political institutions to increasing economic pressure; and (5) extensive changes in the fabric of cultural life. Economic change, then, was not a restricted phenomenon, but profoundly altered most aspects of civilization in the United States. In one way or another, the new America revealed the outstanding characteristics of an industrial society.

ECONOMIC CHANGES

Few aspects of the nation's activities were left untouched by the profound economic changes of this period. From 1860 to 1890, the previously agrarian economy of the United States was transformed into an industrial complex, and the pace of this change seemed to increase constantly. The average American was delighted with the new improvements in transportation such

3

as railroads, but these were usually owned and operated not by local individual entrepreneurs but by big corporations. Instead of conducting his business affairs with a small enterpriser or a local shopkeeper, the average American dealt increasingly with a large, impersonal corporation operating on a national or even world-wide scale. When in need of capital, he once consulted his local banker; by 1890 he found himself more dependent on a few very powerful big-city bankers. The day of the prosperous, small, self-sufficient independent farmer seemed to be passing rapidly as large-scale commercial agriculture, producing cash crops for distant markets, became dominant in many regions. Where small farmers continued their struggle, they found themselves con-tinually more dependent on middlemen, wholesalers, brokers, and warehouse owners who introduced even greater uncertainty and insecurity into what was already a precarious occupation. Thus, within a single generation, the economy of the United States was transformed by the growth of Big Business, Big Fi-nance, Big Agriculture, and Big Labor.

BIG BUSINESS

Among the factors responsible for the growth of Big Business was the emergence of an intricate transportation and communi-cation system in the United States. Expansion of the railway net and the telegraph helps to explain the development of Big Busi-ness during these years. Another force was the expanding popu-lation, which provided not only the labor force necessary for the creation of new industries, but also great new domestic markets, especially in fast-growing urban centers. The availability of capi-tal was also important. Since the average rate of saving in the United States increased by about 5 per cent yearly between 1860 and 1890, economists have estimated that the amount of national saving between 1880 and 1900 totaled approximately $36 bil-lion. A significant portion of this sum became available for investment in new enterprises.[1] Some of these could not have grown without the presence of abundant raw materials in the Western Hemisphere — especially coal and iron, land, and a variety of metals such as lead and copper. Nor can the efforts of

[1]Raymond W. Goldsmith, *A Study of Saving in the United States* (Princeton: Princeton University Press, 1955), Vol. I, pp. 4 – 5.

bold businessmen and entrepreneurs be ignored. Whatever their weaknesses, men like Andrew Carnegie, Philip Armour, and John D. Rockefeller contributed the special skills needed for the creation of great new business complexes. They gathered the capital to establish these ventures on a hitherto unprecedented scale; they devised new forms of organization for management and new methods of production; and they created new organizations and techniques for the distribution of their products. Finally, the rise of Big Business was encouraged by the benevolent attitudes of state and federal governments. Through noninterference, as well as through subsidies, loans, land grants, tariffs, and monetary and tax policies, they did much to hasten the growth of manufacturing.

A combination of these forces transformed the United States from an agricultural nation to an industrial nation. In the value of manufactures in 1859 the United States stood fourth in world rankings, with approximately $1.885 billion. By 1900 it stood first as the world's leader with approximately $13 billion.[2] This expansion was also reflected in the country's rate of economic growth. Between 1880 and 1890 this was about 2.9 per cent annually, but in the ensuing decade it increased to 4.6 per cent. A new economy was on the horizon.

The emergence of Big Business was spearheaded by four major industries — food processing and manufacturing, textiles, iron and steel, and lumbering — all related to the processing of raw materials. As women in the cities went to work in increasing numbers, their needs for prepared foods multiplied. Canned meats, fruits, and vegetables, prepared breakfast foods, and ready-made bread now found large markets. Thus, the expansion of the food-processing industry was phenomenal. Textile products included woven cotton cloth for hosiery, rugs, shirts, and dresses. The steel industry, accorded third rank in manufacturing, was just beginning to be one of the nation's basic industries in 1890. It multiplied the value of its output from $128 million in 1870 to more than $1 billion thirty years later. Toward the close of the century, United States steel mills were producing more than 32 million tons of steel annually, primarily for finished products such as rails, engines, steel pipes, tools and

[2] *Twelfth Census of the United States Taken in the Year 1900, Manufactures* (Washington: United States Census Office, 1902), Part I, p. xlvii.

hardware, and machinery.[3] As new skyscrapers were being built in congested cities, steel became an important structural material. A fourth important industry was lumbering, which doubled its output between 1870 and 1890 to meet pressing demands by builders seeking to satisfy the housing needs of the expanding population. These four industries produced more than one-half of the manufacturing income of the United States in 1890 and employed about 55 per cent of the 5 million workers engaged in manufacturing.

DEVELOPMENT OF FINANCE

Such rapid industrialization was possible only because of the concurrent development of Big Finance. The rise of investment banking houses, securities markets and stock exchanges, and new banks marked this trend. Investment bankers were middlemen who brought investors and businessmen together. Gradually these men assumed a crucial role in promoting the organization of all kinds of enterprises. J. P. Morgan was one of the most successful of this new breed, reorganizing the New York Central Railroad and many other carriers, as well as the United States Steel Corporation. Through these activities, and as director of many of the companies for whom he provided funds, he secured an enormous influence in the world of finance and business. At the same time, the New York Stock Exchange and smaller trading exchanges in other cities responded to the demand for capital by channeling investments into new or expanding corporations. Finally, the increase in the number and size of banks aided in supplying industry with necessary capital. Contrary to popular belief, the business expansion of the period was not directly related to the amount of currency in circulation but to the increasing volume of deposits and the enormous increase of money transactions through the use of checks. Banks facilitated such a flow of money. State-chartered banks grew most rapidly, increasing from a few in 1860 to a total of 4659 in 1900. Federally chartered banks, incorporated under the National Banking Act of 1864, also grew until in 1900 there were more than 3700. But the con-

[3]See statistics in *A Compendium of the Ninth Census (June 1, 1870)* (Washington: U. S. Government Printing Office, 1872), p. 908, and *Twelfth Census, Manufactures,* Part I, p. 9.

centration of banking resources was perhaps the most significant trend of the period. Some of the largest financial institutions in the country, such as the First National Bank of New York, the National City Bank of New York (controlled by Rockefeller interests), and the National Bank of Commerce (controlled by J. P. Morgan), came to control a substantial portion of available credit funds in the United States. In the industrial society that was emerging in the nation, the purveyors of capital were coming to play a crucial role.

AGRICULTURAL EXPANSION

Farmers, like businessmen, were also caught up in the economic transformation that was sweeping America. Revolutionary technological innovations, construction of the railroads, increasing population, and government land policies were all causes for the change. In 1860 many farmers strove for self-sufficiency; by 1890 commercial agriculture based on production of cash crops was becoming characteristic. Production for need was replaced by production for markets.

Agricultural expansion was prompted by various developments. These included many technological improvements such as James Oliver's chilled iron plow, improved reapers for harvesting grain, and mechanical twine binders that eliminated manual chores. The construction of the railroads placed farmers within reach of far-flung markets. And as the country's population expanded through natural increase and immigration in the later nineteenth century, the demand for food and food products likewise grew. Government policies also hastened agricultural expansion. The Department of Agriculture, created in 1862, encouraged increased production by introducing new techniques, by creating standards and inspection programs, and by disseminating information. At the same time, the Morrill Act of 1862 resulted in the founding of the land-grant colleges, which sought to train farmers in scientific methods. Their work was augmented by the Hatch Act of 1887, which provided for the creation of agricultural experiment stations, designed to cope with farm problems through scientific research. As a result of these factors, there was a great increase in total agricultural production as well as a significant rise in yield per acre. In 1870 the total value of

American farm products was $2.450 billion; in 1900 it had risen to $4.717 billion.[4] Productive efficiency increased four to five times during the same period.

American agriculture thus came to take on many of the characteristics of Big Business as farmers in various regions became specialists. After 1860 the middle western states became the heart of the great wheat and corn belt of the United States. The Great Plains witnessed the expansion of the cattle industry, while the South focused on cotton and tobacco. California was just beginning to be the great fruit and vegetable producer for the nation. In most sections of the country commercial agriculture on a large scale came to replace the self-sufficient family-size farm that had been characteristic of an earlier era.

ORGANIZATION OF LABOR

The concentration of economic power as reflected in the rise of Big Business, Big Finance, and Big Agriculture was revealed, too, in the growth of Big Labor. These years witnessed a growing trend towards the formation of national labor organizations in place of the local and regional groups more common earlier. The National Labor Union (1866–1872) was perhaps the first significant effort to unite labor on a national scale. Other attempts followed its demise. The American Federation of Labor (AFL) was founded by Samuel Gompers in 1881 to provide an effective national union for craft workers; within a decade it had almost 200,000 members. An even more ambitious attempt to unite all workers, skilled and unskilled, in one organization was made by Uriah S. Stephens in 1869, when he established the Knights of Labor. This union was really not important until the decade after 1880, when it counted as many as one million members. The day when the individual worker bargained with his boss was rapidly passing. Instead, labor representatives began to negotiate for thousands of wage earners. In an industrial society, centralization of the means of production also affected workers and led directly to the growth of Big Labor. It became an integral part of America's new industrial establishment.

[4]*Compendium of the Ninth Census,* pp. 692–93; *Twelfth Census of the United States, Agriculture,* Part I, p. cxxii.

TECHNOLOGICAL DEVELOPMENTS

Underlying these vast economic changes were striking innovations in technology. The last three decades of the nineteenth century witnessed a technological revolution throughout the western world in which the United States played a leading role. In Great Britain, France, and the United States, this period was one of dramatic improvements in manufacturing techniques, striking advances in the development of transportation and communication networks, and the creation of significant new concepts of management and organization. And the pace of change was rapidly increasing. Until 1860 the United States Commissioner of Patents had issued about 30,000 patents; between 1860 and 1890 he granted more than 440,000. Scarcely a single aspect of American life was left untouched by the impact of this technological revolution. Within the memory of a single generation, it transformed an agrarian America into a complex industrial giant.

EFFECTS ON MANUFACTURING

Among the most visible manifestations of the new technology, the growth of manufacturing industries was pre-eminent. By 1900, as noted, four new major industries were making the United States the world's leading industrial power — food processing, textile and clothing manufacture, iron and steel fabrication, and lumbering. The importance of electric power production was increasing. Each of these industries was stimulated by technological innovations.

Perhaps the most important new manufacturing methods were developed in response to problems encountered by food-processing companies. Dozens of inventors worked on the improvement of canning techniques, refrigeration, and packaging. Their work facilitated distribution of food products to the nation's burgeoning population.

Advances in food preservation after 1860 were truly remarkable. By the 1870's most aspects of the canning process were already performed by machines, and by 1890 it was virtually fully automated. Scores of technicians perfected the preparation of fruits and vegetables for canning. In 1875, for example, Volney Barkley improved a corn-cutting device so that the kernels could be cut from 3000 pounds of corn in only ten hours; by 1895 Warfield Sprague made improvements on the machine which speeded processing to such an extent that one machine cut enough corn to pack 15,000 cans in a single day. By 1885 one Scott and Chisholm pea sheller could remove peas from their pods as fast as 600 hand laborers. The invention of automatic peach and cherry pitters made it possible to distribute fruit to the larger cities during any season of the year at relatively reasonable prices. In almost every aspect of food processing, by 1890 the many operations required by canning processes had been coordinated in a continuous assembly-line system that often increased quality while lowering costs.

Refrigeration was another technological device that profoundly affected the food industries. In the 1870's various engineers pooled their skills to design "ice-boxes on wheels," the first refrigerator cars, which made it possible to ship perishable foods over long distances. This invention had an enormous impact on meat-packing, for it allowed the transportation of meat to distant — and not merely local — markets. As a result, Chicago and Kansas City became great packing centers where meat-packing processes were centralized. Within a decade the industry's great houses (Armour, Swift, Cudahy, Hormel) had mechanized most aspects of meat-packing and processing and developed assembly-line techniques. Indeed, it has been said that Henry Ford visited one of these plants at the turn of the century and was inspired to apply its methods to automobile manufacture.

In a similar manner, technological improvements revolutionized other industries. New machines transformed the textile industry and contributed to its development as Big Business. Most of the inventions in this field contributed to a great speedup of production. As in food manufacturing, manifold operations were increasingly centralized within a single plant. Improvements affected the carding of short fibers for woolens, spinning, weaving, and dyeing. Machines such as the completely automated Northrop loom and the Barber warp-tying device more than doubled the output of each worker, while improving the uniformity and quality of the final product. The weaving of carpets was automated by Erastus B. Bigelow of Boston, who adapted power looms to the manufacture of rugs. The manufacture of cloth into clothing was also revolutionized by technological inventions. After 1875 machines virtually created a ready-made clothing industry, which was rapidly centralized in New York City. Power-driven sewing machines, buttonhole cutters, and mechanical pressers increased by more than one hundred times the volume of clothing that could be produced. George Eastman's straight-knife cloth-cutting machine, for example, could cut 120 layers of material in a single operation.

Technological improvements also laid the groundwork for a major steel industry in the United States. In 1845 a Kentucky ironmaster, William Kelly, perfected an ingenious process for removing impurities from molten iron by oxidizing it with blasts of hot air. Then in 1854 Sir Henry Bessemer in England built a converter furnace that greatly improved the efficiency of the process. In the United States, use of the Bessemer process did not become common until after the Civil War, when Kelly perfected it further to produce steel at the Cambria Iron Works in Pennsylvania. By 1880 the open-hearth furnace made it possible to produce finer types of steel, and within a decade the electric arc process improved the quality and variety of resulting steels even more.

Technological inventions therefore provided a direct foundation for the rise of large-scale industry in the United States, particularly in food processing, textile manufacturing, and the production of steel. By substituting machine power for manpower, inventors and businessmen were able to speed up the volume of production, to coordinate hundreds of formerly separate manufacturing operations, to cut costs by promoting uniformity and standardization, and to improve quality. Since the manifold operations of manufacturing could often be centralized most conveniently under the aegis of a single company, technological devices unwittingly often promoted big business over small.

EFFECTS ON TRANSPORTATION

Technology also helped to revolutionize America's transportation network. In the forty years after the Civil War, the nation was bound together by a transcontinental railway system, by improved waterways, and by better roads. Railroad mileage expanded from about 37,000 miles in 1866 to about 200,000 miles in 1890. Not all waterways prospered, but great canals such as the Erie, Chesapeake, and Delaware continued to be integral links while Great Lakes traffic boomed. Road mileage more than doubled between 1860 and 1890, as new cities and towns were connected by main trunk or through-highways, characterized by vastly improved surfacing and paving to withstand heavy traffic, with feeders into the rural countryside. Five transcontinental railroads were completed during this era: the Union Pacific (1869), Henry Villard's Northern Pacific (1883), the Atchison, Topeka, and Santa Fe (1884), James J. Hill's Great Northern (1884), and the Big Four's Southern Pacific (1882). By 1890 many of the larger carriers were consolidating hundreds of smaller lines. Thus, in the course of the next two decades, the Pennsylvania Railroad came to control about 20,000 miles, almost as many as Vanderbilt's New York Central. So rapid were the mergers that in 1906, four major railroad systems included two-thirds of the rail mileage in the United States, and the seven largest systems collected more than 85 per cent of all rail revenues.

Meanwhile, the rapidly growing urban areas were being knit together by the extension of street railway and trolley lines. The application of electricity to carriages resulted in the first electric street railways by 1870, when New York City also completed its first elevated train lines. These provided rapid transportation within the congested inner city, and between the downtown areas and the suburbs. Thomas F. Ryan, Charles T. Yerkes, and William Elkins became the most important builders of these local railways in metropolitan areas from New York to San Francisco.

Many of the needs of national railroad expansion prompted inventors to make a great variety of technical improvements. After 1870 steel manufacturers perfected the quality of rails so that they could carry heavier railroad cars and locomotives. In fact, the more powerful engines and larger freight cars, as well as special box and tank cars, made it possible for the railroads to carry an increasingly larger volume of passengers and freight. By 1890 great ten-wheel locomotives were hauling long and heavy trains, sometimes with more than fifty cars, and with greater speed. Old Number 999, one of the prize locomotives of the New York Central Railroad, in 1894 achieved a speed of more than 112 miles per hour on a trial run between Syracuse and Buffalo. Understandably, faster trains led to a larger number of accidents and demands for greater safety features. George Westinghouse in 1869 invented the air brake, which enabled the engineer to control the simultaneous braking of all cars on his train. Six years later automatic block signals were installed on many main lines; and in 1886 Eli Jenny's automatic couplers came into use, greatly aiding in the reduction of accidents. The innovation of George Pullman, a former cabinetmaker whose comfortable sleeping car came into wide use after the Civil War, contributed to the increase in passenger travel.

COMMUNICATIONS

The great outburst of technological innovations profoundly affected the field of communications, which helped revolutionize life in America. The telegraph, the telephone, and the typewriter were only three inventions out of many that tied Americans from every region into what was becoming a national community. Federal aid helped spur the completion of the transcontinental telegraph in 1861, making it possible for New Yorkers to communicate with San Franciscans in a matter of minutes. By 1890 hundreds of intracity and local lines provided Americans with a relatively inexpensive and speedy system of communication. Although transatlantic cables between the United States and Europe were open by 1868, it was not until 1881 that Jay Gould built the first wholly American-owned line, forging closer links between the New World and the Old. The telegraph prompted demands for still faster and cheaper communication, especially in cities and suburban areas. Various inventors concerned themselves with this problem, but it was a Scotsman, Alexander Graham Bell, who in June 1876 was granted the first patent for a telephone. Within two years a group of investors headed by William H. Forbes, the son-in-law of Ralph Waldo Emerson, formed the National Bell Telephone Company, which rapidly embarked on the expansion of a national telephone network. By 1900 more than one million miles of telephone wire had been strung. Speedy communication was also furthered by the development of the typewriter. No one man was really responsible for its invention, for Samuel Morse had already experimented with Teletype systems, but credit for the first practical typewriter is usually given to a Milwaukee printer, C. Latham Sholes, who in 1867 built a device with a keyboard. Mark Twain was said to have been one of the first users of the typewriter. His manuscript recounting Tom Sawyer's adventures was perhaps the first typed book manuscript to be published. By 1890 many other individuals such as Franz X. Wagner (Underwood) and the Reverend Thomas Oliver had made significant improvements on the machine. Typewriters had an enormous social impact upon American society, since they opened up a new field of employment for women. By 1890 female secretaries were well on the way toward becoming a vital institution in most American business enterprises.

Meanwhile, another group of inventors produced a veritable information revolution for the emerging mass media by the perfection of photography. Among the most successful was George Eastman, a bank clerk in Rochester, New York. He patented the first commercial film in 1884, made on coated paper rather than on glass. A few years later he manufactured the Kodak camera, one of the first portable lightweight cameras suitable for mass production. Dissemination of pictures on a wide scale became common in the later nineteenth century as the Eastman-Kodak Company took the lead in making photography available for the masses.

The more rapid spread of ideas and information through newspapers was also spurred by new technological devices in the printing trades. Before 1890 William Bullock and others had improved the size, speed, and output of printing presses. On March 4, 1880, the *New York Daily Graphic* introduced a half-tone plate, which inaugurated an era of engraving. Soon many newspapers were using engravings in their daily editions. Meanwhile, Ottmar Mergenthaler developed an automatic typesetter, a Linotype machine, which was first used by Whitelaw Reid of the *New York Herald Tribune* in the July 3, 1886, edition. This invention greatly reduced the amount of time needed to produce a newspaper and, in effect, ushered in the age of the mass media.

IMPACT OF TECHNOLOGY: SUMMARY

Technology, therefore, was one of the key factors responsible for the transformation of the United States in the later nineteenth century. It led directly to the primacy of manufacturing in the national economy; it revolutionized transportation and communications; and it brought about fundamental changes in the organization and management of American business and, indeed, many other institutions. For better or worse, science and technology were bringing a whole train of circumstances in their wake which altered the everyday lives of millions of American men and women.

A CHANGING SOCIETY

One of the direct consequences of the industrial revolution was the dramatic change in the nature of American society; that is, industrialism resulted in diversification to an extent far greater than had existed previously. Three aspects of this diversification appeared very evident indeed. First, the influx of millions of immigrants increased the heterogeneity of the American people. Second, great population movements to the cities constituted an urban revolution and transformed a rural nation into a nation of city dwellers. Third, the social upheavals caused by industrialism altered the prevailing social structure. In the early nineteenth century, America had been a predominantly middle-class society with no great extremes of wealth or poverty with the exception of the black slaves. But by 1890 the rise of industrialism had created a lower-class proletariat in the cities, a white and black rural proletariat mired in poverty, and a new class of millionaires with undreamed-of wealth. In view of such far-reaching changes in American life, it was not surprising that most established values and institutions seemed to be in a state of flux. Diversified population, urban revolution, and a more heterogeneous social structure, then, were only three of the important social changes that stemmed directly from the rise of manufacturing in the later years of the nineteenth century.

IMMIGRATION

The emergence of an industrial complex in the United States acted like a magnet on millions of Europeans anxious to improve their lot. Scandinavians hoped to acquire such new farm lands as were still available; Russians and Poles sought to escape compulsory military service; Jews from Russia and Poland came fleeing from religious persecution; and Germans fled because of political autocracy at home. But the majority of the immigrants who migrated to the United States during these years were eager to escape poverty. They were attracted by the opportunities open for skilled and unskilled labor in a country which was still in the process of building a new society. Whatever their reasons, whether they came because of poverty, militarism, or religious and political persecution, the newcomers poured into the New World in increasing numbers. Two and one-half million arrived in the decade after 1860, and an equal number in the ten years after 1870. Then the pace quickened as 5.5 million landed between 1880 and 1890. In the ensuing twenty years they maintained this rate.

Most of these newcomers composed the "New Immigration": people from southern and eastern Europe rather than Englishmen and northern Europeans, who had composed the immigration group of an earlier period. More than one-half of the total number came from Italy, Greece, Armenia, and other Mediterranean countries, and also Russia, Poland, and the Balkans. Many of them were peasants. And many were Catholics or Jews rather than Protestants. These people provided a labor force that aided native Americans in transforming the agricultural economy. Poles migrated to the coal mines and steel mills of Pennsylvania and midwestern industrial centers like Cleveland and Chicago, Jews migrated to the clothing manufacturing sweatshops in New York and elsewhere, and Italians performed much of the heavy work in the construction industries. The influx of more than 15 million foreigners to the United States from 1860 to 1910 brought heterogeneity to American society.

RISE OF AN URBAN SOCIETY

American society became distinctive for its increasingly urban aspect. The great majority of the new immigrants — along with many farmers' sons and daughters — migrated into urban areas where industry was opening up new opportunities. To be sure, cities were not a new phenomenon in the United States, but the great increases in their population were a departure from the demographic patterns of an earlier rural America. New York, Chicago, Philadelphia, Pittsburgh, Detroit, Cleveland, and San Francisco were emerging as major metropolitan areas with populations of nearly one million people. In 1860 six out of ten Americans still lived in the country. By 1900 this ratio was reversed: six out of ten Americans now lived in towns or cities.

The reasons for the urbanization of America are clear. The desire for economic betterment played a role. As the big new manufacturing corporations grew, they required large numbers of skilled and unskilled workers, as well as access to good transportation facilities and financial institutions. Only large metropolitan areas could provide these essentials in the post–Civil War era. The concentration of industry in or near cities led the masses of immigrants to settle there rather than in the countryside. They went "where the action was," where economic opportunity beckoned, just like the young sons and daughters from native American farm families, who were moving to towns in ever-increasing numbers. New farm machinery drastically diminished the need for hand labor on the farm, and many of those who came were part of a surplus working force created by technological change. In addition, the cultural attractions of cities appeared irresistible. Life there appeared so much more exciting than the hard and dull routine required on most farms. Many rural Americans hungered after the hustle and bustle of a busy metropolis, its nightlife and its entertainments, not to mention the museums, libraries, and theaters. They were eager to exchange the placid rhythm of country life for the exciting and heady atmosphere of the big city. Besides, the educational facilities in urban areas opened a whole new world of opportunity to young people who felt disinclined to follow in the footsteps of their parents on the farm, and unwilling to endure the loneliness and isolation, the hardships, and the risks which were so common to rural life.

The consequences of urbanization were manifold. It led to a distinct change in the nation's accepted values. For three centuries the ideal American had been the self-sufficient farmer, the independent yeoman of whom Thomas Jefferson wrote with such eloquence that he imbedded him deeply in popular folklore and myth. Now that ideal seemed to be shattered and lost forever as millions of young Americans in the new generation of the 1890's turned their backs on the ideals of their fathers and, instead, sought to emulate the manners and mores of city dwellers. The new way of life was not always necessarily an improvement over the past, for a second result of urbanization was the creation of new social problems. Concentration of large numbers of people in congested areas led to dilapidated and inadequate housing, health hazards, and increase of crime. Moreover, city living tended to disrupt the family as a social unit and created problems of social welfare, relief, and poverty, especially for the very young and the very old. Still another consequence of urbanization was a shift of political power from rural areas to the cities. This change was very gradual, since rural legislators resisted the efforts of cities to play a larger role in state legislatures and to practice home rule. Yet the rise of bossism and strong political machines in most American cities during the last three decades of the nineteenth century reflected the increasing political power of the large urban areas. Also, while cities were partly a product of industrialization, they stimulated the pace of economic growth. The concentration of large amounts of capital and managerial skills in a city like New York spurred economic activity in every part of the nation. Finally, cities enriched the cultural life of the nation as they spawned a new generation of writers, dramatists, musicians, and artists. Thus, for most Americans and for millions of immigrants, the American city inaugurated a whole new way of life.

SOCIAL STRUCTURE

The rise of the city also ushered in a new social structure, which had all the earmarks of a status revolution. Visitors to different neighborhoods in the larger cities soon became aware of their diverse social composition. The new class of business tycoons and millionaires was not reticent about display of its recently earned wealth, which was usually reflected in palatial and sumptuous residences. Henry Frick's Renaissance mansion on New York's Fifth Avenue and J. P. Morgan's fabulous New

York home with as many as thirty bedrooms only provided models for thousands of similar ostentatious residences across the land. The brownstones and townhouses of the old American aristocracy, such as the Roosevelts or Schuylers of New York, were more conservative. Their one-time status as the leaders of American society was challenged by the *nouveaux riches* of the business world. Often the neighborhoods housing the old American upper class were not far from the prosperous and comfortable residences of professional men, whose expanding ranks comprised the upper middle class. Many independent farmers or self-employed businessmen still thought of themselves as middle class, and the latter could be seen in respectable frame dwellings on tree-shaded streets in the pleasant but not wealthy neighborhoods of most towns and cities. A walker in the city might have been curious about people "on the other side of the tracks," or the less desirable part of town. There he would have found the dwellings of the working class, the lower middle classes composed of wage earners of native or foreign background who lived in inexpensive, modest dwellings. Finally, an impressionistic view of the urban social structure revealed the presence of the lower classes, an urban proletariat composed of unskilled workers and the unemployed. The urban poor usually lived in congested tenements and slums in neighborhoods characterized by ugliness and filth. Many of these slum neighborhoods had a distinct ethnic character. Newly arrived immigrants tended to cluster together, as in New York City's Lower East Side. Because of racial prejudice, every metropolitan area also had its black neighborhoods. Yet the majority of black Americans were still in the rural areas of the South, and the great migration to the city was still in the future. Thus, the varied neighborhoods of most towns and cities revealed the new diversity in American society, including recent millionaires, the upper class, the upper middle class, the middle class, the lower middle class, and the white and black urban proletariat.

By 1890 industrialization had brought great social changes to the United States. Increasing diversity of the nation's population, the emergence of large cities, and a rapid transformation of the social structure combined to create a new kind of society. The patterns of nineteenth-century rural America were fast disappearing.

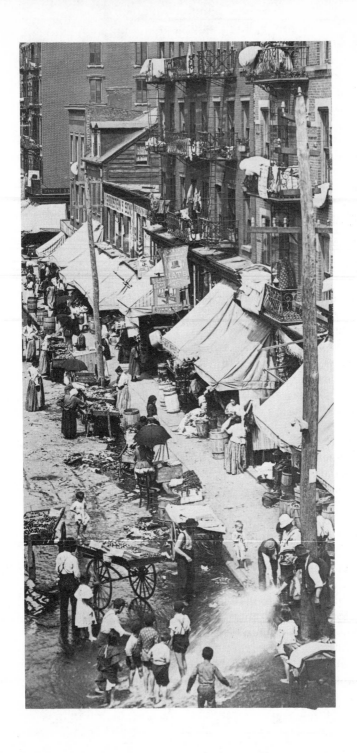

THE POLITICAL CLIMATE

Although it was once fashionable to describe national politics of this period as static and corrupt, it is now clear that such a view was a vast oversimplification. Rather, these years saw energetic, if often faltering, efforts by Americans to adjust their political institutions, fashioned as they were in an agricultural nation, to the very different needs of a rapidly emerging industrial society. In view of the onrush of change, it was not surprising that there were frequent lags in such accommodation. One way in which national politics reflected the force of industrialism was in the increased power of business interests as a pressure group. In addition, inefficiency in the conduct of governmental agencies was often a direct result of an emerging industrial society, as was the growth of a more highly central-

Opposite, *tenements on New York City's Lower East Side about 1890.* *(Brown Brothers)*
Below, *an urban slum dwelling at the turn of the century.* *(George Brayton photo)*

ized political party organization, and a consequent increase in party loyalty and cohesion.

BUSINESS INFLUENCE

During the last three decades of the nineteenth century both of the major political parties showed themselves to be hospitable to the new interests of Big Business. Land grants to railroads, tariff protection for manufacturers, large-scale appropriations for internal improvements, and a general laissez faire attitude toward industrialists were as characteristic of Democrats as of Republicans. Between 1875 and 1887 the Democrats controlled at least one branch of Congress (except in 1881 and 1889) while the Republicans were dominant in the other. Moreover, Republicans controlled the White House between 1868 and 1912 (with the exception of Grover Cleveland's two terms, 1885–1889 and 1893–1897). Yet the presidency was less significant during these years than at other times because Congress asserted itself as the dominant branch of the federal government. Whether in legislative halls or in the White House, however, businessmen found sympathetic listeners.

ADMINISTRATIVE PROBLEMS

Industrialization, which created new and puzzling problems for public officials unprepared to deal with them, led to governmental inefficiency. To be sure, corruption was not absent in this period. Often it was due to confusion about changing standards of the public service, however, beset with unfamiliar problems in finance or industry. Inexperience in the face of new issues was common, particularly since the best executive talents of the age were drawn into business rather than into government service. Moreover, the moral climate of the post–Civil War decades was not especially conducive to high standards of ethics as the age was dominated by postwar reconstruction and intensive economic exploitation. Most federal agencies were also seriously understaffed, and they operated with procedures developed in the Jacksonian period. Congress showed itself to be unwilling to expand the public service to a degree commensurate with the national increase of population. Administrative skills suitable to the management of large-scale organizations, whether in business or government, were still in the process of development. By 1883 Congress began to recognize the need for a better-trained and more highly specialized bureaucracy. Therefore, it enacted the Pendleton Act, which created the beginning of the federal civil service system. This law emphasized expertise and efficiency as qualifications for federal employees instead of advancement through patronage.

Despite the serious lag of governmental services behind the nation's growth, the new industrial society stimulated the expansion of many federal services. In 1861 federal departments and agencies employed only 36,672 persons; by 1891 the number had more than quadrupled to 157,442; and by the turn of the century the force had grown to 239,476.[5] In short, the rise of Big Business led to the rise of Big Government.

PARTY ORGANIZATION

As the large new business corporations increasingly developed vast organizations, the major political parties of this period perfected their party organizations by elaborating centralization from the national level to the local precinct level. Both the Republican and the Democratic parties contained a multitude of factions. Before 1860 party discipline generally had been loose, imposing few restraints on individual politicians. But the failure of the major parties to provide sufficient coherence to preserve national unity in 1860 proved to be a sobering experience for those who lived through the holocaust of the Civil War. It was no wonder that the post–Civil War generation took pains to avoid a recurrence of such a disruption. Thus, the examples of the big corporations and the memories of the Civil War led both Republicans and Democrats to bring greater discipline and order into their party structures. Often they accomplished it through the more rigorous use of party caucuses, through the creation of standing committees in Congress and state legislatures, or through a system of seniority. As shown by election statistics, by 1900 party loyalty was a major determinant of many voters,

[5]U. S. Bureau of the Census, *Historical Statistics of the United States — Colonial Times to 1957* (Washington, 1960), p. 710.

irrespective of their other interests or affiliations. The almost equal division of strength between the Republican and Democratic parties prevented many major problems from becoming public issues, however. But the rapidity of change could not keep some of these from entering the arena of political controversy. Thus, one major trend of this period was the rise of third-party political protest movements that sought to deal with problems created by industrialization.

PROTEST GROUPS

Various factors encouraged the rise of the protest movements. Dissenters were concerned with political corruption and machine politics in local and state governments, or they had economic grievances. Farm groups especially were perturbed about the decline of prices for their products and the failure of the federal government to expand the amount of currency in circulation. Farmers also had a more subtle complaint — they were disturbed about the social decline of agriculture and rural life. Looking to the past but also to the future, the protest movements attracted a variety of followers.

At least five third parties were active during this period. The Liberal Republicans of 1872 were a splinter party especially devoted to the cause of civil service reform to reduce corruption in politics. More significant on the state level were the Grangers, who, in the mid-1870's, pressed for railroad regulation and the formation of cooperatives. A third group was the Greenback Party of 1880, which was primarily devoted to securing an expansion of the currency through federal issuance of more paper money. They were followed in 1884 by the Mugwumps, reform members of the Republican Party. Sick of political corruption, and staunch advocates of a civil service system, they strove for honest enforcement of the Pendleton Act of 1883. Perhaps the most important of the third-party movements was the Populist Party of 1892, which advocated a wide range of reforms including unlimited coinage of silver, government ownership of railroads, federal aid to agriculture, and direct election of United States senators. Although none of these parties ever placed a candidate in the White House, they did achieve the adoption of many of their demands and succeeded in bringing problems created by the growth of industry into public view.

BOSSISM

In state and local politics, bossism — the control or manipulation of democratic institutions by a powerful individual or group — became an accepted fact of political life. Boss Tweed of Tammany Hall in New York City, Boss William Shepherd of the District of Columbia, and Roscoe Conkling of the New York Custom House were among the best-known bosses in the country, but they had their counterparts in every portion of the nation.

Bossism arose because of various pressures. The growth of new interest groups such as Big Business, Big Agriculture, and Big Labor stimulated demands that could not be met quickly by the regular channels of government. It was also a response to the masses of new immigrants in urban areas. With a different cultural and political heritage, many of them were unaccustomed to the ways of democratic institutions and to active civic participation. Moreover, tenement dwellers in the large cities required many social services that existing agencies were unable or unwilling to provide, but that bosses offered in return for votes. The new demands made on governments at all levels as a result of industrialization were rarely met by officials or agencies geared to an agrarian society. City governments were beset by an enormous increase in population; furthermore, many of the newcomers were rural folk not yet adjusted to the ways of urban life or immigrants. Urban officials also had to provide new services such as transportation, gas, sewage, electricity, street maintenance, fire and police protection, and health and housing regulations. It was no wonder that the centralized direction provided by a strong man sometimes promised to be more effective than the manifold efforts of scores of befuddled, harried public servants.

The rise of political bossism acted like a barometer in indicating that democratic governmental institutions fashioned in an agricultural age were often poorly adapted to the needs of an industrial nation.

CULTURE IN FLUX

The fabric of ideas in literature, religion, and education underwent almost as great a transformation as the physical aspects of the nation. Among new concepts, the impact of science was most important. Darwin's theories of evolution were especially significant and reflected the effort of the post–Civil War generation to apply the teachings of science to social phenomena. This movement, known as naturalism, was concerned with scientific facts and the attainment of objective knowledge. With Darwin, the naturalists believed that the laws and principles found in nature could be applied equally well in the social realm of man. Darwin had great attraction for post–Civil War America because of the seeming universality of the doctrine of evolution. The workings of natural laws in the physical world, as well as in the social or moral world of man, suddenly appeared to simplify and resolve most complex issues. Man acted out his role within the framework of institutions over which he had no control.

Darwinism was most brilliantly developed by the British writer Herbert Spencer in his *Social Statics*.[6] It was further popularized by John Fiske, a skillful writer, and William Graham Sumner, professor of social relations at Yale University. Spencer's purpose was to employ Darwin's scientific theories to explain the problems of society. In the years between 1860 and 1890 these doctrines seemed particularly well suited to rationalize the status quo. Spencer offered the hypothesis of the "survival of the fittest." Every society was engaged in a social conflict, he argued, in which only the fittest were able to survive. Yet the process was desirable because it resulted in ultimate, if slow, progress. Spencer thus hailed a highly competitive country such as the United States in which private individuals, rather than institutions like government, were free to solve outstanding problems. If, for example, millions of Americans lived in dire poverty, this was essentially due to their own incompetence or hereditary weaknesses that no amount of government action could ameliorate. Spencer considered such views to be part of the laws of nature. The "rags to riches" novels of Horatio Alger gave widespread popular credence to these beliefs.

A significant group of Reform Darwinists challenged such assumptions. Men like Henry George in his *Progress and Poverty* (1897) and the sociologist Lester Frank Ward in his *Dynamic*

[6]Herbert Spencer, *Social Statics: The Conditions Essential to Human Happiness Specified* (New York: Robert Schalkenbach Foundation, 1954).

Sociology (1883) argued that while Darwin's ideas could well be used to explain biological evolution, they did not explain at all most aspects of human development. What was true of the animal kingdom was not necessarily true of men. They argued that the process of human evolution was not fixed, nor determined by iron laws, and that, therefore, men could change or modify their environment. Poverty was not necessarily the fault of individuals, but of the social system that produced it, and could be remedied by governmental action.[7]

MANAGERIAL THOUGHT

The impact of science had a marked effect in stimulating new ideas about large organizations in an industrial society. Scientific management, organized research, and organizational theory concerning large corporations were some of the fruits of this activity.

The founder of scientific management, Frederick W. Taylor, sought to apply the principles of science to the work habits of the American labor force. An imaginative official at the Midvale Steel Works, he elaborated a series of rules to rationalize and coordinate various operations of the working process in the interest of efficiency. Taylor incorporated these rules into his theory of scientific management, which was designed to increase the output of each worker. His ideas had a far-ranging influence upon generations of corporate managers and gave rise to the fields of business administration and industrial engineering. Businessmen now determined standardized methods for performing necessary work, formulated job definitions, and developed procedures to guide flows of information, statistics, or orders so as to insure a successful performance of all tasks necessary to achieve their organization's stated goals. It was hoped that the principles of engineering could be applied to human beings as well as to machines.

Another product of scientific management was organized scientific research. In the nineteenth century technological de-

[7]See Henry George, *Progress and Poverty: An Inquiry into the Cause of Industrial Depressions* (New York: D. Appleton and Co., 1880); Lester Frank Ward, *Dynamic Sociology: Or Applied Social Science as Based upon Statical Sociology,* 2 vols. (New York: D. Appleton and Co., 1883).

velopment had often been haphazard or incidental as thousands of inventors worked largely under the stimulation of their own imaginations. After the Civil War scientific and technological advances were increasingly organized and coordinated. In fact, frequently they were a direct result of detailed planning. By 1890 most of the large corporations were in the process of creating research units for themselves in which scientists and engineers worked continuously to develop technological inventions and techniques designed to meet that corporation's particular problems. The pioneer in this new research phase was the General Electric Laboratory in Syracuse, New York, which set the pattern for many other industries. As technological advances became cumulative, rather than the product of individual geniuses, organized research came to play a central role in facilitating scientific progress in the United States.

The development of giant corporations during the late nineteenth century was a result of scientific progress. Frequently, new scientific processes or techniques could be applied successfully only on a large-scale basis. As a result, businessmen such as Henry Varnum Poor suggested changes in the structure and organization of industry and development of new ways of marketing.[8] In line with such proposals these new corporations rapidly expanded by consolidation, vertical integration, and creation of vast marketing organizations. Central offices of these industrial empires controlled far-flung operations such as purchasing, processing, accounting, research, and sales. By 1903 a series of corporate mergers had firmly established this pattern of internal corporate organization in American industry as the purchase and production of materials, manufacturing, marketing, and finance came to be directed by one organization. Each major function was managed by a corporate department that was coordinated with others and supervised by the main office. The consolidation of many operations in a single company often lowered production costs, since it allowed large-scale purchasing, rational routing of raw materials and finished products, and systematic plant layout and location. Executives now became specialists — whether in the analysis of market information, purchasing of supplies, finance, or operating departments. These far-reaching changes

[8]Alfred D. Chandler, *Henry Varnum Poor, Business Editor, Analyst, and Reformer* (Cambridge: Harvard University Press, 1956).

in the organization and conduct of American business affected producer, merchant, financier, workingman, and farmer, and revealed the profound effects of technology and scientific thought upon most aspects of American society.

LITERATURE

The rapidity of change in late nineteenth-century America had a direct impact upon a group of literary figures who founded the realist school. They sought to examine critically the influence of industrialism on the lives of Americans of all classes, but especially the masses of wage earners. One of the founders of realism and one of its major figures was William Dean Howells, who set the trend with *The Rise of Silas Lapham* (1885) and *A Hazard of New Fortunes* (1890), novels that dealt at length with the inequality of wealth, class tensions, and the traumatic experiences of Americans who moved from farms to cities. His example was followed by a group of younger writers including Stephen Crane, Frank Norris, Jack London, and Theodore Dreiser.

RELIGION

Religion also revealed the impact of science and industry. Science appeared to contradict many long-held traditional theories in the Bible. Biblical accounts concerning the origins of the world and of man were challenged with increasing frequency as scientific research cast doubt on their plausibility. The findings of this Biblical criticism extended to numerous beliefs and created doubts and conflicts for many Americans. Of the theologians who sought to spread the newer views, Philip Schaff of the Union Theological Seminary in New York was especially well known, since his *Religious Encyclopedia* (1882–1884) reached a wide audience. A more popular version of revisionist views in religion was expressed in 1891 by Washington Gladden, a popular preacher, in his book, *Who Wrote the Bible?*

Many clergymen sought to adjust religious doctrines to the new age. Rejecting the Darwinist emphasis on competitiveness and conflict as antithetical to Christian doctrines, they reasserted the traditional Christian values of cooperation and harmony. Leading Protestant theologians such as Walter Rauschenbush,

Washington Gladden, and Lyman Abbott formulated the Social Gospel, which emphasized the duty of the churches to work for social and economic reform among individuals adversely affected by industrialism. A similar movement arose among Roman Catholics when Pope Leo XIII in 1891 issued his famous encyclical, *De rerum novarum,* in which he condemned laissez faire capitalism and urged churchmen to work for the eradication of social problems it had created. In the United States Father John A. Ryan was among the activist priests who hoped to work for social justice through the organizations supervised by the Roman Catholic Church.

EDUCATION

The process of industrialization in the United States during the later nineteenth century significantly affected education by fostering increasing specialization. This was true in institutions of higher learning as well as in the public schools. The number of colleges and universities doubled between 1870 and 1900. These years also saw the founding of the first graduate schools in the nation at Johns Hopkins, Harvard, and the University of Michigan. Similarly, the first professional schools of law and medicine were created.

Industry's requirements for increasingly greater skills stimulated the expansion of the public school system. The number of pupils enrolled between 1870 and 1900 doubled. The American high school first became important and more than 6000 were operating by the turn of the century. Before the Civil War, training of teachers for schools had been loose and haphazard, but by 1900 more than 175 new specialized teacher-training schools (normal schools) had been created. A more complex, urban nation needed citizens with a greater degree of literacy. Therefore the length of schooling was extended during these years beyond the elementary grade level and the school term itself was lengthened. It was no wonder that illiteracy declined from 17 per cent of the total adult population in 1880 to only 10 per cent of adults in 1900.

Educational specialization was also reflected in the growth of public libraries and adult education forums. Beginning about

1870, more than two dozen states provided tax monies for the support of free public libraries, with 9000 operating by the end of the nineteenth century. In addition, some wealthy businessmen, such as Andrew Carnegie and John Jacob Astor, became library benefactors. Other businessmen supported traveling Chautauquas. Lewis Miller, an Ohio manufacturer, set up such an adult education forum at Lake Chautauqua, New York, in 1874. Established in many communities throughout the nation, the Chautauquas provided a wide variety of general courses for adults. The disruptive strains of industrialism thus affected a wide range of American culture.

PROBLEMS OF THE NEW AMERICA

The industrialization of the United States created a multitude of problems. Among economic problems, at least two stood out. First, the concentration of wealth and the emergence of monopoly became a central issue at the turn of the century, since they threatened the very basis of democratic institutions. In addition, fluctuations in the economy, especially severe depressions like the panic of 1893, were introducing a measure of instability and insecurity into American life quite novel in the national experience. These economic problems were not unrelated to social issues of the period. Urban difficulties were concerned with housing, health, sanitation, education, alcoholism, and prostitution as a consequence of the concentration of population in the cities, and the uncertainties besetting wage earners. The maldistribution of wealth was causing wide concern over a growing gap between the very wealthy and the increasing numbers of the very poor.

Industrialism also created political problems. Corruption in government at all levels cried out for reform. Inefficiency was common in local, state, and federal policies. Crises in American thought remained unresolved. In a word, many of the institutions of American society required a thorough adjustment to the realities of industrialism. To this task the diverse but pragmatic reformers of the Progressive era were to address themselves wholeheartedly.

FOR FURTHER READING

General works covering the late nineteenth century include
SAMUEL P. HAYS, *The Response to Industrialism* (Chicago: University
of Chicago Press, 1957) and ROBERT H. WIEBE, *The Search for Order*
(New York: Hill & Wang, 1968). Technological developments can be
followed in JOHN W. OLIVER, *History of American Technology* (New
York: Ronald Press Co., 1956); A. HUNTER DUPREE, *Science and the
Federal Government* (Cambridge: Harvard University Press, Belknap
Press, 1957); and CARROLL W. PURSELL (ed.), *Readings in Technology
and American Life* (New York: Oxford University Press, 1969). A
fine survey of economic changes can be found in EDWARD C. KIRK-
LAND, *Industry Comes of Age: Business, Labor and Public Policy,
1860 – 1897* (Chicago: Quadrangle, 1967). Social trends are sum-
marized by HAROLD UNDERWOOD FAULKNER, *The Quest for Social
Justice, 1898 – 1914* (New York: Macmillan Co., 1931). Problems of
immigration are discussed by OSCAR HANDLIN in *The Uprooted* (Boston: Little, Brown, 1951), and in a volume edited by him, *Immigra-
tion as a Factor in American History* (Englewood Cliffs, N.J.: Pren-
tice-Hall, 1959). The growth of cities is analyzed in BLAKE MCKEL-
VEY, *The Urbanization of America, 1860 – 1915* (New Brunswick:
Rutgers University Press, 1963); in the old but still useful work of
ARTHUR SCHLESINGER, SR., *The Rise of the City, 1878 – 1898* (New
York: Macmillan Co., 1933); in SAM B. WARNER, *Streetcar Suburbs*
(Cambridge: Harvard University Press, 1962); and also STEPHAN
THERNSTROM, *Poverty and Progress: Social Mobility in a Nineteenth
Century City* (Cambridge: Harvard University Press, 1964). A spright-
ly account of cultural changes of these years is the readable book of
HENRY STEELE COMMAGER, *The American Mind* (New Haven: Yale
University Press, 1950). MORTON G. WHITE, *Social Thought in Amer-
ica* (New York: Viking Press, 1949), and RICHARD HOFSTADTER,
Social Darwinism in American Thought, 1860 – 1915, rev. ed. (Boston: Beacon Press, 1955) also deal with the history of ideas. An excellent work on the history of education is by LAWRENCE A. CREMIN,
The Transformation of the School (New York: Knopf, 1961). ALFRED
KAZIN, *On Native Grounds* (Garden City, N.Y.: Doubleday, 1956)
contains a shrewd and incisive appraisal of naturalism in the literature of the era. Revisionist views of the politics of this period include
the relevant essay by VINCENT DE SANTIS in H. WAYNE MORGAN
(ed.), *The Gilded Age* (Syracuse: Syracuse University Press, 1963)
and H. WAYNE MORGAN, *From Hayes to McKinley: National Party
Politics, 1877 – 1896* (Syracuse: Syracuse University Press, 1968).

2

THE PROGRESSIVE ERA
1890-1914

The years between 1890 and 1914 constitute one of the great eras in the annals of American reform. During this period reformers from every stratum of society sought to improve some aspect of life in the United States. Some labored in the cities where the impact of industrialism seemed most visible; others focused on the state level as the migration of population from farms to the urban areas swelled; still others concerned themselves with national problems. By 1912 virtually all political parties espoused one or another crusade for reform. This burst of reform sentiment was dissipated by World War I, which diverted the attention of many of these activists. As they looked back over the preceding two decades, however, they could take much satisfaction in their work. Collectively they had succeeded in adjusting at least some American institutions to the new needs of an industrial society.

PROGRESSIVE REFORMERS

Progressive reformers had diverse backgrounds. The native American upper class supplied the reform cause with some of its outstanding leaders. Patricians like Theodore Roosevelt were often strongly motivated by their belief in the Puritan ethic, which required them to do right by their less fortunate fellowmen. It has been argued with some justification that they became concerned about their status in American society because they were threatened by masses of newcomers on the one hand and by new millionaires on the other. Whatever their reasons, however, upper-class Americans flocked to a variety of reform causes. Another group of progressives came from comfortable middle-class surroundings, many of them professional men and women. Lawyers like Hiram Johnson of California and Louis Brandeis of Massachusetts were representative of this group, as was the famous settlement worker Jane Addams in Chicago. They were often fired by humanitarian zeal and sometimes with a desire to apply rational principles of science to a broad range of human problems. Less numerous were a third group of progressives with rural and agrarian backgrounds such as Robert M. La Follette of Wisconsin, intent on righting some of the wrongs emphasized by farmers. Finally, spokesmen for the urban immigrant masses contributed to the reform crusade, exposed as they were to the everyday sufferings of poor people in factories and slums. Robert F. Wagner and Alfred E. Smith of New York were among the foremost crusaders for immigrant Americans. Despite his natural caution and restraint, Samuel Gompers helped to introduce European reform ideas to his adopted land. In view of this diversity of backgrounds it is not surprising that the activities of the various reformers were frequently uncoordinated. Progressivism did not result from unified efforts, therefore, but from the activities of many individuals and organizations.

Perhaps the only unifying thread that ran through progressive efforts was an implicit faith in pragmatism. Whatever their background, most reformers believed that the conditions of men were not fixed irrevocably, but that improvements in their environment would eventually lead to the improvement of individuals. Thus they bent their efforts to the betterment of institutions in the hope of building a more perfect society. In the words of one of the leading progressive publicists, Walter Weyl, they strove to build a new democracy. In his confession of faith, *The New Democracy,* Weyl stated his beliefs as follows:

> America today is in a somber, soul-questioning mood. We are in a period of clamor, of bewilderment, of an almost tremulous unrest. We are hastily revising all our social conceptions . . . [and] political ideals. . . .
> It is in this moment of misgiving, when men are beginning to doubt the all-efficiency of our old-time democracy, that a new democracy is born. It is a new spirit, critical, concrete, insurgent.[1]

[1]Walter Weyl, *The New Democracy* (New York: The Macmillan Co., 1913), pp. 1, 4–5.

MUCKRAKERS

Supporting the reformers was a group of journalists known as the muckrakers. In a sense they were the publicity agents for reform. Often not committed to a particular crusade themselves, they nonetheless sensed the timeliness of the issues and exploited them fully. They were similar to the "yellow journalists" who had exploited Spanish policies in Cuba at the time of the Spanish-American War. With a flair for sensationalism they touched upon glaring and visible economic, political, and social problems in numerous articles and books. They criticized monopoly and the concentration of economic power and brilliantly illuminated poverty and vice in the slums, hazardous health conditions, and a wide range of social evils. Others spotlighted widespread political corruption in the cities, in state houses, and in Congress. The exposure movement was spearheaded by the appearance of a new type of inexpensive, mass circulation magazine such as *McClure's Magazine,* which began the trend in 1902, followed by *Everybody's, Cosmopolitan,* and the *American Magazine.*

The muckrakers (so dubbed by Theodore Roosevelt in 1906 in reference to the man with the rake in Bunyan's *Pilgrim's Progress*) focused a great deal of their attention on economic issues. Ida Tarbell set the pace with her sensational articles later collected in *History of the Standard Oil Company,* describing the methods Rockefeller used to secure a monopoly. Burton J. Hendrick exposed scandals in the life insurance business, Charles Edward Russell criticized the beef trust, Ray Stannard Baker concerned himself with railroad abuses, and Thomas J. Lawson wrote about devious transactions in the world of finance. Novelists also contributed their energies: Frank Norris used *The Octopus* (1901) to condemn the alleged injustices inflicted upon California by the Southern Pacific Railroad, and Upton Sinclair dramatized unsanitary conditions in the Chicago stockyards in his best-seller, *The Jungle* (1906).

Many muckrakers dwelt on social evils. Ray Stannard Baker stigmatized racial discrimination in *Following the Color Line,* and William Walling exposed unfair treatment of the black population in the North. George Kibbe Turner successfully dramatized the story of organized vice rings in New York and Chicago, and Sue Ainslie Clark described the problems faced by poor working girls alone in the large cities. Samuel Hopkins Adams busied himself with uncovering patent medicine frauds and dishonest advertising.

One of the most moving indictments of current conditions came from John Spargo, who condemned the exploitation of child labor in a searing exposé, *The Bitter Cry of the Children*. The harsh treatment of criminals was condemned by Jack London, who wrote vividly of the "pen" and how it worsened rather than improved its inmates.

Another group of muckrakers found political corruption their favorite topic. Perhaps the most incisive was the writing of Lincoln Steffens, who brought to light irregular activities by boss-ridden rings and gangs in most major cities. He called it the *Shame of the Cities*. Mark Sullivan concentrated on the Missouri legislature to illustrate the rampant corruption in state capitals, and David Graham Phillips made sensational charges of corruption in Washington, D.C., in his *Treason of the Senate*.

Perhaps the muckrakers exaggerated the evils of which they wrote; perhaps they did tend to stress the seamy aspects of life in the United States, but they helped to galvanize a large segment of public opinion and to turn it to the reformer's cause.

SOCIAL WORKERS

If the revelations of the muckrakers were news to many Americans, the evils they exposed were already well known to the new and rapidly emerging profession of social workers. Before the era of industrialism, social welfare activities had frequently been administered by voluntary agencies. But the increasingly complex nature of social problems required experts for their solution. One of the pioneers of the profession in the late nineteenth century was Jane Addams, whose Hull House (founded in Chicago in 1889) became a model for neighborhood settlement houses in big-city slum neighborhoods throughout the nation. There tenement dwellers could find wholesome recreation, vocational and language training, and medical or counseling services. A close friend of Miss Addams, Florence Kelley, fought for factory inspection legislation and became the first factory inspector in Illinois. In that position she undertook effective enforcement of laws regulating working conditions. Others who came to embrace social work as a profession included Mrs. Josephine Goldmark of the National Consumer's League, an organization dedicated to promoting the welfare of working women. In her youth Mrs. Franklin D. Roosevelt helped

A pioneer social worker: Jane Addams. (Harrison & Ewing)

in the Henry Street Settlement in New York City. Other social workers sought to improve the horrible conditions found in the slums. After Jacob Riis publicized the dreadful existence of many tenement dwellers in *How the Other Half Lives,* professional housing experts and reformers like Lawrence Veillier worked constructively to secure revision of antiquated city and state housing codes and regulations. Some reformers worked for improvement in the treatment of criminals. Judge Ben Lindsey of Denver was a foremost advocate of special institutions for youthful offenders — juvenile courts and homes, and also rehabilitation centers.

LEGAL REFORMERS

Another reform impulse came from the legal profession. The task of adjusting American law to the realities of an industrial society was an enormous one and took at least a generation to accomplish. It consisted of codifying thousands of obsolete and overlapping statutes and of introducing greater flexibility into the interpretation of the law by lawyers and judges. Both of these challenges were brilliantly met by a galaxy of distinguished legal minds in law schools and in the courts. United States Supreme Court Justice Oliver Wendell Holmes, Jr., was one of these pioneers; he interpreted state and federal statutes in light of new conditions. His pragmatic approach to an understanding of American law was well expressed in his book, *The Spirit of the Common Law* (1881). The work he did on the bench was paralleled in legal education by Dean Roscoe R. Pound of the Harvard Law School. He trained a whole generation of lawyers in the precepts of "sociological jurisprudence," the effort to write and interpret law in the light of the sociological circumstances from which it derived, rather than from abstract legal principles. Such a conception was introduced into the lawyer's brief by Louis D. Brandeis, then a young attorney. In the famous case of *Muller v. Oregon* (1908) involving minimum hour regulation for women by state statute, Brandeis emphasized not the legal rules concerning the issue, but the negative effects of long working hours on the health of women. Together, these three men and their co-workers helped to attune American law closely to industrial conditions.

BUSINESSMEN

Business interests also contributed to progressive reform legislation, often motivated by self-interest. In many industries businessmen were becoming increasingly disturbed by intense competition and were seeking ways and means of stabilizing economic fluctuations. One approach to lessening competition was the adoption of uniform rules for business practices, enforced by government authorities. Various businessmen — like George Perkins of the United States Steel Corporation — therefore advocated federal business regulation. This was also true of some railroad executives who favored the Elkins Act (1903) and the Hepburn Act (1906) to lessen intensive rivalries among the carriers. In other words, not all businessmen were opposed to government supervision, especially if they expected to derive benefits from it.

RELIGIOUS REFORMERS

Perhaps it was to be expected that religious groups would be aroused to action by squalor in the great cities. Among Protestants, that concern was reflected in the Social Gospel movement. Through organizations such as the Salvation Army and the Young Men's Christian Association (YMCA), Protestant sects hoped to aid the urban masses by dealing directly with their daily social and economic problems. A number of Protestant theologians such as Walter Rauschenbush and Washington Gladden trained a generation of ministers whose social consciences were closely tied to their theology. Among Roman Catholics there were similar stirrings of conscience, since the parish priests in city slums were constantly exposed to the sufferings of the downtrodden, particularly Italian and Irish immigrants. Father James A. Ryan of the Catholic University of America and James Cardinal Gibbon of Baltimore became the foremost proponents of turning the church's mission into active social work.

INTELLECTUAL REFORMERS

Progressivism also derived much strength from intellectuals and academicians who were changing their orientation in the wake of the new industrialism. Although they differed among themselves on many issues, they were united in revolting against formalism in thought, i.e., against systems of thought based on supposed universal, unchanging principles. Instead, they advocated pragmatism, or principles that varied directly with changes in the cultural or physical environment. This pragmatic revolt was led by such philosophers as William James and John Dewey, who worked out some of the implications of the new theory. In economics the doctrines of the classical economists were flamboyantly challenged by Thorstein Veblen, who disputed the existence of economic laws and emphasized instead the impact of cultural factors in determining the nature of economic institutions. Richard Ely of the University of Wisconsin and Wesley C. Mitchell of Columbia University further elaborated Veblen's attacks on economic orthodoxy. In the field of history Professors Charles A. Beard and James Harvey Robinson of Columbia University questioned immutable laws and stressed relativism in historical interpretation. A similar tendency was revealed in the new field of sociology, where E. A. Ross and Albion Small of the University of Chicago sought to demonstrate the close relationship between social values and environmental conditions. In political science Professor Charles E. Merriam of the University of Chicago urged emphasis, not on the study of abstract rules of politics, but on the political process as it was directly affected by its environment. Anthropologists supported such a relativist outlook. Professor Franz Boas of Columbia University tried to demonstrate that intellectual performance was determined not by unchanging hereditary racial factors but by varying cultural surroundings. Psychologists, too, were discarding the emphasis on heredity developed by their nineteenth-century predecessors. G. Stanley Hall of Clark University introduced Sigmund Freud to the United States in 1911, and his ideas on psychoanalysis attracted much attention in this country. Meanwhile, John B. Watson founded the behaviorist orientation in psychology, which rejected the existence of immutable human behavior patterns and stressed the importance of environment in conditioning human personality. The net effect of this varied intellectual turmoil was to question the status quo, to challenge existing conditions, and to provide momentum for the activists desiring change.

BLACK REFORMERS

No account of progressive reformers can ignore that remarkable band of black Americans who sought desperately

A prominent black American: Booker T. Washington.
(Allyn and Bacon photo)

during this period to improve the conditions of their brethren whom many in white America had consigned to second-class citizenship. The problems of black Americans were so vexing and complex that numerous leaders proposed many alternative solutions. Perhaps the best-known black figure of this period was Booker T. Washington. Born in 1856 as a slave in Virginia, Washington was graduated from Hampton Institute, a vocational school for blacks established during Reconstruction in Virginia, and soon revealed considerable ability as a leader. Pursuing the career of an educator, in 1881 he founded Tuskegee Institute in Alabama, a school that emphasized vocational and teacher training for black Americans. Such a curriculum reflected Washington's belief that the blacks of his generation should strive for no more than a measure of economic improvement, leaving the attainment of political and social rights to some undetermined future date. He gave clear expression to this approach in a famous speech at the Cotton States Exposition in Atlanta during 1895. His program henceforth became known as the Atlanta Compromise. It proposed that racial harmony could be maintained if whites extended some economic rights to blacks, who, in turn, would not demand immediate social and political equality. Many individuals of both races were willing to abide by this doctrine; others found it somewhat difficult to accept. Without doubt, Washington himself believed that the Atlanta Compromise offered a plausible program for his people within the prevailing mood of white society.

The critics of Washington's position were not slow to appear in the early twentieth century. Among the most prominent was Dr. William E. B. DuBois, the distinguished historian and scholar, and the first black American to earn a Ph.D. degree in history (at Harvard University). Believing Washington's approach to racial problems to be too timid, in 1905 DuBois gathered twenty-eight black writers and educators at Niagara Falls, Canada, to found the Niagara movement, a group committed to a more activist policy designed to achieve integration. In view of prevailing apathy on racial problems, during the next four years few whites or blacks joined this band of reformers. Some also feared the displeasure of Washington, the elder statesman of black America. By 1909, however, sufficient funds had been gathered to establish a new organization that called itself the National Association for the Advancement of Colored People (NAACP). Its officers came from both races. DuBois became director of publicity and also the editor of

Crisis, a journal published by the association to discuss its problems and activities. The goal of the association was to strive more aggressively for economic, political, and social equality for black Americans whenever specific circumstances provided opportunity for legal action or publicity. Most members of the group hoped to see the day when integration with white society would be achieved.

Some advocates of integration believed, however, that the National Association for the Advancement of Colored People was frequently more concerned with theories and debate than with immediate reform and practical action. They yearned for an organization that would concentrate on applied social work. Consequently a small group of black and white intellectuals, including Professor E. A. R. Seligman of Columbia University and Dr. George E. Haynes (a black Ph.D. graduate at Columbia) in 1911 formed the National Urban League specifically to aid southern rural blacks who had recently arrived in large northern cities. In seeking to help black Americans to adjust to city life, the Urban League stressed applied social action, vocational training, and the extension of economic opportunities.

Thus, progressive impulses also affected black reformers who sought to improve the condition of their people. Booker T. Washington's Atlanta Compromise could serve only as a temporary program since many blacks and some whites found the prospect of an indefinite period of second class citizenship hard to bear. More in tune with progressives in other spheres of reform were the National Association for the Advancement of Colored People and the National Urban League, which stressed direct action by local, state, and federal governments in pursuit of equal rights and ultimate integration.

POLITICAL REFORMERS

Another group of activists were in politics, seeking action on the municipal, state, and federal level. Since cities bore the brunt of new industrial problems, it was not surprising that it was there that progressive reforms first appeared. In 1894 reformer Seth Low sought to best the Tammany Hall machine in New York City. Just a year later 200 civic leaders met in Chicago to found the Municipal Voter's League, which in 1897 was able to secure the election of reformer Carter Harrison as mayor. A not dissimilar reform crusade in Detroit brought Hazen S. Pingree to the mayor's desk, and in Toledo Mayor Samuel M. "Golden Rule" Jones bested corrupt elements. Perhaps the most colorful urban reformer, however, was Tom L. Johnson of Cleveland. A follower of Henry George, this millionaire introduced methods of efficient municipal administration that provided a model for reformers everywhere.

A progressive Republican leader: Charles Evans Hughes.
(Boston Photo News Co.)

In state houses from coast to coast, leaders of reform causes were able to secure election in the dozen years after 1900. In New York, Governor Charles Evans Hughes set high standards for public officials, and in New Jersey, Governor Woodrow Wilson in 1911 inaugurated a dazzling progressive program. The pattern was similar in the Midwest, where Governor Robert M. La Follette provided a model administration in Wisconsin, which inspired sympathizers across the nation, among whom Governors Joseph Folk of Missouri, Albert Cummins of Iowa, William U'Ren of Oregon, and Hiram Johnson of California were prominent.

From the cities and the states, reformers moved onto the stage of national politics. Many individuals who had gained experience in urban and state areas now sought to exert their influence on federal policies. La Follette, Cummins, and Johnson later went to the United States Senate; Louis Brandeis became Wilson's appointee to the United States Supreme Court; Charles Evans Hughes not only sat on the United States Supreme Court bench but also was chosen as the Republican presidential candidate in 1916; and Theodore Roosevelt and Woodrow Wilson came to occupy the White House. While these reformers differed widely in ideas and programs, many of them believed that the key factor in adjusting the United States to the new conditions brought about by industrialism was the reform of political institutions to allow democracy to function more effectively.

Progressivism thus revealed much diversity; it was not a single unified movement but a mood which sparked the activities of a great variety of individuals and groups.

URBAN REFORM PROGRAMS

In the cities urban reformers found themselves confronted with so many problems that they hardly knew where to begin. One could not walk through the streets of any large metropolitan center without noticing the ineffectiveness of city government, the corruption, filth, crime, and disease, and the great gulf between opulence and poverty. Most reform energies, however, were devoted to programs designed to improve the functioning of city government.

CITY GOVERNMENT

Municipal reformers hoped to make urban political institutions work more smoothly. They urged adoption of a short ballot, which they believed would help eliminate the confusion experienced by the average voter in the polling booth. Lengthy and confusing ballots had long been a favorite device of party bosses to befuddle the average citizen. A second reform sought was the initiative and referendum, which allowed a proportion of the electorate — usually 10 per cent — to present a petition to a legislative body to request a specific proposed law. If the required number of signatures was on the petition, the legislature was obligated to hold a popular referendum on the particular measure, in which all voters could approve or reject it. The obvious purpose of the initiative and referendum was to enable citizens to bypass corrupt legislators, and so to revitalize the power of the voters. A third and less common political device was the recall. It allowed a minority of the electorate to demand the removal of a public official for malfeasance of office, *if* a requisite number of signatures on a recall petition could be secured. Government servants might be recalled for corruption, incompetence, or other weighty reasons. Los Angeles first embodied the recall in its city charter of 1903 and Seattle followed three years later. Another objective of urban reformers was the adoption of home rule. Throughout the nineteenth century state legislators, predominantly from rural areas, enacted laws and regulations for towns and cities. As the urban areas increased in size, this system became awkward and cumbersome. Not only were rural legislators out of touch with the problems of the big cities, but also they were sometimes unable to cope with the large number of pressing issues presented by the rapid growth of metropolitan areas. A key demand of urban representatives thus was for state legislators to delegate many of their lawmaking powers directly to city officials — to grant them home rule — since they were usually more intimately acquainted with the particular problems of city life. By 1900 four states had granted home rule to their urban centers — Missouri, Minnesota, Washington, and California — and by 1914 eight others followed.

Some thoughtful progressives firmly believed, however, that more thoroughgoing reforms were necessary — that indeed the entire structure of city government required renovation. Instead of the prevalent system of mayor-council government, they proposed the creation of a commission of experts to administer municipal affairs. This proposal sprang from the experience of Galveston, Texas, when in 1900 a hurricane and tidal wave destroyed a portion of the city and the corrupt city council found itself unable to undertake the task of rebuilding. The state legislature thereupon appointed a commission of five impartial experts to restore the devastated areas. So successful was their effort that other cities in Texas soon adopted the city commission plan, and it was copied throughout the nation. By 1907 Iowa allowed cities with populations over 25,000 to experiment with this device, which, after much success, also became known as the Des Moines idea. By 1914 more than 1400 cities from coast to coast had opted for it.

Other municipalities experimented with the city-manager plan. In 1913 when the city of Dayton, Ohio, was faced with the problem of rebuilding whole neighborhoods because of a particularly disastrous flood, the city fathers hired a professional manager to administer the various departments. The experiment worked so well that in the next decade 300 cities embraced this new plan for city government.

SOCIAL SERVICES

Meanwhile, urban reformers also sought to enlarge social services. Among the most obvious urban problems, housing congestion in slum neighborhoods — and its attendant social evils — was outstanding. The problem was aggravated after 1879 by the development of the "dumbbell tenement" — a building five to six stories high, subdivided into scores of small rooms, like a railroad car, with windows only for those in the front and rear. All the rest had no direct light or air and there were no individual bathrooms. Into these undesirable quarters landlords would crowd more than 1000 men, women, and children under the most unsanitary conditions. The Lower East Side of New York City was filled with such structures. By 1900 New York had 43,000 tenements housing more than one and one-half million hapless occupants; they constituted two-thirds of the city's total population. Such conditions spurred housing reformers to persistent efforts for improvement. The New York legislature enacted various regulations in 1879, 1887, and 1895, but it was not until the agitation of Lawrence Veillier took root in 1901 that real progress was made. In that year the legislature adopted a comprehensive housing code that insured reform of the dumbbell tenements by requiring minimum standards of light and air for each building, fire escapes, running water, and improved sanitary facilities. Chicago (1905), Boston, Cleveland, and San Francisco (1907), and Baltimore (1908) similarly revised their own housing statutes.

CRIME AND LAW ENFORCEMENT

Urban reformers also attacked vice and crime. New Yorkers were so startled by the prostitution problem that in 1900 a committee of citizens appointed a Committee of Fifteen to investigate conditions. As a result of its work during the next decade, the city council revised hotel and housing regulations and also prescribed revised court procedures — two steps that helped to abate the evil. In Chicago the Federation of Churches persuaded the mayor to appoint a similar committee, and other cities like Pittsburgh, Minneapolis, Portland (Oregon), and Hartford soon followed suit.

Almost as widely discussed was the issue of crime in the streets, particularly in slum neighborhoods. Beggars, thieves, and assorted thugs were particularly active in New York, Chicago, Cleveland, Saint Louis, and San Francisco. Between 1880 and 1890 the number of prison inmates rose by 50 per cent, reflecting a seven-fold increase in murders and homicides to about 8000 annually. In part, the increase of crime was a reflection of the laxity, ineptitude, or corruption of police departments and courts, which were usually ill-equipped to deal with the large influx of newcomers to the cities, including some undesirables. A prime aim of municipal reformers, therefore, was to improve the functioning of law enforcement agencies. In New York City, the Reverend Charles H. Parkhurst of the Madison Square Presbyterian Church enlisted the aid of the New York Society for the Prevention of Crime and secured a legislative investigation that led to the overthrow of the Tammany Hall machine in 1895 and the appointment of Theodore Roosevelt as a crusading reform police commissioner. The reformers also stimulated the reorganization of police departments in many larger cities. Before 1900 most urban police departments were controlled largely by state legislatures in the hope that this would keep them free of local politics and corruption. But the rurally oriented legislatures were not well suited to extend supervision and often made the problem worse. This was true in New York City, Boston, Detroit, Minneapolis, San Francisco, and Denver. Reformers therefore struggled for home rule. Between 1900 and 1914 this movement helped to place control over city police forces in the hands of municipal authorities. New York, Detroit, New Orleans, and Cincinnati were among the first to adopt this reform. When this change in itself did not materially lessen corruption, the reformers urged the appointment of police commissioners with centralized powers to assure greater honesty and efficiency. New York and Detroit (1901), Boston (1906), and Cleveland and Cincinnati (1908) used this method. Meanwhile, police departments in most cities developed improved techniques of crime prevention and detection. Electricity resulted not only in better-lighted and safer streets but also in the installment of burglar alarm systems and emergency street boxes, which citizens could use to summon help. Local police departments across the land began to set up rogues' galleries and exchanged photographs of criminals to track them down more quickly. After 1887 methods for the identification of criminals were greatly advanced in Illinois and Massachusetts by adoption of the French Bertillon system in which detailed body measurements of lawbreakers were recorded. By 1910 fingerprinting augmented the increasingly scientific procedures for apprehending criminals.

Many progressives believed that law enforcement would be most effective through the courts. One of the leaders in the drive to improve court procedures and to establish special courts for juveniles was Judge Ben Lindsey of Denver, who in 1901 was responsible for the establishment of such special juvenile courts in Colorado. He found support elsewhere among Judges Julian W. Mack of Chicago, Curtis D. Wilbur of Los Angeles, Julius Mayer of New York, and Robert M. Foster of Saint Louis. To speed the administration of justice — in view of the exploding population — large cities, like Chicago in 1905, created special new tribunals such as municipal small claims, domestic relations, and traffic courts. Courts in urban centers were confronted with new problems: thousands of cases involving conflicting wage claims, landlord-tenant disputes, marriage and family problems, and industrial accidents. With such inceasing complexity progressives feared that poor people and wage earners would be at the mercy of unscrupulous lawyers. Out of this concern legal aid societies were born. The German Immigrant Aid Society of New York in 1876 first provided free legal advice, and the movement then mushroomed in succeeding years. In 1909 the Detroit Bar Association became the first professional law group to create a legal aid unit, a pattern soon followed by others. By 1918, forty-one legal aid societies were actively functioning in most of the nation's great cities. These measures did a great deal to adapt legal institutions to the pressing needs of a highly urbanized industrial community.

RECREATION

In their battle to improve the daily life of the poverty-stricken urban masses, progressives also strove for the establishment of improved recreational facilities. No "swimming hole" was available for slum children, and new outlets for their playtime had to be developed. In 1898 Mayor Quincy of Boston opened twenty school-yards as playgrounds, designed to keep youngsters off the streets. He felt that such playgrounds would not only promote health of youngsters and provide amusement, but also serve as an instrument to reduce crime among the young. Quincy's plan worked so well that New York City adopted it the next year, and by 1915, 432 cities were operating more than 3300 playgrounds. In addition, most cities now developed parks to provide relaxation for their teeming populations. Boston created a metropolitan park system at the turn of the century, and by 1908 New York, Chicago, Cleveland, and Washington had begun construction of their own systems. Frequently, as in San Francisco, the city fathers attached civic centers or other facilities for outdoor concerts or dramatic productions for the entertainment of the urban masses. A third type of recreation was furnished by urban expansion of museums for the display of art, natural history, or other worthwhile cultural attractions. It was because of insistent appeals from Lower East Side slum dwellers, for example, that in 1891 the New York Metropolitan Museum of Art agreed to keep its doors open on Sundays to allow working people an opportunity to enjoy its treasures. Cleveland's famous art museum started its collections in 1893, and the Boston Museum of Fine Arts began in 1909. Chicago's great Columbian Exposition (1893) provided a building for the Art Institute and stimulated the establishment of the Natural History Museum and the Museum of Science and Industry. The Saint Louis World's Fair of 1904 similarly provided a building to house the city's art treasures. Museums greatly enriched the lives of urban dwellers while definitely establishing the large cities as centers of culture in America.

PUBLIC HEALTH

The very rapid growth of cities brought new problems of water pollution, inadequate facilities for disposal of sewage, and other public health hazards to the attention of reformers. Between 1886 and 1914, state health boards in Massachusetts, Connecticut, Minnesota, New Jersey, New York, Ohio, and Rhode Island developed minimum standards of water supply, sewage disposal, and pollution, which the municipalities had to enforce although the cities varied in the effectiveness of their public health programs. Fewer people died of typhoid fever in New York and Boston than in Philadelphia and Chicago, where the water supply left much to be desired. As burgeoning populations necessitated more intensive fire protection, many cities also created municipally owned and operated water plants. In 1878 only 600 cities had waterworks, but that number grew to 4000 by the turn of the century. Meanwhile many metropolitan areas, including Boston, Philadelphia, and Washington, D.C., greatly extended their sewage lines by building hundreds of miles of new conduits. In 1875 Boston set the pattern for the entire nation by creating a commission to plan an orderly sewer network. By 1914 most urban centers had sewer systems, although New Orleans and Baltimore still depended on open gutters for drainage. During these same years many towns acquired special facilities for the disposal of garbage, usually furnaces.

Following the example of many states, reform governments in the cities also sought to raise health standards. After 1890 most towns established boards of health whose work consisted of investigating the causes of diseases, preventing epidemics, and recommending health measures. In 1897 Rochester, New York, pioneered with the establishment of sanitary standards for milk, a practice soon adopted by other cities. By 1908 New York City and Boston were also providing visiting nurse services, which contributed greatly to the reduction of infant mortality, especially among slum dwellers. In short, progressive reformers advocated a broad range of measures designed to improve the life of the poor in the large urban centers.

ECONOMIC REFORMS

Although the progressive reformers were primarily concerned with political and social problems, they did not completely ignore economic issues. Tax revision and public utility regulation were their two main areas of interest. Best known for such policies was Tom L. Johnson of Cleveland, who succeeded in securing greater equality in tax assessments and in forcing railway and public utility companies to pay a greater share of taxes than in previous years when they had avoided public assessments through bribery and political corruption. Johnson also inaugurated the municipal regulation of utility rates, of transportation fares, and of gas, light, and water charges. His battle for a three-cent trolley fare was one of the highlights of his political career. In one way or another, such struggles were being fought in most cities across the country. Where regulations appeared infeasible, cities built and operated their own utility plants. In 1890 city-owned waterworks numbered 803; by 1915 this number had increased to 3045, or 68 per cent of all such enterprises in operation. Between 1885 and 1914 city-owned electric plants also more than quadrupled, constituting more than a third of those in operation. Practices varied, but in San Francisco, Chicago, Toledo, Los Angeles, and Des Moines, public owner-ship of utilities received widespread support.[2]

ACHIEVEMENT OF URBAN REFORMERS

The work of the progressives in the cities was broad in scope, with emphasis on political and social reforms. Their hopes were higher than their ultimate achievements, yet for many poor people city life was more pleasant in 1914 than it had been in 1890. The credit for many of the achievements of this period must go to the reformers who realized the new significance of the city in American life. They improved the function and form of urban governments. They perceived some of the most pressing social problems created by urban crowding in housing, vice and crime, lack of recreation, and hazards to public health. They improved municipal services by economic regulation or public ownership. Urban problems were by no means solved during the Progressive era, but some constructive beginnings toward their solution were under way.

STATE REFORM PROGRAMS

The experience gained by many reformers in the cities stood them in good stead as they turned their efforts to the state capitals, where political corruption and antiquated laws were as common as on the local level. But state problems were not exactly the same

[2]F. C. Howe, *The Modern City and Its Problems* (New York: Charles Scribner's Sons, 1915), pp. 168–70; C. Woody Thompson and Wendell R. Smith, *Public Utility Economics* (New York: McGraw-Hill, 1941), pp. 602–10.

as those plaguing urban areas. In the states, efforts of progressives touched not only on political and economic reforms but also on social legislation.

POLITICS

Like the urban progressives, state reformers fervently believed that improvement of the functioning of democratic political institutions would, more than any other remedy, revitalize American society and overcome many ills brought about by industrialization. Between 1890 and 1914 they also advocated adoption of the short ballot, the initiative and referendum, and the recall. South Dakota (1898) and Utah (1900) were among the first states to adopt the initiative and referendum, but by 1918, twenty other states had followed in their path. Under William U'Ren's leadership, Oregon made use of the recall device in 1908, and during the next six years at least ten other states did likewise. In addition, progressives were able to secure acceptance of a direct primary system whereby voters could nominate political candidates by popular vote, thus bypassing party caucuses and conventions. Under Governor Robert M. La Follette's leadership, Wisconsin was the first state to adopt the direct primary (1903). Oregon embraced it in 1905, and by 1914 at least thirty states were using it as a device to circumvent boss rule. Twenty states also instituted the primary for preferential presidential ballots.

Other progressive political reforms in the states deserve to be noted. First, there was constitutional revision as many states revised their basic charters to adjust to new conditions created by industrialism. Alabama (1901), Virginia (1902), Michigan (1908), New Hampshire (1912), and Louisiana (1913) framed new constitutions, in addition to the new states of Oklahoma (1907), Arizona (1912), and New Mexico (1912). Altogether, between 1900 and 1920 more than 1500 amendments to state constitutions were proposed throughout the nation. A further demand of progressives was the direct election of United States senators, in place of election by the state legislatures. The Populists had advocated this change in 1892, and Democrats endorsed it in their platform of 1900. At least thirty-two state legislatures approved the proposal, which Congress framed as the Seventeenth Amendment to the Constitution in 1912, and which was ratified within a year. Another progressive reform proposal was women's suffrage. Only four western states (Wyoming, Colorado, Utah, and Idaho) granted voting rights to women before World War I; but by 1912 the Progressive party platform endorsed this reform, which was ratified on a national level as the Nineteenth Amendment to the Constitution in 1920. Administrative reorganization was another desirable progressive reform. Under the spell of Frederick W. Taylor's ideas of scientific management, they strove for efficiency in government as in industry. After 1911 at least twenty states were inspired by President Taft's appointment of a Commission on Efficiency and Economy in Government to establish similar commissions within their own jurisdictions to reorganize the often-outmoded administrative framework of state government. At the same time most states modernized their laws through codification, thereby eliminating many obsolete or inoperative statutes.

It is obvious that the progressive reformers aimed high in their vision of a good society. That they would achieve all their objectives was therefore highly uncertain. The new techniques of direct democracy such as the initiative and referendum, the recall, and women's suffrage did not usher in a period of active participation in everyday politics of the average citizen as the reformers had hoped. And if reformers replaced political bosses in cities and states, this was often only temporary. Yet the American political system was better adjusted to the exigencies of industrialism in 1914 than it had been a generation earlier.

ECONOMIC REFORMS

Meanwhile, reformers in every region of the country were also dealing with economic issues. High on their list of priorities were government regulation of big business and corporations, public control over utility companies and banks, and conservation of natural resources. By imposing certain restraints on the concentrated economic powers, such as legislative and court actions to impede the growth of monopolies and administrative commissions to subject businessmen to scrutiny, they hoped they could restore a greater measure of equality to economic life.

Intensive state control over business corporations was perhaps the most important economic goal of many progressives. This took several forms. In almost every state, reformers fought for stricter railroad legislation, particularly the determination of rates and conditions of service by a state railway commission. As technology revolutionized transportation and communication, the lawmakers extended the jurisdiction of state railroad commissions over gas and electric companies and trolley lines, as well as telephone and water companies. By 1918 forty-five states had transformed their railroad commissions into public utility commissions to undertake their broadened responsibilities of regulation, which now also came to include the award of new franchises, the approval of issues of stocks and bonds by private utility companies, and many details concerning adequate service.

A second type of state control was antitrust legislation in which the operation of monopolies within their borders was prohibited. Twelve states enacted such statutes during the Progressive era. These laws did not accomplish their objective of preventing further business concentration and were far less successful than public utility regulation. There were occasions, however, when they had an important impact. For example, in Texas during 1910 the legislature, through its enforcement of antitrust laws, drove the Standard Oil Company out of the state.

Another area of interest among progressive legislators included banks and insurance companies. State-chartered banks came under much more intensive state regulation during these years than at any previous time. In every state the legislature created a banking commissioner or banking department which inspected banks several times a year to check on adequate reserves or the possibility of fraud. Banks were required to follow hundreds of detailed rules stipulated by state law. Meanwhile, at least twenty states imposed stricter supervision on insurance companies, particularly on the rates they charged, and the provisions of their policies. Their good behavior was under the scrutiny of a state insurance commissioner who was responsible for enforcing detailed regulations. Much of the impetus for this movement came from the famous Armstrong investigation conducted by Charles Evans Hughes in New York (1905), which uncovered many dubious practices by the "big three" of the insurance world and scores of their smaller competitors. Thus, the progressive response to the challenge of concentrated wealth presented by the rise of big corporations was intensified public regulation, both in business and finance.

SOCIAL LEGISLATION

The interests of progressive reformers in social legislation at the state level focused on fields such as labor, public health and welfare, and education.

Labor

Improvement of conditions for working people, especially women and children, was a prime concern and was reflected in six types of legislation. Minimum wage laws for women were initiated by Massachusetts in 1912, with eight states following its example in 1913. By 1917 thirty-nine states also provided for limitations

The evils of industrialism — child labor in a textile mill. (Brown Brothers)

on the working hours of women, usually to ten hours daily during a six-day week. The United States Supreme Court in *Muller* v. *Oregon* (1908)[3] upheld the Oregon Ten-hour Law. Another demand was for the abolition of child labor. In 1900 at least one-half of the states had no age limit for full-time workers, and it was estimated that as many as 2 million children under age sixteen

[3] Muller v. Oregon, 208 U. S. 412 (1908).

were employed. But under the pressure of the National Consumer's League and the National Child Labor Committee, more than thirty-two states enacted various laws to extend some protection to working children. Virtually every state also enacted some form of workmen's compensation in the face of an increasing rate of industrial accidents. By 1915, thirty-five states had such programs. Social reformers also expressed an interest in old age pensions and sickness and unemployment insurance, but only Wisconsin established the rudiments of what might be called a social insurance system in 1911. At least twenty-four states, however, passed factory acts that stipulated minimum standards for safety and sanitary conditions in factories and mines.

Public Health

In view of their broad humanitarian concerns, it was not surprising that the progressives also sought to improve public health facilities. Between 1870 and 1917 every state created a board of health, which investigated the causes of diseases and epidemics and set health standards for cities and counties on such matters as immunization, disinfection, quarantines, and disease control. Following the pattern of New York in 1901, most states adopted rules and regulations for the issuance of licenses to doctors and nurses. Meanwhile, concern for the disabled was reflected in the establishment of state hospitals for the deaf, dumb, and blind, and for other physically disabled persons. Many new public mental hospitals were founded in this period, reflecting the progressives' faith in treatment and rehabilitation and in the efficacy of environmental changes in solving most problems in American society. All of this concern with public health was reflected in a significant reduction of the death rate. New York City's death rate was 28 per 1000 in 1869, but only 13 per 1000 in 1919. Diseases such as typhoid fever, tuberculosis, scarlet fever, and diphtheria were brought under increasing control. Between 1890 and 1914 infant mortality declined by 50 per cent.

Education

The interest of progressives in the welfare of individuals understandably led them to take a special interest in education. Between 1890 and 1914 there was a gradual increase in teachers' salaries. In 1890 many women teachers received no more than $35 monthly; by 1914 the monthly salary reached approximately $65. Legislatures also extended the length of the school year, from about 140 days annually in the late nineteenth century to 160 days by the time of World War I. They also levied additional taxes for school support and augmented their appropriations for education. Increasing urbanization and specialization in industry and the professions prompted extension and expansion of education by the legislators. As previously noted, in 1900 there were about 6000 high schools in the United States, many of them in new urban areas; by 1914 there were more than 10,000. At the same time most states raised teacher standards and required licenses as in the case of other professions. In the field of higher education progressives were successful in extending the benefits of university training to a wider number of people. By 1914 Pennsylvania State University (then a college) and the University of Wisconsin had thousands of students enrolled in extension courses conducted in almost every portion of their respective states.

ACHIEVEMENT OF STATE REFORM PROGRAMS

The progressives' work in social legislation was to set precedents that were elaborated upon in the ensuing fifty years. Their achievements in protective labor legislation, their elaboration of a network of state institutions to guard the public health, and their expansion of educational opportunities to include large segments of society laid a groundwork upon which later reformers were to build. The progressives made welfare a main concern of government.

If the major achievements of progressive reform were primarily on the city and the state level, the lawmakers in the states during this period deserve much credit. Life in America was not so nationalized at the turn of the century as after World War I, and localities and states still figured more prominently in the average American's life than did federal government. State action, therefore, was crucial in any effort to remedy some of the problems produced by industrialism. There were various attempts at political reform; yet as we now recognize, the results were far from adequate. The progressives did not contribute lasting political techniques that would bring voters into closer touch with the big government bureaucracies that were developing at every level. Economic regulation of many types of services and business corporations was extended. They created a pattern that was followed by the federal government in succeeding years. Perhaps the most successful progressive reform was in social legislation, where their contribution was as original as it was sweeping. In all their endeavors the progressives reminded Americans that the democratic tradition required them to have a social conscience.

NATIONAL REFORM PROGRAMS

The ferment of reform in the cities and the states could not fail to affect national affairs. Yet reform on the national level had a different emphasis. While the cities and states were preoccupied with political and social problems, the federal government did relatively little in these spheres. Instead, it became much more concerned with economic issues under Theodore Roosevelt, William Howard Taft, and Woodrow Wilson.

THEODORE ROOSEVELT

On a national scale progressivism emerged during the administration of Theodore Roosevelt. He articulated progressive sentiments at the highest level of policy making. As the nation's number-one muckraker he dramatized and popularized the cause of the reformers. He also made other contributions: he revealed the positive potentials of federal power; he demonstrated anew the flexibility of presidential leadership; and he showed how a strong sense of moralism could be harnessed to the cause of public good. Finally, his formulation of the New Nationalism, a body of ideas synthesizing major strands in progressive thought, crystallized reform sentiments and provided them with a measure of logical consistency.

Roosevelt had had a distinguished career before he assumed his presidential duties in the White House. Born on October 27, 1858, in New York, he was a descendant of an old well-established and prosperous merchant family. After making an impressive record at Harvard College, he received a B.A. degree in 1880, and then embarked on ranch life in North Dakota for several years, largely to build up his weak physique. As the most versatile president since Thomas Jefferson, he devoted part of his time to historical writing, such as *The Naval War of 1812* and *The Winning of the West*, among his more noteworthy contributions. But politics was always his first love, and from 1882 to 1884 he served in the New York State Assembly. In 1885 he was the unsuccessful Republican candidate for mayor of New York City, though he continued in party affairs thereafter. When Benjamin Harrison became president he rewarded the rising young New Yorker by appointing him to the United States Civil Service Commission, where he found outlets for his urge toward reform. Yet he was happier in a more

Theodore Roosevelt on the campaign trail.
(Courtesy Automobile Manufacturers Association, Inc.)

exciting position as police commissioner of New York City (1893-1895), where he gloried in representing "Justice" as opposed to "Evil." After McKinley's election in 1896 Roosevelt moved back to Washington, where he served for a year as assistant secretary of the navy (1897 – 1898). His passion for military glory was vented in that "splendid little war," the Spanish-American War of 1898, when Roosevelt raised a volunteer regiment — the Rough Riders — whom he led to Cuba. He remembered his charge up San Juan Hill just outside Havana as one of the most dramatic moments in his life. Upon his return he was elected governor of New York

(1898 – 1900), and he performed his duties with honesty and efficiency. Since his independence was more than slightly annoying to the Republican party bosses of New York State, they schemed to lessen his influence. An opportunity came during the Republican National Convention of 1900 and the search for a vice-presidential candidate to run with McKinley. Roosevelt seemed a perfect choice. He accepted the nomination with great reluctance, for he was an advocate of the "strenuous life" and the vice-presidency then was anything but that. In most cases it had proved to be a dead end. But Roosevelt's despair was short-lived. When an assassin's bullet ended President McKinley's life in September 1901, the young Roosevelt suddenly found himself the nation's chief executive, the youngest man ever to hold that office. Party regulars like Mark Hanna were aghast to see "that crazy cowboy" in the White House, but that is where he was — and he indicated clearly — where he expected to stay.

As a superb manipulator of political power, Roosevelt was well aware of the limitations imposed on his reform urge by the Old Guard in his party. Consequently he acted with great caution. Starkly realistic, he made strenuous efforts to conciliate Old Guard leaders like Mark Hanna, Orville Platt, and Nelson W. Aldrich by refraining from action to lower the tariff, and similarly handling other touchy issues. Such political realities explain why Roosevelt did not do more to further progressive sentiments on the national scene.

Economic Reform

Like many Americans of his day, Roosevelt was greatly concerned with the rise of monopoly. Between 1897 and 1904 corporate mergers intensified greatly, more so than during any previous period. Of the 318 large corporations in existence during 1904, 236 were organized between 1897 and 1903. Many of these mergers were prompted by the desire of businessmen to secure economies of scale and size, to eliminate cutthroat or wasteful competition, to stabilize prices and profits, or to secure control of an entire industry. Whatever the motive, however, the emergence of these giant enterprises with their enormous economic power created many fears.

Roosevelt reflected such apprehensions and provided leadership for Congress to extend federal controls over Big Business. His motivation was varied and represented a response to diverse pressures. Many businessmen, like Roosevelt's good friend George E. Perkins of the Bethlehem Steel Company, were truly worried about destructive or unethical business practices in their particular industry and urged national policing as one means to bring some order into seemingly chaotic conditions. From another quarter, the National Consumer's League was demanding federal protection of consumers against abuses perpetrated by Big Business. Some progressives feared that the concentration of wealth and power in the hands of a relatively few men would widen the inequalities in American life and constitute a threat to a democratic system. Like Louis Brandeis, they felt that only the national government was powerful enough to challenge the new corporations. Businessmen, consumer groups, and progressives thus had a common interest in federal action to control monopolies.

Keenly aware of these tendencies, Roosevelt activated antitrust measures. He was, indeed, the first chief executive to articulate antitrust sentiments and to propose a campaign for action. In 1903 he took two steps that aroused much attention. At his behest Congress created a Bureau of Corporations in the new Department of Commerce and Labor to collect information on mergers, trusts, and monopolies, and to aid the Justice Department in preparing antitrust cases. In addition, Roosevelt gave his support to the Expedition Act of 1903, which added two new assistant attorneys-general to the Department of Justice primarily to handle antitrust proceedings.

Roosevelt's most dramatic gesture was his revitalization of the Sherman Anti-Trust Act of 1890 in the Northern Securities case.[4] The Northern Securities Company was organized by J. P. Morgan and James J. Hill in 1901 and also included E. H. Harriman, who dominated the Union Pacific and Southern Pacific Railroads. Hill had effective control of the Northern Pacific and the Great Northern railroads, and proposed a giant merger that would allow the group to control approximately two-thirds of the railroads in the United States. Like many Americans, Roosevelt felt that it was undesirable to have fewer than six men exercise control over the nation's railway system. Consequently he instructed Attorney General Philander C. Knox to file a suit for the dissolution of the Northern Securities Company under the Sherman Anti-

[4]U. S. v. Northern Securities Company, 193 U. S. 406 (1904).

Trust Act, charging it with being a combination in restraint of trade. Roosevelt won a great victory in 1904 when the United States Supreme Court, in the Northern Securities case, upheld his contentions and ordered the company dissolved. Meanwhile, in 1902 Roosevelt ordered similar proceedings against the beef trust (Swift, Armour, and Morris) for securing control over independent packers through their National Packing Company. The Standard Oil Company and the American Tobacco Company also came under attack for monopolistic practices. Altogether, under Roosevelt's administration the Justice Department secured twenty-five indictments and eighteen bills of equity (settlements out of court) under the Sherman Act. If Roosevelt did not fully deserve his reputation as a trust buster, undeniably he was the first president to encourage federal antitrust prosecutions.

Roosevelt was also concerned with stricter federal railroad regulation. The Interstate Commerce Act of 1887 had been emasculated by the courts between 1887 and 1900 and had been rendered largely useless. Meanwhile, cutthroat competition and bitter rate wars led many railroad executives, shippers, and state regulatory officials to urge more effective national railway controls. Roosevelt was only too willing to use his great political skills and presidential powers to promote these efforts. The first fruit of his labors came in 1903 when Congress approved the Elkins Act, which prohibited the granting of rebates by railroads. In his annual message to Congress in December of 1904, the president urged more sweeping legislation. This ultimately took the form of the Hepburn Act of 1906, which broadened the jurisdiction of the Interstate Commerce Commission to include terminals, Pullman cars, and pipelines. Secondly, it required railways to adopt uniform accounting practices. Court reviews of commission decisions were limited to United States Circuit Courts and the United States Supreme Court. Finally, the most important provision of the act empowered the Interstate Commerce Commission to fix maximum rates for the carriers. The unilateral authority that railroad companies had exercised in rate-making was now to be shared with the commission. The Mann-Elkins Act of 1910 further strengthened the Interstate Commerce Commission by extending its authority over telephone and telegraph companies, and by allowing it to suspend rate increases subject to its investigation. Through these measures the federal government assumed a large measure of responsibility over the regulation and stabilization of the nation's railroads.

Conservation

As a fervid outdoorsman and amateur botanist, Roosevelt was naturally inclined to be concerned about the conservation of natural resources and pollution of streams and rivers. True, again his words were louder than his deeds, but he did arouse the nation's concern over the depletion of forests, water, mineral lands, and fish and wildlife. Soon after he entered the White House, Roosevelt used his executive authority to triple forest reserves to include 150 million acres of federally owned forest lands and to withdraw in addition 64 million acres of coal lands from public sale. He also gave his support to the Newlands Act of 1902, which made federal aid available for reclamation projects by private individuals, although the pressure of western senators was largely responsible for this measure. In 1905 Roosevelt appointed Gifford Pinchot of Pennsylvania to direct a newly organized Forest Service in the Department of Agriculture. Pinchot was a zealous conservationist who developed imaginative federal programs in timber conservation and elaborate plans for planting future forests. Just before he left office Roosevelt sought to stimulate conservation sentiment by calling a great national conservation conference in Washington during 1908. Delegates included state and local conservation officers as well as representatives from leading organizations that were battling for the cause. They exchanged ideas, garnered much publicity, and adopted resolutions providing guidelines for conservation. The meeting effectively focused attention of the entire nation on what many Americans were surprised to learn had suddenly become a national problem. Thus, through withdrawals of public land, through his appointment of conservationists, and through his unrivalled abilities to secure publicity, Roosevelt dramatized the conservation problem that had resulted from rapid industrialization.

Political Reform

Roosevelt tread more carefully in the sphere of political reform. His concept of a "strong president" who was the steward or custodian of the people's welfare gave new vigor to functions of the executive in the White House. His example set a tone for the administration, emphasizing the function of the president as a national leader. In addition, he took three steps to strengthen good government. First, he maintained high standards for his appointments whether in his cabinet or in lesser posts. Second, he strengthened civil service by extending the number of positions open to competitive examination. And, at his behest, Secretary of War Elihu Root reorganized the War Department and the general staff system.

Social Reform

In the realm of social reform Roosevelt's achievements were relatively few. The passage of the Pure Food and Drug Act of 1906 was not primarily due to his leadership. Many states had already enacted such laws in their own jurisdictions, while the chief chemist of the Department of Agriculture, Harvey Wiley, had been advocating such legislation for over a decade. Moreover, many meat-packing companies desired uniform standards of quality, which they hoped to secure through federal action. Roosevelt paid little attention to pure food problems until he read Upton Sinclair's *Jungle* in 1906, which vividly portrayed the filth in the Chicago meat-processing plants. The book had such a disquieting physiological effect on Roosevelt that he resolved to give his backing to Wiley. Appropriate bills had been pending in Congress for some years, but when the president threw his full support behind them, he provided the impetus for their quick passage. A congressional investigation of conditions in the Chicago stockyards further prompted action, for it disclosed the following conditions:

> Meat scraps were also found being shoveled into receptacles from dirty floors, where they were left to lie until again shoveled into barrels or into machines for chopping. These floors, it must be noted, were in most cases damp and soggy, in dark, ill-ventilated rooms, and the employees in utter ignorance of cleanliness or danger to health expectorated at will upon them. In a word, we saw meat shoveled from filthy wooden floors, piled on tables rarely washed, pushed from room to room in rotten box carts, in all of which processes it was in the way of gathering dirt, splinters, floor filth, and the expectoration of tuberculous and other diseased workers.[5]

The Pure Food and Drug Act of 1906 required honest labeling and stipulated minimum standards of quality with which food and

[5]U. S., *Congressional Record,* 59th Cong., 1st sess. (June 4, 1906), p. 7801.

drug manufacturers had to comply. As for other types of social legislation — whether labor, public health, education, or social welfare — the significant reforms were undertaken in the states. True, Roosevelt used his prestige to endorse labor's position in a coal strike of 1902; he also signed a federal workmen's compensation bill in 1908. But he believed, and perhaps rightly so, that the time was not yet ripe for large-scale federal action in the realm of social legislation.

WILLIAM HOWARD TAFT

Although he was soon to rue his choice, Roosevelt personally picked William Howard Taft to be his successor in the White House. If the Rough Rider was a man of executive mold, Taft had a judicial frame of mind; where Roosevelt rushed to action, Taft deliberated; where Roosevelt gloried in quickness, Taft moved slowly; and where Roosevelt reveled in the strenuous life, Taft preferred the placid life. Certainly Taft was the biggest man ever to attain the presidency, for he weighed 350 pounds before slimming down to 275 pounds in the White House. Perhaps Taft's girth had something to do with his temperament, for differences in temperament rather than deep-seated convictions eventually divided the two men and made them enemies.

Taft's judicial orientation seemed natural in view of his background. Both his father and his grandfather had been judges in their native Ohio, where William Howard Taft was born in 1857. He attended local schools and then went on to Yale University, where he graduated with a fine record in 1878. He then returned to Cincinnati to study law before entering a law office there. From then on, his rise was rapid, largely because of his skill in legal reasoning and his understanding of legal problems. Between 1880 and 1882 he served as assistant district attorney for Cincinnati. His active role in Republican politics also brought him ample rewards. When Harrison assumed the presidency in 1889, he appointed Taft as solicitor-general of the United States, the second-highest position in the Justice Department. He served ably in this capacity until 1892, when Harrison appointed him a United States Circuit Court judge. These were happy years for Taft, who relished his role on the bench. In 1899 McKinley selected him to head the Philippine Commission, whose task was to establish stable government in the recently acquired islands. Taft executed his respon-

William Howard Taft. (Baker Art Gallery)

sibilities with great competence and was rewarded by Theodore Roosevelt with a position in the cabinet as secretary of war (1903–1908). Roosevelt was so impressed by Taft's integrity and his capabilities that he chose him as his standard bearer and virtually forced the Republican National Convention of 1908 to nominate him for the presidency. As Roosevelt's favorite, Taft bested his Democratic opponent, William Jennings Bryan, and moved into the White House. Meanwhile, secure in the belief that Taft would carry out his policies without change, Roosevelt happily left for a tour of European capitals before continuing on to Africa for an exciting safari.

Economic Policies

With the determination of a bulldog, Taft began his administration by placing his support behind economic reform measures. Of these, tariff reduction seemed to be the most pressing. Unlike Roosevelt, who had refused to touch the subject for the sake of political expediency, Taft waded directly into the morass of controversy soon after his inauguration. Unlike his predecessor, he got stuck. Heavy-footed as he was, he soon found himself in trouble. Congressional Democrats introduced bills for tariff reduction, to which Taft was sympathetic, but this embarrassed the president in the eyes of high tariff advocates of his own party. Taft favored only very slight tariff modification, which earned him the enmity of most Democrats, and of all but a minority of Republicans, for different reasons. Consequently, when Taft enthusiastically endorsed the Payne-Aldrich Tariff Act of 1909, he made political enemies by the score, for the act made relatively few downward changes. The net effect of the tariff issue was to weaken Taft's control over the members of his own party.

Despite this political setback Taft continued to advocate various forms of business regulation. He gave encouragement to the work of the National Monetary Commission, a study group working on plans to revise the nation's banking system. Over the opposition of many savings bank executives, Taft successfully persuaded Congress in 1912 to create postal savings banks. This meant that the United States Post Office would accept savings accounts, thus providing direct competition with private banks. He also secured creation of parcel post express service (1912), another instance of government competition with private business — and the exercise of subtle pressure. But most important was Taft's continuation of Roosevelt's antitrust policies. Between 1909 and 1913 his administration initiated sixty-five antitrust suits, exceeding Roosevelt's record. In 1911 the United States Supreme Court handed down its famous Standard Oil decision, in which it decreed the breakup of the Standard Oil Trust into smaller, independent companies. Other decisions that year restricted the size of the American Tobacco Company and the sugar trust. Strangely enough, however, progressives engaged in antitrust crusades were loath to give Taft much credit for his labors.

Conservation

Taft further lost standing with reformers by his clumsy handling of the Pinchot-Ballinger affair in regard to conservation. In 1909 his secretary of the interior, Richard Ballinger, leased some federal coal lands in Alaska to representatives of the Guggenheim interests. Immediately a loud cry of "corruption" went up from Gifford Pinchot, director of the Forest Service, and a great Roosevelt favorite. Taft's careful examination of the accusations convinced him, and later critics feel quite correctly, that Pinchot's charges had little foundation and appeared to be the result of overzealousness. Consequently, Taft quite properly removed Pinchot from his post because of insubordination. But this action was widely interpreted by Pinchot's friends as reflecting Taft's opposition to the cause of conservation. Roosevelt especially was infuriated, and his feelings toward his former protégé, Taft, cooled noticeably. Unfortunately, the rancor and emotionalism that accompanied this feud beclouded the issues. Yet the squabble had the effect of further alienating Taft from the progressives although, in fact, he was seeking to implement Roosevelt's natural resource policies.

Social Policies

Whereas Roosevelt spoke about social reform but did little for it, Taft rarely mentioned the subject but promoted some modest accomplishments in this sphere. In his administration Congress enacted the Mann Act, prohibiting the interstate transportation of women for immoral purposes, a long-standing demand of progressives who were anxious to curtail prostitution. Reflecting the progressives' sympathy for humane treatment of children, Taft encouraged the creation of the Children's Bureau in the Department of Labor (1912). This new agency studied ways and means to improve conditions of youngsters and was particularly concerned with the abolition of child labor. Perhaps the most important reform designed to lessen great inequalities of wealth was the Sixteenth Amendment, authorizing the imposition of an income tax. Taft did not initiate this proposal, but he gave it his undaunted support and meanwhile approved the adoption of a corporate income tax in 1909. The Sixteenth Amendment was ratified in 1913, just as Taft was leaving office.

Political Policies

Taft did not ignore political reforms. He enthusiastically endorsed the Seventeenth Amendment to provide for the direct election of United States senators (1913). But progressives emphasized rather his opposition to the admission of Arizona and New Mexico as states (1912) because Arizona's constitution had a provision for judicial recall, which was anathema to Taft. Yet this was really not a major issue. Possibly Taft's most important contribution in political reform was his appointment of a Commission on Economy and Efficiency in Government (1911) to map plans for a reorganization of the entire federal bureaucratic structure to make it more responsive to the problems created by industrialization. This group of experts made far-ranging recommendations to streamline the machinery and the methods of federal agencies; at least twenty states created similar groups within their own jurisdictions.

Although the president felt at home in administrative and judicial matters, he never felt wholly at ease in the rough and tumble of politics. Repeatedly his lack of timing and political skill led him into political blunders, such as the contest over the house speakership in 1910. A group of progressives in both parties were seeking to oust the dictatorial standpat Republican "Uncle Joe" Cannon, and they solicited Taft's help. Taft was sympathetic but dilatory. The Old Guard in his own party, represented by Senator Nelson W. Aldrich, warned Taft not to desert Cannon. But in 1910 the progressives were able to reduce Cannon's powers without Taft's aid. Thus, the chief executive, because of his straddling and indecision, managed to offend both factions. Such political ineptitude would have been unthinkable on the part of a man like Roosevelt.

ELECTION OF 1912: NEW NATIONALISM AND NEW FREEDOM

As the election of 1912 approached, Taft found himself attacked from many sides. Progressives of his own party — such as Senators Robert M. La Follette and Albert Beveridge — were in open revolt and rejected him. The Rough Rider and his personal followers were vitriolic in their denunciation of Taft, for they believed that he had betrayed most of Roosevelt's major programs, although in fact he had done much to develop them. Old Guard Republicans, on the other hand, were visibly unhappy with Taft's proclivities toward reform. It was no wonder that in 1912 Taft was looking forward to his exit from the White House, and a law professorship at Yale. Slow and deliberate, a great conciliator who often sought to satisfy too many factions, Taft ended his administration by pleasing no one.

The split among the Republicans became real after their national convention in 1912. In a display of power the Old Guard steam-rollered the renomination of Taft, for he was the only candidate they had. By this action they alienated most of the progressives, who angrily stalked out of the convention hall. Yet the Republican platform was a forward-looking document that urged extended government control of business, banking reform, and conservation. But Roosevelt's followers — prompted by their leader, who was seeking a third term under a regular Republican nomination — issued a call for a convention of their own. In an atmosphere of almost religious frenzy, amid chants and group singing, amid the blaring sounds of the "Battle Hymn of the Republic," they founded a new party, the Progressive party. In a dramatic speech Roosevelt shouted to the turbulent throng: "We stand at Armageddon, and we battle for the Lord." Interpreted more realistically, he was asking the delegates to battle for him in the forthcoming election. His nomination by the insurgents had never really been in doubt, despite the efforts of Senator Robert M. La Follette to secure it for himself. The convention then approved a very progressive platform that crystallized many demands of the preceding decade. It advocated women's suffrage, the initiative and referendum, and recall; it urged rigid federal control over corporations and utilities; and it called for protective labor legislation and pension programs. As Roosevelt's personal vehicle the Progressive party had one function — to embarrass Taft; as the highpoint of the progressive movement, it had another.

With the Republicans so bitterly divided it was clear that 1912 could well result in a Democratic victory. It was no wonder, therefore, that when the Democrats met in Baltimore under the hot July sun in 1912, an active struggle broke out over the presidential nomination. It appeared likely that whoever was chosen would be the next president of the United States. When the convention opened, Speaker of the House Champ Clark of Missouri and Senator Oscar W. Underwood of Alabama were leading contenders. Only as they fought to a deadlock did a compromise candidate have an opportunity. For many months various supporters of New Jersey's progressive governor, Woodrow Wilson, had been waiting and planning for just such a moment. Through behind-the-scenes negotiations the Wilson managers were able to win votes for their candidate until the convention gave him the necessary two-thirds majority on the forty-sixth ballot. The platform was a model of progressive sentiments, calling for greater political democracy, destruction of monopoly, and protective labor legislation.

The ensuing presidential campaign witnessed the high point of progressivism. Both the candidates and the platforms of the three main parties espoused most of the demands of progressives at every level of government. The Socialist Party of America, headed by its popular and dynamic leader, Eugene Debs, further added to the temporary national consensus on reform. Roosevelt and Taft aimed bitter barbs at each other, descending often to the level of low insults. Wilson sought to conduct his campaign on a loftier plane and attempted to formulate a concept of the New Freedom, which he tried to contrast with Theodore Roosevelt's New Nationalism.

Eugene Debs, leader of America's Socialists in the early twentieth century. (Harris & Ewing)

The New Freedom and the New Nationalism reflected three major differences. First, Roosevelt proposed to solve many of the new problems of industrialism by action of Big Government, i.e., by the creation of a powerful federal bureaucracy that could best any corporation in the land. Wilson, on the other hand, distrusted the centralization that Roosevelt's ideas entailed and instead urged decentralization, or reliance on Small Government, with much emphasis on state and local action. Only in this manner could Americans regain their freedom, which had been lost to monopoly. Big Government versus Small Government thus came to be one point of contrast between the candidates.

President Wilson on a speaking tour. (Keystone)

A second difference appeared over economic policies. Roosevelt wholeheartedly accepted the permanence of Big Business and urged its national regulation. With his agrarian bias, Wilson believed that economic opportunities for individuals should be restored and that Small Business was to be preferred. He there-fore argued for the dissolution — and not the regulation — of monopoly. Big Business versus Small Business thus was a hotly debated issue — at least in theory.

A third point of contention concerned social policies. Roosevelt believed that social reform should be instigated and administered by the federal government for the benefit of the nation as well as of individuals. Wilson believed that social reform should be left to individuals or the states, lest the fundamentals of democracy be corroded. A vision of the Welfare State versus individual responsibility thus further divided the two men. It would not be quite fair to say that Roosevelt looked more to the future and Wilson to the past, although some contemporaries viewed the debate from this perspective. In a sense, their conceptions constituted Roosevelt's and Wilson's visions of what a future America would be like.

The outcome of the election was as many observers had predicted. Taft and Roosevelt split the normal Republican vote, receiving 3.5 million and 4 million votes, respectively; Wilson secured more than 6 million votes; and Debs accumulated 1 million ballots, the largest ever received by a Socialist. Although Wilson thus had only 40 per cent of the total vote, the division among the Republicans gave Wilson a majority in the electoral college, and thus the presidency.

WOODROW WILSON

The new occupant of the White House, born and bred a Southerner and a Virginian, was descended from an old middle-class family that had included many Presbyterian ministers. Born in 1856, he received much of his schooling at home. He spent a year at Davidson College in North Carolina before enrolling at Princeton University, where he was graduated in 1880. Somewhat uncertain about his future, the young Wilson entered the law school of the University of Virginia and in 1883 opened a law practice in Atlanta. His year in the law was singularly barren, for he had few clients and hated what he considered to be the drudgery of everyday details. During this period he thought seriously about teaching and by 1884 was enrolled in what was then the leading graduate school in the country, Johns Hopkins University. He did quite well in his studies of political science and published his dissertation, *Congressional Government* (1885), which attracted much attention. A criticism of the cumbersome committee system in Congress, it reflected Wilson's disinclination to accept the status quo. After receiving his degree, he accepted teaching positions at Bryn Mawr (1886 – 1888) and Wesleyan University (1888 – 1890), meanwhile establishing himself in his field by writing. In

1890 he was called back to his alma mater, Princeton, where he served as professor of political philosophy until 1902, when the trustees chose him as president. During these years he was as outspoken in his criticism of the rigidity of the curriculum and undemocratic undergraduate living arrangements as he had been in his analysis of the federal government. His bluntness led him into difficulties with colleagues and alumni, so that by 1910 he was glad to leave Princeton and to enter a new phase of his life — politics. In that year he was elected the Democratic governor of New Jersey, where for the next two years he carried through a sweeping progressive reform program. As chief executive of a populous eastern state, as a man of diversified experience, personal attractiveness, and an excellent public speaker, Wilson was a prime prospect for the Democratic presidential nomination in 1912.

Wilson was an exceedingly complex man; yet there are some keys to his personality that in part help to explain his actions. He was a devoutly religious person, thoroughly imbued with the Presbyterian Calvinism of his forebears. Wilson believed in the efficacy of moral standards in this world, and ultimate justification by faith. He also held fast to the doctrine of the elect and seemed to assume that he was one of God's chosen instruments on earth to bring salvation to the masses. Such profound faith often made Wilson highly inflexible since he was unwilling to yield when convinced of the righteousness of his cause. A second key to understanding Wilson is provided by his psychological orientation. It would be difficult to prove that he had an inferiority complex; however, he had a compelling emotional need not only to excel, but to win, with tremendous fear of failure. Possibly this fear was developed in childhood, for he had a domineering father who set high and stern standards for his son. Even in later years the influence of his father probably motivated Wilson to aim for high, and sometimes impossible, goals of achievement.[6] A third key to Wilson lies in his background as a Southerner. As an impressionable teen-ager, he grew up in the ravaged post–Civil War South, saw federal troops of occupation, witnessed destruction and strife, and developed a fear of concentrated power. And since the South of his youth was an agricultural region, he always felt more

[6] Alexander L. and Juliette George, *Woodrow Wilson and Colonel House* (New York: Peter Smith, 1963).

at home in that environment than in the industrial complex which was developing in the United States a half century later.

Economic Policies

Soon after his inauguration, Wilson turned to implement his program, in which economic reforms had high priority. In a dramatic move he called Congress into special session in June 1913 to enact his proposals for control of Big Business. Breaking with a precedent established by Thomas Jefferson, he went to the assembled houses of Congress in person to present his recommendations. "Gentlemen," he proclaimed, "I expect you to fulfill your campaign pledges." Then, in rapid-fire succession, he asked Congress to enact three measures to implement the New Freedom in regard to Big Business. First, he argued for a lowering of the tariff, the tariff that had been called "the mother of trusts" because it was supposedly protecting Big Business from foreign competition. Second, he asked for a reform of the nation's banking system. Finally, he requested further restraints on monopoly and economic concentration.

By brilliant political maneuvers and forceful executive leadership, Wilson was able to secure the first lowering of the tariff in over half a century. The Underwood Tariff of 1913 made large reductions in many rates and duties. To make up for diminished revenues for the federal government, it also included a proviso for an income tax, a measure that many progressives had demanded.

Banking reform proved to be a more complicated matter. Partly as a result of the findings of the National Monetary Commission, Congress had two proposals before it. One was a plan by Senator Nelson W. Aldrich for the creation of a centralized national banking system; the other was a plan offered by Senator Carter Glass of Virginia (who spoke for Wilson) urging a decentralized system. Prolonged debate led to a compromise between these two views, resulting in the Federal Reserve Act of 1914. This created a centralized Federal Reserve Board to supervise a decentralized system of twelve Federal Reserve Banks, one in each region of the country. These "banker's banks" could control lending practices of banks through raising or lowering of rediscount rates for commercial paper (bank notes, promissory notes, and the like). Also, they had power to issue Federal Reserve Notes on the basis of such commercial paper submitted to them by local banks.

This new form of federal currency created a much-needed flexibility for the nation's monetary supply. In times of credit stringency the Federal Reserve Banks could pour additional notes into circulation; in times of inflation they could withdraw their notes. Hopefully, the Federal Reserve System was designed to prevent needless monetary stringencies and panics.

Wilson's recommendations for stronger antitrust legislation were also enacted by Congress. Since the Bureau of Corporations ended its existence in 1913, Wilson was particularly anxious to maintain federal surveillance of trusts. In cooperation with congressional and party leaders, he formulated the Federal Trade Commission Act of 1914. This legislation created the Federal Trade Commission, whose task it was to supervise competitive practices in the American business world and to enforce principles of fair competition. The Clayton Act of 1914 defined some of the practices that constituted unfair competition and also prohibited directors from sitting on the boards of competing corporations. To mollify labor unions, the Clayton Act specifically exempted them from the Sherman Anti-Trust Act of 1890. These measures did not carry through Wilson's earlier plans for breaking up Big Business combinations, but rather tended toward Rooseveltian doctrines of regulated competition.

As a native Southerner, Wilson was more sympathetic to agriculture than his two immediate predecessors in the White House. His administration was responsible for several constructive farm laws. The Agricultural Extension Act of 1914 provided for a federal county agent in every one of the 3000 counties of the United States to demonstrate new farm methods and to explain Department of Agriculture programs. Of a different nature was the Agricultural Credits Act of 1916, which was designed to provide new credit facilities for farmers. It created a system of twelve Federal Farm Loan Banks to extend loans to agricultural associations and banks in rural areas. Another was the Highway Act of 1916, which promised to end the isolation of many rural communities by providing large-scale federal aid for road building. At first, the federal grants-in-aid road program required state governments to contribute one-half the cost of building new roads, but in later years the federal contribution was increased. Since these measures coincided with a rise in farm prices — due to new demands generated by the war in Europe — many farmers had reason to be eminently satisfied with Wilson's leadership.

Wilson rarely expressed great sympathy for labor. Indeed, he acquiesced rather reluctantly to three labor measures enacted by Congress during his administration. This was true, first, of the La Follette Seamen's Act of 1913, which created standards for the improvement of the wretched working conditions endured by sailors on American merchant vessels. In 1916, largely to avoid a national railroad strike, Congress rushed through the Adamson Act, stipulating an eight-hour day in the railroad industry. A third measure, the Keating-Owen Child Labor Bill, prohibited the interstate transporting of goods manufactured by children under fourteen years of age. Wilson was therefore not a great labor crusader. In view of his background, this was hardly surprising.

Social Policies

In many other ways Wilson revealed that his progressivism was perhaps only skin-deep. His conservatism was reflected in his opposition to women's suffrage, and in his sanction of restrictions on free speech during World War I. His social policies evoked protest for he condoned racial segregation; e.g., during his administration federal offices and eating places implemented separation of blacks and whites. If Wilson himself was no rabid racist, he felt that he needed to defer to southern congressmen and senators who held many of the important committee chairmanships in Congress and who were in a position to jeopardize his entire legislative program. Labor leaders were aroused over his veto of a literacy test for immigrants in 1917, for they favored restriction.

Wilson's Contribution to Reform

The entrance of the United States into World War I forced Wilson to shift his energies from domestic to foreign policies. But in his first four years in the White House, Wilson had made significant contributions to the cause of progressive reform on the national level. He had extended the economic regulation of the Roosevelt-Taft era through the Federal Trade Commission Act and Clayton Act, and he had given impetus to the long-needed reform of the banking system. He also did much to make farm credit more easily available. Though not directly related to reform, he contributed to the strengthening of presidential powers by his forceful exercise of executive authority. This was as far as Wilson was willing to go, since he was essentially a conservative who used progressivism for his own ends. Of course many reformers showed their support for his programs by voting for him in 1916. Others criticized the meagerness of his accomplishments as chief executive. They felt that he did not go far enough, and that he left too much unfinished business — especially in the realm of social welfare, in which Wilson's record was rather barren. How much more he might have done if the war had not interfered, no one will ever know. Very likely, by 1916 Wilson had spent most of his reform energies. Yet his achievements should not be minimized unduly, for there is little doubt that Wilson helped to strengthen the reform cause in national politics.

THE PROGRESSIVE ERA: A SUMMARY

World War I helped to bring an end not to progressive reforms, but to an era in which reform had almost become a national pastime. Individuals and groups from a variety of backgrounds, from the urban middle or upper classes as well as from the urban masses, worked toward the adjustment of American life to the realities of industrialism. Often they had little in common except a belief that changes in environment would ultimately lead to the greater happiness of men, and that Americans had it in their power to make a more perfect society. In the cities they concentrated on political and social reform, carrying on warfare against corruption and poverty. In the states, the battlefields were political, economic, and social reform, especially the government regulation of public utilities and other business corporations. On the federal level economic regulation was the most significant component of progressivism. But Roosevelt's New Nationalism clearly heralded an expanding role of the federal government in other areas of public policy.

By the time of World War I American society was by no means perfect; but if it was better attuned to industrialization and its problems than it had been in 1890, a large share of the credit was due to the active efforts of progressives in every part of the nation and at every level of government.

FOR FURTHER READING

Good general surveys include GEORGE E. MOWRY, *The Era of Theodore Roosevelt, 1900 – 1912* (New York: Harper, 1958) and ARTHUR S. LINK, *Woodrow Wilson and the Progressive Era, 1914 – 1917* (New York: Harper, 1954). JOHN CHAMBERLAIN, *Farewell to Reform* (Reprint, Chicago: Quadrangle Books, 1965) reflects the disillusionment of a former Progressive with the results of reform. CHRISTOPHER LASCH, *The New Radicalism in America* (New York: Knopf, 1965), and RICHARD HOFSTADTER, *The Age of Reform* (New York: Knopf, 1955) stress the ideology of reform. A good introduction to the muckrakers is ARTHUR and LILA WEINBERG (eds.), *The Muckrakers* (New York: Simon and Schuster, 1961). Progressivism on the national level can be followed in WILLIAM HARBAUGH, *The Life and Times of Theodore Roosevelt* (New York: Farrar, Straus and Cudahy, 1961). HENRY F. PRINGLE'S *Theodore Roosevelt* (New York: Harcourt, Brace and Co., 1931), and *William Howard Taft*, 2 vols. (New York: Farrar & Rinehart, Inc., 1939) are standard biographies. The definitive long biography of Woodrow Wilson is being written by ARTHUR S. LINK. His book *Woodrow Wilson* (Princeton: Princeton University Press, 1947) is the first in the series. Shorter studies of Wilson include JOHN M. BLUM, *Woodrow Wilson and the Politics of Morality* (Boston: Little, Brown, 1956) and JOHN A. GARRATY, *Woodrow Wilson: A Great Life in Brief* (New York: Knopf, 1956). Among books focusing on state reforms see GEORGE E. MOWRY, *The California Progressives* (Berkeley: University of California Press, 1951) and ROBERT S. MAXWELL, *La Follette and the Rise of the Progressives in Wisconsin* (Madison: State Historical Society of Wisconsin, 1956). Urban politics can be followed in various local studies including WALTON E. BEAN, *Boss Rueff's San Francisco* (Berkeley: University of California Press, 1952); LYLE W. DORSETT, *The Pendergast Machine* (New York: Oxford University Press, 1968); and ZANE L. MILLER, *Boss Cox's Cincinnati* (New York: Oxford University Press, 1968). Particular urban problems are discussed in ROY LUBOVE, *The Progressives and the Slums* (Pittsburgh: University of Pittsburgh Press, 1962), and ALLEN F. DAVIS, *Spearheads for Reform: The Social Settlements and the Progressive Movement, 1890 – 1914* (New York: Oxford University Press, 1967).

3

A NEW WORLD POWER

American Diplomacy, 1890-1917

During much of the nineteenth century United States foreign policy was based on the principle of isolation. Few nations have been as fortunate as the United States in enjoying freedom from foreign invasion or hostile neighbors on its borders. To the east, 3000 miles of ocean separated North America from the intrigues of Europe; to the west, the vast expanse of the Pacific provided a seemingly impregnable barrier to any attack by a potential enemy. To the north and south, the nation had relatively weak neighbors. Thus, America was able to attend to both its domestic and foreign problems relatively untrammeled by fear of outside attacks or threats to its security. But as the nineteenth century drew to a close, America was increasingly losing its favored position of isolation and was forced into the maelstrom of international politics.

THE NEW DIPLOMACY

REASONS FOR CHANGING FOREIGN POLICY

By 1890 various changes were lessening American isolation, thus necessitating a reorientation of United States diplomacy. Technological advances were effectively ending geographical isolation and shrinking the world; the rise of new military powers such as Germany and Japan was creating potential dangers for national security; and the closing of the frontier in 1890 and the end of continental expansion generated pressures for American settlements overseas, beyond the limits of North America. Such demands sprang in part from widely discussed ideas of the period, including Social Darwinism and the concept of the white man's burden. Humanitarian impulses and religious missionary ideals were also powerful motivations of late-nineteenth-century diplomacy. Significant, too, were economic motives — considered by some to be the basis of an American imperialism, as businessmen in new major industries sought overseas markets and commercial expansion. The forces stimulating the United States to greater international involvement were often exacerbated by yellow journalism, which inflamed public opinion and swayed emotions of the masses. Thus, a combination of factors including technology, militarism, Manifest Destiny, humanitarian and religious zeal, economic pressures, and psychological tensions were weaning the United States away from its traditional stance of isolation.

Advances in communications brought the United States closer to international tensions in every quarter of the globe and created new fears about national security, especially because of the rise of new military powers such as Germany and Japan. By 1900 Germany's army was among the most efficient in the world, and its new navy was clearly designed eventually to challenge Anglo-American hegemony in the Atlantic. Meanwhile, German naval and colonizing activities in the Caribbean and in Central and South America posed problems that were immediate and real. Suddenly the United States found a major European power at its very borders, vying for influence and status.

At the same time, after the Sino-Japanese war of 1894 Japan was clearly emerging as one of the strongest nations in the Far East, posing a challenge to American influence there. In 1900 most Americans felt that the United States could easily match these newcomers. But if they ever combined their efforts — as they did after 1941 — the United States would be faced with a simultaneous and serious threat from both the Atlantic and the Pacific. Clearly, the new strategic position in which the United States was placed by the emergence of Germany and Japan required an agonizing reappraisal of American diplomacy.

American awareness of global power politics was heightened by intensification of chauvinism within the United States toward the end of the nineteenth century. Its origins were varied. The closing of the frontier in 1890 meant that the era of continental expansion had ended. The spirit of Manifest Destiny that had driven frontiersmen across the North American continent was now transformed into an urge for overseas expansion. This feeling was also fired by humanitarian impulses and religious zeal which created a desire to spread the benefits of American democracy — whether in the form of political institutions, religion, or economic skills — to peoples across the seas. The vogue of Social Darwinism among some intellectuals between 1880 and 1900 further served as a rationalization for expansion. "We will not retreat . . . we will not repudiate our duty," cried Senator Albert Beveridge, the foremost apostle of United States expansion. . . . "We will not renounce our part in the mission of our race, trustee, under God, of the civilization of the world." [1] Thus, American nationalists and their pleas for modification of an isolationist policy were an important influence in bringing about a metamorphosis in American diplomacy at the opening of the twentieth century.

Rapidly changing economic conditions also induced the shift in United States diplomacy. As technology helped to transform the nation into an industrial society, American businessmen often sought expanding overseas markets in the Far East, Latin America, and Europe, and in underdeveloped areas throughout the world. The rapid growth of Big Business also made investment capital available for foreign nations, where returns were higher than in the United States. Bankers and financiers, such as the House of Morgan, channeled millions of American dollars overseas. In addition, the search for raw materials led some American businessmen into foreign ventures.

The twentieth century ushered in the Age of Popular Diplomacy as the growth of mass media increased the influence of public opinion on foreign policy. By 1900 penny newspapers and cheap magazines were being widely disseminated, and editors like Joseph Pulitzer in the *New York World* and William Randolph Hearst in the *New York Journal* vied with each other in sensationalism to attract as many readers as possible. Their jingoism was designed to appeal to emotionalism rather than to reason, and their shrill tone urged an aggressive, unyielding, and "patriotic"

[1] U. S., *Congressional Record,* 56th Cong., 1st sess. (January 9, 1900), p. 704.

foreign policy. Certainly, the mass media contributed to alerting the policy makers in Washington about the necessities for greater international involvements.

IMPERIALISTS VERSUS ANTI-IMPERIALISTS

In the late nineteenth century, as in later years, the American people were by no means united about the new departure in United States foreign policy. Indeed, a loud debate ensued between the imperialists and the anti-imperialists on lecture platforms, from pulpits, in newspapers and magazines, as well as in drawing rooms and parlors. The imperialists had such vocal advocates as Senators Beveridge (Indiana) and Henry Cabot Lodge (Massachusetts), Secretary of State John Hay, Elihu Root, and Theodore Roosevelt. Their opponents included such distinguished men as William Jennings Bryan, E. L. Godkin, the editor of the influential journal *The Nation,* Senator George F. Hoar, Samuel Gompers, and others. The arguments on both sides were remarkably prophetic in foreshadowing the divisions over foreign policy that would split Americans during the twentieth century.

The imperialists offered the following four arguments for their position. They appealed to national pride, to the necessity for the United States to "find a place in the sun" like other major powers. They also emphasized the supposed economic advantages to the United States, particularly the opening of new markets. "Today we are raising more than we can consume," cried Senator Albert Beveridge, with dubious logic, "we must find new markets for our produce." [2] Another argument was humanitarian: the United States should unselfishly export its beneficent institutions to foreign peoples. This was the American version of the "white man's burden," so well formulated by the English poet Rudyard Kipling. Religious missionaries often supported this idea, since it fit so well with their own objectives. Another proposition emphasized the new and pressing need to safeguard American security. Led by Rear Admiral Alfred Thayer Mahan, one group of imperialists pointed to the need for overseas coaling stations for the navy, for American military bases to protect United States commerce in foreign regions, and for the establishment of a defense

[2] Albert J. Beveridge, "The March of the Flag," in *The Meaning of the Times* (Indianapolis: The Bobbs-Merrill Company, 1908), p. 52.

perimeter around the North American continent. These were some of the most frequently mentioned points made on behalf of the imperialist cause.

The anti-imperialists countered effectively. They stressed a moral issue, for they considered it a violation of American democratic ideals to impose American forms of government or customs on foreign people. They pointed to the economic expense of expansion, for it would require the United States to maintain a large army and navy, and to maintain a costly colonial administrative bureaucracy. They warned against the increasing influence of militarism, which they feared would ultimately undermine the foundations of democratic government. The dangers of a military-industrial complex were clearly discerned by leading anti-imperialists. They also emphasized that foreign involvement constituted a threat to American security, which could be better maintained by the traditional reliance on isolation. International adventures, they warned shrilly — and with a rectitude that offended some of their listeners — would ultimately be detrimental to the entire American way of life.

Both the imperialists and the anti-imperialists thus raised some serious questions. Unfortunately, the American people never had a clear opportunity to make a decision on the issue, although William Jennings Bryan tried unsuccessfully to do so in the election of 1900. In view of this drift, imperialists in powerful positions were able to take the United States down the path of greater international involvement.

FRAMERS OF THE NEW DIPLOMACY

Theodore Roosevelt was pre-eminent among shapers of the new diplomacy. Even before he was President he used his position as assistant secretary of the navy in 1898 to encourage naval expansion. In the White House he was even more effective in putting his stamp on United States foreign policy. Secretary of State John Hay was another key individual to extend American influence abroad, especially in the Far East. The United States Senate counted several important spokesmen for imperialism: Senator Henry Cabot Lodge, who worked closely with Roosevelt, and Senator Albert Beveridge of Indiana, the most vocal spokesman for expansion.

This tightly knit group of policy makers was deeply influenced by a small number of strategists. Among them, Sir Halford Mackinder and Rear Admiral Alfred Thayer Mahan loomed large. Mackinder was a British geographer whose far-ranging imagination gave rise to the new field of geopolitics. In a widely read book, *Democratic Ideals and Reality,* Mackinder also underscored the end of America's historic isolation. In the new world of the twentieth century, he wrote, the globe was divided into two strategic areas. These included Central Europe (Germany and Russia) or the Heartland, and Europe, Asia, and Africa which constituted a World Island. In a famous phrase Mackinder summed up his theory when he noted: "Who rules East Europe commands the Heartland; who rules the Heartland commands the World Island; who rules the World Island commands the World." [3] In this scheme the United States lay only on the fringes of world power and outside the crucial geographical zones that might enable it to affect the destiny of the world. To be sure, Mackinder's theories were theories, and no more. Yet in a disquieting, if dramatic, manner they emphasized the new position of the United States among world powers and contributed to the intensified concern of American statesmen with national security.

If Mackinder raised disturbing questions about the changing strategic position of the United States, Rear Admiral Alfred Thayer Mahan made specific proposals concerning American foreign policy in this new context of international affairs. A close friend and confidante of both Theodore Roosevelt and Henry Cabot Lodge, Mahan was the first president of the Naval War College in Newport, Rhode Island, a postgraduate school for naval officers. Mahan was also the leading military strategist of his day. In several notable books including *The Influence of Sea Power upon the French Revolution* and in scores of popular articles and lectures, Mahan expounded his theory of sea power. As he viewed the rise and fall of nations in the past, Mahan concluded that sea power was the key element in a nation's prowess and directly determined its place in the international community. Naval strength produced more than military might, however. It also extended a nation's commercial interests. Protection of the merchant marine and information about new markets did much to increase the volume of

[3] Halford J. Mackinder, *Democratic Ideals and Reality* (New York: Henry Holt and Co., 1942), p. xxiii.

trade and commerce. In effect, Mahan was urging a revival of mercantilist doctrines in this new age of imperialism.

Viewing America's position at the opening of the twentieth century, Mahan made specific recommendations for the conduct of American diplomacy. He urged American economic expansion overseas as a means of strengthening national military power. In addition, he advocated acquisition of overseas naval bases to provide a ring of defenses around the American mainland. Finally, Mahan called for primary reliance on sea power, which meant the construction of a large navy adequate to protect both coasts, the establishment of naval bases and coaling stations, and federal training programs to provide a large and skilled naval establishment. Mahan lived to see most of his proposals incorporated into American public policies.

Although it is doubtful that a majority of the American people ever supported imperialism in its fullest form, a group of key policy makers exercised their important influence to point United States diplomacy in that direction. Military security and economic expansion were uppermost motives in their minds. For better or for worse they set patterns for American policy from which later decision makers found it difficult to stray.

AIMS AND METHODS OF THE NEW DIPLOMACY

Through discussion, compromises, and planning, the policy makers gradually developed broad guidelines for American diplomacy at the turn of the century. Within the context of the changed world situation they emphasized three aims. First, they emphasized the need for military security. As never before, American strategists were concerned with maintaining an invulnerable fortress America by preventing the intrusion of major foreign powers in the Western Hemisphere, and by building a ring of defenses around the United States. A second and related objective was to maintain the balance of power in Europe and the Far East to avoid potential threats to the New World. A third goal was to increase economic expansion to secure new markets and new outlets for capital investment. Naval strength would be the prime instrument to achieve these three objectives.

To a remarkable extent, this framework for policy governed

American diplomacy from McKinley to Wilson. By one means or another, all of the chief executives sought to establish United States hegemony in the Caribbean and to extend American influence in Latin America. Similarly, they sought with varying success to maintain a power balance both in Europe and in Asia. Between 1890 and 1916 the Departments of State and Commerce as well as other federal agencies strove to extend American influence abroad.

THE McKINLEY POLICIES

CARIBBEAN

The pattern of the new diplomacy could well be observed in President McKinley's Caribbean policies, starting with the Cuban crisis of 1898. As early as 1895, the Cuban people revolted against Spanish rule and as this insurrection continued in succeeding years, it increased in its ferocity. Americans learned not only of the unspeakable barbarities of guerrilla warfare, but also of the Spanish commander's (Weyler) concentration policy. General Weyler's pacification program included the herding of civilians from the countryside into barbed-wire encampments, often under wretched conditions. Such cruel suppression at America's doorstep aroused heated emotions in the United States, particularly in the yellow press. Represented by New York newspapers such as the *Journal* and the *World,* advocates of American intervention clamored for action to save the Cubans for humanitarian reasons, and to maintain American prestige. At the same time some business groups saw opportunities for new markets in Cuba and the Caribbean. Already American capitalists had invested more than $50 million in Cuba's sugar and tobacco plantations. United States trade with Cuba during this period averaged $100 million annually. As the insurrection increasingly led to the destruction of American property, the Department of State received a growing number of requests for protection from businessmen in the United States. Meanwhile, expansionists such as Theodore Roosevelt and Henry Cabot Lodge saw the Cuban imbroglio as an opportunity to secure new American naval bases and to build a protective ring around a possible future isthmian canal. As these pressures coalesced by

1898 they placed President McKinley in a most difficult position.

McKinley was no jingoist, but he was sensitive to the demands of the various individuals and groups clamoring for American intervention. Whether any man could have withstood the aggressive tactics of the imperialists is questionable. Unfortunately, the president's position was made more difficult by two unforeseen incidents. The first of these involved the famous "DeLôme letter" on February 9, 1898. The *New York World* published a letter written by Dupuy DeLôme, the Spanish minister in Washington, to a friend in Cuba. In the letter, DeLôme castigated McKinley by noting that he was "weak, and a bidder for the admiration of the crowd." Amid great furor DeLôme resigned, leaving raw feelings on both sides of the Atlantic. A week after this acrimonious affair an even more disruptive event occurred. A United States battleship, the *Maine,* dispatched to Havana harbor at the request of the American minister in Havana, was lying majestically in the harbor when it was suddenly blown apart by an explosion of mysterious origin. Two officers and 258 crewmen lost their lives. No one knew just how this accident occurred and whether the Spaniards or the Cubans had a hand in it. Despite several exhaustive inquiries, the origins of the blast remained enigmatic. Regardless of who was responsible for the sinking of the *Maine*, many Americans jumped to the conclusion that the Spanish government deserved full blame.

These events narrowed McKinley's choice of action to keep the United States out of a war to expel the Spanish from Cuba, no matter what his own predilections were for a peaceable solution. In the face of a fervent newspaper vendetta against Spain in March of 1898 and the thousandfold repetition of slogans such as "Remember the *Maine*," on March 27 and 29, 1898, McKinley sent messages to the Spanish demanding an end to the concentration policy and asking them to conclude an armistice with the rebels before October. The Spanish government's reply was conciliatory, since it agreed to both of these demands. Thus, any possible pretexts that the United States might have had for a war with Spain seemed to vanish. But the fervor of many Americans was hard to still. On April 10, 1898, McKinley told Congress that his demands to Spain had not been met satisfactorily and that he placed the question of peace in Cuba before Congress. For more than a week the lawmakers debated the pros and cons of a declaration of war. On April 19, 1898, Congress voted to authorize the use of

American forces to aid the Cubans in achieving their independence. At the same time the legislators enacted the Teller resolution, which declared that the United States only sought Cuban independence and would not under any circumstances annex the island. Thus, the United States became embroiled in a war in which its objectives — a mixture of moral and realistic considerations — appeared blurred.

THE SPANISH-AMERICAN WAR

For Americans the military engagements of the 115-day conflict constituted what John Hay termed "a splendid little war." Roosevelt and the American high command hoped to destroy the Spanish navy, and also to occupy Spanish possessions in the Caribbean and the Pacific. At the behest of Roosevelt, Admiral George Dewey and his task force had been cruising in the vicinity of the Philippine Islands since March 1898. With lightning speed, on May 1, 1898, he attacked a Spanish squadron in Manila Bay and utterly destroyed its old and decrepit vessels. Then, for two months, Dewey settled down to a blockade while awaiting American troops. When they arrived, the combined land and sea forces of the United States captured Manila in August 1898 and effectively ended Spanish resistance in the Pacific. Meanwhile, in the Caribbean a strong American fleet under Admiral Sampson and Commodore Schley circled Cuba and on June 1, 1898, began a blockade of Santiago harbor. Within three weeks an American expeditionary force of about 15,000 men under General Shafter landed in Cuba. By July 17, Spanish Governor-General Blano surrendered Santiago and, in the ensuing two weeks, another United States force under General Miles journeyed to Puerto Rico, where they met virtually no resistance. Spain was utterly defeated and on July 18 the Spanish government asked the French Ambassador in Washington to arrange an armistice. After several weeks of negotiation the two countries signed an agreement on August 12, 1898. The document provided for the immediate surrender and evacuation of Cuba by the Spaniards, their cession of Puerto Rico to the United States, and American occupation of Manila.

In the fall of 1898 Spain and the United States carried on peace negotiations in Paris. The American representatives, appointed by President McKinley, were largely expansionists and included former Secretary of State William R. Day, Senator C. K. Davis, chairman of the powerful Senate Foreign Relations Committee, and Whitelaw Reid, bellicose editor of the *New York Tribune*. It was apparent that these men would uphold the imperialist position.

As expansionists, the peace negotiators strove to secure new American possessions in the Caribbean and the Far East. Since the Teller resolution prevented American annexation of Cuba, they sought to obtain independence for that island, but they did want Puerto Rico. Their position on the Philippines was unclear until President McKinley instructed them — after considerable wavering and much deliberation — to demand the cession of the entire archipelago. Final terms were embodied in the treaty of Paris (1898). It provided, first, for the Spanish cession of Cuba; second, the surrender of the Philippines; third, the transfer of Puerto Rico to the United States; and fourth, payment of $20 million by the United States to Spain for the new territories. When McKinley submitted this treaty to the Senate, a furious outcry was heard from the anti-imperialists, many of whom were members of the Anti-imperialist League. Senator Hoar of Massachusetts was an unflinching opponent of ratification. But William Jennings Bryan — who also disapproved of the treaty — urged his followers to vote for it in the belief that it would end the war and further bloodshed. It was his hope that the question of expansion could be placed before the voters in the election of 1900, a hope that proved futile. By the very narrow margin of one vote the Senate ratified the treaty by a two-thirds majority, reflecting the deep split among Americans over the course of their nation's foreign policy.

McKinley and the expansionists thereupon proceeded to consolidate and expand American influence in the Caribbean. While United States troops occupied Cuba between 1898 and 1902, Old Guard Republican Senator Orville H. Platt of Ohio in 1901 was preparing an amendment to the Army Appropriation Act of 1901. Ultimately incorporated into a treaty between Cuba and the United States, and in the Cuban Constitution, the Platt Amendment made Cuba an American protectorate. It provided, first, that Cuba could not enter into treaties with other nations that would impair its independence; that the United States would retain the right of intervention in Cuba to preserve Cuban inde-

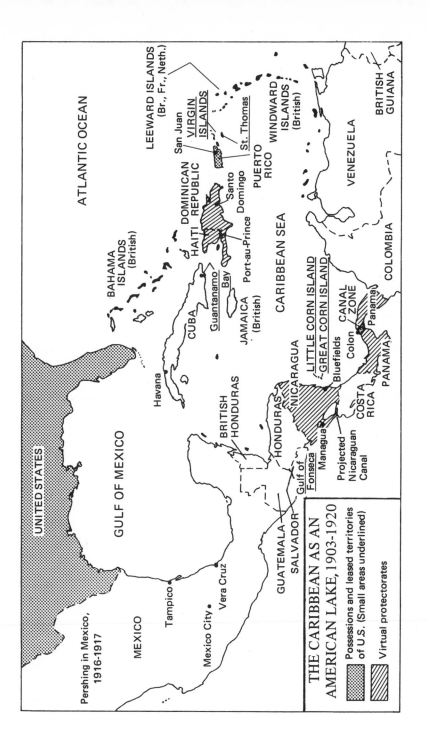

THE CARIBBEAN AS AN
AMERICAN LAKE, 1903-1920

Possessions and leased territories
of U.S. (Small areas underlined)

Virtual protectorates

UNITED STATES

GULF OF MEXICO

MEXICO

Tampico

Mexico City

Vera Cruz

Pershing in Mexico,
1916-1917

GUATEMALA

SALVADOR

Gulf of
Fonseca

HONDURAS

BRITISH
HONDURAS

NICARAGUA

Managua

Projected
Nicaraguan
Canal

COSTA
RICA

Bluefields

LITTLE CORN ISLAND

GREAT CORN ISLAND

CANAL
ZONE

Colon

Panama

PANAMA

COLOMBIA

Havana

CUBA

Guantanamo
Bay

JAMAICA
(British)

CARIBBEAN SEA

BAHAMA
ISLANDS
(British)

ATLANTIC OCEAN

HAITI

DOMINICAN
REPUBLIC

Santo
Domingo

Port-au-Prince

PUERTO
RICO

San Juan

VIRGIN
ISLANDS

St. Thomas

LEEWARD ISLANDS
(Br., Fr., Neth.)

WINDWARD
ISLANDS
(British)

VENEZUELA

BRITISH
GUIANA

pendence, or to maintain a government there sufficient to protect life, liberty, and property; third, that Cuba would sell or lease land to the United States for naval bases; and finally that Cuba could not assume any public debt for which its ordinary revenues were inadequate. Thus, the Platt Amendment accomplished at least two aims of American expansionists — it reinforced American security by establishment of naval stations, and it sought preventive restrictions on Cuban finance so as to preclude possible intervention by major foreign powers who could threaten the United States. Without doubt, it also provided a favorable climate for United States economic development in Cuba.

The process of extending American influence in the Caribbean and excluding other nations was also facilitated by the annexation of Puerto Rico. Under the Foraker Act of 1900 the United States established a civil government there, similar to that created in the territories on the mainland. The president appointed a governor and an executive council of eleven (six Americans) and the Puerto Ricans elected a popular house of delegates. As in Cuba, the United States established naval bases in Puerto Rico, while American capital poured in to develop sugar and tobacco plantations. From the broad strategical perspective of Rear Admiral Mahan, Puerto Rico had its role to play in the American empire as one of the bastions designed to make the Caribbean an impregnable American lake.

EUROPE AND THE FAR EAST

Conscious of the broader dimensions of American diplomacy, McKinley also sought to maintain a balance of power in Europe and the Far East. His dispatch of United States delegates to the international peace conference at The Hague in 1899 reflected an increasing American interest in European peace efforts. His disposition of the Philippine Islands similarly reflected the new global emphasis of United States policy. While the president did not go as far as Whitelaw Reid, who boasted that "the Pacific Ocean is in our hands now," McKinley understood that possession of the islands would enable the United States to play a more influential role in the affairs of Asia. Thus, after weeks of agonizing indecision just after the conclusion of the Spanish-American War, he finally decided upon their annexation. Unfortunately, along with this new possession the United States inherited one of the most vicious guerrilla wars in its history. Native bands under their leader, Aguinaldo, rebelled against American occupation. They had expected, not a change of masters, but independence. It took the United States three years to suppress this war for liberation while the brutalities on both sides horrified people everywhere. With dubious wisdom, and perhaps without a full understanding of the long-range consequences of the new acquisition, McKinley and his advisors took the initiative in involving the United States more closely in the intricacies of Far Eastern politics.

Indeed, with its announcement of the Open Door policy the McKinley administration made a long-range American commitment to participate in the wiles of Oriental diplomacy. The acquisition of the Philippines meant that the United States would no longer be allowed the luxury of ignoring shifts of power in the Pacific. At the turn of the century, especially, the Far East was in a period of enormous flux. After defeating China in 1895, Japan was rapidly emerging as the strongest nation in the area. In addition, many of the European nations, including Great Britain, France, Italy, and Russia, were actively engaged in carving out spheres of special influence for themselves in China. American influence in China appeared to be waning rapidly under such pressures. The McKinley administration was aware of these changes and their detrimental effects on United States economic interests in China, such as they were. Moreover, the British prompted the State Department to take action since they were concerned with German and Russian expansion in China. Partly in response to the urging of two diplomats, Alfred E. Hippisley, an Englishman, and W. W. Rockhill, the State Department's Far Eastern expert, Secretary of State John Hay sent a series of Open Door notes to the major powers in the Far East in September 1899. In essence, Hay asked each of them for a pledge concerning two matters of concern to the United States. He requested their promise (1) to respect the independence and sovereignty of China and (2) to accord free and equal trading privileges to all nations, especially within their spheres of influence. These requests were akin to an intonation requesting the stars to change their courses. That the great nations would accede to the notes was doubtful, and only Great Britain sent an encouraging reply. The others tended to be noncommittal and evasive. But Hay blithely placed the United

States in an exposed and compromising position by declaring in 1900 that he regarded the Open Door policy as an integral part of United States diplomacy in view of the favorable responses he had received. Little did he realize that he was committing the United States to a far-reaching and questionable policy in the Far East — with profound consequences that only gradually became apparent.

The McKinley administration was so concerned with maintaining the balance of power in the Pacific that it was prepared to send American troops to the Asian mainland to preserve United States influence. This became apparent in the Boxer Rebellion of 1900, in which the exploitations of the Western powers goaded many Chinese to violence, especially a small group organized as the Boxer Society, dedicated to expelling the hated foreigners from China. In June 1900 the Boxers attacked European embassies in Peking, massacring more than 200 people. To meet this threat, the European nations dispatched an international military expeditionary force to Peking to quell the revolt, also exacting an indemnity. The United States contributed 5000 marines to this police force, while eventually requiring the Chinese to pay only one-fourth of the indemnity to which it was entitled. With more enthusiasm than prudence, Secretary of State John Hay used the occasion to reaffirm the Open Door policy and the sanctity of Chinese independence.

FOREIGN POLICY UNDER THEODORE ROOSEVELT

As many of his contemporaries expected, Theodore Roosevelt took an even more active role in extending the new American diplomacy. As one of the architects of the policy he sought to spread American influence into the Caribbean, and to maintain the balance of power in Europe and the Far East. Although he was not successful in all of his endeavors, his leadership brought the United States further into the maelstrom of international big power politics.

CARIBBEAN

Roosevelt's Caribbean policies, which reflected the aims and methods of the New Diplomacy, included his stance during the

Venezuelan crisis of 1902, his intervention in Santo Domingo in 1905, his formulation of the Roosevelt corollary to the Monroe Doctrine in that same year, his attempted purchase of the Virgin Islands, and his determination to build an isthmian canal.

The Venezuelan crisis of 1902 provided Roosevelt with an opportunity to apply his imperialist conceptions. In December 1902, the Venezuelan government suspended payment on its bonds held by foreigners. In turn, the German, Italian, and British governments threatened to bombard the main harbor of Port Colombo for they hoped that this would persuade the Venezuelan dictator, Cipriano Castro, to meet the financial responsibilities incurred by his country. Such drastic action was clearly a violation of the Monroe Doctrine. Whether the threat of foreign intervention really was as serious as Theodore Roosevelt later charged is doubtful. In any case, he claimed that he informed the Germans that their proposed intervention would lead to a direct reaction by the United States — perhaps the dispatch of troops. Instead, he offered his services in settling the grievances of European creditors against the Venezuelan government to secure a peaceful settlement. The major powers accepted the president's good offices, and possible violence was averted.

Just two years later, in 1904, Roosevelt intervened in the affairs of Santo Domingo. As early as 1893 an American firm, the San Domingo Improvement Company, had bought a portion of the state debt — receiving in return the privilege of collecting a portion of Santo Domingo's customs duties. The Dominican government repudiated this agreement in 1901, whereupon the company appealed to the State Department for support. Under pressure, the Dominican government then promised in 1903 to resume its payments to the American company and to allow an American financial agent to collect customs if it suspended payments. Such a suspension actually occurred in the following year and thus an American customs agent took over the customshouse at Puerto Plata in 1904. This action led France and other major powers to threaten the seizure of additional customs collection points to assure payments due them. To prevent such possible intervention by foreign nations, Roosevelt negotiated a treaty with Santo Domingo in 1905 (approved by the United States Senate in modified form in 1907) by which the United States lent $20 million to refinance old Dominican debts, but in turn required the installation of an American customs receiver.

Extension of Monroe Doctrine

Roosevelt's experience in this incident led him to a unilateral extension of the Monroe Doctrine. In his annual message to Congress in December 1904 Roosevelt elaborated upon what became known as the Roosevelt corollary to the Monroe Doctrine. He declared to Congress:

> It is not true that the United States feels any land hunger or entertains any projects as regards the other nations of the Western Hemisphere, save such as are for their welfare. All that this country desires is to see the neighboring countries stable, orderly, and prosperous. Any country whose people conduct themselves well can count upon our hearty friendship. If a nation shows that it knows how to act with reasonable efficiency and decency in social and political matters, if it keeps order and pays its obligations, it need fear no interference from the United States.
>
> Chronic wrongdoing, or an impotence which results in a general loosening of the ties of civilized society, may in America, as elsewhere, ultimately require intervention by some civilized nation, and in the Western Hemisphere the adherence of the United States to the Monroe Doctrine may force the United States, however reluctantly, in flagrant cases of such wrongdoing or impotence, to the exercise of an international police power.[4]

Roosevelt emphasized two points. Chronic wrongdoing by Latin American nations could invite foreign intervention; but if such intervention was necessary, only the United States — and not any other foreign powers — would be justified in taking direct action. Thus, he formally claimed the right of American intervention in Latin America, either to preserve political stability or to maintain economic order. Latin Americans naturally questioned the right of the "Colossus of the North" to assume such a paternalistic role. While Roosevelt did not clearly articulate all of his reasons for such a policy, his intent was clear. The United States was intent on restricting the influence of foreign powers in the Western Hemisphere, partly to safeguard American continental security, but also to extend its economic interests.

[4]U. S., 58th Cong., 3rd sess., *House Document No. 1* (Washington: U.S. Government Printing Office, 1905), p. XLI.

Panama Canal

Roosevelt's desire to consolidate American hegemony in the Caribbean was also reflected in his efforts in 1905 to purchase the Virgin Islands from Denmark. Naval experts considered them of strategic importance in guarding approaches to a proposed canal across the isthmus. The Danish Parliament approved a draft treaty prepared by Roosevelt under which the United States would pay Denmark $5 million for the islands. But the anti-imperialists in the United States Senate balked at further expansion and prevented ratification of the treaty. Ultimately Woodrow Wilson consummated the purchase in 1917 when the pressure of war stilled the critics.

The prime aim of Roosevelt's Caribbean policy, however, was the construction of an isthmian canal. To this end all other measures were subordinated. A canal would provide the basis for the new defense strategy envisioned by Mahan and his followers. With naval power as the keystone of the new security system, the canal would enable the United States to defend two long coastlines with a one-ocean navy that could be shifted east or west as circumstances required. Roosevelt had not forgotten that in 1899 it took the battleship *Oregon* 100 days to travel from the Pacific to join the Atlantic squadron, dramatizing the military importance of a waterway across the isthmus. Not only would the canal lower the cost of maintaining an effective striking force, but also it would greatly enhance naval mobility. To a considerable extent, therefore, United States policies in regard to Cuba, Santo Domingo, and the Virgin Islands were motivated by the military importance of these areas as bastions of security for a canal to be built in the near future.

Consequently it could be expected that Roosevelt would bend all of his energies to achieve his prime objective. To succeed, he had to overcome several obstacles. The idea of connecting the two oceans at some point along the isthmus was not original with Roosevelt and had been widely discussed for more than half a century. As early as 1846 the United States had signed a treaty with New Granada (Colombia) that allowed Americans free transit across the isthmus. Four years later the United States and Great Britain concluded the Clayton-Bulwer Treaty, by which both consented not to seek exclusive control over any waterway built across Nicaragua. Prompted by his urge for national security, Roosevelt in 1901 removed this first barrier to exclusive ownership of a waterway by the United States when he helped to negotiate a revised agreement with Great Britain. Under this Hay-Pauncefote Treaty, the British agreed to grant their American cousins exclusive rights to build and operate a canal if they also agreed to allow the vessels of all nations free access without discrimination or inequality in regard to tolls.

A second obstacle was the selection of a physical site for the canal. At least three special commissions appointed to study the problem had recommended a route through Nicaragua. There, the presence of Lake Nicaragua promised to ease the arduous task of construction even though the distance across the isthmus was greater than the alternate southern route across Panama. But the Panama route also had its defenders. One of the most important was Phillippe Bunau-Varilla, a Frenchman, and former chief engineer of the great canal builder, Ferdinand DeLesseps, who between 1881 and 1895 had tried unsuccessfully to build a Panamanian canal for French interests. His company's lease was due to expire in 1904, so, in the hope of salvaging something from the project before this date, Bunau-Varilla journeyed to Washington to plead with Roosevelt and members of Congress for the virtues of the Panama route. His entreaties were so persuasive that both the president and the lawmakers were won over. The resulting Canal Act of 1903 reflected Bunau-Varilla's influence for it provided that the United States would pay Bunau-Varilla's old French company (New Panama Canal Company) $40 million for previous work completed, and for titles, provided that Colombia would give its approval and cede needed land. If these conditions in any manner were not met, the president would be able to fall back on the Nicaragua route. The New Panama Canal Company agreed to the proposal. Meanwhile, Roosevelt had Secretary of State John Hay negotiate the Hay-Herran convention with Colombia under which the United States was to pay that nation $10 million plus $250,000 annually for a 100-year lease over the territory on which the canal was to be located. These acts seemed to clear away the last obstacles to actual construction of the project.

But a third difficulty appeared when Colombia opposed the Hay-Herran convention. Fresh with impressions gained from the Spanish-American War of 1898, the Colombians were simply suspicious of the Americans. Moreover, some of them felt that the proffered compensation was too low, and they hoped for more advantageous terms. In fact, once the lease of the New Panama Canal Company had expired in 1904, the Colombians themselves would be eligible to receive the $40 million which the United States had promised to pay for the existing works. Motives such as these understandably led the Colombian Senate on October 20, 1903, to adjourn without ratifying the Hay-Herran convention. Colombia could well afford to wait.

But Roosevelt felt that he had little time. He was infuriated by this unexpected stumbling block but was determined to get his canal. In the week following the Colombian Senate's inaction the president decided to act on his own initiative. As he noted later: "If I had followed traditional conservative methods the debate would be going on yet, but I took the Canal Zone and let the Congress debate." Certainly some Panamanians were reluctant to lose possible economic advantages which might come to them if a canal was built. Bunau-Varilla maintained contacts with these individuals and also with a revolutionary group in Panama. His machinations were successful. On November 3, 1903, the Panamanian revolutionaries staged an uprising against Colombia and sought the establishment of an independent republic. Meanwhile, four United States naval vessels actively prevented the landing of Colombian troops who sought to quell the rebellion, thus insuring its success. Roosevelt was clearly resorting to direct intervention to achieve his aims. Although the Colombian government suddenly expressed great interest in ratifying the Hay-Herran convention, Roosevelt decided to negotiate with the more tractable new Republic of Panama. Its minister in Washington was none other than Phillippe Bunau-Varilla. On November 18, 1903, this wily Frenchman signed a treaty with Secretary of State John Hay which provided that the United States would pay Panama a lump sum of $10 million and $250,000 annually after 1912, that Panama would grant the United States a perpetual lease to a ten-mile zone across the isthmus, and that Panama would allow the United States the right of intervention. Both governments soon ratified this treaty (Hay–Bunau-Varilla), which removed another stumbling block to the realization of Roosevelt's dream and the attainment of a major objective of United States foreign policy. As the president said, in commenting on his actions: "We, in effect, policed the Isthmus in the interest of its inhabitants and of our own national needs, and for the good of the entire civilized world. Failure to act as the Administration acted would have meant great waste of life [and] great suffering."[5]

The final stage in the canal project was the actual construction, which was not accomplished without difficulties. The president appointed two special canal commissions to supervise the work, but in 1907 entrusted it to the United States Army Corps of Engineers. Health problems were another barrier since the malarial swamps of Panama effectively slowed building progress. Really rapid construction did not get under way until Colonel William C. Gorgas undertook a dramatic program of disease control. Because construction difficulties were so complex, the time needed for completion of the project was much longer than Roosevelt had expected. Instead of half-a-dozen years the task took more than a decade. Its ultimate cost of more than $500 million exceeded original estimates more than fourfold. But the work went on, and in 1914 the United States formally opened the canal to world traffic. The eventual completion of this project reflected the determination of American policy makers to establish naval power as a major goal of the New Diplomacy. With the canal, Mahan's dreams came true as the United States Navy became the nation's first line of defense and a main instrument for wielding American political and economic influence in Europe and the Far East.

EUROPE

In accordance with his broad conception of a "large" policy Roosevelt also envisioned a more active American role in Europe. His prime purpose was to maintain the existing balance of power and to preserve peace on the continent. With these ends in view Secretary of State Hay negotiated a series of treaties between the United States and other nations that provided for arbitration of disputes between them. Roosevelt also sent a United States delegation to the Hague Conference of 1907, which discussed plans for international disarmament. The increased activism of American diplomats was also noted by Europeans during the Moroccan crisis of 1906. Both France and Germany were vying for influence in North Africa and their rivalries had appeared to bring them to the

[5]James D. Richardson (ed.), *A Compilation of the Messages and Papers of the Presidents* (n.d.), XVI, 6918 – 19 (Jan. 4, 1904).

brink of war. In an effort to bring about a peaceful settlement of their differences, the Great Powers called an international conference in Algeciras, Spain, to which the United States also sent representatives. At Roosevelt's direction, American diplomats supported the French position and sought to prevent German influence from becoming too powerful. Although the United States did not play a major role at this conference, the American presence heralded Roosevelt's determination to have the United States assume the stance of a great world power.

FAR EAST

Roosevelt also attempted to maintain a balance of power in the Far East, particularly to restrain Russian influence. With this in mind in 1905 the president accepted the Japanese request to mediate their dispute with Russia over possession of the Kurile Islands, which had led to the Russo-Japanese War of 1905. Roosevelt was unaware that both sides were close to exhaustion and collapse; therefore his offer of mediation was eagerly accepted, especially by the Japanese. The two sides deliberated at the Portsmouth (New Hampshire) Conference and agreed on a treaty by which the Japanese made some territorial gains. Ironically, Roosevelt later received the Nobel Peace Prize for his efforts, although in fact his action only encouraged the Japanese to further expansion and warlike activities.

In fact, Roosevelt quickly grasped the dangers to which American possessions were exposed by Japan's expansion. Fearing for the safety of the Philippines, Roosevelt instructed his secretary of war, William Howard Taft, to conclude an understanding with Taro Katsura, Japan's prime minister. The Taft-Katsura Agreement provided that the United States respect Japanese interests in Korea and that Japan acknowledge American ownership of the Philippine Islands. This was further clarified in the Root-Takahira Agreement of 1908, in which both nations recognized each other's possessions in the Pacific while Japan paid lip service to the Open Door policy and the independence of China. In 1909 Roosevelt sent the United States Navy on a cruise around the world, but its visit to Japan probably aroused as much fear as respect.

Meanwhile, Roosevelt had used all his powers of personal persuasion and charm with the Japanese to avert a serious crisis over the segregation of Japanese schoolchildren in San Francisco.

There in 1906 the school board issued an order directing Japanese youngsters to attend a special school. The Japanese government was furious with what it considered a slur on Oriental racial pride. Roosevelt attempted to assuage their feelings by negotiating the Gentleman's Agreement of 1907. In return for his informal but successful entreaties with the San Francisco school authorities to rescind the order, the Japanese government agreed to restrict the emigration of laborers to the United States. Thus, the Taft-Katsura Agreement, the Root-Takahira Agreement, the Gentleman's Agreement, and the navy's cruise were part of a broad American effort to contain Japanese influence in the Far East. Little did Americans of this decade realize that Roosevelt's policy of maintaining a balance of power in Asia was a precursor to large-scale American intervention in the Far East later in the twentieth century.

ROOSEVELT'S DIPLOMACY: SUMMARY

During his presidency, Roosevelt did a great deal to transform American diplomacy. From an emphasis on isolation he had brought it into the mainstream of international politics. Increasing American reliance on naval strength dictated consequent American domination of the Caribbean. America's new role as a world leader required constant vigilance in Europe and the Far East to maintain a balance of power in these areas. For better or for worse, United States diplomacy was now entangled with the policies of nations everywhere.

TAFT AND THE NEW DIPLOMACY

Roosevelt's successor, William Howard Taft, continued many of his predecessor's policies despite his own inclinations against overly vigorous action. He furthered the construction of the Panama Canal and, even more than Roosevelt, authorized direct American intervention in Caribbean countries wracked by civil wars or disorders. Thus, he sent United States Marines to Nicaragua in 1912 when a revolution against President José Zelaya brought great turmoil. In view of large American mining properties in the country and a remote threat of intervention by a major foreign power, Taft sought to win influence over Nicaraguan affairs by sending troops.

Yet, Taft's predilection was for peaceful means rather than force to consolidate America's position in the Caribbean. Together with Secretary of State Philander C. Knox he formulated the idea of Dollar Diplomacy. This concept was designed to replace European financiers with Americans throughout the Caribbean, since the Panama Canal was nearing completion and the United States was therefore seeking to strengthen its defenses in the area. More effectively than military might, Taft hoped that Dollar Diplomacy could win a preponderant influence for the United States. In accordance with this concept in 1911 Secretary of State Philander C. Knox signed a treaty with Honduras for the refinancing of its national debt through American bankers. Just a little earlier, Knox had also encouraged a New York investment syndicate to invest in the National Bank of Haiti and to rehabilitate the foundering Haitian currency and large public debt.

Unlike the Rough Rider, Taft did not relish active American intervention in European affairs. While also concerned with the power balance on the Continent, Taft preferred to rely on legal means to achieve his objectives. Consequently he encouraged the further extension of the Hay arbitration treaties that had first been negotiated during the Roosevelt administration.

Similarly, in the Far East Taft eschewed the use of American military might. Instead, he utilized Dollar Diplomacy to encourage American financiers to participate in an international Banker's Consortium in 1909 to construct the Manchurian railroad. Some Americans entered this project with great reluctance, and sought the first opportunity to withdraw from the scheme. The risks involved were great, and there were still many fine investment opportunities within the United States. Taft's Far Eastern venture thus was no great success. Indeed, most aspects of Taft's diplomacy lacked the vigor that had characterized the activities of Roosevelt. But despite his placidity, Taft neither reversed any major policy goals or methods of the New Diplomacy nor altered its basic framework.

WILSON'S IDEALISM AND FOREIGN POLICY

The advent of Woodrow Wilson to the White House brought some changes in the rhetoric but not in the design of United States foreign policy. In theory, Wilson hoped to introduce a larger measure of idealism into American diplomacy. In practice, he adhered closely to the patterns established by Roosevelt. Throughout the Caribbean and Latin America he continued direct intervention to preserve United States hegemony and to safeguard the Panama Canal; in Europe the United States strove to preserve peace and to maintain the precarious power balance; in the Far East Wilson continued to strive for acceptance of the Open Door policy and the preservation of the status quo. Thus, American foreign policy under Wilson reflected great continuity with the preceding period.

CARIBBEAN

Wilson's attitude toward Latin Americans was not unlike that of a benevolent father toward his unruly children. He wished fervently that they would adopt democratic political institutions fashioned after his own — or the American — image; if they could only display such virtue they were bound to succeed. If they proved recalcitrant or stubborn he was determined to chastise them, or to use means of persuasion designed to encourage what he considered to be moral behavior.

To be sure, at the beginning of his administration Wilson hoped to turn a new leaf. Intervention was to be fashionable no longer. And Wilson seemed to practice what he preached. First, he settled a developing controversy between the British and the United States over Panama Canal tolls. In August 1912, Congress enacted a law to exempt American coastal vessels from canal tolls, which constituted a violation of the Hay-Pauncefote Treaty. The British government vigorously protested, but Wilson did not act until he felt sure of his mastery over Congress. Then, in 1914 he successfully prevailed upon the legislators to withdraw the exemption. A second reflection of a seeming change in United States policy came with Wilson's effort to woo Colombia. In April 1914, Secretary of State William Jennings Bryan signed a treaty with Colombia under which the United States apologized for the Panama events of 1903 and offered a conscience payment of $25 million. Publication of these terms aroused an enormous furor, especially among the followers of Theodore Roosevelt for it implied a rejection of his methods in securing the Panama Canal. With Roosevelt's urging, the Senate defeated this treaty.

Whatever Wilson's hopes for new policies may have been, however, the record of his administration revealed continued intervention. No president could ignore the responsibility to protect the Panama Canal. Thus, when a turbulent revolution in Haiti once more raised the spectre of foreign intervention late in 1914, Wilson ordered the landing of United States Marines to restore order. Even more contradictory to his professed desires for true Latin American self-determination and independence was the establishment there of American military government in July 1915, and the installation of a native regime under direct American supervision. In addition, the Wilson administration imposed a treaty on Haiti which gave the United States the right of intervention as well as extensive controls over Haiti's finances.

Nor could the citizens of Nicaragua discern any change in United States diplomacy under Wilson. The marines sent by President Taft remained. And the former leader of the anti-imperialists in the United States, William Jennings Bryan, negotiated a treaty with Nicaragua that granted the United States the right of intervention. The United States Senate refused to ratify this agreement, but in 1916 a revised version of the Bryan-Chamorro Treaty did receive the necessary approval. In return for a payment of $3 million to Nicaragua, the United States received the right to construct a possible canal across its territories, and the privilege of building a naval base on the Gulf of Fonseca.

American intervention in Dominican affairs also continued during the Wilson era. Throughout 1914 political disorders continued rife in the Dominican Republic. Wilson sincerely hoped that Dominican leaders themselves would be able to cope with the crisis. He offered them his aid in settling their rivalries and suggested that American control of their constabulary and of their financial institutions could help to establish a measure of stability for the war-torn nation. But the Dominicans balked at giving the United States the right of intervention, which it already had in Cuba and Panama, and violence continued to convulse the island republic. Under these circumstances Wilson acted much as Theodore Roosevelt had before him. Gone were the professions of self-determination for Caribbean peoples as on May 15, 1916, the marines returned to Santo Domingo, seized the capital, and established a military government that displaced the native regime. Until 1922, Santo

Domingo continued to be governed by the benign, paternalistic, but stern arm of the United States.

MEXICO

Perhaps the greatest failure of Wilsonian idealism in the Western Hemisphere occurred in Mexico, where American business interests — especially in oil and railroads — had a direct stake in political stability. During the Wilsonian era Mexico was undergoing a series of revolutions. The violence began in 1910 when a group of liberal reformers headed by Francisco Madero overthrew the thirty-three-year-old oligarchy of Porfirio Diaz. President Taft recognized the Madero regime, but in February 1913, just before Wilson entered the White House, the bandit Victoriano Huerta led a counter-revolution. Huerta's forces assassinated Madero and ruthlessly established their leader in power. Aghast at the use of extra-constitutional methods, Wilson refused to recognize Huerta, who ruled for less than a year. He was succeeded by Venustiano Carranza, in office until 1920. Unfortunately, Carranza found himself unable to restrain various rebellious factions, and so revolution and turmoil in Mexico continued. The depredations of the guerrilla chief Pancho Villa were especially disturbing to Wilson, since they resulted in the loss of American lives and property. Villa's incursion into United States territory made headlines on March 9, 1916, when he raided Columbus, New Mexico, looting and burning as he went. Quite unexpectedly, Mexico presented major diplomatic difficulties for Wilson.

Wilson's diplomacy in this complicated Mexican situation constituted a series of failures. In theory, Wilson had great sympathy for the downtrodden masses of Mexican peasants and their aspirations for improvement. Certainly he was prepared to aid them in the attainment of a more egalitarian society. With his characteristic idealism he made the following statement:

> There can in what we do be no thought of aggression or of selfish aggrandizement. We seek to maintain the dignity and authority of the United States, only because we wish always to keep our great influence unimpaired for the uses of liberty, both in the United States and wherever else it may be employed for the benefit of mankind.[6]

[6]U. S., *Congressional Record,* 63rd Cong., 2nd sess. (April 20, 1914), p. 6909.

But somehow circumstances seemed to conspire against Wilson's good intentions as he appeared to be forced into a policy of direct intervention, at least from the Mexican point of view.

As noted, in 1913 Wilson's first step was to refuse to grant recognition to the government of Huerta. Wilson's sympathies lay with the Madero followers, advocates of constitutional liberalism. The president was truly shocked by Huerta's murder of Madero. Although twenty-seven other nations granted Huerta recognition, Wilson steadfastly refused, hoping that his intransigent stance would eventually lead to Huerta's downfall. Wilson liked to call his policy one of "watchful waiting," and hoped that patience would aid him in achieving his objectives.

Wilson's moral aversion to Huerta was so strong that he did not shrink from using direct military force against him. In February 1914 the United States removed Taft's embargo on the shipment of arms to Mexico. Then, in April 1914, Mexicans were treated to a remarkable display of Wilsonian idealism. When some American sailors from a United States warship off Vera Cruz went on shore to purchase supplies, they were detained by officials of the Huerta government. Although the Mexicans quickly released the Americans, Wilson ordered drastic action. The American commander, Admiral Henry T. Mayo, demanded a formal apology, to which the Mexicans agreed. But Mayo demanded a twenty-one gun salute that was not forthcoming. Since Wilson was willing to resort to war in order to overthrow Huerta, he supported Admiral Mayo's bombardment of the city of Vera Cruz, which killed more than 200 of its inhabitants. American marines then landed to capture the town. A full-scale American invasion seemed in the offing, something feared by Mexicans of every political persuasion, no matter how divided they were at the moment. In the midst of this war crisis, representatives from Argentina, Brazil, and Chile in Washington on April 25, 1914, offered to mediate the dispute. United States and Mexican delegates met at Niagara Falls in Canada between May 20 and July 2, 1914, to negotiate differences. The representatives of the new Carranza government — just coming into power — made it clear that they, too, opposed American intervention in their internal affairs. Wilson still hoped to unify the warring Mexican factions by urging a convention (American style) of revolutionary leaders. The failure of this meeting in November 1914 provided the background for another period of open warfare, especially between Pancho Villa and Carranza. Wilson extended *de facto* recognition to the Carranza regime in October 1915, although he did so with great reluctance.

Despite Wilson's hopes for constitutional government in Mexico, he again felt compelled to authorize direct United States intervention. Villa's raid on Columbus, New Mexico (1916), provoked him to immediate action. He ordered units of the United States Army in Texas to cross the border into Mexico to pursue Villa. Carranza's consent seemed implied. But as Villa eluded his American pursuers Wilson dispatched a punitive expedition into Mexico under Brigadier General John J. Pershing, who roamed more than three hundred miles in Mexico's interior without finding a trace of Villa. As the American army settled down to what appeared to be an occupation, the Carranza regime became increasingly suspicious of Wilson's motives. Was the United States seeking to annex northern Mexico? Wilson's refusal to withdraw the American forces aroused further suspicions. As tensions between the United States and Carranza mounted, Villa continued to roam at large. Only the diversions of the war in Europe restrained Wilson from a full-fledged pursuit. In January 1917 he yielded to Carranza's demand for American withdrawal and two months later extended full *de jure* recognition to his government. Thus, the United States abjured one war to enter another.

By 1917 the ideals envisioned by Wilson in his Latin American diplomacy seemed in shambles. He had fervently sought peace but had engaged in war; he had hoped for self-determination for Mexicans but had increasingly interfered in their internal affairs; he had hoped for stable constitutional government but promoted revolution and chaos. In the process Wilson had alienated a large segment of influential opinion in the Western Hemisphere and added suspicion to the distrust already aroused by Theodore Roosevelt. The course of action into which he was forced by his own miscalculations as well as by the course of events, was unfortunate in contributing to misunderstanding. Yet his policies were not wholly negative in their impact. American intervention in Mexico revealed such a thorny nest of problems that American presidents during the next fifty years sought to avoid direct interference at all costs. In effect, this achieved one of Wilson's professed goals — self-determination. His opposition to dictatorship encouraged the rise of constitutional leaders in Mexico, led to increasingly stable governments, and stimulated domestic reform programs. But the means Wilson used to attain some of these ends were far removed from those which he had envisaged.

FAR EAST

Wilsonian idealism also did not effect any great changes in American diplomacy toward the Far East. The contradictions in United States policies were not resolved, as evidenced by the president's continuing the Open Door policy, on the one hand, while seeking to appease Japan, on the other. In an initial burst of idealism, in 1913 Wilson secured withdrawal of those American bankers who were participating in the consortium to build the Manchurian railroad. Since many of these individuals had shown little enthusiasm for the project in the first place, Wilson had no great difficulty in securing their cooperation. In theory, this action buttressed Chinese independence, although, in fact, other powers continued to infringe upon it heavily.

At the same time Wilson sought to mollify Japan. In 1913 the California legislature passed an Alien Land Law to prohibit Orientals from owning land in the state. This measure was primarily directed at the Japanese, who in the preceding decade had established themselves as an important element among California farmers. The Japanese government protested what it considered to be a racial insult. Wilson seemed powerless to change state legislation, but he sent Secretary of State William Jennings Bryan to Sacramento in a vain attempt to persuade California legislators to modify or repeal the law. The incident created additional tensions between the United States and Japan and perhaps explains why Wilson became especially solicitous to please the Japanese government. His attitude was reflected in the Lansing-Ishi Agreement of 1917. Japan had taken advantage of the outbreak of World War I in Europe to seize German possessions in the Pacific, notably the Marshall Islands and the Shantung Peninsula. In 1915 Japan also made twenty-one demands on China which would have made that nation a mere puppet state. United States protests led the Japanese to modify their demands, but the Lansing-Ishi Agreement provided American recognition of Japan's special interests in China while, incredibly, Japan agreed to respect the Open Door policy and the sovereignty of China. The Wilson administration thus continued to adhere to the fiction of the Open Door policy although implicitly or explicitly agreeing to Japanese expansion in the Far East. Wilson may well have wanted self-determination for the people of the Pacific region, but the record of his administration revealed no appreciable changes in the pattern of United States diplomacy as it had been formulated in the age of Theodore Roosevelt.

WILSONIAN DIPLOMACY IN RETROSPECT

Wilsonian foreign policies thus constituted an amalgam of imperialist and anti-imperialist precepts, of idealism and realism. Wilson's efforts to lift American diplomacy to a high moral or idealistic plane largely failed, although they were not entirely without some impact. His Caribbean diplomacy revealed questionable judgments, but in its basic postulates it continued the programs of his predecessors. In the Far East also Wilson was not too successful in resolving the dilemmas of American policy, and continued the guidelines he found upon entering the White House. The commitments of the past, the pressure of events, and also his own ambivalence led Wilson to the path which he trod in the diplomatic sphere.

SUMMARY

Between 1890 and 1917 American foreign policy had undergone great changes. From a decided preference for isolation, the nation had come increasingly to rely on expansion and internationalism, as befitted a world power. The reasons for this shift were varied. Industrialization of the country and the new needs of national security wrought by far-reaching technological developments were major factors. Such considerations led McKinley, Roosevelt, Taft, and Wilson to follow policies designed to establish American dominance in the Caribbean, and to maintain a balance of power in Europe and Asia. The ideals of these men, their methods, and their personal styles varied greatly, but their different actions revealed a remarkable pattern of similarity and continuity. By 1917 Wilson discovered — with great reluctance — that even greater American involvement was required if the United States was to maintain a balance of power in Europe favorable to its own interests.

FOR FURTHER READING

On the new departures in American diplomacy after 1898 ERNEST R. MAY, *Imperial Democracy: The Rise of America as a Great Power* (New York: Harcourt, Brace & World, 1961), is highly informative. GEORGE F. KENNAN, *American Diplomacy, 1900 – 1950* (Chicago: University of Chicago Press, 1951) is critical of the ambiguities of American foreign policy during this period. ROBERT L. BEISNER, *Twelve Against Empire: The Anti-Imperialists, 1898 – 1900* (New York: McGraw-Hill, 1968) is one of the first books to discuss this important movement at length. Two biographies that stress President McKinley's moderation are MARGARET LEECH, *In the Days of McKinley* (New York: Harper, 1959), and H. WAYNE MORGAN, *William McKinley and His America* (Syracuse: Syracuse University Press, 1963). A short, popular account of the Spanish-American War is by FRANK FREIDEL, *The Splendid Little War* (Boston: Little, Brown, 1958). JULIUS PRATT, *The Expansionists of 1898* (Baltimore: Johns Hopkins University Press, 1936) stresses the importance of Manifest Destiny in American overseas expansion. Roosevelt's diplomacy in the Far East is discussed in detail by HOWARD K. BEALE, *Theodore Roosevelt and the Rise of America to World Power* (Baltimore: Johns Hopkins University Press, 1956). SAMUEL FLAGG BEMIS, *The Latin-American Policy of the United States* (New York: Harcourt, Brace and Co., 1943) is an older but very reliable survey of the subject. Among biographies of American policy makers consult JOHN A. GARRATY, *Henry Cabot Lodge* (New York: Knopf, 1953) and WILLIAM E. LIVEZEY, *Mahan on Sea Power* (Norman: University of Oklahoma Press, 1947). PAOLO COLETTA has completed a fine biography, *William Jennings Bryan*, 3 vols. (Lincoln: University of Nebraska Press, 1964 – 1969).

4

THE UNITED STATES IN
WORLD WAR I

In Europe the spring of 1914 brought not hope, but tension; not peace, but an open outbreak of hostilities. Problems that had been accumulating over decades crystallized in the dramatic events surrounding the assassination of Archduke Francis Ferdinand of Austria by a Serb on June 28, 1914, at Sarajevo (Serbia). This set the stage for one of the great conflicts in world history as Austria and Germany faced Russia, France, and Great Britain. As a recent newcomer to the ranks of major powers, the United States could hardly fail to be affected by the threatened disruption of the Continent and the Atlantic community.

Some of the same forces that had driven the United States into the war with Spain in 1898 were operating to bring the European nations into conflict. Extreme and belligerent nationalism was one cause. Whether expressed in strident Pan-Germanism, shrill French cries of "revenge" against the Germans, Russian Pan-Slavism, or some of the more regional hostilities in the Balkans, nationalism proved to be a disruptive factor in European affairs. Overseas, too, economic imperialism brought rivalries between the great powers as they competed for economic concessions and markets in such faraway places as China, Africa, the Middle East, and Latin America. Perhaps some of these rivalries could have been muted, but a third factor, virulent militarism throughout Europe, encouraged open conflict. The influence of military men on diplomatic negotiations, and the presence of large standing armies and navies, boded ill for peace. A fourth precipitating factor was the network of entangling alliances and treaty systems, which hastened the juggernaut of war as France, Great Britain, and Russia banded together in the Triple Entente to confront Germany, Austria-Hungary, and the Ottoman Empire (Turkey), bound in the Triple Alliance. The assassination of Archduke Ferdinand brought mutual suspicions to a head. By August 1914 the major European nations were at war with each other as they followed their treaty obligations.

During that summer of 1914 few Americans believed that the outbreak of hostilities in Europe would seriously affect the United States. President Wilson's reaction was perhaps characteristic when he revealed concern primarily for his personal and domestic problems. His first wife, Edith Bolling Wilson, had just died in July 1914, and he was plunged into a prolonged period of grief and mourning. Moreover, since Congress had recently enacted the major portions of his domestic program, he was concerned with planning domestic legislation in the immediate future. The new problems that emanated from the European conflict soon diverted his energies as he was forced to shift attention to foreign policy. In his own changing interests he mirrored the concerns of millions of Americans.

THE UNITED STATES AND WARTIME PROBLEMS

EFFECTS OF BRITAIN'S INVOLVEMENT

The war's effect on Anglo-American relations chiefly concerned infringement on the property rights of Americans. Almost immediately after the outbreak of hostilities the British established a naval blockade of Germany, as they sought to impede the flow of supplies to members of the Triple Alliance. German naval activities, on the other hand, affected the safety of American lives as the Kaiser's submarines roamed the oceans to destroy British and neutral ships in order to isolate the British Isles. In both cases a neutral nation like the United States was bound to be caught in the middle.

British policies during the first year of the war created several problems for Americans. The British blockade seriously interfered with neutral shipping involving trade with the Continent. The mining of the North Sea by the Royal Navy hindered

American trade with Baltic and Scandinavian nations, not to mention Germany itself. In addition, the British engaged in visit and search of neutral vessels, bringing back memories of the War of 1812. If Americans were no longer as conscious of British infringement of their rights as neutral carriers than in an earlier age, they still resented the boarding of their merchant ships by British sailors who searched their cargoes for possible contraband bound for Germany. Such activities could not fail to arouse resentment. This practice also led to a problem concerning the clear definition of what goods constituted contraband. According to the British interpretation, foodstuffs, medical supplies, or virtually anything else that could be used by German consumers could be designated as contraband liable to confiscation. The State Department, on the other hand, adhered to the traditional definition of contraband: only munitions and other implements of war. In hundreds of cases between 1914 and 1917 British and American claims clashed on this question. Irritating also was the British practice of blacklisting and thus prohibiting British trade with American corporations engaged in commercial dealings with German, Austrian, or Turkish firms. As neutrals, Americans had every right to trade with whomever they pleased, and this attempted pressure by the British provided another disrupting factor in Anglo-American relations. Finally, thousands of Americans were disturbed by the British practice of censoring United States mail bound for Triple Alliance nations. Often the Royal Navy would seize mail sacks on American or other vessels. The eyes of British censors fell not only on personal or confidential communications, but also on business and trade secrets of Americans engaged in overseas transactions. In these diverse ways the British government was interfering with American property rights on the high seas and creating new problems between the two countries.

STRAINS IN AMERICAN-GERMAN RELATIONS

At the same time the United States was encountering serious difficulties with Germany. While the disputes with Great Britain usually centered on interference with American property, those with the Kaiser's government often concerned destruction or interference with American lives. The most serious issue undoubtedly was the unrestricted submarine warfare begun by Germany on February 4, 1915, in an effort to cut off the flow of American supplies to England. The new policy meant that, contrary to principles of international law, Germany would sink vessels without any regard for the safety of passengers and crew. The Germans were driven to this practice because the light construction of their submarines made them peculiarly susceptible to ramming and destruction by larger ships. If a submarine could not take advantage of the element of surprise, it lost its effectiveness as a weapon. Thus, soon after the announcement of unrestricted submarine warfare, the German admiralty began to sink ships of all nations without prior warning. While its campaign was aimed primarily at Allied vessels, the German U-boat captains did not always take sufficient care to identify the nationality of the ship under attack, hurried as they were in such dangerous circumstances. Thus, American vessels soon became involved in this Atlantic warfare. On May 1, 1915, a German submarine torpedoed the United States tanker, the *Gulflight,* with the resultant loss of two American lives. Meanwhile, United States citizens traveling on Allied ships were subjected to even greater dangers. Most serious was the German sinking of the giant British luxury liner, the *Lusitania,* on May 7, 1915, off the coast of Ireland. Of the 1198 people who lost their lives in this tragedy, 128 were Americans. On August 17, 1915, two Americans died when the British ship *Arabic* was attacked by a German submarine. On March 24, 1916, a French vessel, the *Sussex,* succumbed to German torpedoes; three Americans lost their lives. Unrestricted submarine warfare, therefore, was seriously infringing on United States neutrality.

At the same time many Americans became annoyed with German espionage efforts in the United States, which were designed to impede the flow of supplies to Great Britain. It was widely believed that the German ambassador in Washington, Count Johann von Bernstorff, headed a German spy ring in the United States that included as many as 3000 agents. The German military attaché, Franz von Papen, spent much of his time in actual supervision of this force. Some of the details concerning such clandestine activities came out into the open in the Heinrich Albert case. Heinrich Albert, the German consul in New York City, absent-mindedly left his briefcase on a Third Avenue elevated train. When the bag was discovered, it was found to be packed with compromising materials revealing various phases of German espionage activities in the United States. Even more disturbing were the attempts of German agents to resort to violence as revealed in the foiling of a plot by German agents to blow up production facilities at the Bethlehem Steel Company plant in Pittsburgh, Pennsylvania. More damaging was the Black Tom Docks explosion in 1916, on the docks of the Erie Railroad in New Jersey, where supplies were being loaded on board ships bound for England. Although the physical damage was not great, it brought a sense of fear — if not hysteria — to many Americans concerned with future targets of German saboteurs. German submarine warfare and, to a lesser extent, sabotage activities were therefore straining relations between the United States and Germany.

STAGES OF WILSONIAN DIPLOMACY

With the United States caught between two turbulent groups of belligerents, as chief of state Wilson had the unenviable task of steering an even course through the troubled waters. His role was difficult as he tried to reconcile his avowed long-range idealism with every day short-range problems. In view of the limited policy alternatives, it is questionable whether or not another man in the White House would have acted differently than he in shaping American diplomacy.

Wilson's cautious course in response to problems posed by Great Britain and Germany evolved through at least five stages. In the first phase (August 1914 to February 1915) Wilson sought to maintain a position of complete neutrality. With the beginning of unrestricted German submarine warfare in February 1915, Wilson turned United States foreign policy into a second stage characterized by diplomatic warnings (February 1915 to August 1916). Hoping to ease the increasingly burdensome problem of American neutrality, Wilson embarked on a third phase as he tried personal mediation between the combatants to end the conflict (December 1915 to December 1916). For a while his strenuous peacemaking efforts appeared to have some success, but the resumption of unrestricted submarine attacks by

Germany in February 1917 forced him to shift his stance. Thus, Wilson entered upon a fourth phase of his war diplomacy in February 1917, when he took the nation into a period of armed neutrality (February 1917 to April 1917). With the country already engaged in a shooting war, Wilson's alternatives seemed to shrink even further. In April 1917, therefore, after days of agonizing contemplation, Wilson came to the reluctant conclusion that the only course left open to him was a declaration of war against Germany. "It is a fearful thing," he noted in his war message to Congress on April 2, 1917, "to lead this great peaceful people into war." And somewhat unrealistically, but true to his idealism, he added: "The world must be made safe for democracy. Its peace must be planted upon the tested foundations of political liberty."[1] But the patterns of United States diplomacy were clearer than Wilson acknowledged at the time. America entered World War I to restore the balance of power on the European continent as it had already tried to do by peaceful means in the preceding two decades.

FIRST STAGE — NEUTRALITY

At the outbreak of the war in the summer of 1914 Wilson advocated a complete neutrality for the United States. Cognizant of George Washington's role in another European conflict (1793), Wilson's first reaction was to issue a Neutrality Proclamation on August 4, 1914, in which he called upon Americans to be impartial in word and deed, and to refrain from possible involvement. As he said: "No person within . . . the United States shall take part in the [European] wars, but . . . shall maintain a strict and impartial neutrality."[2] Wilson's Secretary of State, William Jennings Bryan, took additional measures to maintain neutrality. In October 1914 he announced an informal policy of the State Department to discourage American loans to any of the belligerents lest they entangle United States citizens with foreign causes. At the same time Congress took another measure to insure neutrality by enacting the Tonnage Act of 1914, which provided

---

[1] U. S., *Congressional Record,* 56th Cong., 1st sess. (April 2, 1917), p. 104.

[2] *New York Times,* August 5, 1914.

federal aid for the increased construction of American merchant ships. Hopefully this would relieve American shippers from using foreign vessels and from becoming embroiled in disputes with the warring powers on the high seas. Thus, the president, the State Department, and Congress each acted with determination to maintain the nation's neutrality, and rigorously to abstain from any action that could involve the country in the European war.

SECOND STAGE — DIPLOMATIC WARNINGS

As the conflict increased in tempo, Wilson's problems multiplied and he embarked on a phase characterized by diplomatic warnings. In response to the British declaration in the fall of 1914 closing the North Sea to all traffic, the president sent a vigorous protest in which he upheld American neutral rights in international waters. He also sent notes to the British in which he protested their interpretation of contraband and interference with American mail. In their replies the British usually hedged, pleading necessity, but they refused to modify their policies.

At the same time, the German announcement of unrestricted submarine warfare on February 4, 1915, also prompted a Wilsonian response. In a vehement communication to the German government on February 10, 1915, Wilson blended moralism and realism by declaring that he would hold them to "strict accountability" for any losses of life or property suffered by Americans due to clear violations of international law. This "strict accountability" note clearly placed the United States in direct opposition to the German policy of unrestrained U-boat attacks. Secretary of State Bryan reiterated this position after the sinking of the British ship *Falaba* in March 1915, resulting in the loss of one American. But Wilson's policy was put to a real test by the sinking of the *Lusitania*. Frustrated by the failure of his attempt at peaceful persuasion, Wilson now took a stronger stand. In eloquent language he declared:

> American citizens act within their indisputable rights in taking their ships and in traveling wherever their legitimate business calls them upon the high seas, and exercise those rights in what should be the well-justified confidence that their lives will not be endangered by acts done in clear violation of universally acknowledged international obligations, and certainly in the

confidence that their own Government will sustain them in the exercise of their rights.[3]

Nevertheless, Wilson was far more conciliatory than many newspapers and periodicals which were clamoring for war. In a series of three "*Lusitania* notes" (May 1915) Wilson used strong language to demand that the Germans cease their sinkings without prior warning. Bryan considered Wilson's tone to be so provocative that he resigned from the State Department rather than sign his name to these diplomatic dispatches. He himself felt that Americans should be restrained from traveling on foreign ships or in foreign seas. Wilson, however, was convinced that his policy of strong diplomatic protests to Germany was successful. In his communications he hinted that the United States would break diplomatic relations with Germany unless it ceased practices that were clearly illegal under international law. Although the replies by the German government were evasive, Wilson considered them to be a conciliatory acceptance of his demands.

But he was disappointed a few months later when on August 19, 1915, a German U-boat sank the *Arabic*. This new crisis led Wilson to take a stronger stand. He threatened a direct break of diplomatic relations between the United States and Germany unless unrestricted submarine warfare was stopped immediately. Such a strong demand led the German government to yield. On August 26, 1915, it gave the "*Arabic* pledge," promising not to sink unarmed vessels without due warning. The Germans kept this commitment until March 24, 1916, when a German U-boat raider sank the *Sussex*. As Wilson prepared to implement his earlier threat to break diplomatic contacts, the German government hastened to give the "*Sussex* pledge," in which they agreed not only to cease sinkings without warning, but also to accept the American demand that they visit and search vessels before destroying them. Wilson's great patience and determination to rely on diplomatic warnings rather than force to secure recognition of American rights seemed at last to have succeeded. Throughout 1916 he was hailed as having preserved the peace, and for keeping the United States from entering a needless war.

[3] *Foreign Relations of the United States, 1915* (Washington: U. S. Government Printing Office, 1928), Supplement, pp. 394–95.

Indeed, in the election of 1916 Wilson campaigned under the slogan "He kept us out of war." Republicans like Theodore Roosevelt and other advocates of forceful action and preparedness castigated Wilson as being too mild. They supported Charles Evans Hughes, the distinguished former governor of New York and associate justice of the United States Supreme Court, who was the Republican presidential candidate in 1916. Hughes urged the nation to adopt a stronger policy than Wilson's to maintain neutral rights. After a close and hard-won election Wilson could feel justified, however. His victory at the polls reflected the desire of perhaps a majority of the American people who hoped that the United States could remain aloof from the European conflict.

THIRD STAGE — PERSONAL MEDIATION

A feeling that Wilson had kept the United States out of the World War was reinforced by his diplomatic efforts to bring about mediation. As early as January 1915, he had sent his trusted confidante, Colonel E. M. House, to London and Berlin to ascertain their respective attitudes on possible peace terms. In London the diplomats demanded German evacuation of Belgium before any kind of talks could commence; in Berlin authorities were equally recalcitrant on this question and refused to make any concessions as a price for negotiations. Thus, the adamant stance of both sides left a deadlock. Nevertheless, at Christmastime, 1915, Wilson tried again. Once more House journeyed to the European capitals, and once more he found his peacemaking efforts rebuffed. Wilson made another attempt shortly after his election victory in 1916 when he offered his good services as a mediator to the belligerents. The Germans were sympathetic, but both the Central Powers and the Allies were planning new campaigns that, each was certain, would bring a final victory. Thus, neither side was in a serious mood to allow American mediation.

FOURTH STAGE — ARMED NEUTRALITY

Within a few weeks after this last failure to bring about mediation Wilson found himself taking the nation into a stage of armed neutrality. Indeed, his re-election in 1916 constituted an enormous irony. He had been elected because of his peacekeeping efforts, and yet within five months thereafter the nation was at war. The force of events was leading the president into reluctant actions from which it was difficult to turn back. This was true of the period of armed neutrality, which was a step on the road to war, as during February and March 1917 German submarines openly attacked American vessels.

Steps taken by the German government during the first three months of 1917 narrowed Wilson's alternatives and led him to embark on this armed neutrality. Most disturbing was the resumption of unrestricted submarine warfare after February 1, 1917. In a desperate effort to win a smashing victory, the German government announced that it would sink all vessels in the vicinity of Great Britain, France, and Italy without previous warning. One American ship weekly was to be allowed to sail between New York and Falmouth, England, provided that it had clear markings. This threat was no idle bluster for the declaration was quickly followed by a succession of sinkings. On February 25, 1917, the British ship *Laconia* was sunk, with the loss of American lives. On March 18, 1917, German torpedoes sank three United States merchant ships without warning, resulting in death and destruction. A third step that forced Wilson's hand was the Zimmerman telegram. On February 25, 1917, the American ambassador to Great Britain, Walter Hines Page, sent the president word of a message from the German foreign secretary to Arthur Zimmerman, the German minister to Mexico. In these instructions, which the British had intercepted, Foreign Secretary Bethman-Hollweg noted that if Germany and the United States were at war, Zimmerman should urge the Mexicans to declare war on the United States. Germany would support them in recovering the territories they had lost in the Mexican War of 1848, including Texas, New Mexico, Arizona, and California. To Wilson and many Americans this communication revealed German intentions in the New World more accurately than most other events in the preceding two decades. Former fears appeared to have become realities.

Yet Wilson still hoped to keep the nation out of war even though the odds seemed against him. Following up his earlier threat in the Sussex note of 1916, he broke off diplomatic negotiations with Germany on February 3, 1917, because of the resumption of unrestricted submarine attacks on merchant shipping. Wilson prayed that this measure would deter Germany from further hostile activities, but the events of February 1917 discouraged him. Just a day after publication of the Zimmerman telegram, Wilson asked Congress for authority to arm American merchant vessels for self-defense and to provide them with protection. But a small group of isolationists in the United States Senate, including Senators Robert M. La Follette, Hiram Johnson, and William Borah, filibustered this request to death. As Congress adjourned without taking action on the president's request — and as German submarines began attacks even on American war vessels — Wilson used his presidential powers to issue an appropriate executive order on March 18, 1917. Once again, as in 1793 and 1807, the United States had become involved in an undeclared naval war.

FIFTH STAGE — WAR

Throughout March 1917 Wilson was anxiously groping with problems that led him into his final phase of World War diplomacy — a declaration of war. He could not ignore direct German attacks on American ships, especially after more than two years of protest. Moreover, the collapse of the Czarist government in Russia during March 1917 changed the nature of the Triple Entente. With the elimination of absolutist Russia many Americans came to view the Allied cause as an alliance of democratic nations arrayed against authoritarian regimes. The withdrawal of Russia also weakened the Allied military effort and necessitated a rapid choice by Wilson — either he would spring to the aid of Great Britain quickly with large-scale military aid, or he would run the risk of a German victory in the near future which would ultimately leave the United States to face an impregnable Germany alone. The range of choices open to American diplomatists was narrowing.

Wilson and his advisors agonized over a decision for weeks. Then, convinced that he had no other course before him, on April 2, 1917, Wilson went before Congress to ask for a declaration of war against Germany. As he said:

> We shall fight for the things which we have always carried
> nearest our hearts — for democracy, . . . for the rights and

liberties of small nations, for a universal dominion of right by such a concert of free peoples as shall bring peace and safety to all nations and make the world itself at last free.[4]

Then he proceeded to catalog countless German infractions of American neutrality and urged war as a means of self-defense. But his strong Calvinist convictions prompted him to find moral justification for his action. Thus he argued that the world had to be made safe for democracy — an impossible task for any man or nation — for righteousness, and for a universal dominion of peace through the concert of free peoples. In view of later disillusionments it was unfortunate that he stressed moralism rather than realities that had led him to this fatal step. Indeed, he failed to inform the American people of the realistic and pressing considerations that had brought the nation into war. This failing was to have serious consequences in later years.

REASONS FOR UNITED STATES ENTRY INTO WORLD WAR I

In truth, three other reasons help to explain American entrance into World War I, apart from Wilson's insistence on making the world safe for democracy. First came the needs of national security. Certainly the German submarine menace constituted a threat to the security of the United States and the Western Hemisphere. Nor could the United States ignore the possibility of one major nation dominating the European continent and posing an eventual threat to American political and economic interests there. The maintenance of the balance of power in Europe was closely tied to the safeguarding of American security. A second reason for United States entry into the war was economic. Submarine warfare threatened to have a serious effect on American commerce, one which the United States could not remain indifferent to for long. The maintenance of neutral rights and commercial independence was fundamental to the framework of American diplomacy. A third reason was related to moral factors, especially the ideal of spreading the beliefs and institutions of American democracy to other nations of the world, a mission which would be seriously impeded by a Ger-

[4]*New York Times,* April 3, 1917.

man victory. The United States therefore went to war to safeguard its national security and to maintain neutral rights and commercial independence, realities which were bolstered by a degree of moralism. But Wilson did not speak of self-interest as a motivating factor in bringing the United States into the war. In keeping with his nature he chose to stress high-blown selflessness and abstract ideals that, in time, would fail to find a wide measure of support among most Americans.

Historians have argued long and hard about the reasons for American entry into the First World War, stressing now one, then another, of the factors already noted. That economic pressures led the United States to express sympathy for the Allies seemed eminently plausible. Didn't J. P. Morgan and other big bankers make extensive loans to the British? And did not thousands of American manufacturers benefit from the flood of Allied orders? Indeed, did not munitions makers, in particular, have a vested interest in seeing the United States at war? No matter how plausible such suggestions may appear, they have not been substantiated. Until now, historians have failed to find any evidence to indicate that economic motives were primary or direct determinants of United States policy, or that they swayed Wilson, Lansing, and other important policy makers.

DOMESTIC MOBILIZATION

American entrance into World War I necessitated a vast mobilization effort. The conflict was not fought primarily by a professional army, so it affected the lives of most Americans whether at home or abroad. As the advocates of preparedness had argued for many months, modern warfare required a comprehensive centralization of the domestic economy to a degree unprecedented in the American experience. Industry, transportation, finance, agriculture, and labor all had to be harnessed to wartime needs no less than public opinion and civil liberties. Although few could foresee it at the time, this mobilization effort was to have a profound influence on federal control of the economy in postwar years and to provide many precedents for the New Deal and World War II.

In addition to domestic mobilization, the war demanded creation of a large military establishment virtually overnight. Few had thought it possible, but within less than a year the United States could boast of an army of more than 2 million men, in addition to a powerful navy. The combination of an enormously effective domestic mobilization with an astounding military contribution made the United States effort crucial to the Allied victory.

INDUSTRY

During his first year as a wartime president, Wilson created a number of new agencies to facilitate industrial mobilization. As early as 1916 he created a committee of cabinet members that he designated as the Council of National Defense. Their task was to make an inventory of manufacturing facilities and to advise businessmen seeking to convert to war production. The Council of National Defense appointed a large number of advisory committees composed of representatives from major industries. After Congress declared war, however, this loose organization required greater cohesion. In July 1917 Wilson created a War Industries Board with the prominent Wall Street financier, Bernard Baruch, as its head. The functions of this Board were threefold. First, it attempted to stimulate production of goods needed for the war effort, often through a system of priorities for the allocation of scarce raw materials. Second, it coordinated the purchasing activities of hundreds of federal agencies and of the Allied governments, which bought goods in the United States. A third responsibility was price-fixing, although Baruch was reluctant to use this power which was designed to prevent inflation. As the War Industries Board gradually consolidated its activities, it achieved a comprehensive mobilization of American industry for the war. Its work was supplemented by another new agency created by Wilson, the United States Fuel Administration, headed by Harry A. Garfield, son of the former president. This agency was charged with increasing the production of coal and oil, and with coordinating their distribution. Most Americans came to know of its work through a campaign of "heatless Thursdays," designed to preserve the nation's precious fuels.

TRANSPORTATION

The Wilson administration also found it necessary to extend federal controls over transportation. As accelerated production schedules in thousands of factories across the land resulted in a growing volume of freight, by the summer of 1917 the nation's railroads were placed under increasing strain. Often their schedules were wholly uncoordinated, so that desperately needed boxcars might be standing idly at some remote spur or siding while war goods were piling high in a busy depot. Or the congestion of train traffic en route to the East coast was so great that many long trains would wait' for days to secure track clearance on main lines. The heavy traffic also placed a tremendous strain on railroad equipment so that breakdowns, due to excessive wear or careless maintenance, became frequent. By December of 1917 these conditions had become so serious that the country's railroad system came to a virtual halt. Wilson had little choice, therefore, if he was going to prevent a stoppage of the flow of supplies to the Allies. In December 1917 he created a United States Railroad Administration and appointed Secretary of the Treasury William G. McAdoo, his son-in-law, as its director. The federal government thus took over the operation of all the nation's rail carriers, meanwhile keeping all of the incumbent managers and personnel, paying rent to the private owners, and refurbishing the equipment. But consolidation of all lines into one system brought about needed coordination, which vastly improved efficiency and broke many of the bottlenecks that had impeded the smooth flow of heavy traffic during the preceding year.

FINANCES

Problems related to the financing of the war led Wilson to extend federal powers over finance through the Capital Issues Committee, the War Finance Corporation, the United States Treasury's Liberty Loan Drives, and tax policies. In an effort to avoid runaway inflation Wilson created the Capital Issues Committee in 1916. Although without direct formal powers it gave or withheld its approval to corporations seeking to issue new stocks and bonds. The committee encouraged the expansion of businesses directly involved in war production and sought to discourage others. Once the United States had entered the war, however, many corporations found the problem of securing capital for quick expansion a real stumbling block. Only direct federal intervention could help them in this dilemma. Recognizing their difficulties, Wilson created the War Finance Corporation in 1917. Congress provided it with $1 billion to make loans to those industries which were seeking to convert to war production. This government corporation also made loans to the United States Treasury and bought federal securities to stabilize their value in the open money markets. The Treasury found such services of inestimable value, since it was engaged in borrowing large sums to finance the war. It raised a significant portion through public subscription in the four Liberty Loan drives it conducted. Altogether the Treasury sold $21 billion worth of Liberty bonds.

Meanwhile Congress was becoming increasingly conscious of its taxing powers as a means of financing large-scale federal expenditures. The War Revenue Act of 1917 increased the rates of graduated individual taxes as well as corporate income taxes, imposed an excess profits tax (from 20 to 60 per cent), raised excise and luxury taxes, and boosted the estate tax to a minimum of 25 per cent. Through these varied methods the federal government was able not only to prevent runaway inflation, but also to pay for a substantial portion of war costs. Of total war expenses amounting to $33 billion, it secured $10.5 billion through taxes — paid mostly by corporations and wealthy individuals — and the remainder through borrowing. The World War I experience revealed dramatically what enormous fiscal and monetary powers the federal government could wield in an industrial society.

FOOD ADMINISTRATION

The food requirements of American military forces and the Allies also led Wilson to mobilize American farmers for the war. For this purpose he created the United States Food Administration, directed by Herbert Hoover. Its activities were similar to those of other emergency agencies. To stimulate food production, Hoover inaugurated programs to pay federal subsidies to producers of wheat, corn, cotton, sugar, and hogs. To encourage prudence among consumers, Hoover proclaimed a series of meatless Fridays. The Food Administration also bought up crop surpluses as a means of maintaining price levels, which would tend to spur maximum production. These methods were remarkably successful. Between 1917 and 1919, for example, American hog producers doubled their output, and crop producers were not far behind. Altogether, United States food exports during 1918 to 1919 were three times as great as they had been in the immediate prewar era.

LABOR

The federal mobilization effort could not have succeeded without the loyal cooperation of American labor. To avoid disruption of war work by strikes or other interruptions, the Wilson administration took on new responsibilities in settling disputes between employers and employees, and in creating national labor standards. To achieve these objectives, the chief executive created the National War Labor Board, composed of representatives of industry and labor, and headed by its co-chairmen, former president William Howard Taft and Edward P. Walsh, a labor lawyer. This board was extremely effective in settling more than 1200 labor disputes between 1917 and 1919. In addition, it worked out uniform labor standards to be followed by both management and workers. The guidelines included recognition of labor's right to organize and to engage in collective bargaining, the adoption of an eight-hour day, and the attainment of an adequate living wage. Such standards provided precedents for many federal agencies in developing their own labor policies during the war. Wilson also authorized the establishment of special labor adjustment boards for particular industries. One of these was the Shipbuilding Labor Adjustment Board, which supervised federal shipyard workers, and which was headed by Assistant Secretary of the Navy Franklin D. Roosevelt. The president also created a National War Labor Policies Board to coordinate the diverse labor policies of scores of governmental agencies. To balance the supply and demand of labor he established the United States Employment Service, not only to help workers find jobs, but also to insure an adequate labor supply for every region of the country. As never before, the federal government came to exercise a powerful influence on labor problems in World War I.

FEDERAL CONTROL OVER PUBLIC OPINION

To the surprise of many, Wilson also undertook to control public opinion and freedom of expression as a means of furthering the war effort. As the United States moved along the path to belligerency, millions of "hyphenated Americans" of diverse ethnic and national backgrounds found themselves confronted with conflicting loyalties. Many newcomers from Ireland, Central Europe, Russia, and the Balkans were not yet fully assimilated and still had strong ties to their native lands. In addition, the Socialist Party of America led by Eugene Debs strenuously opposed American intervention in the war. As a means of solidifying public opinion behind him, in April 1917 Wilson created the Committee on Public Information (CPI) with George Creel, an experienced newsman, as director. Creel instituted a voluntary but effective self-censorship by newspapers, and inaugurated a far-flung propaganda campaign to instill patriotism in all Americans while urging them to hate the Germans. Through pamphlets, fiery speakers, and lurid posters depicting alleged atrocities Creel sought to highlight what he considered to be the idealistic Allied crusade for freedom, which contrasted with the cruel, authoritarian, and land-hungry goals of the imperial German government. Creel's program was successful in developing what came to be a veritable anti-German hysteria in America.

More controversial was the administration's program to stifle dissent through a series of new laws. These included the Espionage Act of 1917, which gave the postmaster general broad discretion to ban the sending of periodicals or of any mail that in his opinion contained statements advocating treason or opposition to established statutes. In addition, the measure stipulated imprisonment or fines for any person who attempted to interfere with army recruitment or the draft, or who made false reports that could aid an enemy. Under the Justice Department's direction this law was administered particularly to stamp out radical opinions. Perhaps the most symbolic indictment was made of Eugene Debs for a speech made in June 1918 in which he expressed his own opposition to American involvement in the war.

A second relevant measure was the Trading-with-the-Enemy Act of 1917, which allowed the postmaster general to censor foreign language newspapers. Still another piece of legislation in this sphere was the Sabotage Act of 1918 directed largely at the International Workers of the World (IWW), a radical labor union. The act made sabotage of war production or transportation facilities a federal crime. Most drastic, perhaps, was the Sedition Act of 1917, which prohibited disloyal, profane, or abusive remarks about the United States government or its war efforts. More than 2000 persons were indicted under these laws, which tended to promote mass fears and hysteria and led to the suppression of criticism and dissent.

SUMMARY: SUCCESS OF DOMESTIC WAR EFFORT

Viewed in its entirety, the domestic war mobilization effort was a huge success. Industrial production reached all-time highs as industry after industry accomplished phenomenal production records. Financial management of the war by the Wilson administration was extremely shrewd, since one-third of the total cost was financed by taxes, while inflation was held to a minimum. Agriculture was galvanized into an unprecedented efficiency. Federal support of national labor standards brought achievements for labor which years of independent struggle had been unable to achieve. Ironically, Wilson had implemented many of Theodore Roosevelt's theories proposed in the New Nationalism. Only in the realm of free speech was Wilson's record clouded. Otherwise, the achievements of World War I domestic mobilization stood as a shining example to succeeding generations who, during the New Deal and World War II, paid the highest tribute to their predecessors by seeking imitation.

THE MILITARY FRONTS

Mobilization of the home front was more than matched by the vast military operations of the United States on land and sea. Few had thought it possible for the United States to raise a large army in a short period of time. Indeed, the German government had made its decision for unrestricted submarine warfare on the assumption that it would take the United States several years to raise an army and several more to transport the bulk of it to Europe. Yet more than 2 million Americans were under arms by early 1918, and by the middle of that year more than 2 million were on the European battlefields. Moreover, they proved themselves to be outstanding combat soldiers and were directly responsible for tilting the balance of power in favor of the Allied cause. At the same time the United States Navy proved itself extraordinarily adaptable in meeting the U-boat menace. In fact, where other nations had failed to cope with submarines, the United States Navy succeeded brilliantly within a single year. The American military effort therefore was no minor contribution but proved to be a decisive factor in the war.

The creation of an American army and the dispatch of an American Expeditionary Force (AEF) to Europe were major accomplishments of the Wilson administration. In Congress a bitter struggle ensued in 1917 between the proponents of a volunteer force and those who advocated national conscription. Some Congressmen, in addition, were supporting Theodore Roosevelt's demand for the creation of volunteer units. Roosevelt himself, although physically weakened, hoped to lead a modernized version of his Rough Riders of 1898 into the fray, an effort that surely would have been suicidal. The first Draft Act of May 18, 1917, was the result of a compromise between divergent views. All males between 21 and 35 became eligible for the draft. Volunteer units up to 500,000 men could be added to the regular forces. More than 9 million Americans registered under this law, including more than a million black Americans who were expected to serve in segregated units. The urgency for speed soon led Congress to make revisions. The result was the second Draft Act of August 1917, which extended the age limits of eligible men to include all those between 18 and 45. Of the 24 million who were considered, about 3 million were inducted. The other 5 million Americans who were mobilized consisted of volunteers. To command the 2 million men who ultimately comprised the AEF in France, President Wilson appointed John J. Pershing, whose ideas of offensive strategy contrasted sharply with the defensive psychology of the British and French generals on the Western front.

To the surprise of the German general staff and the Allied

commanders, the United States Army proved itself to be an enormously effective fighting instrument on the European battle-fronts. Accompanied by the melodious strains of George M. Cohan's popular tune "Over There," thousands of American troops began to stream into French ports in the very first year of American involvement. By the beginning of 1918 there were 2 million American soldiers in France, and in the spring of that year they were engaged in large-scale actions. As the Germans launched their last and great desperate offensive of May 1918, designed to win a final and decisive victory, the crucial contribution of American forces to the Allied cause became clear. Certainly a repulse of the German threat could not have been possible without the United States Army. One of the first dramatic encounters in which Americans won a decisive victory was at Château-Thierry (May 28, 1918), when United States Marines drove German attackers back across the strategic Marne River. Just a week later at the Battle of Belleau Wood (June 5, 1918) United States forces took the offensive and inaugurated the long drive that was to result in final German defeat. Their maneuver was perhaps decisive in producing the Allied break-through at the Second Battle of the Marne, which ended the German threat to Paris. After August 1918, American units fought independently and were no longer attached to French or British forces. Their great prowess was shown in the Battle of St.-Mihiel (September 12, 1918), which prevented German disruption of Metz, a vital railroad and transportation hub. The greatest battle of World War I in which American troops were engaged was the Battle of the Meuse-Argonne (September 26, 1918). This resulted in breaching the string of fortifications along the Franco-German border known as the Hindenburg Line. This decisive victory led to a headlong rush of the AEF toward Germany itself, and the virtual collapse of the Kaiser's vaunted army. Thereafter, only time waited upon a formal surrender.

Meanwhile, within a year after American entry into the war, the United States Navy greatly diminished the sinking of Allied vessels by submarines in the Atlantic. This it did partly by developing an effective convoy system. The British Royal Navy itself had an insufficient number of craft to ferry merchant vessels across the ocean, but the addition of United States destroyers made such protection feasible. Another contribution of the navy

Over the top: American troops in action during World War (National Archives)

The costs of war: General Pershing paying homage (1925) to Americans who died in the First World War. (Wide World Photos)

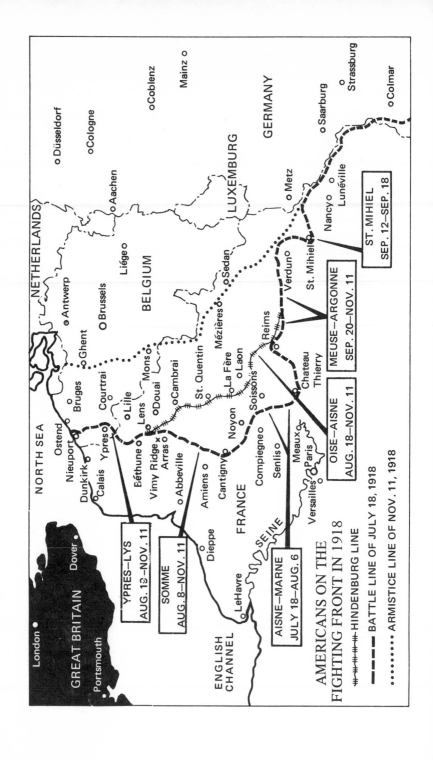

AMERICANS ON THE
FIGHTING FRONT IN 1918

╫╫╫╫ HINDENBURG LINE
━━━ BATTLE LINE OF JULY 18, 1918
••••••••• ARMISTICE LINE OF NOV. 11, 1918

YPRES–LYS
AUG. 19–NOV. 11

SOMME
AUG. 8–NOV. 11

AISNE–MARNE
JULY 18–AUG. 6

OISE–AISNE
AUG. 18–NOV. 11

MEUSE–ARGONNE
SEP. 20–NOV. 11

ST. MIHIEL
SEP. 12–SEP. 18

was its antisubmarine mine barrage in the North Sea, which impeded German naval movements there. By 1918 the navy inaugurated air patrols to aid in detection of underwater raiders. Meanwhile, American shipyards began to turn out specially built submarine chasers whose deftness and maneuverability constituted an important threat to U-boat captains. Finally, the navy made a major contribution by ferrying men and supplies to Europe. In April 1917 it had perhaps no more than a dozen ships available as troop carriers. But within a year frenzied mobilization activity began to manifest itself as 150 vessels became available to carry nearly 1 million United States troops to France without the loss of a single man — a feat that had been considered nearly impossible. The navy also transported almost all necessary supplies for the army with a minimum of losses.

The navy's efforts practically eliminated German submarines. In March 1917 the U-boats had been sinking as much as 600,000 tons monthly, and April 1917 was a particularly bad month for the Allies as they lost 880,000 tons. By April 1918 the navy had reduced such losses to less than 200,000 tons monthly, and the total steadily diminished. In every way the navy lived up to the expectations of the strategists and planners.

These brilliant victories on the sea, and the rapid advances made by Americans on land led the Germans to seek an armistice. The American war effort had been little short of remarkable. At home, the Wilson administration, in the short space of a single year, had mobilized virtually every aspect of the American economy and had bent the energies of millions of men and women toward the successful prosecution of the war. Abroad, on short notice the United States raised a large new army whose discipline and effectiveness as a fighting force proved itself second to none. Before 1914 the great powers of the world had tended to belittle the military prowess of the United States; after 1918 they had become convinced that its enormous potential could be harnessed effectively to tilt the balance of power in its favor.

PEACEMAKING, 1919

By September 1918 it was clear to all sides in the war that the end of German resistance would come soon. Thus the thoughts of Allied leaders turned from war to peace, from the making of battle plans to strategies of peacemaking. Certainly, more than the others, Wilson became preoccupied with problems surrounding the conclusion of the conflict, "with ending this war to end all wars." As he was to discover, his views diverged increasingly from those of the British and the French. In the making of the armistice, and in the formulation of the final peace treaty, Wilson suddenly found himself alone.

As the Allied armies swept France clear of foreign soldiers, various German groups sought negotiations for an armistice. Some of the military leaders like General Ludendorf, the German chief of staff, hoped to secure a breathing spell that would allow them to regroup their forces. Many civilians were tired of the war, however, and planned a definite end to the fighting and bloodshed. These pressures led the Kaiser to flee to Holland in October 1918, leaving a new government headed by Prince Maximilian of Baden free to contact the Allies. Wilson demanded the withdrawal of all German troops from France and Belgium, but did not insist on an unconditional surrender. British and French statesmen, however, hoped to impose more stringent terms on the Germans. Discussions between Allied and United States representatives on this problem stretched out during the month of October. It was not until early in the following month that they could agree on a tenuous compromise, which was forwarded to the German government. It provided that a peace treaty was to be negotiated on the basis of Wilson's earlier recommendations, but that discussions of freedom of the sea and German reparations to France were to be wide open. The Germans had little alternative but to accept these Allied terms. On November 11, 1918, the armistice became effective, thus ending the bloodshed that had resulted in one of the costliest wars in world history.

Wars frequently create more problems than they solve, and World War I was no exception. News of the cessation of fighting produced a flurry of activity in Washington. Now the president and his advisors had to ready American peace proposals and to make the difficult preparations for American participation in an international peace conference. The last months of 1918 posed a real challenge to Wilson's highest capabilities as a statesman.

FOURTEEN POINTS

Certainly the president had been contemplating various peace plans ever since his re-election to the White House. One of the earliest suggestions came from the League to Enforce the Peace, a group of distinguished Americans including Elihu Root, William Howard Taft, and others who were concerned about a stable postwar world. The most important of their proposals envisaged the formation of a world organization to maintain peace and to settle international disputes. By 1916 Wilson had been attracted to this program and incorporated it into his own thinking. As the war attracted an increasing amount of his time and attention he himself began to formulate a peace program. He made his first proposal in a Peace without Victory speech in January 1917. A postwar settlement, he declared, should not result in victors and vanquished. It should be a peace of righteousness. As he said, "The treaties and agreements which bring [the war] to an end must embody terms which will create a peace that is worth guaranteeing and preserving, a peace that will win the approval of mankind."[5] After the United States had entered the war, Wilson felt compelled to develop his suggestions further. The most significant of his pronouncements came in the Fourteen Points speech on January 8, 1918, when he enunciated terms which he considered vital to a peace treaty. In elaborating his earlier views he urged the following comprehensive program:

Point I. Open covenants of peace, open diplomatic negotiations

Point II. Freedom of the seas

Point III. Removal of economic barriers and freedom of trade

Point IV. Reduction of armaments

Point V. Self-determination for colonial peoples

Point VI. Self-determination for Russia

Point VII. Self-determination for Belgium, and its evacuation

Point VIII. Evacuation of France and restoration of Alsace-Lorraine

Point IX. Self-determination for Italians

[5] *New York Times,* January 23, 1917.

Point X. Self-determination for Austria-Hungary

Point XI. Self-determination for Balkan nations

Point XII. Self-determination for peoples of Turkey

Point XIII. Independence of Poland to include access to sea

Point XIV. A league of nations

The Fourteen Points could be reduced to four essentials. First, Wilson insisted on open rather than secret diplomacy. Second, he urged adherence to the principle of freedom of the seas. Third, he advocated self-determination for subject peoples; and fourth, he pleaded for establishment of a league of nations.

Unfortunately, Wilson's peace plans differed from those of Allied leaders, who were seeking a peace *with* victory. Lloyd George, Clemenceau, and the Italian premier, Vittorio Orlando, all hoped to supplement secret treaties that their respective nations had concluded among themselves during the war. All of these agreements included ambitious plans for the carving up of Germany, Austria-Hungary, the Ottoman Empire, and their possessions, in addition to other spoils of war. Thus, a Franco-Russian treaty promised Constantinople and the Dardanelles to Russia; a treaty between Great Britain and Italy promised the latter control of the Adriatic and the Alpine passes to Austria; England and France agreed that Alsace-Lorraine was to be returned to France while England was to get the German colonies; Great Britain and Japan arranged to divide German Pacific territories between them, Japan to secure those north of the equator (in addition to the Chinese province of Shantung) while Great Britain would take over all those south of the equator.

The persistence of the Allied war effort was due in large part to their anticipation of dividing up the spoils once victory had been secured. When Congress had declared war on Germany in April 1917, British Foreign Minister Earl Grey hurried to Washington with a bulging briefcase to acquaint President Wilson with the various Allied commitments. But the chief executive — intent on his own plans for a postwar world — brusquely waved them aside and refused to consider their contents seriously. He hoped eventually to develop an entirely new approach to peacemaking for the postwar world. Unfortunately, Wilson made a great tactical mistake, for in April 1917 he might have forced the Allies to revise their secret protocols as the price of

United States support. After the end of the war, however, Wilson no longer had the same effective leverage to secure concessions. Thus the Allied plans for a peace with victory were bound to clash with Wilson's plans for a peace without victory.

PEACE NEGOTIATIONS

During October 1918, in anticipation of forthcoming peace negotiations, Wilson asked Americans to elect a Democratic Congress. Desiring an expression of confidence in his policies, Wilson made a partisan appeal as William McKinley had done before him in 1898. He declared:

> My fellow countrymen: The Congressional elections are at hand. They occur in the most critical period our country has ever faced or is likely to face in our time. If you have approved of my leadership and wish me to continue to be your unembarrassed spokesman in affairs at home and abroad, I earnestly beg that you will express yourselves unmistakably to that effect by returning a Democratic majority to both the Senate and the House of Representatives.[6]

Unfortunately Wilson's call was ill-timed since, by implication, it reflected unfavorably on important Republicans who had given their unswerving support to the administration's wartime program. The president's request fell on deaf ears; the voters returned Republican majorities to both houses of Congress in the November elections. Later analysis of the results revealed that the return of midwestern farmers to Republican ranks, due to their concern over the decline of farm prices, was an important factor in determining the outcome. But many Americans, and also a large segment of Europeans, interpreted the election results as a repudiation of Wilsonian leadership. This attitude boded ill for the president's success in the forthcoming peace negotiations. Yet he himself stubbornly refused to reconsider either his program or his strategy in the light of the electoral results and simply continued with previously determined preparations.

These preparations also involved crucial decisions concerning United States representation at the peace conference. By

[6]*New York Times,* October 26, 1918.

the fall of 1918 Wilson had decided that he personally would lead the American delegation to insure acceptance of his program. Such a decision constituted a calculated risk, which had both advantages and dangers. Obviously Wilson's presence would lend great prestige to the American point of view. On the other hand, Wilson was narrowing his range of alternatives as he placed the great weight of the presidency solely behind the Fourteen Points. Had he remained in the White House during the negotiations and practiced a certain measure of aloofness, he could perhaps have exercised a greater influence in Paris — and might have had more options available — through chosen representatives. But for better or for worse Wilson made his decision. He himself would go to Paris to lead the United States delegation.

His selection of delegates for the American commission was no less debatable than his decision to go to Paris. Many Americans hoped that the president would select a broadly representative group composed of Republicans as well as Democrats, of legislators, diplomats, cabinet members, public figures, academicians, and experts. Certainly many leading Republicans such as William Howard Taft and Elihu Root had played the role of a loyal opposition and deserved recognition. Moreover, since any eventual treaty to which the United States would be a party required approval of the United States Senate, it seemed wise to have at least one representative from that august body. But Wilson was stubbornly intent on choosing associates who would be clearly subservient to him. In addition to Secretary of State Robert Lansing he selected General Tasker Bliss, his personal military aide, and Henry Wilson, a relatively obscure career diplomat. No prominent Republican and no United States senator found a place in the delegation. In addition, Wilson appointed the Inquiry, an advisory group composed of several hundred experts on European and Far Eastern problems, many of them college and university professors. Although they made innumerable detailed and informative studies, the president largely ignored their work. Clearly, he was planning to assume almost the entire burden of peacemaking himself.

His preparations for the peace conference completed, in January 1919 Wilson proceeded to Paris amid tumultuous acclaim in Europe where the masses considered him as a savior who would usher in a new age of peace and justice. With his strong Calvinist background, Wilson relished his role and looked hopefully to exercising his powers at the negotiating table. At no other time, perhaps, did he enjoy greater prestige as a world leader than during those first weeks of 1919 in Paris. Women threw flowers in his path; his picture, large and small, adorned public buildings and thousands of private homes as he was hailed as a messiah from the new world who would right the wrongs of the old. For Wilson, it was an exhilarating experience.

Once the formalities and celebrations were concluded, however, Wilson found himself with a great deal of hard work. Gathered at Paris were representatives of twenty-seven nations — with Germany excluded — including such luminaries as Prime Minister Lloyd George of Great Britain; Georges Clemenceau, the fiery premier of France (also known as "the Tiger"); Prime Minister Vittorio Orlando of Italy; the famous pianist, Ignace Jan Paderewski, representing Polish interests; Field Marshall Jan Smuts of South Africa; and the Czech leader, Jan Masaryk. Russia, dominated by the Bolsheviks since November 1917, was not invited. The conference, meeting in the Hall of Mirrors at Versailles just outside Paris, proceeded through three stages. In the initial phase (January 12, 1919, to February 14, 1919) world leaders were concerned with organizational matters and agreements concerning a league of nations. During the technical phase (February 14, 1919, to March 14, 1919), specialized committees worked out technical details for the arrangement of proposed new territorial boundaries. The third period of the conference was the bargaining phase (March 14, 1919, to June 28, 1919), when the deliberations over final terms took place.

Initial Phase — Organization

The initial phase stretched over the period of one month. Since a gathering of delegates from more than two dozen nations was unwieldy, the conference soon left many problems to be discussed by a Council of Ten (the former Supreme Allied War Council). This still made the negotiations difficult, and so the leaders of Great Britain, France, the United States, and Italy organized themselves as a Council of Four. When Prime Minister Orlando walked out in a huff over the Adriatic question, he left only the Big Three: Wilson, Lloyd George, and Clemenceau.

The Big Four at Versailles Peace Conference, 1919.

With only a stenographer to record their conversations, their talks resulted in the major provisions of the final treaty. During this early period Wilson insisted, as a prerequisite to the discussion of all other issues, on securing the acquiescence of the Allies to the establishment of a league of nations. As George and Clemenceau soon surmised, Wilson was ready to make many other compromises to secure acceptance of the league in the proposed peace treaty, since nothing else was quite so close to his heart. Day after day, in his face-to-face talks with George and Clemenceau, he fought stubbornly and single-mindedly for this goal, which to him seemed essential for any lasting peace. His efforts bore fruit by mid-February when the others agreed to the creation of a world organization. Then the conference temporarily adjourned, and Wilson, flushed with victory, sailed back to the United States for a brief stay, during which he hoped to acquaint legislative leaders with the results of his first weeks of bargaining. His reports were generally received with sympathetic interest and he returned to Paris in an optimistic mood.

Technical Phase — Establishing Territorial Boundaries

While Wilson was away, fifty-two special committees were hard at work in Paris drawing up proposed new boundaries for western and central Europe. In seeking to apply the principle of self-determination, these specialists attempted to devise a tentative map of Europe based on the nationalist aspirations of its myriad minorities. They determined the borders of a new independent Poland and the Saar and Alsace-Lorraine along the Franco-German frontier. Then they delved into the complicated rearrangement of lands once in the Austro-Hungarian monarchy, which involved the creation of an independent Czechoslovakia, cession of the Tyrol (between Austria and Italy) to Italy, the disposition of the Adriatic port of Fiume for which both Italy and Yugoslavia (the former Serbia) were striving, the exact definition of borders for Yugoslavia, and the creation of a German-speaking Austria. The technical problems involved in redrawing European boundaries along ethnic lines were certainly difficult. But the final disposition of these issues was political rather than technical and was left to the heads of state.

Third Phase — Bargaining

Perhaps the most important period at Versailles was the third, or bargaining phase. Most of the vital decisions were made by the Big Three in the spring of 1919 when they met almost daily to squabble over knotty problems. While the European leaders strove for punitive action, Wilson sought to uphold the ideals and principles of the Fourteen Points. The treaty that emerged from their oftentimes heated and acrimonious discussions represented a compromise between their divergent views.

Disposition of Germany

The Big Three dealt with four major problems. Obviously the disposition of Germany was high on the agenda. Lloyd George, who had just been re-elected in England on a platform promising "to hang the Kaiser on a sour apple tree," joined Clemenceau in urging the breakup of the German empire, and the creation of a series of buffer states along the Franco-German frontier. To this proposition Wilson was bitterly opposed, since it violated his cherished principle of self-determination. Instead, he urged the preservation of existing German boundaries. The three leaders argued long and hard until they could agree on a compromise. Wilson did achieve his prime goal — to prevent the breakup of a united Germany. He agreed, however, that Germany should return Alsace-Lorraine to France (which had lost it to Germany in 1871) and that the Rhineland, although remaining with Germany, should become a demilitarized zone for twenty years. To allay French fears, Wilson further promised to support a Franco-American defense treaty under which the United States would be obligated to come to the aid of France in case of a future German attack. Unfortunately, the United States Senate later refused to ratify this agreement.

Reparations

A second issue concerned reparations. Lloyd George and Clemenceau strove to have the Germans pay for the entire costs of the war, including pensions and hospital expenses for Allied veterans. Wilson was opposed to the levy of such a punitive and staggering sum, which he also considered to be unrealistic. Disagreement among the Big Three was so great on this question that they decided to leave the precise determination of damages to be paid by the Germans to a special reparations commission, which was to determine a total figure after intensive examination of the problem.

Disposition of German Colonies

A third matter requiring settlement was the disposition of the German colonies. Both British and French sentiment was strongly in favor of despoiling Germany of all overseas possessions and transferring their ownership to the Allies. The territories in question included the Marshall and Gilbert islands in the Pacific, and Togoland, the Cameroons, and German Southwest Africa. Decisions about these areas were also likely to affect a settlement concerning the division of the Ottoman Empire. If the secret treaties of the Allies were to be implemented, division of the spoils would also carve up Turkey. But Wilson — eager to sustain his "peace without victory" — hoped to ignore the secret arrangements and opposed colonial acquisitions by the Allies. To secure any kind of compromise between two such divergent positions was difficult. The deadlock was broken only when General Jan Smuts of South Africa prepared a plan envisaging mandates, or trusteeship territories. Under this arrangement, former colonies of the Central Powers were to be held in trust by various Allies for a period of years until the native populations appeared ready for self-government. At such time the mandating power was to give up its jurisdiction and to let its former pupil exercise full sovereignty and independence. Wilson, Clemenceau, and Lloyd George eventually agreed to this proposal. Great Britain became the mandating nation for German colonies in Africa, Japan assumed responsibility for those in the Pacific, and France for Turkish territories in the Middle East (except for Palestine, placed under British mandate since it had received Britain's promise to establish a Jewish homeland).

One of the most acrimonious disputes at the Versailles Conference broke out between the United States and Japan concerning the disposal of the Shantung Peninsula in China. This area had been a German sphere of influence and was valued for its trade. By 1915, when Japan made the so-called twenty-one demands on China, these also included a provision for dominant influence in Shantung and even its annexation to Japan. Wilson, committed to the Open Door policy and the principle of self-determination, was resolutely opposed to any such plan. The Japanese were determined, however, and threatened to boycott the League of Nations if their demand was not met. To Wilson's dismay, Great Britain and France were not unsympathetic to Japanese aggrandizement. Rather than see any disruption of the League, Wilson yielded with very great reluctance and secured a compromise of sorts. Japan agreed not to annex Shantung, which was nominally to remain under Chinese sovereignty. But the Japanese were allowed prime economic influence in the Shantung Peninsula, to the great anger of the Chinese, who refused to sign the final treaty because it included these concessions. For after all, it was not China who bargained away Chinese territories, but the representatives of foreign nations. The Shantung settlement was perhaps one of the most questionable in the Versailles negotiations.

Independence for Poland

A fourth problem that proved thorny was the establishment of a free, independent Poland. Divided and occupied by foreign powers for centuries, Poland's boundaries were particularly difficult to draw. On the one hand, Clemenceau urged the inclusion of all of east Germany in the new state; on the other, Wilson argued for the right of self-determination for thousands of Germans who had moved into Polish lands over the centuries. The debates among the Big Three ultimately resulted in an agreement that sought to integrate the divergent views. Poland did not receive east Germany, but a Polish "corridor" was created, a strip of territory ten miles wide, stretching across east Prussia in order to allow Poland its only direct access to the Baltic Sea. To appease the Poles further, the Big Three agreed to designate Danzig, a major German port on the Baltic, as an international city. Though this compromise was less than perfect, it resulted in the establishment of an independent Poland and, essentially, recognition of the principle of self-determination.

FINAL TREATY

Their work completed, on June 28, 1919, the delegates gathered in the Hall of Mirrors at Versailles to affix their signatures to the final treaty. It contained provisions that were the essence of the compromises made by the Big Three. These included, first, the covenant of a League of Nations with an assembly in which each nation had an equal vote, and a council with nine members (five great powers and four elected smaller nations). League members were not to resort to war until three months after the League of Nations had made a decision on an issue of controversy, under threat of economic reprisals. Military action against a violator could also be sanctioned by the council. Second, Germany was allowed to retain her boundaries, but the Rhineland was to be demilitarized; Alsace-Lorraine was returned to France; and a plebiscite was to be held to determine the future of the Saar. Third, Poland was to be re-established as an independent nation with access to the sea through the Polish corridor, and with Danzig as an international city. Fourth, the mandate system was created, providing for trusteeships for former German and Turkish territories. Japan secured a mandate over Shantung and predominant influence there. Reparations were to be determined by a special commission (which reported a sum of $33 billion in 1921). The treaty had many other clauses of which the most famous, or infamous, was Article No. 231, the war guilt clause, under which Germany assumed full responsibility for starting World War I. Representatives of the new German government were not consulted about any of these terms but, instead, were called in only to affix their names to the formal document. Under the circumstances they had little choice. This peremptory demand by the Allies was to have profound consequences in the future as millions of Germans vowed to avenge this humiliation.

Was the Treaty of Versailles a harsh peace settlement? It was not a Draconian peace such as the Allies had planned if they had been able to exact the terms of their secret treaties. On the other hand, it was not the idealistic "peace without victory" that Wilson had desired. Instead, it represented a compromise between the secret treaties on the one hand, and the Fourteen Points of Wilson on the other. Certainly it would have been a much harsher document if Wilson had not constantly striven to mitigate its punitive aspects. Yet it fell short of achieving the ideal new order that the president desired. It represented the best terms that could be secured under the weight of conflicting pressures in 1919. As a man-made document it was full of imperfections, yet not wholly devoid of idealistic aspirations.

THE CRISIS OF 1919

In a mood of confidence Wilson returned to the United States in early July 1919, unaware that his administration was entering a period of crisis both in foreign and domestic policies. Already the opponents of the president were gathering their strength to oppose Senate approval of the treaty for which he had labored so arduously. At the same time, his preoccupation with diplomacy led him to a serious neglect of reconversion problems at home. Indeed, Wilson virtually abdicated his leadership in bringing the nation through the painful transition period from war to peace. In doing so he contributed greatly to the gravity of the agonizing foreign and domestic crisis of 1919.

SENATE FIGHT FOR TREATY OF VERSAILLES

In his fervent desire to secure acceptance of the treaty, Wilson hoped to rally both the Democratic party and a substantial portion of the American people. Physically he was exhausted by six months of negotiations at Versailles. In addition, he had never completely thrown off a cold infection that had bothered him in Paris early in the winter of 1919. Nevertheless, Wilson planned an intensive speaking tour in July 1919 to explain the treaty to Americans throughout the land. His plan was not unrealistic, for a substantial body of public opinion was behind United States participation in some sort of international assembly. In addition to Wilson's own supporters in the Democratic party (including forty-three United States senators) many prominent Republicans approved of the treaty. Men as eminent as William Howard Taft, Philander C. Knox, General Leonard Wood, and others favored Senate approval, although they urged inclusion of some reservations. The support in the states was also overwhelming. Thirty-three governors went on record along with thirty-two state legislatures as supporting some version of a league. More than two-thirds of the nation's newspaper editors were similarly inclined. It seemed as if Wilson's pleas had struck roots in the hearts and minds of millions of Americans.

Yet opposition to Wilson's peace plans had also developed. Much of it crystallized in the person of Senator Henry Cabot Lodge, the powerful chairman of the Senate Foreign Relations Committee, who favored substantial amendments to the treaty. Staunch isolationists and nationalists also objected to American participation in an international organization. Their most influential spokesman was Senator William E. Borah of Idaho, a very effective speaker whose intransigence became notorious. Many of his views were applauded by some of the "hyphenated Americans," those who were recent immigrants or first generation Americans with strong ethnic loyalties overseas, whether of German, Irish, Czech, Polish, or Balkan backgrounds. Resenting one or another provision of the Treaty of Versailles, they hoped to see its defeat in the Senate.

In the legislative battles over the treaty, Wilson, Lodge, and Borah emerged as the three leading protagonists. Wilson was determined to see the treaty approved just as he had brought it back from Paris, without any amendments. Whatever weaknesses it might have, he felt, could eventually be settled by the League, but the immediate important task for the United States was to assume its responsibilities as a great power to maintain world peace. Senator Lodge did not fully share these views. Apart from the personal animosity he felt toward Wilson, he also believed that United States participation in a world organization should be hedged with various safeguards to assure the United States freedom of action and full exercise of independence and sovereignty. Moreover, like many members of Congress, he felt strongly that the Senate should play an important role in shaping the Treaty of Versailles, especially since Wilson had largely ignored the lawmakers during his dealings in Paris. Senator Borah supported his colleague, though for different reasons. As an ardent isolationist and leader of about a dozen like-minded senators, he opposed any kind of American involvement in international affairs such as League membership would entail. Together, Lodge and Borah controlled at least forty-nine Republican votes in the Senate. Thus, these three men, each stubborn, determined, and recalcitrant, set the stage for congressional consideration of the treaty.

Process of Ratification

The process of ratification underwent three stages including a period of delay (July 1919 to October 1919), a period of deliberation (November 1919 to February 1920), and a period of defeat (March 1920). During the first stage the strategy of Lodge and other opponents of the treaty was to engage in delaying tactics in order to gain time for rallying hostile sentiment. Beginning in July 1919, Lodge took up more than two weeks on the floor of the Senate to read the text of the treaty, 264 pages in all, line by line, word for word, slowly and deliberately. In August and September he slowed consideration of it further by holding hearings before the Senate Committee on Foreign Relations. Meanwhile, in September a very tired and weary Wilson embarked on his nationwide speaking tour to win support for his cause. Everywhere he spoke to enthusiastic audiences and appeared to be making headway in his fight to have the treaty accepted without appreciable changes. Close on his heels Lodge and Borah operated as a Republican "truth squad," seeking to present their point of view to audiences that had just listened to the president. But they did not have long to go. After a speech at Pueblo, Colorado, on September 25, 1919, Wilson collapsed and within ten days suffered a coronary attack and stroke. He was rushed back to Washington where, partially crippled, he never again arose from his sickbed. Thus, his personal campaign for the treaty came to a sudden — and perhaps fatal — end.

Meanwhile, the Senate Foreign Relations Committee was listening to testimony concerning amendments to the treaty. Most important were the so-called Lodge reservations, essentially four in number. Contemporaries as well as later critics debated whether they would have changed the very substance of the Treaty of Versailles and the League, or whether they merely would have altered some procedural details. Wilson himself was convinced that they would destroy the League. The Lodge reservations emphasized the sanctity of the Monroe Doctrine. No action of the League was to infringe upon any principle of the Monroe Doctrine. Domestic problems were to be excluded from League jurisdiction as the world organization was to be specifically excluded from dealing with domestic issues in the United States, an eventuality that seemed highly unlikely. Third, congressional approval was to be required for all League actions in which the United States participated. Finally, the reservations provided for American nonintervention in international disputes. This was the famous Article X, which, Wilson felt, cut out the heart of the treaty. Under it, the United States would not automatically intervene in any action authorized by the League to uphold the territorial integrity of a foreign nation. In other words, the United States would not assume its responsibilities of enforcing the peace-keeping functions of the League. Congress was to judge each case on its own merits and to decide upon the desirability of American intervention. Thus, the Lodge reservations proposed significant changes in the treaty as Wilson had fashioned it in Paris. Lodge's great influence led the Senate Foreign Relations Committee to recommend acceptance of the Treaty of Versailles, but with the Lodge reservations and some forty-five other sundry amendments.

Ironically, the Senate rejected the treaty with the Lodge reservations when it came to its first test. From his sickbed Wilson remained adamant in rejecting all amendments and ordered loyal Senate Democrats to vote against it. They were joined by the Irreconcilables, the isolationists who were totally opposed to American membership in the League. When the final tally was made in the Senate on November 19, 1919, it was found that fifty-five senators had voted against the treaty, and only thirty-nine for it.

The defeat of the treaty in November 1919 ushered in a period of deliberation. Leading Democrats such as William Jennings Bryan and Colonel E. M. House urged Wilson, without success, to relent and to accept the Lodge reservations. Nor were important Republican internationalists able to persuade Lodge to soften his views. The British government naturally was greatly disturbed by the seeming deadlock and sent Sir Edward Grey to Washington, where Wilson refused to see him. Yet millions of Americans were hoping for a compromise between Lodge and Wilson since seventy-seven members of the Senate favored a League of Nations in some form. Neither man was willing to budge, so many of the discussions and proposals for compromise came to naught.

The period of defeat for the treaty came in March 1920 when the Senate took a final vote. Once again the Senate Committee on Foreign Relations submitted the treaty with the Lodge reservations. With a two-thirds majority required for its approval, once again the Wilsonian Democrats and a few isolationist Irreconcilables combined to vote down the treaty with forty-nine "yeas" and thirty-five "nays." A switch of only seven Democratic votes would have resulted in approval of the treaty, but Wilson's stern admonitions to wavering Democrats kept them in line. As in 1918 he hoped that the voters at the forthcoming elections (1920) would justify his position. On May 15, 1920, Congress simply enacted a joint resolution ending the formal state of war between the United States and Germany. Wilson's great dream seemed to have been shattered.

POSTWAR DOMESTIC PROBLEMS

Many of the divisions wrought among Americans by the fight over the League were multiplied by domestic problems of reconversion as the nation struggled to shift from war to peace. President Wilson, preoccupied with the Treaty of Versailles and then incapacitated by his illness, virtually abdicated his responsibility for leading the country smoothly through demobilization at home. Thus, 1919 was a year of crisis and of turmoil for the United States. Political crisis developed as presidential leadership and direction dissolved and as the White House allowed sudden random dismantling of scores of wartime agencies. Economic crisis came because the rapid shift from a war economy produced a major depression affecting agriculture, business, and labor. Social crisis grew directly from such political and economic changes and was reflected in race riots, labor strikes, and antiradical hysteria. In many ways, the crisis of 1919 was a harbinger of similar and more serious crises that were to plague Americans later in the twentieth century, involving the powers of the presidency, depression, and racial strife.

Political Crisis

Immediately after the armistice, Wilson revealed his determination to abolish all wartime agencies as quickly as possible. He gave little thought to any plan of gradual dismantlement or postwar planning that could tide the nation over this most difficult period of readjustment. Perhaps because of his intensive preoccupation with the League during these months, his concern with domestic questions was minimal. Although he had grandiose schemes for the reorganization of the world, he had none for avoiding chaos and confusion at home. His prime concern, he said, was to reduce the number of federal agencies in operation so as to restore the status quo of the prewar era. By June 1919, therefore, the Wilson administration had abruptly abolished the War Industries Board, the United States Food Administration, the National War Labor Board and its related agencies, the United States Fuel Administration, and dozens of lesser boards. Congress returned the nation's railroads to their owners under the Transportation Act of 1920. Despite the expressed concern of businessmen, farmers, labor leaders, and many government officials, Wilson ruthlessly pushed forward with his helter-skelter process of dismantling, and ignored all pleas for federal guidance to facilitate gradual adjustment. Even before his illness, Wilson revealed extraordinary obstinacy and conservatism, which seriously hampered the effectiveness of his postwar leadership.

Wilson's collapse left the United States without an effective president at the very time when a strong hand was needed in the

White House. Isolated in his sickroom, the stricken chief executive's only contact with the outside world came through his second wife, who transmitted written or oral messages to him, or so it was believed. Whether his mind was directly affected by his affliction is not clearly known, but it is possible that this forced confinement further blunted his sense of realism. Confident that his policies would be endorsed at the polls in the election of 1920 — and striving for a third term in the White House — Wilson turned deaf ears to all pleas that he change his course. Meanwhile the Senate was so preoccupied with the Treaty of Versailles that it devoted little time to pressing domestic problems. An incapacitated president and a lagging Congress produced a lack of leadership that resulted in the political crisis of 1919.

Economic Crisis

The lack of federal guidance between 1919 and 1921 helped to foment a deepening economic crisis. Wholesale prices dropped by more than 50 per cent in some areas of the economy as unemployment mounted. It was not difficult to find the reasons for this depression, which had been predicted by many skilled economists. The absence of federal planning for postwar reconstruction was of course one factor. The cancellation of a large number of government contracts had an enormous impact in reducing markets for American producers. The reappearance of foreign competition further heightened their dilemma. Then, just as domestic demands appeared to be slackening and production in some industries declined, the very rapid demobilization of more than 3 million men in the armed forces swelled the number of job seekers and created unemployment. Thus, businessmen experienced a decline of exports, falling prices, and cancellation of orders. Farmers were especially hard hit as an abrupt decrease in demand led to plummeting prices. Wheat, cotton, and corn brought only half as much in 1920 as in the preceding year. The sudden abandonment of the United States Food Administration's purchasing and subsidy programs greatly aggravated the seriousness of the agricultural depression. Labor did not fare much better. The influx of returning war veterans, just as many factories were decreasing production, resulted in a disillusioned and restless group of at least 5 million unemployed. Those who did have jobs in 1919 had to struggle with a burgeoning inflation, involving more than a 20 per cent increase in prices during 1919 and the sudden removal of all federal supports for labor standards or organization. Everywhere Americans were adversely affected by the severe economic crisis of 1919.

Social Crisis

It was hardly surprising that these disruptive factors in the everyday lives of millions of Americans resulted in severe social tensions. A rash of major strikes in 1919 reflected the undercurrent of discontent. To many conservatives the most frightening was the Seattle general strike of 1919, which for a brief time paralyzed the city. That work stoppage generated such a fear of radicalism that Mayor Ole Hanson requested the state militia to suppress it. Just a few months later, in June 1919, 100,000 members of the steelworkers' union went on strike for higher wages and fewer hours. Led by William Z. Foster (in later years the leader of the American Communist Party), the steelworkers faced mounting violence as state and federal troops limited picketing and protected more than 30,000 strikebreakers. Defeated, the union men returned to their jobs in January 1920, after eighteen had been killed in scuffles. While this bitter dispute was raging, newspaper readers learned of an unprecedented strike by the Boston police department on September 9, 1919. Three days of rioting and looting broke out, which hastily organized citizens' vigilante committees were unable to quell. At that time Governor Calvin Coolidge called out the National Guard and announced tersely that there is no right to strike against the public good by any one, at any place, at any time. Amid congratulations from President Wilson and other national leaders, his action effectively broke the strike. Mayor Andrew Peters of Boston refused to rehire any of the police officers and instead installed an entirely new force. The Boston police strike made the whole nation jittery, and Americans were shaken further a few weeks later when the United Mine Workers struck for higher wages in November. In the face of a fuel shortage during the oncoming winter, Attorney General Mitchell Palmer secured an injunction that prohibited the work stoppage, and threatened to use federal troops to operate the mines. Under such pressure the union withdrew its demands. United Mine Workers' president John L. Lewis then reluctantly ordered his men back to work. The year 1919 therefore closed as it had begun — marked by disruptive and virulent strife between labor, management, and government.

Postwar tensions were reflected not only in labor violence, however, but also in a series of race riots. During the war, large numbers of black men and women from southern rural areas had moved to northeastern and middle western urban centers, drawn by the lure of well-paying jobs in war industries. Others had served in the armed forces, where the inequities of racial discrimination also had jarred them. In addition, organizations like the National Association for the Advancement of Colored People and the Urban League were urging black Americans to assert their full rights as United States citizens. This new militancy aroused the fears and apprehensions of many whites, especially in industrial cities where the races were actively competing for jobs and housing. The economic depression and other fears of the postwar period only worsened the antagonisms.

The result was a rash of severe race riots. Most serious was the Chicago race conflict, which lasted almost two weeks. It began on July 27, 1919, when a group of blacks sought to use a beach along a section of the Chicago lake front usually frequented by whites. As the whites pounced on the blacks, violence erupted and spread, leading to thirty-eight deaths (fifteen whites and twenty-three blacks) and leaving at least 510 persons injured. A similar disturbance rocked East Saint Louis, Illinois, where racial unrest had long been rife. Racial disorders also broke out in Omaha, Knoxville, Detroit, and Pittsburgh. Farther south, black-white relations experienced renewed tensions as the number of blacks lynched by whites in 1919 jumped to seventy-four, compared with thirty-four in 1917. Longview, Texas, experienced a particularly bitter armed clash between the races. These racial conflicts clearly revealed the intensity of postwar fears and tensions.

Many of these same insecurities were also reflected in the wave of antiradical hysteria that swept the nation at the conclusion of the war. One manifestation of such feelings was Attorney General Mitchell Palmer's "Red Raids." At his instigation, in December 1919 the Labor Department deported 249 suspected Communists, while Palmer also secured the arrest of approximately 3000 persons who were aliens or who were suspected of being Communists. Then, on New Year's Day, 1920, Palmer's agents rounded up 6000 other suspected leftists. Asserting that the United States was faced by a great Communist conspiracy and that the menace was immediate, Palmer unsuccessfully urged enactment of more drastic sedition legislation. His actions were widely applauded. Meanwhile, violence seemed to increase. Palmer received bombs in his mail, reportedly sent by radicals. Similar packages were sent to J. P. Morgan and John D. Rockefeller. Another manifestation of antiradical sentiment came in the form of direct confrontations. On May Day, 1919, at least 400 war veterans marched into the New York offices of *Call,* a leading Socialist newspaper, and administered a merciless beating to the staff. Elsewhere, American Legionnaires clashed on the streets with radicals and their sympathizers. Prevailing tensions were also seen in legal prosecutions of leftist dissenters. Most revealing, perhaps, was the trial of Victor Berger, a Socialist congressman from Milwaukee, who was convicted under the Sedition Act of 1917 and denied his seat by the House of Representatives. Such manifestations of antiradical sentiment reflected deep-rooted anxieties in American society.

OVERTURE TO TWENTIETH-CENTURY PROBLEMS

Thus, the crisis of 1919 shattered the tranquility of many Americans. They had been promised a great new world by Wilson, but the war left them with the apparent shattering of the old order. Conflict between capital and labor, between city and country, between black and white, between government officials and dissenters all had a disturbing impact upon millions of Americans who had been led to believe that their mission was to make the world safe for democracy. Unfortunately, these conflicts were but an introduction to new major domestic problems with which Americans in the twentieth century were to be confronted. As a nineteenth-century man, Wilson largely failed to grasp some of the new divisions in American society. The crisis of 1919 was merely a prelude to similar and greater crises that were to rock the United States over the next fifty years.

World War I had an enormous impact on life in the United

States. In foreign affairs, the war brought the nation into closer involvement with European and Far Eastern diplomacy than in any previous period. In the economy, it hastened the further development of Big Business and the extension of federal administrative regulation which brought the beginnings of a planned economy. In politics, the war revealed the tremendous powers inherent in the presidency during the twentieth century and the dangers that beset public policy when the chief executive was incapacitated. In social life, the conflict crystallized new conflicts in American society involving rural-urban tensions, racial strife, and radicalism. In many ways, therefore, World War I was like an overture to a full-scale drama about the major issues confronting twentieth-century America.

FOR FURTHER READING

Wilson's diplomatic policies are favorably appraised in CHARLES SEYMOUR, *American Diplomacy During the World War* (Baltimore: Johns Hopkins University Press, 1934), and less approvingly from a pacifist point of view in WALTER MILLIS, *Road to War: America, 1914 – 1917* (New York: Houghton Mifflin Co., 1935). ERNEST R. MAY, *The World War and American Isolation, 1914 – 1917* (Cambridge: Harvard University Press, 1959) is judicious and detailed. BARBARA TUCHMAN, *The Guns of August* (New York: Macmillan, 1962) provides a colorful account of Europe on the eve of the First World War. A general survey of America's wartime military activities can be found in EDWARD M. COFFMAN, *War to End All Wars: The American Military Experience in World War One* (New York: Oxford University Press, 1968). Aspects of the peace movement are touched on in MERLE CURTI, *The American Peace Crusade* (Durham: Duke University Press, 1929). Good studies of the domestic scene in wartime are still needed. PIERCE G. FREDERICKS, *The Great Adventure: America in the First World War* (New York: Dutton, 1960) is a popular survey. The story of the navy's role is recounted in THOMAS G. FROTHINGHAM, *The Naval History of the World War*, 3 vols. (Cambridge: Harvard University Press, 1925 – 1926). Propaganda activities are detailed in JAMES R. MOCK and CEDRICK LARSON, *Words that Won the War: The Story of the Committee on Public Information* (Princeton: Princeton University Press, 1939). HARRY R. RUDIN, *Armistice, 1918* (New Haven: Yale University Press, 1944) is a detailed analysis of that topic. THOMAS A. BAILEY, *Woodrow Wilson*

and the Great Betrayal (New York: Macmillan, 1945) furnishes a
critical but not unsympathetic view of America's role in peacemaking. The crisis of 1919 is discussed in JOHN D. HICKS, *Rehearsal
for Disaster* (Gainesville: University of Florida Press, 1961) and
ROBERT K. MURRAY, *Red Scare: A Study in National Hysteria, 1919 –
1920* (Minneapolis: University of Minnesota Press, 1956). ELLIOT
RUDWICK, *Race Riot in East St. Louis, 1919* (Carbondale: Southern
Illinois University Press, 1967) is one of the best studies of racial
tensions at the close of World War I.

5

DECADE OF CONTRASTS

The 1920's

Halfway between 1890 and World War II, the 1920's reflected many characteristics of industrial America while at the same time revealing many features of post–World War II technological America. It was then that more Americans first became concerned with the growth of Big Government and bureaucracy, the rise of an affluent society, the attempted integration of ethnic and racial minorities into the mainstream of American life, the rejection of pre–World War I moral standards and values, and the attempt to assume a major role in the international community. To many older people who, like William Jennings Bryan, were born before the Civil War, it seemed as if the rural, agrarian America they had once known was disappearing, if not already irretrievably lost. Middle-aged Americans like Herbert Hoover, in established positions in many spheres of life, were concerned with grafting the image of the United States in their own youth (1890 – 1914) upon the generation moving into adulthood in the 1920's. The youth of this period, however, were repelled by this emphasis on the past by their elders. Amid the revolutionary changes wrought by a technological society they looked more to the future, but without the optimism of their fathers. Instead, they were often nagged by doubts and insecurities and not at all sure of their sense of direction.

Thus, in the 1920's the United States represented a nation of contrasts. A period of such rapid changes inevitably produced a clash between the old and new. American politics witnessed a contrast between normalcy and progressivism. The American economy reflected a further decline of agriculture and other "old" industries and the growth of mass production and distribution on a hitherto unprecedented scale. Social changes were no less profound as millions of older people imbued with the values of rural agrarian America clashed with their fellow citizens living in urban industrial centers, many of them young, or members of ethnic or racial minorities with different sets of values. Similar cleavages were revealed in American culture and thought as a younger generation of writers and artists largely rejected traditionalism and embarked on a search for new standards that could be adapted to a technological civilization. The conflict between the old and the new was also reflected in United States foreign policy, where the advocates of isolationism carried on a continuing debate with the defenders of internationalism. In every aspect of American life in the 1920's, therefore, the contrast between the old and the new underscored the rapid change engulfing the United States as technology, urbanization, and immigration were transforming it into a modern mass society.

POLITICS IN THE 1920'S

Politics accurately reflected divergent tendencies in America, taking the form of normalcy and progressivism, respectively. To many Americans normalcy signified Small Government and bossism, and progressivism was characterized by a faith in Big Government and bureaucracy. During the decade the presidents mirrored these trends. Without question, Warren Harding and Calvin Coolidge represented nineteenth-century rural America from whence they came. Yet neither was wholly impervious to the winds of change during his tenure in the White House. In Congress and many state houses a similar dichotomy existed between old and new.

ELECTION OF 1920

The election of 1920 set the stage for the politics of the era. Among the Republicans, the division between Roosevelt progressives and advocates of normalcy was clear. In the presidential convention General Leonard Wood, once a loyal follower of Teddy Roosevelt, was a leading contender for the presidential nomination, but he was opposed by Old Guard elements in the party who favored a more conservative contender such as the highly respected governor of Illinois, Frank O. Lowden. The deadlock between Wood and Lowden presaged the selection of a compromise candidate who could attract votes from both the progressive and Old Guard wings of the Republican party, such as Senator Warren G. Harding of Ohio, who had always been careful to try not to offend anyone. Thus, on Friday evening, June 11, 1920, a group of Republican leaders met in a smoke-filled room at the Blackstone Hotel in Chicago and, prodded by Harding's manager, Harry Daugherty, agreed on Harding as a likely presidential choice. His selection did not come as a result of a conspiracy or a corrupt deal, nor as an attempt to foist an unwanted candidate upon the convention, but rather as a practical solution to a political deadlock. Moreover, Harding was popular with the rank and file of Republicans. As his running mate the convention chose Governor Calvin Coolidge of Massachusetts to provide geographical balance for the ticket.

The Democrats reaffirmed Wilson's domestic and foreign policies. President Wilson, although incapacitated, was eager for a third term, but his paralysis prevented an active race. Nevertheless, his influence was still great enough to persuade the Democratic National Convention to select candidates pledged to implement Wilsonianism. For the presidency the Democrats chose James M. Cox, the progressive governor of Ohio; and for the vice-presidency they picked Franklin Delano Roosevelt of New York, Wilson's handsome and debonair assistant secretary of the navy.

The campaign of 1920 reflected the ambivalent feelings of many Americans concerning the old and the new in American politics. In an atmosphere of disenchantment with Wilson's foreign policy, rather than with his domestic program, a Republican victory seemed certain. Senator Harding thus contented himself with "front porch" electioneering as he graciously met visitors at his home in Marion, Ohio, and restricted his speech-making tours to a minimum. As party leaders had hoped, he appealed to both traditionalists and progressives, to men as diverse as Andrew Mellon and Charles Evans Hughes, Robert La Follette, and William Howard Taft.

Cox and Roosevelt, on the other hand, traveled far and wide into every section of the country. Everywhere they espoused the cause of domestic reform, but especially United States member-ship in the League of Nations. The voters (including millions of women who cast ballots for the first time) distrusted Wilsonian rhetoric and idealism. They found Harding's placid stance more appealing. By a very large majority they gave Harding an over-whelming victory. Gathering 62 per cent of the popular vote, he received the largest plurality in the annals of American elections.

HARDING ADMINISTRATION

The president was a product of the nineteenth-century rural and small town Middle West. Born in New Caledonia, Ohio, in 1865, he was one of eight children in a farm family. He received only a limited education in country schools before attending Central Ohio Academy from 1877 to 1882. Meanwhile, he secured

Warren G. Harding. (Harris & Ewing)

odd jobs as a railroad laborer and farmhand. In 1882 he moved to the larger town of Marion (20,000 population), where he became an insurance salesman while dabbling in the law. Within two years he had drifted into journalism and had begun working for the *Marion Mirror*. He bought the *Marion Star* in 1886 and embarked on an independent publishing career. During this period he became well known about town, for he was handsome, friendly, and outgoing — indeed, one of the gay young blades of Marion. After his marriage in 1891 to Florence De Wolfe, a wealthy widow, he became more affluent and enjoyed increasing prestige in the community. As a result, he was chosen a director of the Marion County Bank and the local lumber company, and he served as a trustee of the Trinity Baptist Church. With his pleasing appearance and success as a small-town publisher, he was a natural candidate for a career in politics. Harding's first effort, in 1898, resulted in his election to the Ohio State Senate, where he served for two terms. In the state capital of Columbus he met Harry Daugherty, an astute politician who became his close friend and political mentor. Daugherty had high hopes for Harding's political career. In 1902 his aid proved to be valuable when Harding was elected lieutenant governor of Ohio and gradually became known throughout the state. Harding ran for the governorship of his native state in 1910 and suffered his only major political defeat, though he continued to be active in Republican politics. Urged on by Daugherty, in 1914 he was elected a United States senator and served until 1920 with no special distinction. A modest man who was keenly aware of his own limitations, Harding viewed his ascent to the White House with some fear and trepidation. Kind, good-natured, and of average intelligence, he knew that forcefulness was not one of his major virtues. As in the earlier years of his career, by nature he was inclined to look two ways, thus securing support from Old Guard advocates of normalcy as well as from progressive factions in his party.

Harding's cabinet reflected his ambiguous nature. On the one hand, he selected a group of political hacks and local courthouse politicians sometimes known as the "Ohio Gang." These men would have cast discredit on any administration. On the other hand, the president also surrounded himself with a very distinguished array of progressive Republicans who could easily be designated as the "Washington Statesmen." The "Ohio Gang" was frequently seen in the White House, where they joined Harding on many an evening for the poker games he loved so well. Included in the group was Harry Daugherty, whom the president now appointed as his attorney general. Also present at many of these unofficial functions was Ed Scobey, the former sheriff of Pickaway County in Ohio, who became director of the United States Mint. Daniel R. Crissinger, a Marion lawyer, was chosen to be comptroller of the currency and later a member of the Federal Reserve Board. Charlie Forbes, the new director of the Veterans Administration, was another one of Harding's cronies. These men were typical of small-town courthouse politicians whose vision was often restricted to local issues if they were absolutely honest, as unfortunately was not the case with some of Harding's associates.

The "Washington Statesmen" whom Harding appointed to his cabinet consisted of a number of leading Republican personalities. They included extraordinarily able progressive Republicans such as his secretary of state, Charles Evans Hughes, former governor of New York. His secretary of agriculture was Henry C. Wallace, publisher of *Wallace's Farmer,* one of the major farm periodicals in the United States. Wallace was one of the nation's leading authorities on agricultural problems. The new secretary of commerce, Herbert C. Hoover, was then regarded as one of the most promising and outstanding younger men in public life for not only had he made an impressive record as a member of Wilson's war administration, but also he had won world-wide renown for his international relief programs. Harding also appointed William Howard Taft as chief justice of the United States, a choice that received widespread acclaim. The men around Harding, therefore, represented both normalcy and progressivism in American politics.

Political Scandals

Unfortunately, the political scandals of the Harding administration overshadowed its many constructive achievements. Corruption in government after conclusion of a war was no new occurrence for Americans; it had appeared after the American Revolution and the Civil War. The moral letdown after World War I was therefore not wholly unexpected, but it nevertheless created widespread shock. Five important scandals rocked the Harding years. First to be publicized was the case of Jess Smith, known primarily as a "fixer" in Washington. As a friend of Daugherty's, Smith became a vital contact man between bootleggers or tax dodgers who wanted easy access to the Department of Justice. Before news of his dubious activities could reach Harding's ears, Smith returned to Ohio where he fatally shot himself. A second scandal involved Charlie Forbes of the Veterans Administration, who was found to have received bribes and kickbacks from government contractors who were building hospitals. His legal advisor committed suicide, and Forbes himself was later (1925) convicted of fraud. A third scandal involved Alien Property Custodian Thomas Miller, who in 1927 was found guilty of having received bribes from foreign companies (such as the American Metals Company) desiring return of properties taken over by the United States government in World War I. His activities were related to a fourth questionable case involving Harry Daugherty himself. Investigation revealed that Daugherty had a joint bank account with Jess Smith, who was also involved in the American Metals Company case in which Miller was implicated. Daugherty refused to testify before a United States Senate committee about his transactions, and in fact instructed the Federal Bureau of Investigation (FBI) to trail committee members.

The most sensational scandal was the Teapot Dome Affair, involving Secretary of the Interior Albert Fall. A New Mexican who had served in the United States Senate (1913 – 1920), Fall persuaded Harding to transfer two naval oil reserves, Teapot Dome (Wyoming) and Elk Hills (California) to the jurisdiction of his department in 1921. Then he leased these properties to two of his friends, Harry F. Sinclair and Edward L. Doheny, respectively, both prominent oil operators. Subsequent testimony before a Senate investigating committee headed by Senator Thomas Walsh of Montana revealed that Fall had received a loan of $100,000 from Doheny, and a similar payment of more than $300,000 from Sinclair. Although Fall claimed that these sums constituted loans and that they were not directly related to his award of the leases, nevertheless in 1929 a federal court convicted him of accepting bribes although — somewhat inconsistently — it acquitted the two oil men of having offered them. Fall resigned from the cabinet before the transactions were brought to light, but his name became a national household word to symbolize corruption in the Harding administration. However, later investigators suspected strongly that Teapot Dome was not a case of outright corruption on the part of Fall but rather a case of poor and questionable judgment.

Reform Programs

Unfortunately, the sensationalism surrounding Teapot Dome and political corruption overshadowed the constructive and progressive-minded policies of the Harding administration in the realm of economic, political, and social reform. Certainly the president and his advisors were far more sensitive to postwar problems than Woodrow Wilson had been after Versailles. In many areas of public policy they were compelled to carry on where Wilsonian reform had left off before American entrance into the war.

One such area of economic reform concerned farm policies. Secretary Wallace and many agricultural economists believed that insufficient credit was a major source of the farm depression and that the federal government should step into this gap. Thus, in cooperation with the farm bloc in Congress — a group of United States senators from farm states led by Senator Arthur Capper from Kansas — the Harding administration promoted three measures. In 1921 Harding revived the War Finance Corporation to extend more than $1 billion in agricultural loans and subsidies to farmers and cattlemen to alleviate immediate distress. He approved the Packers and Stockyards Act of 1921, which authorized federal regulation of grain exchanges and more rigid federal inspection of meat packers. Finally, he authorized the creation of a new system of agricultural banks to ease the difficulties many farmers had in securing credit. This new system of Federal Intermediate Credit Banks, which provided for twelve such institutions in as many regions, extended loans to agricultural cooperatives and banks in rural areas.

Harding also continued several economic reforms that had been begun in the Progressive era but which were delayed because of the war, such as the Highway Act of 1916. Thus, Harding became the first chief executive to put a large-scale federal road program in operation. Under his prodding Congress allocated new funds for this purpose in the Highway Act of 1922, which effectively got the federal program under way. Harding also continued the antitrust campaigns of his predecessors as the Justice Department filed twenty-three suits during his tenure in the White House to enforce the Sherman Anti-Trust Act. Another area of action was public power. Harding put into operation the Power Act of 1920, which gave the federal government greater authority to regulate power rates and standards of service, and created a Federal Power Commission to administer the law. Various officials in the Harding administration were also sympathetic to Senator George Norris of Nebraska in his attempts to secure a public power project in the Tennessee Valley. They successfully opposed an offer by Henry Ford to purchase and operate federal power facilities at Muscle Shoals, Alabama, later to become the nucleus of the Tennessee Valley Authority. Finally, the president himself went on a speech-making tour of Alaska to promote the cause of natural resource conservation, particularly the prudent use of minerals, water, and forests.

Harding was not insensitive to the needs of labor. In the face of increasing joblessness in the depression of 1921 he called a national Employment Conference, which brought together representatives of employers and employees to discuss ways and means of alleviating unemployment. Though this conference did not result in concrete action, it did reveal a new concern by the federal government to alleviate the plight of the unemployed. Meanwhile, with little success, the president was urging the adoption of an eight-hour day in the steel industry, where he met strong resistance on the part of management.

Nor did Harding completely ignore the progressive political tradition. Although the work of streamlining and modernizing federal revenue procedures had been in preparation for more than a decade prior to the enactment of the Budget and Accounting Act of 1921, it was the Harding administration that had to create precedents and to put it into operation. The ascendancy of Harding also brought an end to the Red Scare of A. Mitchell Palmer. Harding helped to lessen antiradical hysteria by granting an executive pardon to Eugene Debs, the Socialist leader who had been languishing in prison for his opposition to American entrance into World War I.

Despite its achievements, the Harding administration ended in a cloud of scandal. In the face of impending revelations of wrongdoing, the president embarked on an Alaskan tour in June 1923. Already tired and worn from the cares of office, Harding made a long succession of speeches in Alaska pleading for improved conservation. In late July he was struck down with a suspected case of ptomaine poisoning and was rushed back to San Francisco, where he died of a stroke on August 2, 1923. Rumors that he had been poisoned by his wife, who supposedly suspected him of unfaithfulness, were without foundation.

COOLIDGE

The death of Harding automatically elevated Calvin Coolidge to the White House. At the time, Coolidge was vacationing in rural Vermont, where, on the morning of August 3, 1923, he took the presidential oath of office from his father, a justice of the peace, attired in an old-fashioned nightcap and flowing gown. In many ways the ceremony was symbolic because the new chief executive represented the traditional Puritan values of rural New England. Born in Plymouth Notch, Vermont, on July 4, 1872, near the general store owned by his parents, he came from some of the first settlers in New England. A serious and taciturn young man, he graduated from Amherst College in 1895 and soon entered the practice of law in Northampton, Massachusetts. With great diligence he applied himself to specialization in real estate and mortgage problems. Meanwhile, his sense of duty led him into politics, where he commenced a slow and steady — if somewhat unimaginative — climb. In 1898 he was elected to the Northampton City Council; by 1906 he was a member of the Massachusetts House of Representatives; in 1910 he returned as mayor of Northampton; from 1911 to 1915 he served in the state Senate; in 1915 he became lieutenant governor of Massachusetts; three years later he was elected governor and gained national prominence through his handling of the Boston police strike. In the Republican National Convention of 1920 progressives were not unsympathetic to him as a vice-presidential choice, since his integrity was beyond question. Although outwardly bland, he had a dry wit, and possessed considerable political finesse and astuteness. He believed in frugality and thrift, morality and pietism, individualism and industriousness — in short, the qualities often associated with the Puritan ethic.

More than Harding, Coolidge was an exponent of normalcy. He had little sympathy for farmers who had been in the throes of a depression ever since the end of World War I. When the farm bloc in Congress succeeded in securing the passage of the McNary-Haugen Bill in 1927 and 1928 — proposing a plan to market surpluses overseas to maintain price levels in the United States — Coolidge exercised his veto on both occasions. Nor was he friendly to the development of public power. His response to Senator George Norris's bill for regional resource development in the Tennessee Valley was a pocket veto. The president also upheld traditional Republican attitudes toward the tariff by seeking to keep it high. In 1924 when the United States Tariff Commission issued a report recommending selective tariff reductions, Coolidge, in his inimitable quiet way, had it sidetracked.

To a limited extent Coolidge supported some of the programs advocated by progressives. He was not deaf to the pleas of conservationists, and in 1924 created the Federal Oil Conservation Board to advise him on ways and means to preserve the nation's oil supply. Nor was he averse to extending federal controls over new communications media. He approved creation of the Federal Radio Commission in 1927 to supervise and assign the nation's air waves. He was also sympathetic to pleas for immigration restriction and signed the National Origins Act of 1924, which set up quota systems that allowed no more than about 150,000 immigrants to enter the country yearly. Coolidge's tax policies also answered some of the demands of progressive reformers. In fact, he was one of the first chief executives to relate taxation directly to the federal government's efforts to stimulate economic growth. The Revenue Act of 1924 provided for the reduction of taxes on high incomes in the hope that such encouragement would stimulate new investments. It also lowered taxes on small incomes. The Revenue Act of 1926 reduced levies even further as a means of providing incentives to investment. Without Theodore Roosevelt's sense of drama, Coolidge favored continuation of antitrust policies and corporate regulation. During his presidency he encouraged the increase of antitrust prosecutions by the Justice Department, which secured forty-eight consent decrees and initiated 130 proceedings under the Sherman Anti-Trust Act. In addition, he appointed W. E. Humphreys chairman of the Federal Trade Commission. That controversial figure believed in closer cooperative relationships between the federal government and Big Business and emphasized regulation by collaboration and advisement rather than by dissolution of large corporations.

Coolidge was not particularly active in securing social legislation. He did speak out for needed laws to prohibit child labor and he was also sympathetic to the cause of racial equality, although he did little more than discuss the question. Otherwise, he did not believe that the federal government had major responsibilities to secure social justice. "The business of America," he once remarked, "is business."

Thus, Coolidge represented the old and the new in American life during the twenties, with emphasis on the former. In his own person he symbolized normalcy — the values of nineteenth-century America. Yet he had too much Yankee shrewdness to ignore some of the reform pressures of his own times. Together with his predecessor, Warren Harding, he reflected the rapid changes that were sweeping almost every aspect of American civilization during the decade and which explain its contrasts and tensions.

AMERICAN ECONOMY OF THE 1920'S

If agriculture was declining during this period, its passing confirmed what many Americans already sensed — that business had become the mainstay of the American economy. Anyone who drove through the countryside in most sections of the nation could see evidence of the decline of rural life. Here could be found shrinking populations, abandoned farmhouses, stagnant villages, seemingly impoverished schoolhouses and churches, and, above all, a lagging spirit — a feeling that this civilization had a past but not a future. On the other hand, visitors would find a striking contrast in urban and suburban areas. There, in the midst of bustling activity, the population was visibly increasing, new buildings were in various stages of construction, large schools, imposing churches, museums, and public buildings met the eye, and one could sense a feeling of optimism, opportunity, and hopefulness in the air. Coolidge may have oversimplified his remarks in considering business as the business of America, but there was a measure of truth to his observation. These years saw the emergence of an affluent society in the United States characterized by mass production and distribution. To be sure, the benefits of this affluence were not as yet equally distributed among the various groups in the United States, but its effects were visible. Total wealth of the country (measured by gross national product) between 1919 and 1929 increased from

$74 billion to $104 billion. This meant a per capita increase from $710 to $857 in this same period.[1] As the United States entered an age of rapid technological development, nineteenth-century industrialism and agrarianism appeared to be fading.

THE FARM PROBLEM

The reasons for agricultural decline were threefold. First, there were technological changes; second, there was an increase in indebtedness; and third, there was a decline of available markets, which contributed directly to the crux of the farm problem. This farm problem was revealed in the decline of the value of farm products between 1919 and 1929, from $14.754 billion to $8.077 billion. In these same years farm debt rose significantly as the average value per farm declined from $12,084 (1920) to $9,103 (1930).[2] No wonder that the number of individuals engaged in farming dropped appreciably.

How did technology — such a boon to most farmers — also create serious problems for them? Essentially, it tended to increase productive capacity much faster than new market outlets, thus creating temporary surpluses and consequent falling prices. Production was greatly boosted by the replacement of horses by tractors, by increasingly automatic plows, harvesters, and threshing equipment, and efficient new machines for milking. Such innovations led to the expansion of crop lands from 955 million acres in 1920 to 987 million acres in 1930; and the productivity of farm workers increased by 25 per cent in the same period. But this rapid mechanization also greatly increased the farmer's debt.[3] Understandably, farmers frequently needed loans or installment credit to buy new machines and equipment. In addition, an expanding population tended to drive up land values and, with it, state and local taxes. The value of farm machinery used by each worker rose considerably between 1919 and 1929 as farmers bought labor-saving devices.[4] Unfortunately, their growing debt came at a time when markets for agricultural products were shrinking.

[1] U. S. Bureau of the Census, *Historical Statistics of the United States — Colonial Times to 1957* (Washington, 1960), p. 139.

[2] U. S. Bureau of the Census, *Abstract of the Fifteenth Census of the United States, 1930* (Washington, 1933), pp. 501, 644.

[3] *Ibid.,* pp. 526, 589.

[4] U. S. Bureau of the Census, *Fifteenth Census of the United States: 1930, Agriculture* (Washington, 1932), IV, pp. 535 – 43.

There are several reasons for the decline of marketing outlets as related to increased production. First, there was a relative decline in domestic demand due to a decrease in the rate of population growth, as an increasingly urbanized society reflected a lower birth rate. With the decrease of immigration this lag became even more noticeable. Another factor was the change in American dietary habits. Increased numbers of Americans lived in more congested surroundings in the cities and led a more sedentary life; thus, they shifted to different foods, usually from a diet based on carbohydrates (bread and potatoes) to one containing more fruits and proteins (meat and eggs). The fashion trend toward higher hemlines for women resulted in figure-consciousness and, consequently, new dietary habits. Shorter skirts and more revealing clothing created changing modes of dress as the chemical industries developed new synthetic fibers, bringing a pronounced shift from cotton to rayon stockings (which directly affected cotton farming). Meanwhile, the recovery of European farmers provided Americans with stiff competition; at the same time newer areas of the world such as Canada and Australia became major wheat producers, while Argentina emerged as an important cattle grower, and Egyptian cotton was shipped all over the globe. Thus, at a time when technological aids were enabling United States farmers to increase their production, their available market outlets decreased appreciably.

Inevitably, farm prices declined. Wheat dropped from $2.19 per bushel in 1919 to $1.04 per bushel ten years later. Similar figures for corn were $1.49 to $0.76, and for cotton from $1.76 per bale to $0.85 per bale.[5]

As a result farm income was drastically reduced. What made the decline particularly serious was the concomitant rise in farm debt, which caught the farmer in a squeeze.

Understandably, American farmers protested loudly about their increasingly marginal position in the economy and advocated various proposals to ease their plight. In Congress the farm bloc worked persistently for remedial legislation. In the election of 1924 a third party, the Progressive party, offered Senator Robert M. La Follette as a presidential candidate. Many of the 5 million votes he received came from farmers who felt that the efforts to help agriculture by the major parties were inadequate. The Packers and Stockyards Act of 1921, the Federal Intermediate Credit

[5] *Ibid.*, p. 714.

System Act of 1923, and various lesser measures were put into law. To stabilize prices the farm bloc also supported the McNary-Haugen bills (developed by George N. Peek of the Moline Plow Company) for marketing surpluses overseas, but these bills succumbed to Coolidge's veto.

Since farm income continued to decline throughout the twenties, the farmers were disappointed with these efforts. Apparently the roots of agricultural depression lay deeper than in the insufficiency of farm credit; shrinking markets and mushrooming production appeared to have a more direct bearing. But the experience with farm legislation in the 1920's revealed that abuses of middlemen were not necessarily the cause of the farm problem. Rather, this seemed to lie in the nature of agricultural production and distribution in an industrial economy. Thus, the farm programs of the twenties paved the way for new ideas and new programs in the years ahead.

RAILROADS AND OTHER "SICK" INDUSTRIES

The fate of American agriculture was shared by a number of other "old" or "sick" industries that entered a period of decline during the decade. The most important were the railroads, whose high overhead costs contrasted sharply with their declining profits. Despite great increases in the volume of business transactions in the country, their volume of freight remained almost constant. Newer and competing forms of transportation were grasping the bulk of this new business, especially the booming truck industry, which made survival for the railroads difficult.

No less troubled was the coal mining industry, as competing sources of energy plunged it into deep depression. Electricity was rapidly replacing steam and other coal-powered machinery in factories across the nation. By 1920 most railroads had completed their conversion from coal-powered locomotives to electric engines or to diesel fuel. Meanwhile, householders across the nation were converting their coal-burning furnaces to fuel oil, further diminishing coal consumption. In this decade coal production declined by more than 100 million tons annually, resulting in the displacement of at least 200,000 miners. The textile industry was in a similar predicament since it had to meet competition not only from foreign manufacturers but also from the new synthetic fibers like rayon, which adversely affected wool and cotton producers.

To cut costs many textile mills moved from New England to the South, where labor costs were cheaper. This rapid shift created numerous pockets of poverty in the Northeast — areas of unemployment whose condition was also worsened by not dissimilar conditions in boot and shoe manufacturing. The striking decline of agriculture and the "old" industries during the twenties reflected profound changes in the nature of the American economy.

NEW INDUSTRIES

On the other hand, development of a new economy based on mass production and distribution presaged an affluent society which suddenly emerged during this period. If national wealth grew by leaps and bounds during the decade, it was due to the rise of major industries based not on the processing of raw materials but on technological innovations. These industries spurred the whole economy.

First and foremost among the newcomers was automobile manufacturing, which was revolutionized by Henry Ford's adaptation of assembly line techniques and by applying standardization to the manufacture of motor cars and trucks. Between 1921 and 1929 annual production exceeded 5 million vehicles, resulting in a total value of almost $4 billion in 1929 and totaling 12 per cent of all manufacturing output in the United States.[6] In many ways the auto industry acted like a trigger mechanism for prosperity because it gave rise to a number of other important auxiliary industries such as road construction, which boomed with millions of new cars on the move. The enormous increase in automobile traffic precipitated unprecedented demands for concrete and asphalt and other highway construction materials. The petroleum industry was invigorated by the new markets opened by motor transportation, especially for gasoline and lubricants. Millions of cars also spawned a large-scale rubber tire industry. The addition of millions of new vehicles during the decade created major new service industries such as gasoline stations, repair shops, and restaurants. To a lesser extent, the nascent aviation industry promoted similar trends.

The manufacture of electrical appliances was another of the

[6]U. S. Bureau of the Census, *Abstract of the Fifteenth Census, 1930*, p. 762.

spectacular new industries. For the first time American factories were turning out millions of consumer items such as refrigerators, stoves, washing machines, electric irons, and toasters. Hardly less amazing was the emergence of large-scale radio manufacturing. Originally Enrico Marconi's invention and Lee DeForest's vacuum tube (1910) were mere gadgets; in 1919 the Radio Corporation of America began manufacturing radio receivers, however, resulting in sales of more than a million sets each year during the twenties. The widespread use of radio in turn stimulated the organization of a broadcasting industry. By 1924 there were 562 radio stations, many affiliated with the new National Broadcasting Company (NBC).

Such technical advances contributed to making the entertainment business a major industry, particularly with the development of motion pictures. More than 20,000 new motion picture theaters were constructed in the 1920's as Hollywood became the glamour center of the nation. By 1929 more than $2 billion was invested in various spheres of movie-making and theaters.

Another major new industry grew around chemicals. Before World War I the United States had been largely dependent on outside sources for many of its needed chemicals. The war stimulated E. I. Du Pont and many smaller companies to double their production and to diversify in order to meet demand. Synthetic foods and fibers as well as plastics became important products.

The business boom was also paced by the expansion of some older industries, notably construction, which added 6 million new industrial and residential housing units each year, and the steel industry, which vastly increased its output. Thus, automobiles, electric appliances, radio, movie, and chemical industries sparked the economic advance of the 1920's, aided by growth in some older industries.

MASS DISTRIBUTION

Such brilliant growth in America's productive capacity would scarcely have been possible had it not also been accompanied by a veritable revolution in the methods of mass distribution. The day of the small shopkeeper — so characteristic of the nineteenth-century United States — was clearly passing. Striking innovations in retailing brought about the change and ushered in a consumer-oriented society. Advertising became a major business, evidenced by annual revenues exceeding $1 billion. It was argued that advertising generated new wants and through its establishment of brand names helped to stabilize consumer demand, thereby contributing to general economic prosperity. One of the pioneers in this field was Bruce Barton of the advertising firm of Batten, Barton, Durstine and Osborne, which helped to make advertising an integral part of the American economy.

A second innovation in distribution was installment selling. Though it was not an entirely new business practice, it was now becoming widespread. Reliable estimates in 1926 noted that almost 70 per cent of all automobiles were sold on time payments, as were one-fifth of all retail goods. The new mass production industries could not have found ready market outlets for the vast quantities of goods they produced if it had not been for the technique of installment credit, which created millions of new customers.

A third characteristic of retailing during the decade was the development of chain stores, which were often able to achieve great economies because of their very large volume of sales. By 1929 chain stores had captured almost one-third of the nation's retail business in urban areas and started a significant new trend in retailing. Chains such as Safeway and Piggly-Wiggly achieved important positions in food distribution, and Sears, Roebuck and Company and Montgomery Ward began to open their first retail outlets. With the new concepts of merchandizing, which stressed big volume and low prices, they began the rapid displacement of individually owned stores throughout the country.

Thus, the business landscape of the United States was being transformed in the 1920's. The locally owned general or specialty store, owned by a proprietor who took pride in knowing his cash-paying customers and who catered to their individual tastes, was disappearing. In its place rose the company-owned establishment with a standardized store front, staffed by hired employees who provided standardized service for all customers, many of whom were persuaded to buy goods because of advertising and the availability of installment credit.

The Stock Boom

To a considerable extent, the evolution of mass production and distribution was reflected in the New York stock market.

The decade witnessed a stock boom that erupted into an increasingly wild speculatory binge after 1926. People in every walk of life, from housemaid to tycoon, were engaged in stock speculation. Two million stocks were traded on the New York Stock Exchange in 1924; by 1929 the figure was more than 7.5 million. Stock prices rose appreciably. Some of this growth represented real increments in productive capacity. But by 1927 the average price of stock had risen to three times its asset value. Meanwhile, stock transactions were increasingly marked by abuses. Purchases on margins as low as 10 per cent (buying stock with only a 10 per cent down payment), rigging by insiders, and artificial sales drove prices up to unrealistic levels. This orgy of speculation was also draining funds away from investments in productive enterprises, thereby endangering the stability of the whole economy.

ECONOMIC CHANGE: A SUMMARY

The American economy during the twenties therefore presented stark contrasts between old and new. On the one hand, the old industries that had prompted economic growth in the nineteenth century were in decline, notably farming, coal mining, textile manufacturing, and railroading. On the other hand, a group of new industries was stimulating the rapid surge of the economy during this decade, transforming it into an affluent consumer-oriented society. Automobiles, appliances, radio, movie, and chemical industries were among the new leaders in manufacturing production, accompanied by significant innovations in retailing such as advertising, installment credit, and chain stores. These fundamental changes in the economy were to affect most phases of American life during the next fifty years.

SOCIAL TENSIONS

Old and new America was revealed starkly in the many social tensions that beset the United States during the decade of the twenties. The population of old America had been predominantly white, Anglo-Saxon in origin, Protestant, and native-born. In addition, by background and orientation they were predominantly rural. Since the United States had a relatively homogeneous population in the nineteenth century, it was not surprising that before 1914 most Americans shared common values, many of which were embraced in the Protestant ethic. This stressed the desirability of success and material wealth, thrift, diligence, integrity, and hard work. But in the twentieth century the United States found itself a heterogeneous nation, as 24 million immigrants poured into the country between 1860 and 1920, introducing greater diversity into American life. In contrast to the old Americans these newcomers were often of east or south European stock, and this new component of the population contained more Catholics and Jews. In the twenties, the population included many foreign-born or first generation Americans; many of them were city dwellers. In addition, large numbers of black Americans from southern rural areas moved to northern and midwestern cities. They too added to cultural diversity as they brought their own social values to formerly white communities.

Although the American melting pot absorbed many of the immigrants, it did not do so without sustaining an effect on values ingrained in the Protestant ethic. The immigrants left their own impact on prevailing American norms. This decade therefore witnessed the commingling of two generations. One comprised white rural Anglo-Saxon Protestants; the other contained urban immigrant Catholics, Jews, and black Americans. Understandably, the values of these diverse groups often differed, thus setting the stage for contrasts and conflicts. The inherited Protestant ethic of the nineteenth century was to clash with the "ethnic ethic" of the twentieth century.

The rivalry between rural and urban America, and between native and foreign-born Americans was reflected in many social problems of the decade. It could be observed in controversies over standards of personal behavior, especially involving sex. It was also revealed in the re-emergence of nativism in most sections of the United States, directed at ethnic minorities and black Americans. It was seen in the noble experiment of Prohibition, and in the struggle over religious beliefs and orientation. The social issues of the period were the reflections of fundamental changes in the composition of American society.

THE CHANGING MORALITY

To many Americans it appeared as if the nation was undergoing a revolution in sex standards. Though the changes were not as novel as they appeared at the time, they did herald a new age. In nineteenth-century America, the accepted standards of etiquette and behavior had been reasonably well defined. A woman's place was in the home, and relations between the sexes were shrouded in privacy and silence. In the twenties, however, these patterns underwent a rapid transformation. Women now entered the fields of law, medicine, and business. To dramatize their newly found freedom many women adopted new styles of dress (skirts, now two inches above the knee, had been eight inches below the knee in 1919), they cut their hair short (like men), smoked cigarettes in public (a privilege once reserved only for men), and on occasion used language hitherto spoken only by men. They also enthusiastically took up new — and to old Americans shocking — dances like the Charleston, which displaced the more sedate waltzes of an earlier age. The Reverend William J. Porter expressed the dismay of an older generation when in 1922 he wrote a book entitled *The Dangers of the Dance,* in which he flayed the "syncopated embrace" of modern youth. Moreover, discussions of matters pertaining to sex became increasingly frank. Perhaps the changing conceptions of the modern woman were aptly reflected in contemporary movie idols. Before World War I "America's sweetheart" had been Mary Pickford, a symbol of the shy, demure, sweet, innocent young lady exemplifying the "highest type" of American womanhood. America's movie idol in the twenties was Clara Bow, the "it" girl, who became famous for her brash, bold personification of flaming sex. The span of only ten years constituted a gap between generations.

Indeed, a preoccupation with sex seemed characteristic of the United States in the twenties. One index to the new attitude was the rise of popular magazines in which the subject was discussed as openly as possible. The model for these journals was *True Story,* founded in 1919 and dedicated to the exploitation of sensational personal affairs. It soon had a circulation exceeding 2 million. Moving pictures also emphasized romance and sex to a far greater extent than in previous years, and Rudolph Valentino became the prototype of the great screen lover. Novelists and story writers became more explicit in their discussions of sex than at any previous time. James B. Cabell's *Jurgen* (1919), an erotic novel of the new genre, was a huge success, perhaps because it was banned in many towns and cities. No less shocking to many Americans was the behavior of some (not all) young people who could be observed kissing and necking in public. They were promptly dubbed "flaming youth." An increase in the number of automobiles gave them a new freedom and mobility as more couples embarked on joy rides. Now they could escape the scrutiny of their elders to which they had been subjected in the days when young men and women had traditionally courted in their family's front parlor. The suspicions of the older generation were especially aroused because the new mobility of youth allowed them to revolt more effectively against the authority of their parents. Moreover, the older ideal of premarital chastity was being openly challenged with increasing frequency. Without doubt, mores governing personal behavior were undergoing rapid change. The clash between the old and the new values was bound to create social tensions. And while the expression of such tensions varied greatly, changing behavior patterns were perhaps the most visible manifestation of great changes in the values held by a large number of Americans.

Why did the twenties witness such shifting moral standards? The rise of a technological society enormously increased the mobility of individuals, and so was bound to affect their patterns of behavior. The automobile certainly played a big role in encouraging a veritable revolution in the manners of Americans. Urbanization was another factor. Quite obviously, the behavior of a nation of city dwellers — of individuals living in close proximity to each other in congested areas — was bound to differ from that of a nation of rural farmers in which the family constituted an important and closely knit social unit (which was not as true in cities). The influence of immigrant and minority groups was also significant as multicultural behavior patterns affected prevailing American standards to some extent. Nor could the impact of Freudian psychology be ignored. To be sure, Freud was more widely discussed than read. Right or wrong, it was generally believed, however, that Freud counseled uninhibited expression of sexual desires, and that repression would result in mental illness. Such an assumption directly challenged traditional Judeo-Christian behavior standards, which were being questioned by individuals, in public forums, and in the press. Finally, it may well be that the postwar disillusionment felt by some Americans resulted in a modified form of self-centered hedonism in the twenties. But, in one way or another, these factors contribute to an understanding of the rapidly changing moral standards of the decade.

NATIVISM

The social tensions of the period were also reflected in nativism, which resulted from the clash between the customs of old Americans and those of newcomers. In the large ethnic conclaves of the big cities many of the more recent immigrants continued to follow their own cultural traditions and to lead lives that differed from those of native Americans in rural areas. They spoke their own language, read their own newspapers, continued to attend Catholic, Jewish, or Moslem houses of worship, ate seemingly strange and exotic foods, had their own forms of recreation, and followed incomprehensible, strange customs. To make matters worse, sometimes they espoused radical political theories, which they brought with them to the New World. The prospect of tolerating these apparent strangers and aliens in their midst seemed too much for some Americans.

The tensions of the postwar period hastened the reappearance of nativism in the United States as it brought many latent fears and hostilities toward foreigners to the surface. Such nativism was revealed in legislation to restrict the entrance of additional immigrants, in the revival of the Ku Klux Klan, patriotic journalism, and court trials. These reflected a deep current of mistrust concerning minority groups — white and black — in American society.

The sentiment for immigration restriction was turned particularly against peoples from southern and eastern Europe and the Far East. Such feelings manifested themselves in the Immigration Act of 1921, which restricted the annual number of new arrivals to 2 per cent of any ethnic group already in the United States in 1910. This law was tightened by the more important National Origins Act of 1924, which prohibited Orientals from entering and established a quota system for others, limiting annual inflow to 2 per cent of the foreign born living in the United States in 1890. It therefore allowed larger quotas for English and north European peoples than for those from southern and eastern Europe. Altogether, after 1927 the quotas did not allow for more than 150,000 newcomers annually.

Fear and dislike of foreign elements in American life also prompted resurgence of the Ku Klux Klan. After Reconstruction in the South had ended (1877), this secret and violent organization had become defunct. But with the growth of antiforeign and anti-Negro sentiment in World War I the Klan was called back to life. Its prime appeal, as might be expected, was in regions where "old" Americans were a majority. Thus the Klan was strong in relatively rural areas or places where native-born white, Anglo-Saxon Protestants, usually lower middle class, felt that immigrants and blacks were threats to the American way of life. After William J. Simmons founded the new Klan at Stone Mountain, Georgia (1915), he embarked on an active membership campaign. By 1920 he found an enthusiastic response in the Middle West, the South, the Southwest, and the Far West. In 1925 the Klan was estimated to have about 5 million members, with particular strength in Indiana, Alabama, Oklahoma, Texas, Oregon, and California. The Klan's program was simple. It opposed Catholics, Jews, and blacks while reaffirming the purity and patriotism of its own members. Absorbed in secrecy and ritual, the Klan favored open violence and intimidation of minorities, whether through floggings, midnight rides, burnings, kidnapping, and, at times, murder. By 1929 these methods had evoked revulsion among large numbers of Americans. But its success in the twenties revealed the vehement fears that alien elements aroused.

These feelings also appeared in patriotic journalism. In every part of the country some newspaper or magazine editors became self-appointed guardians of "One Hundred Per Cent Americanism." In Chicago Colonel Robert R. McCormick performed this function by using the *Chicago Tribune* to uncover "unpatriotic" statements in American history textbooks. In Michigan, Henry Ford used the pages of his *Dearborn Independent* to give vent to his virulent anti-Semitism by publishing the forged "Protocols of the Elders of Zion," which purported to document an alleged Jewish conspiracy to control the world. After a court suit Ford later retracted the accusations. Various state legislatures, notably New York, Wisconsin, and Oregon, enacted laws designed to insure patriotism in school books.

Antiforeign sentiment was also evident in one of the sensational court trials of the decade, the famous Sacco and Vanzetti case (1927). Both of the defendants, Italian immigrants and also professed anarchists, were accused of a payroll robbery and murder in Braintree, Massachusetts. Many observers believed that their conviction by the courts was based on prejudice against their alien and radical backgrounds rather than on a careful scrutiny of the evidence. Whether or not they were guilty of the crime with which they were charged has never been decisively determined. But many liberals felt, along with Professor Felix Frankfurter of the Harvard Law School, that the two men had become the victims of a miscarriage of justice because of hostility against immigrants. The Sacco-Vanzetti case crystallized the issue of nativism as did no other issue of this decade.

PROHIBITION

Among the habits of foreigners that offended many native Americans, indulgence in alcoholic beverages was prominent. In the congested urban slums heavy drinking was common among many newcomers. Irish-Americans, for example, had no aversion to the use of alcohol. Moreover, in the absence of pleasant homes or other convenient social gathering places, they made the corner saloon a very important meeting place and social center. Catholics from southern and eastern Europe also brought their traditional wine-drinking habits to the New World. Jews had always had a low incidence of alcoholism, although they used wine in their rituals. Whatever individual differences might be, however, the new immigrants brought drinking habits to the United States that sometimes differed from those of native Americans.

Certainly the consumption of alcohol was not a new phenomenon in American life. During the nineteenth century, Americans had been a hard-drinking people, as reflected in their high per capita consumption of whiskey, ale, cider, and other strong liquors. After 1842, however, the Puritan ideal of abstinence reflected itself in an active temperance movement that resulted in laws prohibiting the sale and consumption of alcoholic beverages in at least ten states. The demand for abstinence grew stronger after 1860 as many rural youths moved to the cities where the temptations of drink were greater and where it was more easily available, or so it was believed. By 1900 the Women's Christian Temperance Union (WCTU) had been organized to demand not merely temperance but outright prohibition. The success of this group was remarkable. By 1918 three-fourths of the states were dry. With the drafting of large numbers of young men into the armed forces and the emotional fervor and patriotism aroused by

World War I, the antiliquor forces strove harder than ever for national prohibition. Their influence led to the adoption of the Eighteenth Amendment (1918) and the Volstead Act of 1919, which forbad even the consumption of beer. The motives of the Prohibition forces varied, but some of their main objectives were clear. Prohibition served as a vehicle by which rural Americans (who still controlled state legislatures) could seek to impose traditional Protestant values, such as abstinence, on urban dwellers. Extension of Prohibition was also an attempt by native white Americans to impose their own moral standards on the immigrant masses of the cities. It was also a convenient device for social control, i.e., an instrument to Americanize the foreigners. In addition, Prohibition may have been a reflection of class antagonisms as middle class Americans strove to fasten their values on lower class workingmen of the great cities.

The "noble experiment," as it was sometimes called, was not a great success, however. Urban dwellers (and drinkers) were increasingly becoming a majority outnumbering the rural drys. Widespread violation also led to the failure of enforcement. Everywhere Americans frequented "speak-easies," restaurant or bar establishments which sold and served liquor in defiance of the law. Home stills also became more popular, leading to many legends about "bathtub gin." Another reason for the failure of Prohibition was the development of bootlegging and the increase of crime. As Prohibition was widely flaunted, gangsters moved in to control the supply of illegal liquor for speak-easies and individuals. Their bootlegging operations provided avenues to other types of crime. The problems that country dwellers faced in adjusting to city life, particularly in festering slums, together with greater ease in transportation, drove up the crime rate. Theft, arson, robbery, personal assault, and murder became more frequent. Indeed, crime was becoming more professional. It was no longer characterized by the lone gunman but by highly specialized gangs that sometimes operated like corporations or big business enterprises. The most notorious of these was Al (Alphonse) Capone's Chicago-based crime empire, which had branches across the nation. Capone, a Sicilian immigrant who became the vice king of Chicago, employed more than 900 gangsters specializing in various types of crime, including the infamous "Murder Incorporated." His income was reputed to be as high as $60 million annually, and his activities contributed heavily to the failure of Prohibition.

Another reason for the failure of Prohibition was inadequate enforcement. The Prohibition Bureau in the Department of Justice had only 1520 agents in 1920, and 2800 agents a decade later. This small force was hardly adequate to assure observance of the Prohibition laws by more than 100 million Americans. For these various reasons, within a few years the attempt to enforce the nation-wide ban on alcohol broke down completely.

FUNDAMENTALISTS AND MODERNISTS

The contrast between old and new currents in American society was also manifested in religion during the twenties. In the nineteenth century rural Americans had frequently embraced a faith based on literal interpretation of the Bible, a faith often fanned by the heat of religious revivals. Some of their descendants sought to carry on this heritage. Just after World War I, William Jennings Bryan became one of the leading spokesmen for orthodoxy (a fundamentalist Christian creed). He was joined by some of the great revivalists of the decade, especially the dynamic Billy Sunday and the flamboyant Aimee Semple McPherson. Convinced that modern doctrines of science were undermining the traditional moral codes and values of Christianity, the evangelists thundered against the evils of modernity. Darwin's doctrine of evolution, which contradicted the Biblical explanation concerning the origins of man found in Genesis, was one of their special targets. Bryan himself undertook a speaking tour before state legislatures to urge adoption of laws that would prohibit the teaching of evolutionary doctrines. Florida and Tennessee responded to his appeal in 1923, North Carolina in 1924, and Texas in 1925. The Tennessee statute was challenged in the famous Scopes trial of 1925 when John T. Scopes, a high school biology teacher in the small town of Dayton, Tennessee, was accused by the state of teaching Darwinian doctrines. Bryan rushed to Tennessee to defend the statute, which prohibited the propagation of such theories. The famous trial lawyer Clarence Darrow, himself an agnostic, volunteered his services to defend Scopes. The resulting courtroom trial promised high drama but ended briefly with Scopes' conviction. The significance of the case far exceeded its local importance, for it revealed the wide gulf between traditional and modern religious values and created greater antagonisms between the advocates of these respective points of view.

The efforts of Bryan and his followers to preserve existing Christian beliefs conflicted with the modernism that was sweeping many Christian churches in the United States. Such modernism was based on a broad and loose interpretation of the Bible, with emphasis on its symbolic rather than its literal meaning. It also incorporated the results of half a century of Biblical criticism and scholarship that rejected portions of the Bible as inaccurate in the light of more recent scientific findings. Many advocates of modernism also favored the social gospel and stressed the social reform activities of Protestant churches more than doctrinal interpretations. Indeed, those who favored secularization of the churches often sought to incorporate the findings of Freudianism and psychology into Christian doctrines. One of the most popular national exponents of this phase of modernism was Dr. Harry Emerson Fosdick, pastor of the magnificent Riverside Church in New York City, whose sermons were carried to the entire nation via radio. Thus, the clash between religious orthodoxy and religious modernism precipitated real tensions among millions of Americans who were confronted with the difficult task of making a choice between them.

BLACK AMERICANS

The cultural conflicts that created tensions in American life during the 1920's also left their stamp on white-black relations of this period. Many Americans were content to view the black man as a second-class American citizen and to adjudge him, explicitly or implicitly, as an inferior. Thus, the chief executives during this decade expressed their sympathies for the strivings of blacks, but they were not as yet prepared to do much more. As Calvin Coolidge noted with some complacency:

> In the less than seventy years that the negro [sic] race in America have been in the enjoyment of freedom, they have made marvellous progress. That progress is shown not only in the property they have acquired . . . but most of all in the honest, industrious way in which the great body of their people have performed the plain everyday duties of life. Their greatest contribution lies in the fact that they have helped to do the work of the nation.[7]

[7]Calvin Coolidge, *The Price of Freedom* (New York: Charles Scribner's Sons, 1924), p. 275.

Coolidge did urge Congress to enact an anti-lynching law, but without much success.

Within the black community a number of aggressive leaders rejected acceptance of second-class status and strove for absolute equality, or perhaps even independence. One of the most striking personalities was Marcus Garvey, a Jamaican who was an early advocate of Black Power. A founder of the Universal Negro Improvement Association, by 1921 he was preaching a doctrine of racial pride. Garvey asked American blacks to forsake hopes of achieving equality with whites in the United States and instead to return to Africa. To accomplish this purpose he founded the Black Star Steamship Line as well as other black-operated enterprises. But Garvey was soon in trouble with the law. Charged with embezzlement, ultimately he was deported to Jamaica. Yet he succeeded in giving black Americans a new sense of self-respect, a positive identification with blackness, and brought the whole question of racial equality into the forum of public discussion.

Racial consciousness such as Garvey aroused also found an outlet in a burst of black cultural activity known as the Harlem Renaissance. During this period New York's Harlem became the intellectual center of black America as a talented group of black artists, writers, and thinkers made it their home. Among them were literary figures such as James Weldon Johnson, Alain Locke, Langston Hughes, Countee Cullen, and Claude McKay. Johnson edited *The Book of American Negro Poetry* in 1922, in which he gathered together some of the best contemporary black poetry. A few years later he also collected two notable volumes of Negro spirituals. McKay was a West Indian who came to the United States just before World War I and who attended Tuskegee Institute and the University of Kansas. His book of verse, *Harlem Shadows* (1922), dealt boldly with racial problems such as lynching and discrimination. He also wrote a novel about black life in New York City, *Home to Harlem* (1928). A writer of considerable versatility, McKay was adept in various forms of literary expression. Perhaps Langston Hughes enjoyed an even greater reputation, although he was not as preoccupied with racial themes. The author of many verses, his *Weary Blues* (1926) and his novel, *Not Without Laughter* (1930), won wide acclaim from many literary critics. Not all black writers dealt with the poor and oppressed in their midst. Jessie R. Fauset, a well-educated, middle-class black herself, wrote with insight about the black middle class in her novel,

There is Confusion (1924), in which she touched on the essential humanity that should bind blacks and whites together. Three younger writers were also associated with the renaissance. Jean Toumer published a collection of sensitive short stories about black America, *Cane* (1923). Countee Cullen wrote poetry as well as novels that focused on arousing racial consciousness. Walter White, in later years active in the National Association for the Advancement of Colored People, revealed considerable literary talent. *Fire in the Flint* (1924), his novel about the struggle of blacks in the South, was well received, as was his factual account of lynching, *Rope and Faggot: A Biography of Judge Lynch.*

The decade also saw the development of a black theater in Harlem, and black performers on Broadway. Companies such as the Lafayette Players presented a wide repertoire in Harlem. Black actors such as Charles Gilpin, Paul Robeson, Ida Anderson, and Clarence Muse appeared in varied productions. Gilpin gave a memorable performance in Eugene O'Neill's *Emperor Jones* and Robeson in O'Neill's *All God's Chillun Got Wings.* One of the most popular Broadway productions with a black cast was Marc Connelly's *Green Pastures* (1930), a fable about the black man's conception of the Old Testament. Black performers were notably successful in musicals. *Shuffle Along* (1922), written and produced by black artists Aubrey Lyles, Noble Sissle, and others, ran successfully for over a year. It overshadowed other black musicals such as *Put and Take, Liza,* and *Runnin' Wild. Chocolate Dandies* (1924) introduced Josephine Baker to American audiences as one of the world's outstanding stage and night-club entertainers. *Dixie to Broadway* (1924) featured the beautiful Florence Mills, perhaps the most gifted black dancer and musical comedy star of the decade. Vocalist Ethel Waters and dancer Bill Robinson were also building their reputations during these years. Meanwhile, singers like Paul Robeson, Roland Hayes, and Taylor Gordon revealed the increasing tide of black racial consciousness by devoting entire concerts to the performance of American Negro spirituals. The emergence of cultural nationalism among black Americans indicated that many of them would no longer be content with slavish imitation of white standards, and that, indeed, they were searching for different values and a cultural identity.

In politics, however, many black leaders still had faith in integration and advocated racial equality. Compared to Booker T.

Washington, they displayed a greater degree of militancy. Dr. William E. B. DuBois of the National Association for the Advancement of Colored People believed that only through aggressive protest — and not through meek submissiveness — could the Negro win his full rights as a citizen. Walter White, who became secretary of the National Association for the Advancement of Colored People, placed his own faith in legal action to secure the lessening of discrimination. The Urban League was primarily concerned with practical problems arising from the adjustment of rural blacks to urban life, mainly through economic means.

The increase in black-white tensions during the 1920's can be attributed in part to the fact that World War I opened new visions of equality and opportunity for thousands of black Americans. Their service in the armed forces and their assignments in Europe led them to question the treatment they received in many parts of the United States. Another factor was the increasing flood of southern rural blacks, often displaced by machines, into northern and midwestern cities. There the newcomers often met white hostility as they competed for jobs, housing, and other facilities. The slow progress of blacks in the professions and in business also whetted demands for greater gains. It was estimated that in 1930 there were no more than 1000 black lawyers in the country, and the number of physicians was not much higher. Less than 1 per cent of the nation's businesses were owned by blacks, and these were usually insurance companies or undertaking establishments that provided services for the black American community which whites were not anxious to furnish. The frustrations of second-class citizenship could hardly fail to arouse racial tensions.

INTELLECTUAL TRENDS

The contrast between old and new in American life was perhaps most clearly reflected in the realm of culture, which witnessed a clash between traditionalism and modernism. A revolt against traditionalism had already been begun by intellectuals before World War I, but the movement did not come to full fruition until the 1920's. Then artists in many fields including literature, art, music, philosophy, and academic disciplines undertook an attack on formalism, or rigid doctrines of all kinds. The rebels were not always certain just how they would replace the values which they were rejecting, but they were willing to experiment in their search for new standards.   /

LITERATURE

Perhaps the tensions generated by these controversies contributed to making the twenties a Golden Age of American literature. The turmoil in the minds and hearts of so many writers over acceptance or rejection of new concepts and beliefs brought out their most creative impulses. This is not to say that all writers turned against the American past; many continued to use themes and forms that revealed a reliance on traditionalism. Yet a significant number turned their backs on the United States and went into voluntary exile — mostly in Paris, but also in Taos, New Mexico, and other remote areas. These were the members of the "lost generation," who were sure about their rejection of contemporary values in American society but who were not quite so sure about alternatives to replace them.

A varied array of talented writers continued to express ideas in a traditionalist framework. Important among them were the southern regionalists — a group of young novelists who reaffirmed many of the values that had guided the nineteenth-century South and which included John Crowe Ransom, Allen Tate, and Robert Penn Warren. Other writers continued in the realist tradition — notably Willa Cather, whose *Death Comes to the Archbishop* dwelt on familiar themes in a dazzling style. Some of the most remarkable poets of the decade also chose to reaffirm traditional values. Robert Frost, Archibald MacLeish, and Edwin Arlington Robinson essentially reaffirmed Jeffersonian humanism in their works. T. S. Eliot, on the other hand, in *The Waste Land* and other works, experimented with varied standards until he found the stability he was seeking in medieval Christian doctrines. Literary critics like Paul Elmer More and Irving Babbitt championed humanism and the Christian ethic as values for Americans in time of stress, as did Van Wyck Brooks in his literary history of the United States. In essence, the defenders of Western humanism were quite vocal, although they tended to be overshadowed by the brilliant products of the "lost generation."

The spotlight of American literature in this decade was on

those writers who repudiated American values. They criticized the crass materialism of their own age and of values that seemed to put man at the mercy of machines. Sometimes they relayed their message in the framework of well-known literary techniques; at other times they pioneered with new forms of expression. A sizable number of the expatriates in Paris frequented the salon of Gertrude Stein, who in addition to her own experiments with the English language served as the godmother of a whole literary generation. Ernest Hemingway was one of the most brilliant of the lost generation. In *A Farewell to Arms* he mirrored the revolt of his contemporaries against the false ideals of American society. John Dos Passos in *Three Soldiers* and *The Big Money* severely criticized the emphasis on material success in the United States. Others used a regional setting to convey a similar message — notably William Faulkner, whose *Sound and the Fury* pilloried the false ideals of the southern aristocracy and their descendants. Sherwood Anderson provided criticism of the Middle West in *Winesburg, Ohio,* as did America's first Nobel Laureate in literature, Sinclair Lewis, whose *Main Street* presented a bittersweet indictment of materialism in the American heartland (1920). The feelings of alienated youth were strikingly documented by two brilliant and tragic young writers of the period. F. Scott Fitzgerald in *This Side of Paradise* caught the feeling of confusion, disillusionment, and drift of many of his generation better than any other author; his own life revealed the current attempt to escape into hedonism. Thomas Wolfe, in his lengthy and overwritten *Look Homeward, Angel,* beautifully expressed the emotions of those who felt trapped in their contemporary age, reluctant to look into the past, and afraid to look into the future. Most of these writers found it difficult to accept the values inherited from the nineteenth-century American tradition and embarked on a not-always-successful search for substitutes.

Other realms of literature witnessed a similar rejection of old standards. Ezra Pound eschewed traditional forms of poetic composition and in his *Cantos* imaginatively sought new combinations of words that would synthesize psychological insights and symbolic logic. A conflict of values also provided an agonizing birth for the first great dramatists in the United States. Eugene O'Neill, who joined the Provincetown (Massachusetts) Players in 1916, strikingly adapted Freudian themes to attack what he considered to be the perversities of American life. *Desire under the Elms, Strange Interlude,* and *Mourning Becomes Electra* dramatized a disillusionment that sometimes bordered on nihilism. Elmer Rice, a playwright whose talents were perhaps not fully appreciated by his contemporaries, condemned the dehumanization of man by technology in *The Adding Machine,* and Maxwell Anderson decried war in *What Price Glory?*

MUSIC

The world of music also mirrored the clash between old and new. Classical and romantic composers of the nineteenth century were dramatically presented by Walter Damrosch, conductor of the New York Philharmonic Orchestra, who provided a model for at least seventy similar orchestras throughout the nation. Numerous young American musicians began to revolt against traditional forms of music and began to experiment with new modes of expression. Deems Taylor wrote one of the first American operas, *Through the Looking Glass,* and Howard Hanson made a similar effort in *Merry Mount.* Aaron Copland reflected an innovative genius as he boldly departed from classical forms of composition to adapt the modes of Igor Stravinsky and Arnold Schoenberg to American themes. Perhaps George Gershwin was the most successful composer of the twenties to develop daring new styles without complete rejection of the past. His *Rhapsody in Blue* and *An American in Paris* achieved a brilliant new effect through their subtle blend of American folk music, classical form, and jazz. Jazz itself was first widely developed during this period and represented a departure from traditional types of music — indeed, a revolt against established patterns. William C. Handy, composer of the "Saint Louis Blues" and sometimes known as "the father of the Blues," set the new style during World War I. Louis Armstrong, Bix Beiderbecke, and others brought jazz from New Orleans to Chicago and New York, and then to the entire nation.

ART

Contrasts between traditionalism and modernism also dominated art in the period. Whatever their particular mode of expression, the painters of the decade were seeking new subjects, new techniques, and new color combinations. In the later nine-teenth century the French Impressionists had exercised a profound influence on Americans. They made Paris an art center to which scores of painters from the United States had gone for inspiration. The post–World War I generation of Americans, how-ever, strongly reacted against the Impressionists. Perhaps the rebellion began with the New York Armory Show of 1913 and was further developed through at least two forms of protest. The emergence of abstraction in American art was significant — whether expressed in cubism, surrealism, or primitivism. Among the leaders of this movement John Marin and Max Weber stood out because of their daring and imaginative experiments with color. Another reflection of protest was the realist school, popu-larly represented by the "Ashcan" group including George Bellows and Rockwell Kent, who used art as a form of social protest by focusing on lower-class life and problems in the large cities, whether in barrooms, tenement houses, or prize fights.

ACADEMIC DISCIPLINES

The revolt against formalism also shook academic subjects taught in colleges and universities. During the nineteenth century, in one way or another, each of these disciplines had been char-acterized by the discovery of laws or principles. Newtonian laws dominated physics, the Daltonian classification shaped chemistry, and Darwinian theories influenced biology. Historians prided themselves on their scientific certainty as expressed by Leopold von Ranke and his American disciples, Herbert Adams, John Vincent, and others, all of whom stressed political and military history. Political scientists were preoccupied with finding laws of political behavior, using Walter Bagehot's *Physics and Politics* as a guide. Economists were concerned with the framework elab-orated by Adam Smith and the classical school, just as sociologists admired Auguste Comte and his attempts to find scientific laws of behavior. In short, most scholars then were engaged in the search for general principles or laws.

During the twenties, however, many Americans developed a different approach to their respective fields, characterized by pragmatism. Although the breakdown of traditional concepts had already begun in the Progressive era, the movement was accelerated in the decade after World War I. In physics, Albert Einstein's theory of relativity (1906) had already modified Newtonian concepts. In 1927 Werner Heisenberg's discovery of irregularity in the behavior of electrons led him to elaborate the principle of uncertainty. This further diminished the faith of many in the absolute exactitude of scientific principles and encouraged a relativist or pragmatic view toward scientific phenomena. In chemistry Robert A. Millikan's researches on cosmic rays and the relative weight of electrons cast doubt on many accepted "laws."

Among historians there was a similar revolt against the scientific approach of Leopold von Ranke as James Harvey Robinson, Charles A. Beard, and Arthur M. Schlesinger, Sr., advocated a "new history" that would be relevant to contemporary problems instead of revolving about formal laws. They placed a special emphasis on economic and social issues. Similarly, political scientists directed their energies to matters of contemporary interest rather than to an analysis of "scientific principles." Economists followed a parallel development: Wesley Clair Mitchell and the National Bureau of Economic Research (which he founded in 1924) turned to the use of contemporary statistics and the study of business cycles instead of dwelling on classical economic doctrines. Sociologists largely abandoned their previous search for iron-clad laws and concentrated on examination of the social behavior of contemporaries. The outstanding example of the new approach was Robert S. and Helen M. Lynd's *Middletown,* a study of American behavior patterns in a small midwestern town. Other sociologists — for example, William F. Ogburn — studied urban issues. Florian Zaniecki, in *The Polish Peasant in America,* seriously examined the acculturation of immigrants.

Developments in psychology were within the context of these other disciplines. Throughout the nineteenth century psychologists had been working along lines laid out by the French pioneer, Alfred Binet, in which hereditary factors and "laws" were considered to be prime factors in understanding mental illness. In the twenties two major new orientations challenged this approach, with emphasis on experimentation. Behaviorists, led by John B. Watson, focused on development of new theories by scientific experiment and by relating physical and environmental (relative) factors to mental behavior. The Freudians, who enjoyed an enormous vogue during the decade, also emphasized a pragmatic experimental view, as evidenced in particular by their analysis of irrational behavior, which they believed could often be traced to sexual maladjustment.

INTELLECTUAL CLIMATE OF THE TWENTIES

If the range of academic research was broad and diverse in the twenties, one thread of unity that characterized the work of scholars in most fields was their passionate revision of dogmatic or rigid principles and theories. Thus, in most spheres of American intellectual life, the conflict between old doctrines and new departures created contrasts and tensions. The revolt of writers was only one phase in the movement to substitute pragmatism for formalistic theories. Similar tendencies affected fields as diverse as music, art, history, social science, natural science, and psychology. Perhaps the twenties were such an exciting period intellectually and culturally because the dilemmas which the decade presented to so many individuals brought out some of their most creative energies.

AMERICAN DIPLOMACY IN THE 1920'S

The contrasts so vivid in most spheres of American life in the twenties also appeared in American foreign policies. A whole generation of Americans born in the nineteenth century had grown to consider the principle of isolation as a basic guideline for the conduct of the nation's diplomacy. Senator William E. Borah was a spokesman for this view, and his adherents were disturbed by the increasing internationalism that characterized United States policy after 1898. The experience of World War I only confirmed the isolationists' belief that extensive overseas involvements were detrimental to the national interest. Meanwhile, some of those who had favored United States intervention in World War I were also disillusioned in the aftermath and disinclined to favor large-scale involvements.

Nevertheless, it should not be assumed that after World War I the United States retreated into an isolationism of the kind that had characterized the nineteenth century. Many international commitments simply could not be abandoned; and, as a consequence of the nation's great power, the impact of American actions was still felt throughout the world. Rather, both isolationism and internationalism coexisted in the diplomacy of the decade.

EUROPEAN POLICY

Certainly both elements existed in United States policy toward Europe. Isolationism was revealed in the American attitude on war debts and reparations. As a result of the Allied war effort, European nations owed the United States $10 billion in debts, and $3 billion in private loans had to be repaid. The Allies hoped that the United States would cancel a large share of these obligations, since they had been incurred in a common cause. Likewise, more than 90 per cent of the funds had been spent in the United States. But Congress and the chief executives during the twenties insisted on repayment, since the United States had been an "associated" rather than an Allied power in World War I. Such an attitude was later revealed to be shortsighted, for the financial strains it caused contributed to the increasing disruption of European economies.

The American attitude on German reparations was similarly inflexible. Two special commissions studied the problem at first hand. When German finances collapsed in 1923, the Dawes Commission of 1924 arranged for a revised schedule of payments for international loans that would enable Germany to resume payments. Public opinion was too much opposed to possible cancellation. Continuing difficulties led to the appointment of the Young Commission is 1929, which worked out another scheme for repayment, providing for American loans to enable the Germans to continue their installments. In effect, the United States was extending funds to Germany with which to pay the United States — a somewhat illogical procedure.

American desire for aloofness was seen in other policies as well. The closing of open entry for immigrants by the National Origins Act of 1924 was another example. The fears of the Irreconcilables also explain the refusal of the United States to join the World Court. Ironically, this tribunal had been created largely because of American pressures in 1919 and with the help of Elihu Root, William Howard Taft, John Bassett Moore (a distinguished expert in international law), and other policy makers. But throughout this decade Borah and other isolationists on the Senate Foreign Relations Committee prevented approval of any treaty that would have led to United States membership in the World Court, despite recommendations for such membership by Presidents Harding (1923), Coolidge (1925, 1927), and Hoover (1930).

At the same time, however, United States withdrawal from world affairs was not complete. Unofficial American interest in League activities was common and persistent. Although the United States did not join the world organization and took no responsibility for its actions, the State Department did send five unofficial observers to Geneva after 1922 to report on proceedings. In addition, the United States participated in some forty conferences held under League auspices, showing special interest in the regulation of traffic in arms and drugs, and in the International Labor Organization. American interest in disarmament was also pronounced. Prominent Americans such as James T. Shotwell (a professor of international relations at Columbia University) were instrumental in formulating the Kellogg-Briand Pact of 1927, in which the United States and thirty other signatories agreed to outlaw war in the settlement of international disputes. The United States also sent delegates to the naval disarmament conferences in Geneva (1927) and London (1930) with Great Britain, France, and Japan, although these meetings did not result in lasting or long-term agreements.

FAR EASTERN POLICY

Contrasting strands of isolationism and internationalism were reflected as well in American policies toward the Far East. One indication of isolationism came during the period from 1919 to 1920, when President Wilson withdrew American military forces from an international expedition to Siberia whose purpose was to overthrow the Soviet government in Russia. Nor did the United States make an effort to secure control over former German colonies in the Pacific, but agreed to let Japan become a trustee for the Mariana and Marshall Islands. The exclusion of Orientals under the National Origins Act of 1924 seemed a further indication that the United States had few intentions of extending close ties with Far Eastern nations.

Yet internationalism in American–Far Eastern relations

was not dead. United States ownership of the Philippines and the verbal commitment to the Open Door policy did not allow a complete withdrawal. The defeat of Germany, the decline of Great Britain's power, and the collapse of Russia in 1917 left a clear power vacuum in the Pacific that Japan was anxious to fill. The State Department was virtually forced into an effort to maintain the balance of power in the Orient lest Japan dominate the area completely. With such considerations in mind, President Harding and Secretary of State Hughes made arrangements for the Washington Conference of 1921 to develop new treaty arrangements that would maintain a power balance as well as the Open Door. Great Britain, France, Japan, and other nations with interests in the Far East were invited.

The work of the conference bore fruit in at least three important treaties. A Four Power Treaty (United States, Great Britain, France, Japan) provided that the signatories would respect the territorial integrity of their respective possessions in the Pacific. Its prime purpose, as far as the United States was concerned, was to maintain the balance of power and to restrain Japan from further expansion. A Five Power Treaty (United States, Great Britain, Japan, France, Italy) provided for a ten-year suspension in the construction of capital warships and a limitation of total naval tonnage to 500,000 tons each for the United States and Great Britain, 300,000 tons for Japan, and 175,000 tons each for France and Italy (a ratio of 5:5:3:1.75:1.75). For the United States, the major purpose of this agreement was to limit naval armaments in the Pacific. Hopefully this would help to preserve the status quo and to prevent the extension of Japanese influence. A Nine Power Treaty (United States, Great Britain, Japan, France, Italy, Holland, Portugal, Belgium, and China) stipulated that the signatories would recognize the Open Door policy and respect the independence and sovereignty of China. This arrangement, too, was designed to maintain the balance of power and to secure a reaffirmation of the Open Door policy. The agreements at this conference led Secretary Hughes and American policy makers to the illusory conclusion that they had succeeded in building a new alliance system in the Far East that would maintain the prevailing balance of power and extend American influence through the principle of the Open Door. For the moment it did seem that they had accomplished just that. But in historical perspective, the work of the Washington Conference was highly unrealistic, since Japanese power could not be contained by mere "scraps of paper."

POLICIES TOWARD LATIN AMERICA

A strange mixture of isolationism and internationalism was also revealed in United States policies toward Latin America in the twenties. It became clear that neither aloofness nor a big stick policy was useful as an instrument of United States policy here. Various reasons can be given for the changing role of the United States in the Western Hemisphere. Economic considerations played a part as American capitalists were now actively seeking overseas investments. Technological improvements in transportation and communication made closer ties between Western Hemisphere nations feasible. Also, military considerations became more important. American military planners came to place less stress on naval power — especially since Great Britain and Germany had declined as major naval rivals. Proportionately, the importance of the Panama Canal decreased. In addition, psychological considerations were significant. Latin American feelings of hostility toward the United States had developed in part because of Theodore Roosevelt's intervention policies. Finally, moral feelings could not be wholly neglected, for the anti-imperialists and other critics of United States diplomacy in the Western Hemisphere after 1898 constituted a large minority in American public opinion whose criticisms were unrelenting. In 1922 Secretary Hughes voiced the hopes of many Americans when he reiterated the American desire to apply the principle of self-determination in South America.

United States–Latin American policies thus revealed a new emphasis, combining aloofness with cooperation. The new policy of nonintervention reflected this new mood. The attempted withdrawal of United States Marines from Haiti in 1922, their actual withdrawal from Santo Domingo in 1924, and from Nicaragua in 1925 revealed an American restraint not present in the previous decade. At the same time the Republican administrations placed greater emphasis on mutual cooperation, especially in regard to Mexico. Already between 1921 and 1927 Harding and Coolidge had exercised self-control in rejecting the demands of United States investors and religious groups for direct interference in the internal affairs of Mexico. During these years the Mexican government was confiscating the properties of Americans, while also involved in a comprehensive program to divest the Roman Catholic Church of its powers. This policy of closer cooperation was further solidified in 1927 when President Coolidge appointed Dwight Morrow as United States Ambassador to Mexico. A former businessman, and proficient in the Spanish language, Morrow wove a network of contacts with Mexicans at all levels of society which provided a basis for more harmonious relationships between the two nations. Already the United States was seeking to develop the image of a good neighbor to replace its widely heralded reputation as a bad bully.

In various quarters of the world, then, American diplomacy revealed the old and the new, isolationism and internationalism. This ambiguous policy was applied to European diplomacy by virtue of the United States' decision not to join the League of Nations, while continuing to show an active interest in its work. It was also characteristic of American policies in the Far East, where on the one hand policy makers eschewed a strong stance to stop Japanese expansion but, on the other, sought to weave a network of paper treaties that would maintain important American influence in the region. United States policy toward Latin America reflected a shift from intervention at the same time that a search for closer cooperative relationships gathered momentum. In the twenties Americans tried to have their cake in diplomacy and to eat it, too. They sought to exercise power without taking on responsibility. As the years passed they found to their dismay that it was rarely possible to separate these two factors.

SUMMARY

The twenties were a period of pronounced contrasts. If this was a decade marked by tensions, they were usually prompted by a clash between old and new factors in American civilization. In politics, normalcy contrasted with progressivism as these two trends combined to produce the major issues of the period. Similarly, the American economy was beset by a declining agriculture, on the one hand, and the emergence of mass industries on the other. At the same time, American society revealed a clash between old rural elements as opposed to the new urban masses, each with a differing set of values. The conflicts also affected intellectuals in a wide variety of fields; traditional standards came under attack by a younger generation that rejected a large part of their cultural inheritance. American foreign policy also reflected the contrast between old and new as isolationism and internationalism became two major threads in the determination of United States policies overseas.

In almost every aspect of American civilization, the inheritance of nineteenth-century America came into conflict with the new trends developing in the twentieth century. Absolute values went into decline; relativism or pragmatism came to be more widely accepted. The tensions created by these clashes unleashed much creative energy. By the end of the decade it appeared that the new trends would become dominant in American society in the next few decades. The twenties, therefore, were halfway between industrial America (1877 – 1940) and technological America (1941 – 1970), reflecting many characteristics of the United States in the nineteenth century, but also revealing a way of life that was to become more familiar to Americans in later years.

FOR FURTHER READING

General surveys of the decade include WILLIAM E. LEUCHTEN-BURG, *The Perils of Prosperity, 1914 – 1932* (Chicago: University of Chicago Press, 1958) and JOHN D. HICKS, *Republican Ascendancy, 1921 – 1933* (New York: Harper, 1960). FREDERICK LEWIS ALLEN, *Only Yesterday* (New York: Harper & Brothers, 1931) stresses social trends in a characteristically engaging style. Until a definitive biography of Harding is written, ANDREW F. SINCLAIR, *Available Man: The Life and Times of Warren Gamaliel Harding* (New York: Macmillan, 1965) can be consulted. ROBERT K. MURRAY, *The Era of Warren G. Harding* (Minneapolis: University of Minnesota Press, 1970) is excellent. An admirable biography of Coolidge is DONALD R. McCOY, *Calvin Coolidge* (New York: Macmillan, 1967). A brief survey of economic changes in the twenties can be found in THOMAS C. COCHRAN, *The American Business System: A Historical Perspective, 1900 – 1955* (Cambridge: Harvard University Press, 1957); a more detailed, older account is by GEORGE SOULE, *Prosperity Decade, 1917 – 1929* (New York: Rinehart, 1947). JAMES W. PROTHRO, *Dollar Decade: Business Ideas in the 1920's* (Baton Rouge: Louisiana State University Press, 1954) stresses changing patterns in business thinking. A contemporary account is by the President's Conference on Unemployment, *Recent Economic Changes in the United States,* 2 vols. (New York, 1929). Among studies of social problems during this decade, one of the best, dealing with nativism, is JOHN HIGHAM, *Strangers in the Land: Patterns of American Nativism, 1860 – 1925* (New Brunswick: Rutgers University Press, 1955). ANDREW F. SIN-CLAIR, *Era of Excess: A Social History of the Prohibition Movement* (New York: Harper & Row, 1964) attempts to provide a fresh view of the noble experiment. DAVID CHALMERS, *Hooded Americanism: The Ku Klux Klan in America, 1865 – 1965* (Garden City: Doubleday, 1965) is a comprehensive volume. Among more recent works dealing with the Sacco-Vanzetti case see ROBERT H. MONTGOMERY, *Sacco-Vanzetti* (New York: Devin-Adair Co., 1960). FREDERICK J. HOFFMAN, *The Twenties* (New York: Viking Press, 1955) surveys literary achievements. On the other hand, literary critic MALCOLM COWLEY presents his personal recollections of the writers in the twenties in *Exile's Return,* rev. ed. (New York: Viking Press, 1951). On diplomacy consult the relevant chapters in FOSTER REA DULLES, *America's Rise to World Power, 1898 – 1954* (New York: Harper, 1955).

6

THE GREAT DEPRESSION
1929-1933

The era of prosperity that affected so many Americans during the 1920's came to an end with the Great Crash of October 1929, which soon developed into the Great Depression. A disaster of unprecedented proportions, it brought poverty into the everyday lives of millions of Americans. Everywhere one could see men and women living in tent cities or shantytowns, sleeping in parks or other public places, begging for a handout or a meal. Jobless youths roamed the city streets and the countryside when they were not taking to the rails. Few aspects of life remained untouched by the economic crisis. And black Americans, first to be fired and last to be hired, experienced particularly great suffering in the depression. Every evening perhaps as many as 20 million Americans went to bed feeling pangs of hunger. Children stayed away from school because they had no shoes or because their clothing was in tatters. Almost overnight, prosperous America gave way to desperate America as the former mood of optimism changed to desperation.

PRELUDE TO CRISIS: THE ELECTION OF 1928

As they went to the polls in November 1928, few Americans anticipated that in just another year the nation would be plunged into the Great Crash and the depression crisis. On the surface, or so it appeared, much was right in the country in 1928.

The presidential campaign reflected some of this smugness. Republican candidate Herbert Hoover pledged himself to continue the era of prosperity by promising every American family "two chickens in every pot and two cars in every garage." He also declared his intent to help farmers with their special problems, and vowed to continue the noble experiment of Prohibition. The Democratic standard-bearer was Governor Alfred E. Smith of New York, the first Roman Catholic to secure the presidential nomination of a major party. Urging the repeal of Prohibition, Smith advocated a variety of reforms, including public works projects for the unemployed. With his New York accent, his immigrant antecedents, and his Catholic religion, Smith appealed more to the urban masses than to Protestant rural America, especially the South and the Middle West. Consequently, Hoover handily won the election. At the time it was thought that Smith's religion was a prime factor in his defeat, but later analysis of the election statistics revealed that very likely religion was not the decisive factor in the outcome. The association of prosperity with the Republican party, and especially with Herbert Hoover, was a major consideration for many voters. Hoover's ascendancy to the White House in the fall of 1928 presaged what many Americans expected to be the continuation of affluence and prosperity.

THE GREAT ENGINEER

As Americans looked eagerly to their national leaders for guidance, they turned confidently to Herbert Hoover. A man of very broad experience in dealing with great social and economic problems on a vast scale, the Great Engineer presented an image that exemplified the American genius for efficiency and scientific planning to the world. At the start of the depression a substantial part of the nation expressed confidence in Hoover's ability to best the economic crisis. As economic conditions worsened after 1930, and as the once vaunted image appeared to be a myth, admiration and respect turned to bitter hatred and contempt. Ironically, by 1932 Hoover had become one of the most vilified presidents of the twentieth century. During his four years in office he worked hard to alleviate economic and social problems stemming from the depression; however, no man could have wrought the miracles that were expected of him. Hoover greatly worsened the impression he made upon contemporaries by his political ineptitude, and by a most unfortunate inability to communicate with individuals at every level of society. Thus, the election of 1932 witnessed an overwhelming repudiation of his leadership. Meanwhile, the blighting effects of the depression deepened, and the nation seemed to drift further into seeming chaos.

ORIGINS OF THE DEPRESSION

Black Thursday — October 24, 1929 — was a memorable day on Wall Street, for it initiated the Great Crash and the consequent depression. For several months before, the boom in stock prices had appeared increasingly unrealistic and precarious. By September 1929 some stocks were declining as much as thirty points. Although the market began to sag on Wednesday, October 23, 1929, the psychology of fear did not grip traders until the following day when panic gripped them and created a major crisis. More than 13 million shares changed hands, resulting in a great decline of stock prices. On succeeding days a group of financiers representing J. P. Morgan and the First National Bank of New York sought to stem the tide. But on Tuesday, October 29, 1929, another selling spree gripped the market, and many stocks sold for less than one-half of what they had cost a few months before. During the next four years, far from staging a recovery, the market declined much further. By 1933 the average price of securities on the New York Stock Exchange fell from $89.10 per share to $17.35. The total market value of all stocks dropped from $67.5 billion in 1929 to less than $23 billion four years later. As this stock market decline was followed by an increasingly deepening depression, some economists realized that it was only a symptom of graver ills in the economy.

CAUSES OF THE CRASH: DOMESTIC AND INTERNATIONAL

What factors were responsible for the crash and the consequent depression? Contemporaries and later critics cited elements in both domestic and foreign conditions that created the basic problem: an imbalance between production and consumption.

Several weaknesses in the domestic economy seemed to be operating: (1) maladjustments created by technological changes; (2) un-
equal distribution of the national income; (3) stock market
abuses; (4) weaknesses in the structure of large corporations; and
(5) questionable policies of the federal government.

In addition to these trends at home, the international economic crisis also affected the United States. In a sense, the American depression was but one phase of a world-wide depression.
Every major industrial nation except Soviet Russia — whether
Great Britain, France, or Germany — was suffering widespread
unemployment, decline of production and trade, bank failures, and
monetary instability. In a world connected by rapid transportation and communications as well as intricate financial arrangements, the United States could not fail to be touched by this
international crisis. It brought about a direct decline of United
States trade; it resulted in a sharp drop of foreign investments
in the United States; and the disorganization of various national
currencies seriously disrupted foreign debt and reparations payments to the United States and thus, willy-nilly, affected the
soundness of the dollar. The consequences of the international
economic crisis thus added materially to domestic weaknesses
which were contributing to the development of a depression.

Technology's Adverse Effects

While the rapid pace of technological progress during the
1920's had laid the basis for the mass production industries,
it also created some maladjustments in the economy. As has already been noted, the new technology created a group of "sick"
industries that were rendered increasingly obsolete, including
some forms of agriculture, coal, and textiles. These declining
industries were usually localized in certain areas such as New
England, Appalachia, and portions of the South and the Middle
West. The influence of their decline on regional economic activity was often pronounced and created pockets of unemployment. If the coal industry forced out more than 200,000 men in
the twenties, the textile manufacturers failed to hire proportionately larger numbers of employees after modernizing their manufacturing equipment. Indeed, technological unemployment was
a consequence of technological change. Although the displacement of men by machines was most visible in farming, it was

duplicated in many other industries that were affected by a succession of new technological inventions. In fact, between 1919 and 1929 manufacturing industries experienced a gain of 50 per cent in output while employing the same number of workers. To be sure, technological displacement was usually only temporary, since in the long run machines tend to create new jobs. But during the Great Depression these temporary displacements were sufficiently disruptive to lead to chronic unemployment; one worker out of seven was unemployed, or about 5 million people yearly. As the purchasing power of these individuals shrank, so did their function as consumers. In short, as the number of potential customers diminished, the producer's stock of goods increased, creating a growing imbalance between supply and demand.

Unequal Distribution of Income

The gap between production and consumption was further widened by the persistence of poverty and underconsumption in the United States caused by a maldistribution of personal and corporate incomes. During the twenties production grew at a much faster rate than the relative number of potential new consumers. In 1929, 60 per cent of American families had annual incomes below $2000, which was then considered as a minimum for self-sufficiency. This large group of individuals was increasingly unable to buy desired goods. On the other hand, 1 per cent of the population received 19 per cent of the national income in 1929 (compared to 12 per cent in 1919); 10 per cent of the highest income earners garnered 40 per cent of the national income. Unfortunately these wealthy individuals provided an extremely limited market for consumer products. If income had been more equitably distributed among a larger number of people, the number of potential customers for consumer items would have been vastly increased.

Oligopoly

Another reason for the deepening depression was found in the weaknesses and policies of the great corporations. As noted, the twenties witnessed the emergence of oligopoly as a characteristic of American industry. A few giant firms — such as General Motors, Chrysler Corporation, and Ford in the auto business — tended to dominate production in an entire industry. By 1929 the 200 largest corporations in the United States (out of a total of about 400,000 corporations) controlled 49 per cent of all corporate assets and received 43 per cent of all corporate income. The 1350 largest corporations secured 80 per cent of all corporate profits. Corporations were being transformed from private into quasi-public institutions whose economic power no longer merely affected private individuals but the entire American economy.

How did oligopoly contribute to the depression? First, it tended to lead to price rigidity. Secure in their control of a significant portion of their particular industry, oligopolies tended to set arbitrary "administered prices," i.e., those not determined by supply and demand. In a period of declining economic activity and shrinking purchasing power, their rigidity in maintaining artificially high prices rather than making downward adjustments contributed to the growing imbalance between supply and demand. A second way in which corporate structure contributed to the depression was through the abuse of holding companies, or companies that held stock in hundreds of subsidiary corporations, following a practice known as pyramiding, especially in the field of public utilities. In the case of Samuel Insull, the leading public utility magnate in Chicago, parent companies frequently followed policies that were detrimental to firms they controlled. If one had financial troubles, it might affect all the others in the system. Consequently, the whole pyramid could collapse, as happened to the utility empire of Insull after he encountered financial difficulties in 1929. As a result, the unsound structure of some large corporations operating as holding companies introduced an element of instability into American industry. A crisis such as the crash of 1929 could set off a chain reaction. The collapse of a great corporation easily created further unemployment, thus shrinking the purchasing power of the workers. The imbalance between consumption and production then grew only wider.

Speculation

An unsound corporate structure also contributed to the depression by fostering a declining rate of investment in new enterprises. The concentration of capital in the hands of only a few hundred huge companies made their investment decisions crucial to the welfare of the entire economy. During the twenties large individual and corporate investors were not quick enough in plowing their surplus back into new productive enterprises in the United States. Many of these funds found their way into risky enterprises overseas or stock market speculation. Meanwhile, beset with a lagging rate of investment, the nation's economic growth rate grew sluggish.

To some extent, excessive speculation on the stock market contributed to the outbreak of the Great Depression. After 1925 the speculative orgy gathered momentum. In that year, 300 million shares were traded on the New York Stock Exchange; in 1926, 451 million shares; in 1927, 577 million shares; and in 1929, more than 1 billion shares. During this period the market value of all stocks jumped from $27 billion to $67.5 billion. That some of this increase represented speculative expectation rather than real earning power was reflected in the ratio of corporate earnings to the market price of stocks. Although ten to one was considered to be a safe ratio, by 1929 this average had climbed to sixteen to one. The speculative surge was also fired by many frauds and abuses. Speculators would often engage in "wash sales." By buying and selling to each other, they would frequently drive up the price of a particular issue; then they would unload it before more gullible investors became wary. In other cases, insiders in possession of special information would act on confidential information concerning a particular stock and reap great profits.

Such conditions clearly contributed to the depression. Investment capital was diverted from economic growth industries, which might have opened new sources of employment, into nonproductive speculation. Stock speculation helped to weaken the banking structure of the nation, since many banks were heavily involved in extending loans to speculators. When the crash came, they were directly drawn into the whirl of failures. Speculation also created a tight money and credit situation. As interest rates for loans increased, less speculative enterprises found it increasingly difficult to secure loans themselves or to raise necessary capital. Although stock market speculation did not of itself initiate the depression, it did aggravate existing weaknesses in the economy.

Passivity of the Federal Government

Another reason for the economic crisis was the attitude of the federal government in the twenties. Neither President Coolidge, nor the Congress, nor the Federal Reserve Board felt a responsibility for taking vigorous action to remedy some of the more obvious weaknesses in the American business and corporate structure, inequalities of income, or stock market abuses. Despite warnings from economists, for example, President Coolidge refused to dampen the increasingly reckless spirit of speculation. Instead, in 1928 and again in February 1929, he publicly stated that in his estimation, stock market prices were not unusually high. Nor did the Federal Reserve Board take note of the danger signals. Although it had the authority to raise reserve requirements of member banks of the Federal Reserve System (and so to limit their capacity for making loans for speculative purposes), and although it could raise the rediscount rate for loans, it refused to do so. In fact, during 1927 it lowered its rediscount rate from 4 to 3.5 per cent, making it easier rather than more difficult to secure credit for stock speculation. Very likely the Board could have braked the stock market boom by raising margin requirements (the percentage of down payment required for stock purchases), or by official statements advising caution. Coolidge was not wholly unaware of the nation's need for sustained economic growth, or of unemployment problems stemming from technological change, or of corporate abuses. But he took little direct action to deal with these issues or to alert Congress for necessary legislation. Since the federal government seemed passive in the face of emerging economic problems, it appears that its inaction contributed to the economic debacle of 1929.

International Crises

Whatever domestic conditions contributed to the outbreak of the depression, these were worsened by the international dimensions of economic crisis. By 1929 the economies of Great Britain, France, Germany, and most European countries were beset with large-scale unemployment. Almost all of them sought to mitigate their problems by erecting trade barriers against their neighbors. The result was a further decline in world trade, which brought additional economic strains. Since the United States was tied to the international economy, it, too, was affected by these trends. One of the most direct effects was a great decrease in American trade between 1929 and 1932. United States exports declined from $5 billion to a mere $1 billion in 1932. At the same time that American businessmen found their domestic markets shrinking, therefore, the number of their foreign customers was rapidly dwindling as well.

Another effect of the world economic depression on the United States was the withdrawal of foreign funds. As financial stringency affected the European economies, many European bankers and investors called back monies they had invested in American enterprises. As the New York Stock Exchange boom became more precarious in 1929, foreign stockholders in American corporations began to sell their shares in large numbers, thereby adding to the selling wave after Black Thursday. The net result of this European liquidation of United States holdings was twofold. It placed a great strain on American banks by depriving them of an important source of credit. Also, the large volume of stock sales by Europeans added to the psychology of panic on Wall Street in 1929 and further demoralized stock prices on the Exchange.

Another effect of the international depression resulted from the instability of foreign currencies, which unsettled the dollar. With heavy war debts and reparation payments, most European nations staggered under their burdens and suspended debts owed to the United States. Perhaps the vicious cycle began in Germany, which between 1924 and 1932 underwent the most severe fluctuations in monetary cycles, from extreme inflation to deflation. Since the Germans were obligated to make large reparation payments to the Allies, their plight directly affected the others. By 1931 the currencies of most European countries were in disarray. A common remedy for many of them was devaluation, and one after another they abandoned the gold standard. In 1931 the Bank of England began the trend and was followed in rapid succession by France, Austria, Italy, and Belgium. Because of these international disturbances, American investors in overseas enterprises lost a substantial portion of their original investment as devaluations made previous monetary values worthless. Trade and commerce suffered because of the uncertain values of various national currencies. Finally, the world monetary crisis placed a drain on United States gold reserves and thus threatened the

soundness of the dollar. Since the United States was also expect-
ing European nations to make regular payments on their debts —
payments they suspended after 1929 — this added to the strains
on America's supply of gold.

Review of Factors Causing Depression

The Great Depression thus resulted from a combination of
foreign and domestic factors. Certainly, in the world of the twentieth century, economic problems were no longer confined to
the boundaries of one particular country but also affected its
neighbors. The depression that broke out in Europe after 1927
could not fail to leave its impact on the United States. Within
the American economy, the dislocations of technological development, inequalities of income, imperfections in corporate business policies, wild stock market speculation, and a lack of government economic leadership were all laying the groundwork for
the most severe economic crisis in the experience of the United
States.

EFFECTS OF THE DEPRESSION

The economic crisis had a profound impact on almost every
aspect of American society. It disrupted the economic system;
it brought serious dislocations into the everyday life of most
Americans, whether in town or country; and it threw politics into
a turmoil. Wherever one listened in on the conversation of Americans in 1930, 1931, or 1932, in factories, in offices, in church
groups, or in breadlines, the topic was the same. Why did the
richest nation on earth witness so much poverty, suffering, and
desolation?

ECONOMIC SLOWDOWN AND INDIVIDUAL POVERTY

The economic impact of the depression could be gleaned
from statistics, to be sure, but perhaps more poignantly from
everyday occurrences in the lives of ordinary people. Statistics
reveal that between 1929 and 1932 a chain reaction slowed the
economy, producing an ever-wider gap between production and
consumption. Production dropped from a total value of $10

billion in 1929 to $3 billion three years later. Bank loans declined from $36 billion to $22 billion in this period, while business failures increased fivefold. Agricultural prices in 1932 were only one-third of their already low 1929 levels.[1] Perhaps the most important result of the economic slowdown was unemployment. In 1930 approximately 4 million people were without jobs; during the next year this total rose sharply to 11 million people; and in 1932 the number had swelled to 15 million people, or one-third of the entire labor force. Moreover, this total did not include the millions who had only part-time work. Possibly one out of two Americans in 1932 was without a job or with no visible means of support. In a mobile society such as the United States, a job had often been more than merely a means of livelihood. It provided a sense of status and identity; it determined one's friends, interests, and major conversation topics. The Great Depression swept all this away and thus brought about a far-reaching disruption in the lives of millions of Americans.

The depression also made poverty a reality for a substantial portion of the population. Shantytowns arose in most places, near refuse dumps or along waterfronts. There one could see the tar and paper shacks or tents occupied by the homeless. Soon the swelling army of unemployed who dwelt in these dingy hovels dubbed them "Hoovervilles," a living monument to the seeming failure of the administration to relieve the plight of the poor. Thousands of others were not so fortunate as to have a roof over their heads. They slept in open parks, railroad terminals, hallways, abandoned houses, or in public buildings. In Chicago it was reported in 1932 that perhaps as many as 20,000 persons were sleeping in the parks, including some homeless women.

While many Americans did not have a decent roof over their heads, they and many others also suffered from malnutrition or starvation. Long breadlines and soup kitchens could be seen in every town and city as the Red Cross, the Salvation Army, and other private agencies sought frantically to relieve this distress. Their doles were often given to well-dressed individuals, middle-class Americans who suddenly faced destitution and

---

[1]John K. Galbraith, *The Great Crash* (Boston: Houghton Mifflin, 1954) is one of the most readable surveys of the economic effects of the depression.

hunger. By 1931 the sheer weight of numbers made the task of voluntary relief agencies nearly impossible. Meanwhile, begging on the streets became a familiar sight, as did the appearance of jobless men on street corners selling apples or shining shoes. Frequently their well-kept business suits and coats served as a reminder of their more affluent status in the recent past. In rural areas of the South and the Southwest malnutrition was widely prevalent. There the lean, haggard faces of tenant farmers told a tale of abject poverty and hunger, a tale reinforced by the bloated bellies of their underfed children. Cases of outright starvation were not unknown, and newspaper reports concerning them were common.

Another result of the depression was to force thousands of homeless youths to take to the roads. They clogged railroads and highways in search of jobs, food, clothing, or sometimes just to drift. Often driven from their homes by circumstances, they were forced into a way of life that few relished. As one of them noted to a reporter: "I ride the rails because I have to. But a lot of people think that I am a bum, and I don't want to be a bum." The poverty brought by the depression tended to degrade human personality and left a lasting impression on thousands of young people at the time. In abject poverty even pride had its limits, and the Great Depression was rapidly depriving countless Americans of that pride.

Psychological Effects

The depression also seemed to heighten the tensions of many Americans. Increased crime statistics told part of this story; a rise in the suicide rate revealed other strains; and the divorce rate shot up and brought additional tensions. A situation in which families moved in with each other and lived in congested quarters, and husbands and sons lingered around the home each day if they were unemployed, could lead only to anxieties and short tempers.

Summary of Depression's Effects

The effects of the Great Depression were manifold. It brought the slowdown of the economy — in business, agriculture, and large-scale unemployment. It brought poverty to a substantial portion of the American people. It brought insecurity and lack of self-respect to a large number of hitherto affluent members of the middle class, and caused psychic injuries. Few other events in the first half of the twentieth century so shattered the lives of millions of Americans.

HERBERT HOOVER AND ECONOMIC CRISIS

In this great catastrophe, the eyes of countless millions turned hopefully to Herbert Hoover for leadership and guidance. Many facets of Hoover's personality and background seemed to suggest that he was superbly fitted to deal with the economic and social problems facing Americans. But in the years between 1929 and 1933 the president seemed bewildered by the ramifications of the depression. Although he embarked on a variety of programs, Hoover failed to win the nation's confidence for the course of action he charted.

Until his bout with the economic crisis, Hoover's life had been a chronicle of success. Born of Quaker parents on an Iowa farm in 1874, he was orphaned before he was ten years old and sent to live with an uncle in Oregon. In 1891 he entered Stanford University to study mining engineering, while working his way through college by a variety of campus enterprises such as a laundry service, newspaper deliveries, and arrangement of lecture series. Upon graduation in 1895, he entered the engineering profession and during the next ten years worked in Australia and China. By 1905 he had established a recognized reputation in the field and formed his own consulting firm, meanwhile authoring a standard text on mining (1909). His professional skill and shrewd investments made him a wealthy man by the time of World War I — a living personification of the rags-to-riches ideal in America. For the next fourteen years he devoted his energies to the public service. He served well in providing relief for Americans stranded in Europe by the outbreak of World War I and then as United States food administrator under Woodrow Wilson (1918 – 1919). At the end of the war he took on a new responsibility as director of emergency relief, in which job he kept thousands of people from starvation. In 1920 he was prominently mentioned as a presidential possibility by both major parties. Just a few months after the election, President Harding appointed him as secretary of commerce, a post in which he served forcefully and effectively for the next seven years (1921 – 1928). Although he had held a number of important positions by 1928, his nomination and election to the presidency in that year was the first to be secured by popular vote, all the others having been appointive. If ever a man had shown himself to be capable of dealing with large and complicated problems, however, in 1929 many Americans felt that that man was Herbert Hoover.

While the years before 1928 had highlighted Hoover's virtues, the succeeding four years laid bare his weaknesses. That he was resourceful, energetic, and possessed managerial ability was clear. But only during his presidency did he clearly reveal himself to be inflexible and dogmatic, with a particularly poor sense of political timing. Moreover, he showed himself to be very sensitive to criticism, and increasingly vindictive. Perhaps his greatest failing as chief executive was his inability to communicate with masses of people.

Since Hoover liked to think of himself as a man of principle, his philosophy cannot be ignored. A professed Quaker, he was a profound believer in individualism as a basis for the American system of government. With this faith came his advocacy of voluntary cooperation among individuals as a solution to most of their major problems.

Soon after the stock market crash, Hoover applied his theory of voluntary cooperation to the new economic problems then emerging. The plight of business, agriculture, and labor first attracted his attention. Nor was he insensitive to the need for long-range social reforms, including the amelioration of the conditions of poverty and the building of a prosperous society. Unfortunately the severity of the immediate crisis prevented him from carrying out his intended programs, occupied as he was by the pressing issues of the moment.

BUSINESS

To deal with the decline of business, Hoover proposed several measures. His first reaction was to call a series of conferences in the hope of stimulating voluntary efforts of cooperation to meet the problems of the depression. On November 19, 1929, he called a meeting of railroad presidents, whom he urged to cooperate in continuing expansion policies that would prevent further unemployment. Two days later he presided over a similar gathering of financial leaders, who agreed to pool their resources to prevent more bank failures and to avert greater shortages of credit. On November 23, 1929, labor leaders came to see the president to give their pledge not to seek wage increases and to cooperate in his program by discouraging strikes. In addition to such conferences, Hoover envisaged a second remedy in a higher tariff. Despite a petition from 1000 economists who pleaded with the president to lower tariffs as a means of stimulating trade, Hoover remained steadfast in his belief that a high tariff would protect American industry and would bring a revival of business. As he said: "The protective tariff . . . is the very first line of defense of the American standard of living."[2] Thus, the administration secured the Smoot-Hawley Tariff of 1930 — the highest in American history. Unfortunately it had disastrous consequences, since it led to foreign retaliation and a further decline of American trade and commerce. A third measure proposed by Hoover was banking reform. Although Congress was unwilling to pass his proposals (the House was Democratic after 1930), the banking bill of 1932 contained many provisions enacted during the New Deal. Finally, in 1931 Hoover recommended voluntary cooperation to extend credit to ailing banks and businesses. He urged financiers to form a voluntary National Credit Corporation — a money pool — for this purpose. When this experiment in self-help failed by October 1931, Hoover reluctantly agreed to the creation of the Reconstruction Finance Corporation, a government corporation that in 1932 extended more than $1 billion in loans to big banks, railroads, and corporate businesses.

FARM POLICIES

The president's belief in voluntary cooperation was also reflected in his farm policies. During the election campaign of 1928 he had promised to aid rural Americans already caught in a severe agricultural depression. The Agricultural Marketing

[2] A convenient compilation of Hoover's views on tariffs can be found in Ray Lyman Wilbur and Arthur M. Hyde (eds.), *The Hoover Policies* (New York: Charles Scribner's Sons, 1937), pp. 181–92.

Act of 1929 was the result. This law created a Federal Farm Board with $500 million at its disposal. Its purpose was to make loans to farmers organized in agricultural cooperatives to enable them to hold crops off the market until they could receive reasonable prices. In addition, the Board itself bought up surpluses in what proved to be a vain endeavor to raise farm prices. As the Federal Farm Board's experience indicated, the major reason for falling prices appeared to be production in excess of demand — not insufficient credit. The Board's programs for voluntary restriction of production in 1930 and 1931 unfortunately did not work at all. The administration's farm program thus proved to be an ignominious failure.

UNEMPLOYMENT

Hoover's emphasis on voluntarism also boded ill for his attempts to relieve unemployment. He firmly believed that relief of unemployment was not a responsibility of government but of private and voluntary agencies. Soon after the Great Crash he organized the President's Committee for Unemployment Relief, composed of prominent public figures who made appeals for contributions to individuals in the hope that they would raise relief funds for the jobless. By 1931, however, the existence of more than 11 million unemployed made all such voluntary programs futile. But the president continued to make appeals for private and state donations. In October 1930 he appointed another committee, the Emergency Committee for Employment, to develop new job opportunities. Its chairman, Arthur Woods, resigned in 1931 because he considered Hoover's efforts wholly inadequate. A third remedy tried by Hoover was to expedite federal public works expenditures. Although he resolutely opposed legislation in Congress offered by Senator Wagner of New York to authorize the spending of more than $900 million annually for federal works projects, he approved a doubling of existing annual appropriations of $150 million yearly because he was preoccupied with balancing the budget. On the other hand, he vehemently resisted all proposals for direct federal relief for the unemployed. He vetoed the Wagner Bill to re-establish a United States Public Employment Service, a service that he believed should be carried out by private enterprise. He also vetoed the Rainey Bill, which would have authorized $300 million of federal monies for direct relief, and he severely criticized the La Follette-Costigan Bill of 1932, which proposed the distribution of $450 million to alleviate suffering. Hoover inflexibly clung to his belief in voluntary cooperation. He strongly felt that direct federal grants to the unemployed would undermine individualism and self-respect of the average citizen, qualities upon which the very foundations of the Republic rested.

SOCIAL REFORM

Within the framework of his philosophy Hoover hoped to further his plans for social progress. Ironically, he had hoped to conduct a war on poverty, but a war to be waged by private individual efforts. Soon after his election he appointed a President's Committee on Social Trends to investigate social evils that impeded the development of a good society in America. This able group delved into subjects such as crime and law enforcement, educational facilities, urban problems, equality for women, problems of the aged (including pension plans), and unemployment insurance. Unfortunately the sage recommendations of his committee were lost amid depression controversies between the president and Congress. Moreover, Hoover believed that the social issues highlighted by the Commission could be implemented without much governmental action. The president also called a National Child Conference in 1930 to recommend ways and means for improving conditions of children. To a very limited extent he favored federal grants to rural health agencies to facilitate disease control among youngsters. However, he felt much of this task could be accomplished by private efforts. He also called a National Housing Conference in 1930 to recommend methods of improving living conditions for millions of Americans. Finally, the chief executive supported congressional revision of bankruptcy legislation, designed to ease the lot of the honest, but impoverished, debtor.

As a Quaker, Hoover was a passionate believer in equality, including racial equality for black Americans. Consistent with his belief in voluntary cooperation, however, he felt that this problem must be solved by individual private efforts, and not by governmental action. The prime instrument with which equality could be achieved was education. An admirer of the work of Booker T. Washington, and a believer in a process of gradual integration, Hoover felt that the decline of black-American illiteracy, the increase of home ownership, and the growth of Afro-American churches signified real progress for the race. Yet many black Americans were hostile toward President Hoover because of the large gap between his words and his action. Traditionally, black Republicans had been awarded various posts in southern states as a fruit of patronage. Hoover, however, seemed to follow a "lily white" policy unlike his predecessors in the twenties. He failed to appoint black men to hundreds of lesser patronage jobs held by them for many years in previous Republican administrations. His reasons were difficult to discern and led some to question the sincerity of his professed beliefs.

Nevertheless, it is apparent that Hoover was not completely without social vision, for he held before him the ideal of a democratic affluent society that could provide the good life for a majority of its citizens. But the implementation of this vision was circumscribed not only by his political ineptitude, but also by his dogmatic and inflexible belief in the supreme virtue of voluntary cooperation. Yet in later years, as the welfare state became a reality, and as individuals appeared to be overwhelmed by masses, Hoover felt more than ever that he had been right in upholding the primacy of individualism over all other values of American society.

Hoover's stumbling efforts to relieve poverty led him into political embarrassments. It was indeed ironic that, while he had made a world-wide reputation for relieving human suffering and starvation in many corners of the globe, he seemed unable to duplicate this feat in his own native land. A good example was the severe drought of the summer of 1930 that affected at least thirty states, of which Arkansas was the hardest hit. There, in July and August, the rainfall was less than one-half the normal amount, and the temperature climbed to over 100 degrees on more than thirty successive days. With acute suffering, many drought-ridden farmers hoped for federal aid in the form of loans and, perhaps, distribution of direct relief and food supplies. Although the president was understandably sympathetic, he did not do much beyond urging voluntary relief activities. In August 1930 he called a conference on the drought and appealed to private charity organizations to aid the plight of Dust Bowl farmers. Hoover relied particularly on the Red Cross in this situation. Meanwhile, he actively opposed congressional efforts to grant at least $60 million in direct federal loans to farmers affected by the drought; only under direct pressure did he assent to an act of Congress allotting $45 million for these purposes. Whatever feelings Hoover may have had on the drought of 1930, his action put him in an unfavorable light. He conveyed the image of an opponent to the relief programs designed to alleviate poverty and distress.

BONUS EXPEDITIONARY FORCE

Even more damaging to Hoover's public stance was his clumsy handling of the Bonus Expeditionary Force (BEF) — a poor people's march to Washington, composed largely of unemployed war veterans, hard hit by the depression. Just after World War I, Congress had authorized special bonus payments for veterans, issued in policies that were to be paid in 1945. Caught in the throes of the depression, many veterans' organizations advocated the immediate payment of the bonus, whether in part or in full. Congress responded to this pressure as 2 million veterans signed a petition requesting necessary legislation. The result was the Veterans' Bonus Act of 1931, which provided for immediate payment of 50 per cent of the bonus. Anxious to balance the budget, President Hoover vetoed this measure, but Congress passed it over his objections. Nevertheless, as the depression worsened, many veterans urged immediate full payment of the sums to which they were entitled as embodied in the Patman bill in Congress. To emphasize their support for the measure, a group of 300 men in Portland, Oregon, decided on a 3000-mile march (by train) to Washington to impress congressmen and the president with the earnestness of their cause. They persuaded poverty-stricken veterans in all parts of the country to join them, and expected about 20,000 to converge on Washington. On May 29, 1932, about 1300 of the marchers set up a tent city in the District of Columbia parks and slept in abandoned Treasury buildings as they prepared to petition Congress and the president in support of the Patman bill. Hoover was increasingly concerned about the presence of the BEF and refused to confer with any of its leaders. By late July the Senate had defeated the Patman bill, although the House had given it approval. But the BEF stayed on, and the president now panicked. He offered the BEF $100,000 in loans to pay for their homeward-bound transportation, the sum to be deducted later from their bonuses. When this proposition did not result in a rapid dismantlement of the tent city, Hoover called out the District of Columbia police and also the United States Army. Under the leadership of General Douglas MacArthur, soldiers and tanks stormed the defenseless veterans' quarters, routing men, women, and children with tear gas and rifle fire. Two veterans were killed in the assault and several babies injured by the tear gas. The BEF was scattered, but at an enormous price to the president's prestige. Once touted as a great humanitarian, Hoover's image was indelibly tarnished after the BEF affair. Rightly or wrongly, he was accused of being brutal and insensitive to desperate cries of poverty.

ECONOMIC REFORMS

In analyzing the reasons for the depression and consequent unemployment, President Hoover liked to emphasize the primacy of foreign difficulties, for he believed that the American economy was sound. He felt that he could do little to improve conditions at home unless he dealt with the more significant problems of international depression. As in the domestic sphere, voluntary cooperation would be a prime vehicle for economic recovery on a world-wide scale. With this perspective, he contemplated measures to relieve economic distress. First, he initiated a series of conferences with foreign dignitaries to reduce war debts and reparations, and perhaps to secure agreements concerning monetary stabilization. In November 1931 he met with Premiers Laval (France) and Grandi (Italy) to work out an agreement. But he was stymied by Congress. Moreover, he himself opposed any lowering of tariffs or other trade barriers. Hoover also made public appeals to Americans to lend money to distressed European nations. Pressed by their own difficulties, few Americans heeded this call; American loans to Europe declined from $905 million in 1930 to $229 million in the following year. Another Hoover measure, the Moratorium of 1931, was worked out in collaboration with Secretary of State Henry Stimson and Secretary of the Treasury Andrew Mellon. This presidential order provided for a one-year suspension of all debt and reparations payments owed by foreign nations to the United States. Within the year, Hoover hoped, the international economic crisis would right itself. Finally, Hoover enthusiastically supported disarmament, in part because a reduction of expenses for naval armaments would aid him in balancing the budget. After a visit to the United States by British Prime Minister Ramsay McDonald in October 1929, Hoover agreed to the meeting of a London Naval Conference in 1930 to develop formal treaties. Unfortunately this meeting accomplished almost nothing.

Despite Hoover's efforts, the depression deepened. His belief that the origins of economic crisis were world-wide was not wholly amiss. But as in the domestic sphere, the remedies proposed by Hoover fell far short of ameliorating existing problems. He was therefore compelled to bear further frustrations as his critics mercilessly criticized his policies as inadequate.

PROTESTS

Despite much activity in the White House, 1932 witnessed a worsening of conditions in almost every aspect of American life. It appeared that the American system had broken down and failed and that a revolution might be at hand. Economic activities reached new lows, the building industry declined to one-half of the level of the preceding year, and automobile production was no more than one-fifth of what it had been in 1929. As many as 15 million people were unemployed, while most voluntary and state programs to provide relief had bogged down completely, in view of the magnitude of their task. Poor people's protest marches became common in many cities. In New York City during September 1932 — where 200,000 families were destitute — the Communists sponsored mass protest meetings; in Chicago at least 20,000 marched to dramatize their plight; similar demonstrations took place in Detroit, Saint Louis, and other towns and cities.

Violent protests also ran through the rural areas. Midwestern farmers especially were concerned about the constant decline of farm prices and resorted to direct action. In May 1932 under the leadership of Milo Reno they organized the National Farmer's Holiday Association. This organization sponsored farm boycotts of the cities, preventing the delivery of produce for urban dwellers with the intent to raise prices. In August 1932 Reno's men blockaded roads and highways near Sioux City, Iowa, and threatened other farmers who were not in sympathy with them and who sought to sell their farm products in the city. Elsewhere farmers also resorted to direct action to prevent thousands of mortgage foreclosures as they gathered with clubs and pitchforks to prevent bank agents from dispossessing neighbors whom the depression had forced to become delinquent in their payments. In some states like Nebraska and South Dakota, farmers dumped their crops rather than sell them at ridiculously low prices. On farms as in cities, an increasing number of Americans appeared to be prodded into desperate action.

All the while, worsening economic conditions heightened social tensions. Local relief rolls swelled; forced sale of homes and farms increased; begging and petty thievery rose sharply; and more than 2 million individuals were drifting — without homes, without friends, without jobs. Often families would double up for economy, and others began to barter as their supply of money was exhausted. By the fall of 1932 many wondered just how much longer the fabric of American society could stand the brutal strain of the depression.

EFFECTS OF THE HOOVER POLICIES

The effects of the Hoover policies were fourfold. First, they accelerated a shift of political power from rural America to a new urban coalition. Such a shift had already been evident in the twenties as it reflected the burgeoning growth of the nation's cities. The economic crisis hastened a new alliance between pressure groups that represented some of the disadvantaged peoples of America — the "forgotten men." Wielded into potent political groups by big city bosses, they included ethnic minorities, black Americans in the city slums, industrial (blue collar) workers, small businessmen, and the unemployed. Many farmers were ready to support this coalition. A second result was to make Hoover a convenient scapegoat. No man could have been expected single-handedly to provide rapid solutions to depression problems, but Hoover was frequently blamed for just such a failure. Also, the Hoover policies made the president a political liability for the Republican party. Already in the congressional elections of 1930 the Democrats secured control of the House of Representatives, although the Senate remained in the hands of Republicans. In the spring of 1932 no one knew exactly who the Democratic presidential nominee might be, though one point was certain — whoever he was, he was likely to defeat Hoover in the forthcoming presidential balloting. Finally, the Hoover policies encouraged the revival of splinter parties. The Communist party increased its strength between 1929 and 1932, as did the Socialists. In addition, various messiahs appeared with simple solutions for the complex difficulties brought by the depression. Often they gathered large followings like the popular radio priest, Father Charles E. Coughlin of Detroit, and former Governor Huey Long of Louisiana. It seemed as if the Hoover policies had polarized the major economic groups in the United States and added to the sharpening of tensions already wrought by the Great Depression.

The unemployed — a breadline during the depression. (UPI photo)

PROTEST AND THE ELECTION OF 1932

Understandably, Republicans looked to the election of 1932 with gloom. Some influential contributors to the party's campaign chest seriously considered drafting Calvin Coolidge for the presidency. But Hoover was determined to run again and to seek justification of his record. With his characteristic lack of political realism, he failed to realize that his image as the Great Engineer had been tarnished, and that in 1932 he had come to symbolize failure and frustration. The Republican platform in 1932 had few fresh ideas but proposed continuation of the Hoover policies. Sensing a political defeat, a group of progressive Republicans including Senator George Norris, Henry A. Wallace, Harold Ickes, and Hiram Johnson refused to give their endorsement to Hoover and turned instead to the Democrats.

For the first time since the Wilson era, the Democrats smelled victory in the air. Their national convention witnessed keen rivalry among several contenders including Huey Long, Newton Baker, Governor Franklin D. Roosevelt of New York, Alfred E. Smith, William G. McAdoo, and John Nance Garner. After extensive deliberations and bargaining, the political finesse of Roosevelt's manager, James A. Farley, bore fruit as the convention nominated Roosevelt, a distant relative of the Rough Rider. The Democratic platform, like that of the Republicans, contained no new suggestions for dealing with depression problems, although it condemned Hoover for lack of leadership and advocated the repeal of Prohibition. Yet the Democratic candidate injected personal magnetism into his appeal to the voters, which his opponent largely lacked. At the very beginning of the campaign, Roosevelt broke precedents when he flew directly from Albany, New York, to the National Democratic Convention meeting in Chicago in a DC-3 to accept the presidential nomination in person. In a dramatic and rousing speech to the wildly cheering delegates, he promised to inaugurate a "new deal" for the American people. Although he did not spell out his program in great detail during succeeding months, his enormous enthusiasm and unbounded energy exuded an attitude of buoyant optimism and hope that seemed infectious. Probably any Democrat would have won in 1932; but Roosevelt proved to be an unusually good campaigner.

Apostle of individualism — Herbert Hoover. (Wide World Photos)

The election itself proved to be one-sided. Roosevelt received 23 million votes; only 15 million votes went to Hoover. The electoral count revealed an even more decisive repudiation of Hoover: he received only 59 votes compared with 472 for Roosevelt. By a very clear majority, the American electorate had opted for a change of leadership.

President Franklin D. Roosevelt delivers a fireside chat.
(Allyn and Bacon photo)

THE CRISIS OF THE INTERREGNUM

New leadership was not scheduled to begin operations until March 1933. The Twentieth Amendment, which provided that a new president should be inaugurated in the January after his election, was not to be effective until 1936. The four months between the election in November 1932 and the inauguration of the new administration in March 1933 thus constituted an interregnum that witnessed an intensification of the depression crisis. As unemployment increased further and as bank failures multiplied, the functioning of government in Washington came to a virtual halt. During this period Hoover sought to commit his successor to numerous policies already in force. When Roosevelt refused, relations between the two men became quite strained. In a series of formal and terse conferences at the White House late in 1932, Hoover demanded that Roosevelt pledge his adherence to a balanced budget, to banking reform, and to federal insurance of bank deposits. He also wanted a commitment to the reduction of war debts, for international monetary cooperation, and participation at the London Economic Conference to be held in July 1933. Roosevelt did not wish to pledge himself to a specific course on any of these issues, nor to associate himself with an administration that the voters had just thoroughly repudiated at the polls. He preferred to reserve judgment on all these matters until he himself exercised the powers of the presidency.

The suspension of governmental action during these four crucial months added to the gravity of the depression. It also embittered personal relations between Hoover and Roosevelt to an extent perhaps unprecedented in American history. At a White House reception early in 1933, Hoover studiously let Roosevelt stand in line for more than half an hour, although the wait was pure agony for Roosevelt, who wore more than thirty pounds of steel braces on his legs. Whether or not this delay was intentional cannot be known, but Roosevelt resented it deeply. When the two men drove to the inauguration ceremonies in the same car, as was the custom, observers noted that they were virtually not on speaking terms with each other. The interregnum thus paralyzed the wheels of government at a time when quick and effective action was needed to stem the breakdown of the economy.

SUMMARY

The Great Depression thus constituted one of the major crises in the nation's history. Brought about by technological changes, an imbalance in the distribution of the nation's income, corporate maladjustments, stock market abuses, and questionable governmental policies, it affected most spheres of life in America. In the economy it created mass unemployment, a decline of production, and consequent business and banking failures. It brought poverty, misery, and insecurity to millions who were left without adequate food, clothing, housing, and health care. The emergence of such problems on an unprecedented scale created a unique situation for Herbert Hoover, who had made his reputation as an engineer, solving tough problems that were seemingly insoluble for others. But in this, his greatest test, Hoover did not succeed. He worked patiently and conscientiously, to be sure, but narrowly within the framework of his personal conviction of voluntary cooperation as the primary means of alleviating depression. After four years of Hoover's administration, most Americans had lost faith in his ability to provide the leadership necessary to bring the country out of economic crisis. Whatever virtues Hoover had, and whatever constructive measures he elaborated, he found himself unable to lessen the impact of this major disaster upon the lives of millions of Americans. Thus, they repudiated him roundly in the election of 1932. Whether or not the new administration would bring improvement could not be known until March 1933, because of lateness in ratification of the Twentieth Amendment. For millions of individuals in that grim winter of 1932, the inaction of the federal government due to the change in administrations meant only more and greater suffering. Facing the stormy winter winds they wondered, What would the New Deal bring?

FOR FURTHER READING

A lucid and well-written analysis of depression causes is JOHN K. GALBRAITH, *The Great Crash* (Boston: Houghton Mifflin, 1954). With the opening of the Hoover Library in West Branch, Iowa (1962), serious studies of Hoover are just getting under way. Meanwhile,

HARRIS G. WARREN, *Herbert Hoover and the Great Depression* (New York: Oxford University Press, 1959) and ALBERT V. ROMASCO, *Poverty of Abundance: Hoover, the Nation, the Depression* (New York: Oxford University Press, 1965) are informative. A good collection of contemporary comments on life during the early years of the depression is in DAVID A. SHANNON (ed.), *The Great Depression* (Englewood Cliffs, N.J.: Prentice-Hall, 1960). Hoover explains himself in his *Memoirs,* 3 vols. (New York: Macmillan, 1951 – 1952), in *The Challenge to Liberty* (New York: Charles Scribner's Sons, 1934), and in WILLIAM STARR MYERS and WALTER H. NEWTON (eds.), *The Hoover Administration: A Documented Narrative* (New York: Charles Scribner's Sons, 1936). FRANK FREIDEL, *Franklin D. Roosevelt: The Ordeal* (Boston: Little, Brown, 1954) and *Franklin D. Roosevelt: The Triumph* (Boston: Little, Brown, 1956) are valuable biographical studies that tell much about the early depression as seen through Roosevelt's eyes.

7

FRANKLIN D. ROOSEVELT
AND THE NEW DEAL
1933-1939

On a grey and rainy day, suitably somber for the occasion, Franklin Delano Roosevelt stood before Chief Justice Charles Evans Hughes in front of the Capitol in Washington, D.C., and took the presidential oath of office. Then, in a stirring inaugural address he set the tone for his administration when he told the assembled dignitaries, and the American people listening on their radios, "I am certain that [you] expect that on my induction into the presidency I will address [you] with a candor and a decision which the present situation of our nation impels. . . . So, first of all, let me assert my firm belief that the only thing we have to fear is fear itself — nameless, unreasoning, unjustified terror which paralyzes needed efforts to convert retreat into advance." He conveyed a mood of optimism although as yet he did not have a carefully thought out comprehensive program to remedy the ills brought by the depression. But his confident attitude infused a new surge of energy into millions of Americans who had given up hope. Roosevelt's appeal stirred them to try again to grapple with the serious difficulties brought on by the economic crisis. Now they would no longer be alone, but would be joined by a sympathetic federal government in a common cause. And in ensuing years the masses of American voters gave their overwhelming support to Roosevelt, often only because they felt — rightly or wrongly — that he had a sympathetic understanding of their particular individual problems.

THE NEW ADMINISTRATION

Within a few months after entering the White House, Roosevelt translated his spirit of vitality into the New Deal. As his policies gradually developed they came to constitute the three R's — Relief, Recovery, and Reform. Roosevelt tried first to alleviate immediate suffering and distress; then, with less success, he tried to lead the country out of the depression; finally, he mapped long-range reforms, many of them designed to prevent the recurrence of another depression crisis. These efforts aroused widespread support but also created dissent on the left and right. The president himself considered his administration to be slightly left of center — an accurate self-appraisal for his own time, although after 1965 New Left historians condemned his conservatism. Despite a mixed record of successes and failures, however, the New Deal revived the faith of a vast majority of voters in the American system of economy and government.

The new president was born on the Roosevelt estate in Hyde Park, New York, on January 30, 1882, the only son of a wealthy merchant and investor. Raised by a doting mother, he was educated at home by a succession of governesses and tutors until 1896 when he entered Groton, the nation's most exclusive preparatory school. There he showed himself to be an average student, well liked by colleagues and teachers. In 1900 he went on to Harvard, where he engaged in a wide variety of social activities, including a stint as editor of *The Harvard Crimson*. His record was not outstanding, usually not rising above the "Gentleman's C" often earned by the sons of the wealthy during this era. In 1905, shortly after graduation, he married his fifth cousin, Anna Eleanor Roosevelt, in a gala ceremony. She was President Theodore Roosevelt's favorite niece, and the former chief executive insisted on giving away the bride. After two desultory years at Columbia Law School, Roosevelt dropped out, practiced law for a while, and in 1910 secured election to the New York State Senate as a progressive Democrat. An admirer of Woodrow Wilson, Roosevelt served as Assistant Secretary of the Navy between 1913 and 1920, a post also held by Uncle Theodore. He became sufficiently well known to receive the Democratic vice-presidential nomination in 1920. His active campaigning that year made him a national figure, but his promising career was seemingly cut short when in the following year he was struck down with polio. Largely because of the encouragement of his wife, and his close confidante, Louis Howe, Roosevelt made a determined effort to re-enter public life although he never regained full use of his legs. In 1928 he was elected governor of New York; in this position, for the next four years he initiated a model state program to fight the depression. This program embraced public works and public power projects, unemployment insurance, employment exchanges, and closer regulation of banks and corporations. As the successful chief executive of the nation's most populous state, in 1932 Roosevelt was in a prime position to ascend to the presidency.

Roosevelt's outlook on the world was far more flexible than that of Herbert Hoover and reflected various characteristics. Three were prominent: he was a conservator of traditional American values, he was a pragmatist who preferred common sense to abstract theories, and he was a master politician. Although sometimes accused by contemporaries as undertaking a revolution, Roosevelt's ends and means were designed mainly to preserve the American democratic system. His prime purpose, he was often eager to explain, was to serve as a doctor who sought to cure, not to transform, an ailing patient. As an American aristocrat, like Theodore Roosevelt he held to the old Puritan doctrine of stewardship, to the idea that the privileged members of society had a moral obligation to improve the condition of their less fortunate brethren. This general concept was tempered by his pragmatic outlook, for he was a doer, a practical man, rather than a thinker. If a proposal worked, he was glad to incorporate it into his policies; if it failed, he did not hesitate to abandon it and try something else instead. When once asked by a reporter about his philosophy, he replied: "Philosophy, philosophy? I have no philosophy. I am a Christian and a Democrat. That's all." While not an original thinker himself, he had the knack of picking the brains of others and of combining the bits and pieces that he found into a politically workable synthesis. He read much, yet he was even more adept in learning from conversations with others than from books. Finally, he was one of the most skillful politicians of his time. Few presidents had his rare combination of traits — he had the ability to compromise, and he was always willing to make a concession for the attainment of some broader goal. Critics considered this tendency to be Machiavellian, but Roosevelt himself relished bargaining as an act of statesmanship. He also had a superb sense of timing, an uncommon gift of communicating with Americans of all ages in every stratum of society. His radio voice was one of the most magnificent of his generation and his sense of drama was superb. He had much personal charm as well, which he exuded with persons of both high and low position. In combination, these qualities made him an extraordinarily effective chief executive.

Roosevelt was not without faults, however. Some accused him of lack of candor, for he often liked to keep his real motives hidden from even his closest friends. Others pointed to his lack of principle, for he seemed always willing to experiment. The president was also charged with irresponsibility, as he sometimes applied his own carefree attitudes to public policies. His experiments with the gold standard were a case in point. Indeed, during his lifetime "Roosevelt-hating" came to be fashionable for some of the very rich, and for extremist groups.

Although Roosevelt always reserved the power of ultimate decision for himself, he was particularly adept at choosing able advisors and co-workers. Some were his personal confidantes, others constituted his Brain Trust, and still others served in his cabinet. Perhaps none of his aides was more important than Louis Howe, who devoted his entire life to furthering the career of his chief, even living with Roosevelt in the White House. After Howe's death in 1936 Harry Hopkins, a former social worker, became Roosevelt's closest informal advisor. In addition, during the early days of his administration Roosevelt relied on his "Brain Trust," a group of university professors who drafted much of the initial New Deal legislation. They included Columbia University professors Raymond Moley and Adolph A. Berle, agriculture experts Rexford Tugwell and M. L. Wilson, speechwriter Samuel Rosenman, and others who were called in for special problems. They would meet with Roosevelt on weekends and informally discuss ideas, programs, and proposals from which he would formulate more concrete recommendations for direct action. Often the Brain Trust had a greater influence on the president than his official cabinet, although in some fields Roosevelt relied heavily on his secretaries. These included Cordell Hull in the State Department, Harold Ickes in the Department of the Interior, Frances Perkins in the Department of Labor, Henry A. Wallace in the Department of Agriculture, and after 1940 Henry L. Stimson in the War Department.

Roosevelt's approach to depression problems after his inauguration was cautious. His first objective in 1933 was to provide relief for the immediate crisis that faced the nation; after the threat of total collapse of the American economy was averted, he turned his thoughts to programs designed to bring about economic recovery; then, as various dissident groups clamored for more comprehensive action in 1935, Roosevelt embarked on a series of long-range reforms. By 1938 the domestic phase of reform was virtually completed. Thereafter, problems of foreign policy increasingly occupied the president's attention.

THE NEW DEAL: RELIEF

When Roosevelt became the nation's chief executive in March 1933, the country found itself at the lowest point of the depression. As he described the situation in his first inaugural:

> Values have shrunken to fantastic levels; taxes have risen; our ability to pay has fallen; government of all kinds is faced by serious curtailment of income; the means of exchange are frozen in the currents of trade; the withered leaves of industrial enterprise lie on every side; farmers find no markets for their produce; the savings of many years in thousands of families are gone. More important, a host of unemployed citizens face the grim problem of existence, and an equally great number toil with little return. Only a foolish optimist can deny the dark realities of the moment.[1]

In the midst of this stark crisis, Roosevelt remembered his not entirely dissimilar experiences with the war mobilization program of Woodrow Wilson in 1917 – 1918. To a considerable extent, Wilson's war mobilization program provided a model for Roosevelt's relief measures during the spring of 1933. The 1000 days of preparedness under Wilson (1916 – 1919) paved the

[1] *New York Times,* March 5, 1933.

way for the famous 100 days of relief legislation (March – June 1933) during Roosevelt's first term in office.

ECONOMIC POLICIES

Finance and Business

Roosevelt began his relief program by turning his attention to finance and business. Among his first official acts was an executive order closing all banks for a period of one week. This was designed to prevent an expected panic, since hundreds of banking institutions were threatened by anticipated "runs." On March 12, 1933, the president broadcast the first of his famous "fireside chats." These talks were designed to explain his actions in clear and simple language to millions of Americans hovering around radio receivers in living rooms across the land. Many banks would not have survived without this breathing spell, which allowed them to put their finances in order. In addition, Roosevelt pleaded for an end to the hoarding of money at home by individuals who feared possible bank failures. His plea was eminently successful: within a month more than $1 billion came back into circulation, slightly alleviating the shortage of money in financial institutions. The president also made use of the "Trading with the Enemy Act" of 1917 to prohibit the export of gold bullion on March 25, 1933. This action partially took the United States off the gold standard and was a deliberate effort to promote inflation.

Meanwhile, Raymond Moley and other advisors were working furiously to draft legislation designed to prevent the imminent collapse of business. They were considering various plans that had been suggested by individuals and groups such as Gerard Swope (of General Electric) and the United States Chamber of Commerce for the suspension of the antitrust laws to allow cooperation among businessmen for achievement of stability. The result of their labors was the National Industrial Recovery Act of June 16, 1933, which was designed to bolster many failing industries. It created a National Recovery Administration to supervise cooperative activities in every sphere of business. It directed the National Recovery Administrator, in cooperation with representatives from each industry, to frame codes of fair competition for each of more than 500 industries. These codes were to restrict competition by limiting production. They also empowered the administrator to fix prices where he deemed it feasible and to include standards concerning wage scales and labor conditions. The NRA permitted cooperation and consultation among businessmen which would contribute to economic revival. To direct the NRA President Roosevelt appointed General Hugh S. Johnson, a protégé of Bernard Baruch. In World War I, Baruch had brilliantly channeled the energies of American industry into mobilization as chairman of the War Industries Board. During the summer of 1933 Johnson held hearings at which various representatives from affected industries presented their views on each proposed code. He also embarked on a vast publicity campaign to secure public cooperation with the NRA, urging Americans to patronize only those enterprises that were cooperating with the program. A Blue Eagle became the national emblem of the NRA and served as an insignia to identify businesses cooperating with NRA policies. By the fall of 1933 the whole nation eagerly watched this experiment and hoped that it would spark recovery. In creating the NRA Roosevelt was consciously falling back on his World War I experience and hoping that the success of the War Industries Board in mobilizing American industry in a common cause could be repeated in the face of this new crisis fifteen years later.

Farm and Labor Problems

During these same hectic months, administration leaders were readying legislation to deal with farm and labor problems. By 1933 they had the advantage of the hindsight gained during the Hoover years. Though they had no sure solutions, at least they knew which policies had been tried and which had been found wanting. Certainly the experience of Hoover's Federal Farm Board revealed that federal aid in the distribution of agricultural products by itself achieved little in raising farm prices or farm income. Farmers tended then merely to increase their production, and the surplus only drove prices down further. Thus, Roosevelt's farm experts, including Henry A. Wallace, Rexford Tugwell, and M. L. Wilson, turned their attention to control of production. The fruit of their labors was the Agricultural Adjustment Act of 1933, designed to bring a better balance between the production and consumption of farm products.

It stipulated the imposition of production controls. These were applied by the Agricultural Adjustment Administration (AAA), which agreed to make "benefit payments" to compensate farmers who consented to take a portion of their acreage out of production. Essentially the AAA made commodity loans to farmers who restricted their output. The act also authorized the establishment of marketing quotas (the amount each farmer could sell in the open market) if at least two-thirds of the producers of a particular crop voted to establish these at a special referendum. The AAA made farm credit available, too, continuing the policy of the Republican administrations of the preceding decade. All federal farm loan agencies were consolidated in a new body, the Farm Credit Administration. Another feature of the act was its provision for federal purchase of surplus farm products by a new government corporation, the Commodity Credit Corporation. This was based on the model of the United States Food Administration during World War I and on the experience of the Federal Farm Board of 1929. Finally, the AAA directed crop destruction. In 1933 it ordered farmers to plow under one-fourth of the cotton crop, and to slaughter 6 million pigs as a way to raise prices. At a time when millions of Americans were in the throes of poverty and hunger, such action understandably aroused considerable criticism. Hunger amid abundance seemed senseless, but the administration was unable to devise other methods that might avoid this dilemma, especially because of the need for rapid action. Moreover, the farm legislation of the New Deal tended to benefit medium-scale or big farmers primarily rather than the poorest segments of the American agricultural community. Thus, the National Grange and the Farm Bureau Federation enthusiastically endorsed the AAA, whereas the National Farmers' Union and other organizations representing tenant farmers or migratory workers viewed it with skepticism. Until the United States Supreme Court declared it unconstitutional, however, the AAA, aided by droughts, reduced production of cotton, wheat, and corn by about 30 per cent, raising farm prices and doubling national farm income in just two years.

Within a short time circumstances forced Roosevelt to consider the problems of unemployment and labor. His World War I experience as a labor administrator stood him in good stead as he drew upon this knowledge to fashion a hasty program.

Prodded by Senator Robert Wagner of New York, Roosevelt's advisors inserted Section No. 7A into the National Industrial Recovery Act. Its purpose was to strengthen labor's bargaining power and, indirectly, its share of the national income. It stipulated that NRA codes of fair competition should include provisions for a forty-hour work week, a guarantee of labor's right to organize and to bargain collectively, and the prohibition of child labor. During World War I the federal government had successfully enforced these standards. To administer these provisions the president appointed a National Labor Board, chaired by Senator Robert F. Wagner. By 1934 this board had settled more than 5000 disputes and had appreciably fostered the growth of union membership.

Railroads

In the frenzied pace of the first 100 days Roosevelt also remembered the successful consolidation in 1918 of the nation's railroads under federal supervision. In May 1933 he appointed a Federal Coordinator of Transportation to try to coordinate the nation's ailing railroads and to improve the efficiency of their operation. Roosevelt chose an expert for the post, Interstate Commerce Commissioner Joseph Eastman. His responsibilities were mainly advisory and embraced the formation of plans and recommendations for coordination of railroads, and for facilitating federal loans to struggling carriers through the Reconstruction Finance Corporation.

SOCIAL POLICIES

To relieve the plight of the unemployed, Roosevelt improvised several emergency measures to extend desperately needed financial help. Unlike Hoover, he did not oppose direct federal grants to individuals. Aided by Frances Perkins, Harry Hopkins, and others, in April 1933 he created the first of a succession of temporary relief agencies. These included the Federal Emergency Relief Administration (FERA), which made available to the states more than $500 million in federal funds to be distributed to needy persons. As the chilly fall of 1933 presaged a severe winter — particularly for the 15 million people who were unemployed — Roosevelt listened to the pleadings of Harry Hopkins to establish still another welfare agency. This was the Civil Works Administration (CWA), which received $400 million from Congress to undertake small-scale public works projects to provide temporary employment for more than 4 million persons. At the same time, the administration sought to deal with the thousands of young people who were drifting throughout the country, by creation of the Civilian Conservation Corps (CCC). One of the most successful of all New Deal projects, the CCC enrolled young men between the ages of eighteen and twenty-five and placed them in work camps under supervision of the War Department and the United States Army. In addition to food and lodging they received $1 per day. Their prime responsibility was to work on useful natural resource conservation projects involving reforestation, reclamation, and irrigation. Between 1933 and 1935 the CCC recruited more than 500,000 boys and men and paid out more than $300 million in wages. Its success inspired a later generation to create the Peace Corps and the Job Corps.

As the first 100 days drew to a close, a phase of the New Deal — the Relief New Deal — had been clearly inaugurated. With extraordinary speed the president and Congress had cooperated in the enactment of a succession of measures designed largely to cope with the immediate crisis. Although many of these laws were hastily drawn, they had been discussed in one form or another for several years before Roosevelt's ascendancy to the White House. To a considerable extent, in 1933 the president relied on his World War I experience to mobilize the nation for the crisis. The NRA, including its Section No. 7A, the AAA, the suspension of gold exports, and the attempted centralization of the transportation system, bore vivid testimony to the earlier heritage. To some extent, also, Roosevelt drew on the program he had developed as governor of the state of New York between 1928 and 1932, particularly welfare measures such as the FERA and CWA. Nor did Roosevelt completely neglect Hoover's experience — especially with farm legislation — although he revealed much greater flexibility in experimenting with untried means. The Relief New Deal thus was based heavily on experience gained in war mobilization during World War I, Roosevelt's governorship, and some aspects of the Hoover program.

THE NEW DEAL: RECOVERY

The Relief New Deal was only a prelude to the Recovery New Deal, for the central problem of depression still remained. Since the economic crisis reached unprecedented depths, the president had no well-established guidelines before him. In this predicament he revealed an extraordinary talent for improvisation. Unlike Herbert Hoover, who felt himself bound by principles and doctrines, Roosevelt had great flexibility in experimenting with a myriad of solutions to spur recovery. Experimentation thus became the key to understanding the Recovery New Deal. As Roosevelt himself noted:

> It has been remarked of late . . . that those who are today in charge of your national Government are guilty of great experimentation. And they are right. If I read my history correctly, the same suggestion was used when Englishmen, two centuries ago . . . founded new colonies in the American wilderness as an experiment.[2]

Between 1933 and 1934 Roosevelt's experimental mood was seen in several measures. Perhaps the most important was his attempt to induce controlled inflation through manipulation of the nation's money supply by trying to take the nation off the gold standard. By decreasing the amount of gold in the dollar and by raising the price of gold he hoped to bring about a rise in prices. His nationalization of gold and the prohibition of its export in March 1933 began the process. He intensified the effort between October 1933 and March 1934 when he pegged the gold price at $35 an ounce. Roosevelt would sit in his bed during the morning hours poring over dozens of newspapers. Then, Secretary of the Treasury Henry Morgenthau would appear to discuss gold prices with the president. "How high shall they be today, Henry?" roared the president. At times Morgenthau was perturbed by Roosevelt's exceedingly informal manner in dealing with such a complicated problem, but this scene reflected the chief executive's penchant for experimentation.

[2] *New York Times,* November 19, 1933.

Nevertheless, by the middle of 1934 the effort to bring about controlled inflation had shown itself a failure, and Roosevelt abandoned the idea. Other nations had devalued their own currencies to correspond to changes in the American dollar, therefore leaving the international trade balance much where it had been before. Since the total supply of money did not increase, the anticipated rise in prices did not materialize.

Monetary Stabilization

Related to the president's dabbling with the gold standard was his flirtation with international monetary stabilization as it was discussed at the London Monetary Conference of July 1933. In the spring of that year Roosevelt had not yet decided whether the United States should seek to stabilize its currency without regard to other nations or whether it should cooperate with them in fighting the world-wide depression. Was nationalism or internationalism to be the guide of American monetary policies? During April and May of 1933 the president seemed to lean toward internationalism; he appointed Secretary of State Cordell Hull, a free trader, as American delegate to the London Economic Conference to negotiate an agreement on international monetary stabilization. Hull duly attended the conference in the early days of July. Meanwhile, Raymond Moley was persuading the president that a go-it-alone policy emphasizing nationalism would be more effective in bringing the country out of the depression. Roosevelt was undecided, but Moley's persuasive arguments finally won him over. Thereupon the president dispatched Moley to the London conference to inform Hull and other United States delegates of his change of mind. On July 5, 1933, Roosevelt sent his "bombshell message," announcing to the conference that the United States could not participate in any international efforts to stabilize the currency at that time, because it was preoccupied with putting its own house in order. This action wrecked the conference and demonstrated Roosevelt's experimental, and sometimes hesitant, approach in dealing with recovery problems.

Roosevelt's use of fiscal policy as a device to alleviate the depression was also experimental. Like Herbert Hoover, Roosevelt was committed to a balanced budget in 1933, though he was not averse to deficit financing, if it served as a useful tool to extricate the nation from the depression. His fiscal experimentation began in June 1933 when the administration secured the creation of the Public Works Administration. Endowed by Congress with $3 billion, this new agency was to undertake construction of public works on a large scale, including roads, bridges, and public buildings. Unfortunately the PWA, guided by Secretary of the Interior Harold Ickes, spent its money far too slowly, so that the impact of its expenditures upon the economy was negligible. Indeed, many economists believed that Roosevelt was not injecting sufficient quantities of new funds into the country's money and credit system to end the depression. In 1935, John Maynard Keynes, the famous economist and foremost advocate of "pump priming," visited the president in an effort to persuade him to embrace his doctrines. Roosevelt, a supreme pragmatist who eschewed theories, listened politely, but was not converted. Since college days he had distrusted abstract economic theories, and preferred a piece-meal experimental approach. When the PWA obviously failed to spur large-scale recovery, Roosevelt was ready to abandon deficit financing, but the recession of 1937 forced him to continue it on a moderate scale.

Unemployment

Roosevelt's recovery efforts were also aimed at the unemployed. By 1935 temporary relief agencies such as the FERA and the CWA went out of existence, but unemployment continued. Roosevelt therefore felt compelled to try other methods to achieve recovery. He experimented with the creation of another temporary agency, the Works Progress Administration (WPA), largely the brainchild of Harry Hopkins. Congress appropriated more than $11 billion for it between 1935 and 1941 to engage in small-scale work projects, which provided employment for at least 5 million persons each year. Most of its activities were concerned with construction, but unemployed musicians and artists were also encouraged to practice their particular skills in free performances for the public. The WPA differed from previous emergency relief agencies in that it was designed to do more than provide subsistence grants for individuals. Roosevelt and his advisors hoped that it would stimulate a real recovery by training men and women in new skills, and by rehabilitating many who had become unaccustomed to a work discipline. The WPA achieved these goals well, but it could not bring about a national recovery from the depression by itself.

Supplemental to the WPA was the National Youth Administration (NYA), which aimed to help high school and college students. The NYA also provided work projects and made small monthly grants to students to enable them to remain in school. Roosevelt's purpose was not only to provide subsistence allowances, but also to keep young people off the already saturated labor market as long as possible, and so to spur economic recovery.

THE NEW DEAL: REFORM

The failure of the Recovery New Deal to bring about the long-awaited return of prosperous times generated many pressures to seek more far-ranging reforms. Indeed, by 1935 Roosevelt shifted from the Recovery New Deal to the Reform New Deal. Why this change? In the first place, though the depression was still very much with Americans, the threat of immediate economic collapse had been averted. Second, the presidential election of 1936 was approaching, and Roosevelt was concerned about another term. Third, the United States Supreme Court's invalidation of more than a dozen major New Deal laws including the NRA and the AAA added fuel to the fires burning for reform. Finally, and perhaps most important, the threat of various dissident groups persuaded Roosevelt to incorporate some of their demands in his own program. Most important were Huey Long's share-the-wealth movement, Francis Townsend's old-age pension scheme, and Father Charles E. Coughlin's social justice movement. Thus, the year 1935 witnessed a third stage of the New Deal as it came to place prime emphasis on reform.

This third phase of the New Deal embraced a broad spectrum of economic and social reforms. It reflected a recognition that the rural way of life for most Americans was gone and that henceforth they would live in a highly urbanized industrial society. Since the Great Crash had bared many weaknesses in the economy, reform centered on banking, business, agriculture, and labor. Even more significant was the attack on poverty as revealed in social legislation affecting unemployment insurance, old-age pensions, health care, and prohibition of child labor. The administration's efforts to secure political reforms were more limited in nature.

What were the sources of the Reform New Deal? Many of the measures enacted between 1935 and 1939 had developed from precedents created before Roosevelt's advent. First, the tradition of Progressive reform (1890 – 1916) created some basis as Roosevelt elaborated upon the work of two of his heroes, Theodore Roosevelt and Woodrow Wilson. To some extent, the New Deal embellished the New Nationalism and the New Freedom. Second, the tradition of state reforms in the twentieth century provided guidelines as the New Deal shifted major responsibility for economic and social policies away from the states, and to the national government. A third source was the pragmatic tradition in American life, for some of Roosevelt's reforms had few antecedents, but were practical responses to new, immediate, and pressing problems.

ECONOMIC REFORMS

One of the New Deal's most carefully wrought reforms was the Banking Act of 1935. In preparation for more than two years, it embodied changes recommended by President Hoover during his tenure. This measure made the most far-reaching amendments to the Federal Reserve System since its creation (1914), and tended to centralize the authority of the Federal Reserve Board. It provided for the issuance of new forms of bank notes by the Board, gave it authority to engage in direct open market operations (to buy and sell government bonds on security exchanges to maintain their price levels), allowed it to regulate reserve requirements of member banks, and set the rate for discount rates (of bank notes and paper presented by commercial banks). This enlargement of the Board's powers enabled it to play a greater role as a central banker and as a more effective instrument of federal fiscal policies. Though these reforms had been long overdue and were not originally conceived by Roosevelt, he provided the political skill that led to their enactment.

Public Utilities

Since public utilities became increasingly important in a highly urbanized industrial society such as the United States, the Roosevelt Administration devoted a large share of its energies to their regulation. One of the most significant reform measures in this field was the Holding Company Act of 1935, affecting electric light and gas companies. It provided that the Securities and Exchange Commission (established in 1933 to regulate truthfulness in advertising of corporate stocks and stock exchange practices) approve all their security issues; it instructed the Federal Power Commission to further the consolidation and integration of private power companies; and finally, in the controversial Section No. 11a, the act prohibited holding companies beyond the third degree. These provisions were designed to simplify and to stabilize corporate structure in the public utility field and to increase the efficiency of light and power companies so that they could render better and cheaper service to millions of urban consumers. Such public regulation was not a brand new departure, but represented a shift from state to federal regulation.

Congressional leaders such as Speaker Sam Rayburn of Texas, who had fought hard to secure stricter federal controls over utilities, also strove for tighter regulation over the distribution of electric power. The Federal Power Act of 1935 enlarged the jurisdiction of the Federal Power Commission over transmission of power across state lines and particularly endowed it with authority to set rates. This act reflected an acute awareness of the importance of millions of city dwellers, consumers, and manufacturers who were becoming increasingly dependent on electricity for a thousand different uses.

In fact, one of the most significant New Deal reforms was creation of the Tennessee Valley Authority, a milestone in the history of public power. The TVA had been proposed for more than a decade by Senator George Norris of Nebraska. Not until 1933, however, did Norris find a sympathetic ear in the White House that would make his dream a reality. Roosevelt was enthusiastic about the enterprise. The TVA was a federally owned government corporation responsible for the integrated resource development of a seven state area (40,000 square miles) in the Southeast. Using the World War I United States nitrate plant at Muscle Shoals, Alabama, as a base, the TVA was to produce cheap and plentiful electricity for the inhabitants of the region. But that was only one of its many responsibilities. The three directors who managed the enterprise were to plan production of power in relation to flood control, the manufacture of fertilizers and prevention of soil erosion, the improvement of navigation on streams and lakes, the construction of recreational areas, and re-forestation. Roosevelt and Norris hoped that such a regional concept of integrated resource development could be applied to other parts of the United States. They hoped, too, that it would provide a model — a yardstick by which private utilities could measure their services and rates. The TVA very quickly proved itself a great success as it stimulated economic development throughout the Tennessee Valley. New, cheap electricity brought new industries, new employment opportunities, and increased incomes to the area.

Transportation

In view of pressing problems created by the emergence of new forms of transportation and the extension of existing facilities on a nationwide scale, Roosevelt sought a corresponding shift from state to federal regulation. Congress enacted three measures in the light of these changing needs. First, the Motor Carrier Act of 1935 subjected trucks to the same kind of regulation to which railroads were already held by the Interstate Commerce Commission. This agency was now instructed to develop standards of service for trucking companies, to license interstate truck routes, and to determine commercial truck rates. The ICC received similar powers over inland waterways, including canals and rivers, which were passageways for a significant amount of freight. A second reform was the Merchant Marine Act of 1935. It created the United States Maritime Commission, whose responsibilities included the encouragement of private ship owners through direct subsidies, and the leasing of federally owned vessels. The third proposal was the Civil Aeronautics Act of 1938, which established the Civil Aeronautics Board with jurisdiction over air carriers. It received authority to assign airline routes, to regulate standards of service, and to determine rates. The Roosevelt administration, as well as the nation's railroad managers, hoped that the extension of such federal regulation would enable railways to compete more suc-cessfully with the newer forms of transportation, thereby improv-ing their own perilous financial status. Moreover, considerations of national defense required a connected national transportation network that, unlike the World War I system, would allow rapid national mobilization in a time of crisis.

Antitrust Campaign

The New Deal's efforts to reform American business were implemented in the vigorous antitrust campaign conducted by Roosevelt between 1937 and 1941. The demise of the NRA, as well as the persistence of the depression and increasing hostility of the business community to the New Deal, led the president to experiment with the progressive panacea of trust-busting. In 1937 he appointed Yale law professor Thurman Arnold as an assistant attorney general in charge of antitrust activities and ordered him to increase the number of federal antitrust prosecutions in the courts. Arnold undertook 215 investigations of alleged violations of the Sherman Anti-Trust Act by business firms and instituted formal court actions. A second weapon in Roosevelt's antitrust campaign was his creation of the Temporary National Economic Committee (TNEC) in 1938. This group of experts made an exhaustive study of the degree to which economic concentration and monopoly were characteristic of American industry. In 1941, the committee's report concluded that economic concentration had increased during the past thirty years, despite the existence of antitrust laws. Altogether though, the New Deal's antitrust campaign achieved little. The outbreak of World War II led to the virtual suspension of all antitrust prosecutions and shifted public attention away from domestic issues. Moreover, it became increasingly clear to Roosevelt and his advisors that the relation between economic concentration and depression was not necessarily always direct. Economic factors other than monopoly were responsible for the persistence of the depression. The results of the New Deal's antitrust program were therefore highly inconclusive.

Agriculture

The reform surge of the New Deal also touched agriculture. In one way or another, the legislation was designed to fight rural poverty. Perhaps the most successful of the measures affecting farmers was creation of the Rural Electrification Administration (REA) in 1935. The agency granted loans to farm cooperatives to enable them to extend power lines into rural areas not served by private companies. Within six years the REA succeeded in bringing electricity to 90 per cent of American farm homes, more than a fourfold increase. The second major farm measure of the Reform New Deal was the Bankhead-Jones Farm Tenancy Act of 1937, designed to help the most disadvantaged of the nation's farmers. It made loans available to farm tenants seeking to become land owners, and also provided for some federal aid for migrant agricultural workers. Before World War II, however, the act had virtually no impact because of the opposition of the major farm organizations as well as administrative difficulties in its execution. The second Agricultural Adjustment Act (1938) was more effective. Since the United States Supreme Court had declared the first AAA unconstitutional, the administration framed a substitute bill that proved not to be objectionable. The AAA of 1938 instituted production controls by stipulating that farmers who took their land out of cultivation would receive federal payments for "soil conservation." Marketing quotas could be put into effect if two-thirds of the producers of a given crop voted to impose them, and federal loans would be made available to farmers for holding crops off the market and for the purchase of surpluses.

Labor

While in his reform mood, Roosevelt also wrought considerable gains for labor. Like many former progressives, Roosevelt held no special sympathies for labor unions. But the president was pushed into action by the continuance of large-scale unemployment, increasing difficulties in administering Section No. 7A of the National Recovery Act, and restlessness of the American Federation of Labor, in which dissidents sought to organize an industrial union. By 1935 he was ready to support Senator Robert F. Wagner's efforts to provide for federal encouragement of labor organizations. The result was the enactment of the Wagner Act (1935), sometimes known as labor's Magna Carta. There were several important provisions: it guaranteed labor the right to organize and to bargain collectively; it outlawed company unions (yellow dog contracts, which required an employee's promise not to join a union as a condition of employment, had already been outlawed by the Norris-LaGuardia Act of 1932); it contained a list of prohibited "unfair labor practices" by employers (such as blacklisting of men active in union activity); and it created a National Labor Relations Board to administer these stipulations, and to supervise elections for union representatives and the settlement of labor-management disputes. The Wagner Act was a landmark in labor legislation and was responsible for the enormous increase in union membership during the decade following its passage.

In view of the continuation of unemployment, especially during the recession of 1937, Roosevelt undertook to shift responsibility for minimum wage legislation from the states to the federal government. One of the last accomplishments of the Reform New Deal was the Fair Labor Standards Act of 1938, which created national minimum wage standards (starting at 25 cents per hour in 1938), a maximum forty-hour week, and the longstanding progressive demand for the prohibition of child labor. Although Roosevelt had not begun his presidency in a pro-labor mood, his administration was nevertheless maneuvered into a pro-labor stance by a variety of pressures so that many of labor's rights and privileges previously recognized in only a few selected states were now incorporated into national policy.

The economic measures of the Reform New Deal therefore touched upon a multitude of problems. As a great consensus maker, Roosevelt crystallized and implemented many long-standing demands for change, and incorporated them in legislation that found support among a wide spectrum of interest groups. In almost every instance the precedents set by Theodore Roosevelt, Woodrow Wilson, and progressives in the states were further developed by Roosevelt on a national scale. This was true of reform in banking, the regulation of business, many phases of the farm program, and labor legislation. The Reform New Deal was both old and new — the content of many of its reforms was familiar, but the assumption of so many new regulatory responsibilities by the federal government was new.

SOCIAL REFORM

The social policies of the Reform New Deal, which helped to lay the groundwork for the welfare state in the United States, were also striking. Since his early days as a New York State senator, Roosevelt had expressed an interest in social welfare and the attack on poverty, but he had never been a crusader. In fact, perhaps his wife did more than any other person in developing his sense of social awareness, for she had been involved all her life in a great variety of humanitarian causes. Between 1933 and 1935 many groups and individuals advocating one or another social reform increased their influence, however, and prodded Roosevelt into action. Millions joined Huey Long's "share the wealth" movement, which openly espoused the redistribution of wealth in America and federal aid to education, health, and social service agencies. Francis Townsend's revolving pension scheme attracted millions of older people who supported their leader's demand for a federal old-age pension system. Father Charles E. Coughlin, the popular radio priest, approved of these proposals while advocating more extensive deficit spending. In addition, some intellectuals supported social reform schemes advocated by Socialist leaders like Norman Thomas and Upton Sinclair, or by Communist chief Earl Browder. As the election of 1936 drew nearer, Roosevelt realized that in order to stifle the possibility of serious political opposition, in some way he had to satisfy these yearnings. Certainly the president was aware of precedents in Ohio, Wisconsin, and New York, which had inaugurated limited pension or unemployment insurance schemes after World War I. Indeed, throughout the twenties social workers and professors such as Paul Douglas (of the University of Chicago), Elizabeth Brandeis of Wisconsin, E. E. Witte, Arthur Altmeyer, and others had campaigned actively for federal pension and unemployment insurance plans. By 1935, it appeared that Roosevelt was ready to steal the thunder of the Left, the Right, and the professional social workers.

The major weapon of the Reform New Deal's war on poverty was the Social Security Act of 1935. This far-reaching measure was a milestone in New Deal social legislation. It created a system of unemployment insurance based on contributions by employers into a fund administered by the states. Second, the legislation granted small federal stipends for dependent persons such as parentless children, the blind, the deaf, the mute, and the crippled. Third, it created an old-age pension program. To be sure, it provided far less than Francis Townsend had demanded, but it constituted a beginning. The plan called for establishment of a pension fund on the basis of regular contributions from employers and employees. After the age of sixty-five, workers were eligible for modest old-age pensions, depending on the size of their contributions.

Though there was no major redistribution of wealth in the United States during the New Deal as Huey Long demanded, the Revenue Act of 1936 sought to make the tax system more progressive. It stipulated higher tax rates on large incomes, maintained inheritance taxes at a high rate, and gave a decided tax advantage to the low-income earners.

The pressures for social reforms also led Roosevelt to advocate federal action in the fields of housing and health. In his well-known second inaugural address the president lamented:

> I see a great nation, upon a great continent, blessed with a great wealth of natural resources. . . . I see a United States which can demonstrate that, under democratic methods of government, national wealth can be translated into a spreading volume of human comforts hitherto unknown, and the lowest standard of living can be raised far above the level of mere subsistence.
>
> But here is the challenge to our democracy: In this nation I see tens of millions of its citizens — a substantial part of its whole population — who at this very moment are denied the greater part of what the lowest standards of today call the necessities of life.
>
> I see millions of families trying to live on incomes so meager that the pall of family disaster hangs over them day by day.
>
> I see millions whose daily lives in city and on farm continue under conditions labeled indecent by a so-called polite society half a century ago.
>
> I see millions denied education, recreation, and the opportunity to better their lot and the lot of their children.
>
> I see millions lacking the means to buy the products of farm and factory and by their poverty denying work and productiveness to many other millions.
>
> I see one-third of a nation ill-housed, ill-clad, ill-nourished.[3]

One effort to improve this situation was the Wagner-Steagall Act of 1937, which created the United States Housing Authority. It was licensed to spend up to $1 billion for loans to public housing agencies in the cities and the states and also granted them direct subsidies for building public housing projects. Such money was allocated only if minimum federal housing standards were met by the local and state governments. Within four years the United States Housing Authority had contributed to the building of 160,000 new housing units.

Roosevelt's proposals for national health insurance did not fare as well. A furious battle broke out in Congress over

[3] *New York Times,* January 21, 1937.

the National Health Bill, designed to make federal funds available for medical care, as the administration lacked the votes to secure its enactment.

The social measures of the Reform New Deal have been subjected to a variety of criticisms. Conservatives frequently berated the president for bringing the federal government into the field of social welfare. They castigated Roosevelt for establishing the welfare state in America with all the evils of paternalism that are frequently associated with Big Government. On the other hand, radicals charged that the administration did not go far enough — that, indeed, it did little more than to make minor adjustments in an inequitable system. Such strictures on the right and left usually reveal more about the prejudices of the accusers than they do about Roosevelt's social reform accomplishments. Considered in the context of their time, the 1930's, they struck a consensus among a large variety of groups and had a place in the president's favorite playing position in the field of politics — slightly left of center. Judged by the standards of the time, the Social Security Act of 1935 and the Housing Act of 1937 constituted notable advances in promoting the welfare of millions of Americans.

POLITICAL REFORMS

Roosevelt's stunning victory at the polls in 1936, reflecting the voters' endorsement of his program, encouraged him to seek at least three major political reforms, all of which had precedents in state reform legislation of the Progressive era. Most important was his plan for the reorganization of the United States Supreme Court. By 1935 the Court had invalidated more than a dozen key New Deal measures including the NRA (*Schechter* v. *United States*) and the AAA (*United States* v. *Butler*). Thus, at this time Roosevelt feared that the Wagner Act and the Social Security Act would be next to incur the Court's wrath. Soon after his triumphant re-election Roosevelt fostered the Judicial Reorganization Bill in Congress (1937), which authorized the president to appoint up to six new Supreme Court justices whenever incumbent judges did not retire at the age of seventy. An accompanying Retirement Bill proposed the payment of full salaries to justices who took advantage of the retirement option. Much to Roosevelt's surprise, his proposals aroused a loud outcry of protest from virtually every quarter, despite the fact that in the Progressive era many states and localities had adopted judicial recall laws designed to make judges more responsive to public opinion. Critics charged the chief executive with seeking to "pack" the Court, and to impair its independence. Even staunch supporters of the president deserted him in this bitter dispute and the plan was unable to muster a majority in Congress. Yet, if the president lost the battle, he won the war. During the next two years at least four of the justices either died or retired, giving Roosevelt an opportunity to make his own appointments. Moreover, between 1937 and 1941 the Court passed favorably upon a number of important New Deal laws, thus seeming to remove the sense of urgency that had prompted the court reorganization proposal in the first place.

Other phases of political reform were less controversial. In 1937 the president appointed a Committee on Administrative Management headed by public administration expert Louis Brownlow. Its purpose was to simplify the bureaucratic structure of the federal government, particularly the morass of new agencies that had come into existence after 1933. Frequently overlapping functions created much confusion in the day-to-day work of scores of federal offices, creating the need for reorganization. Within two years Congress implemented some of the suggestions of the Brownlow Committee to streamline the executive departments. Also, Congress adopted a third political reform, the Hatch Act of 1939, which imposed federal controls on contributions to political parties in order to prevent corruption.

THE NEW DEAL: BLACK AMERICANS

The Reform New Deal did little specifically to improve the black American's position in the United States. But since black people constituted a significant proportion of the economically underprivileged and unemployed, the relief programs instituted by Roosevelt could not fail to benefit them. In some parts of the rural South, however, racial discrimination impeded such assistance, especially in WPA programs. Nevertheless,

Roosevelt showed himself to be more sensitive to the demands of the black community than Hoover, and he sought to establish channels of communication with it. He did just that through an informal organization of about forty black advisors — many of them federal employees — who became known as the Black Cabinet. As early as 1933 black leader Charles S. Johnson of Fisk University and some of his friends urged Roosevelt to appoint someone to look after the interests of black Americans in the administration's programs. Roosevelt agreed and asked Secretary of the Interior Harold Ickes (a former president of the Chicago chapter of the National Association for the Advancement of Colored People) to appoint such an advisor. Ickes chose Clark Foreman, a white Atlantan, who picked a black assistant, Professor Robert C. Weaver of North Carolina Agricultural and Mechanical College. By 1936 Weaver had succeeded Foreman in his position. In the Department of Commerce Eugene Kinkle Jones of the Urban League became a special advisor; in the Department of Justice Robert L. Vann looked after the interests of black people; in the Farm Credit Administration Henry Hunt was concerned largely with the special problems of black tenant farmers; William H. Hastie became Assistant Solicitor in the Department of the Interior; Lawrence Oxley was the Department of Labor's consultant on black matters; and Mrs. Mary McLeod Bethune brought an awareness of the special problems of blacks into the programs of the National Youth Administration, as did Ira DeA. Reid in the Social Security Administration.

The Black Cabinet constituted a group of articulate spokesmen for black interests, and also helped the New Deal to attract black American voters. To be sure, the Black Cabinet lacked real and effective power to implement its demands; but this was the first time that the White House had deliberately developed channels of communication with the black community in order to hear their grievances. During the New Deal, the voice of the black American was at least heard.

Blacks benefited from many of the New Deal programs, although there were exceptions. The proportion of black Americans on public relief rolls was greater than that of whites. Blacks constituted 10 per cent of the population, but they comprised 18 per cent of those on relief. In southern states local officials sometimes discriminated against blacks. In Atlanta during 1935, for example, white relief recipients were receiving $32.60 each month, while blacks were paid only $19.29. Between 1933 and 1936 some local agencies excluded blacks from the Civilian Conservation Corps. Only in the latter year did the percentage of black Americans in the CCC equal their proportion of the total population, i.e., 10 per cent. And in many camps the War Department enforced segregated quarters. Many NRA codes also had loopholes that made it possible for employers to pay lower wages to black men and women. Of 1000 black employees in the NRA itself, only one rose above the rank of messenger. Similarly, the Tennessee Valley Authority sometimes conformed to Jim Crow practices in southern areas which it served, but it made an energetic effort to employ black Americans in proportion to their percentage of the population.

Some New Dealers went out of their way to advocate greater integration. In the Department of the Interior Harold Ickes desegregated all departmental cafeterias. Almost one-half of the Public Works Administration housing projects in the South were for blacks, partly because of the insistence of Harold Ickes. Construction contracts issued by the federal government, especially by the PWA, required the employment of black workers, creating precedents which the United States Housing Authority and other federal agencies soon followed.

Another champion of racial equality was Mrs. Franklin D. Roosevelt, who appeared frequently in public with black Americans and belonged to a variety of interracial groups. In a dramatic expression of her feelings, she invited Marian Anderson, the famous black singer, to perform at the Lincoln Memorial in 1939 after the Daughters of the American Revolution had denied Miss Anderson the use of their Constitution Hall in Washington, D.C., because of her race.

During the New Deal, Congress was not disposed to enact civil rights legislation. Partly as a reaction against the twenty-one lynchings that marred 1930, Senators Wagner and Costigan introduced an anti-lynching bill in the United States Senate in 1933 in response to a plea by the National Association for the Advancement of Colored People. This bill reappeared in succeeding Congresses until in 1938 a group of southern senators filibustered it to death. As for the president, he evinced real concern for civil rights, but was forced to weigh political consequences carefully. The great importance of Southerners in Congress where they were entrenched in committee chairmanships because of the seniority system required Roosevelt to be extremely cautious lest he jeopardize his entire legislative program.

Later critics of Roosevelt criticized him for a lack of fervor in the cause of civil rights, yet one must judge men by the standards of their own age, not solely by those of a later era. In Roosevelt's own day millions of black Americans felt that he was one of the best friends they had ever had in the presidential chair. Their feelings were manifested in the overwhelming black vote for the Democrats in the dozen years after 1932, as blacks deserted the Republicans in large numbers. In 1944 at least 90 per cent of black Americans in the United States cast their votes for Roosevelt.

ACHIEVEMENTS OF REFORM NEW DEAL

By 1939 the zeal of the Reform New Deal had spent its force. Its accomplishments lay in a body of substantial legislation, much of which transferred government regulation from the states to the federal government. Economic reforms included further federal controls over banking, public utilities, development of private as well as public power, transportation, antitrust activity, agriculture, and labor. Social reforms embraced the Social Security Act of 1935, the Fair Labor Standards Act of 1938, and the Wagner-Steagall Housing Act of 1937. Political reforms revolved around the ill-fated reorganization plan for the Supreme Court, administrative reorganization, and the elimination of political corruption. Various activities of the executive branch were designed to lessen the inequalities between white and black Americans. The Reform New Deal was broad and varied, and despite failures and omissions, it accomplished much.

PROTEST GROUPS AND THE NEW DEAL

There were many individuals and groups who felt that the New Deal did not go far enough, or that it went too far. The onset of the depression initiated a questioning of American

values and the system they had created — in its political, economic, and social manifestations. From the far left to the far
right, individuals and groups challenged a civilization that seemed
to have collapsed under the weight of the depression. On the
Marxian left, the Communists, Communist fronts, and the Socialists were vocal; more important was the radical left which included Selden Rodman's Revolutionary movement, Father
Charles E. Coughlin's Social Justice crusade, Huey Long's Share
the Wealth movement, Francis Townsend's old-age revolving
pension scheme, and the "End Poverty in California" (EPIC)
campaign of Upton Sinclair in California during 1934. On the
right of the political spectrum the American Liberty League and
the American Fascist Party drew small numbers of the malcon-
tents into their ranks. In addition, the pressures generated by the
depression produced several fringe groups that attracted thousands of the befuddled, such as the Ham and Eggs movement in
California, Technocracy, and the "I Am" fad. These varied
protest movements presented plans and programs that offered
alternatives to the New Deal and drew in millions who had given
up hope in the existing system.

LEFT-WING GROUPS

Communist influence during the depression was reflected
in the work of several groups. The Communist Party of the
United States was a small, disciplined group dedicated to the
overthrow of the American economic system. During the thirties
the Party was led by William Z. Foster and Earl Browder, with
no more than perhaps 15,000 members. Its influence extended
beyond its card-carrying cadres, however, since its program
appealed to many of those who were simply disillusioned with
American society. The Communist program called for the abolition of private enterprise and a multi-party system. It rejected
the experimentation that characterized so many of the New Deal's
efforts to combat the depression, and instead called for adoption
of Marxist theories as the basis for a Communist state. In addition to the formal party the Communists sought to further their
cause through an underground espionage group, which sent secret
information to Moscow. Several dozen federal civil servants
(Whittaker Chambers, for example) participated in such clan-

destine activity during the New Deal. Finally, the Communists sought to spread their influence through front organizations. Idealistic high school and college youths were attracted to groups such as the American League against War and Fascism, the American Youth Congress, and the Young People's Socialist League, which were controlled by reputed Communists like Gus Tyler and Gil Green. The American Writer's Congress, which the Communists helped to organize in 1935, attracted a large number of leading writers who were disillusioned by the Great Depression. But this effort to mobilize American intellectuals soon failed because most of them were unwilling to subscribe to a rigid ideology. Nevertheless, the vigor and élan of the Communists during the depression contrasted sharply with the seemingly stumbling and halting efforts of the New Deal.

Surprisingly, the Socialist Party of America in the thirties never regained the popularity it had enjoyed during the Progressive era, although Norman Thomas, the beloved Socialist leader and perennial presidential candidate, polled 900,000 votes in the election of 1932. This may have been due to divisions within the ranks, making it difficult for Socialists to present a united front. One faction, led by veteran orthodox theorist Morris Hillquit, favored emphasis on theory. Another segment, represented by Norman Thomas, urged activism. In fact, through lectures, speeches, and writings, Thomas focused public attention on problems largely neglected by the New Deal. In particular, he was concerned with the serious plight of the sharecroppers and tenant farmers in the South, largely bypassed by New Deal farm programs. The Socialists also brought up discussion of civil rights questions. Norman Thomas was one of the few well-known public figures during the New Deal era who chose to dramatize the condition of black Americans.

There were several leftist critics of the New Deal who did not feel bound by ideological considerations, such as the Revolutionaries, a non-Marxist group. Founded in 1932 by Selden Rodman and Alfred Bingham, two wealthy young men of upper-class background who had recently returned from Soviet Russia, the Revolutionaries appealed primarily to intellectuals dissatisfied with the seeming drift in American life of the period. Through their magazine, *Common Sense,* and through Rodman's book, *Insurgent America: The Revolt of the Middle Classes,* as well as by organizing clubs known as the American Commonwealth Federation, they fashioned a program designed to pull the United States out of the depression. Essentially, Rodman and Bingham urged the nationalization of most means of production and distribution in the United States, and the creation of an elitist managerial class that would have responsibility for administering a rational economic system.

FATHER CHARLES E. COUGHLIN

More appealing to the masses was Father Charles E. Coughlin and his National Union for Social Justice, which presented other alternatives to the New Deal. Coughlin was the famous radio priest of the thirties who broadcast his messages every Sunday from Detroit to as many as 10 million listeners. Colorful and vitriolic, Coughlin attacked Hoover, Roosevelt (after 1935), J. P. Morgan, the Mellon family, and the Rothschilds, as well as Jews in general. In one form or another his theme was concerned with the economic inequalities that were bred by capitalism, especially since they affected the unemployed and the small wage earners. As an alternative to what he considered the increased bungling of the New Deal, Coughlin urged the nationalization of banks, and of public utilities. Above all, he urged Roosevelt to bring about inflation by resorting to very liberal coinage of silver and federal issuance of paper money. Since Roosevelt had veered away from such panaceas by 1936, Coughlin actively opposed his re-election. At the height of his popularity in the mid-thirties, Coughlin effectively vented the frustrations of many who yearned for faster and more effective remedies for the depression than the New Deal was able to provide.

HUEY LONG

Millions of Americans also listened to the forceful attacks on the New Deal emanating from the brilliant demagogue, Senator Huey Long of Louisiana. Long served as governor of his state from 1928 to 1932, where he undertook a program of comprehensive social and economic reform. He built roads and bridges and new public buildings; he increased expenditures for education and health care; and he increased taxes on corporations and the wealthy. At the same time he established a virtual political dictatorship, a prototype of a fascist state, so that he effectively controlled state affairs even after 1932 when he left for Washington to take his seat in the United States Senate. There he founded the national Share the Wealth Movement in 1934, which he hoped would catapult him into the presidency. Proposing "to make every man a king," he advocated the equalization of wealth in America through confiscatory taxes on the wealthy and on corporations. With sufficient funds he expected to create a welfare state in which poverty would be abolished. He advocated an elaborate system of public works, the limitation of working hours to overcome unemployment, and public aid to education, health, and the rural as well as urban poor. In addition, he came out for federal old-age pensions. Long's brilliant fiery oratory won him followers in every section of the nation. In 1935 he posed a direct threat to Roosevelt's re-election, but his life was cut short by an assassin's bullet.

FRANCIS TOWNSEND

While Long was appealing to young and middle-aged voters who were dissatisfied with the New Deal, Francis Townsend (himself over sixty-five) was becoming the hero of the aged. The Long Beach (California) dentist saw the ruthless impact of the depression on older people at first hand when he worked as a county health officer. He found senior citizens who had no friends or relatives, no savings, and no visible means of support. In a highly urban society, the elderly were frequently cast adrift — unlike the situation in the nineteenth century, when the older citizens had lived out their declining years in the circle of their families. Townsend was determined to help the aged by focusing the attention of the entire nation on their special problems. In 1934 he developed the old-age revolving pension scheme and founded hundreds of local clubs devoted to the promotion of his plan. He was also adept in utilizing the radio, a corps of speakers, and a flood of special publications to spread his message. Within two years he had more than 4 million followers. His plan contained three main points. First, it called for the compulsory retirement of all workers at the age of sixty; second, it proposed federal pensions of $150 monthly for everyone over sixty who would spend this sum; third, it advocated a national sales tax which would raise the money necessary to cover the estimated cost of the scheme (about $4 billion annually). Townsend's ideas sent shivers down the backs of many taxpayers, but his pressure and lobbying tactics in Washington were so effective that President Roosevelt and Congress were persuaded to throw their support behind the Social Security Act of 1935. Indeed, perhaps Townsend deserved more credit for enactment of this law than the president or his advisors.

EPIC

The EPIC campaign of 1934 in California also reflected prevailing discontent with New Deal programs. At the time, Upton Sinclair, the famous muckraking journalist who had won fame with his portrayal of the Chicago stockyards in *The Jungle,* decided to make a race for the governorship of California. He felt strongly that a program more effective than the New Deal was needed to end the depression and poverty in America, and he spelled out a plan in his book, *I, Governor of California, and How I Ended Poverty.* More than 200,000 copies were sold throughout the nation in 1934. The volume provided a slogan for his campaign, "End Poverty in California" (EPIC), which led to his capture of the Democratic gubernatorial nomination. His platform called for government operation of idle factories, for the establishment of workers' communities, and for the creation of state land colonies to take care of some of the unemployed. He also advocated the formation of more cooperatives to relieve distress and urged extensive government issue of paper money to resuscitate the economy. The wide appeal of this program frightened many conservative Democrats and Republicans, and they combined their forces to defeat Sinclair narrowly in the elections of 1934. Even so, Sinclair garnered 1 million votes (of a total of about 2.3 million), reflecting the attraction of his proposals for large numbers of California voters.

RIGHT-WING GROUPS

Criticism of the New Deal also came from right-wing forces. In fact, some of the wealthiest individuals in the United States feared that Roosevelt was undermining the capitalistic system and joined together to organize the American Liberty League. They included people like the Du Ponts, financier Felix Warburg, banker Winthrop Aldrich, and others. Finding almost everything about the New Deal abhorrent, they charged that Roosevelt was leading the nation into socialism. To counter this trend they advocated a reaffirmation of private enterprise.

Various fascist groups were more overt in their opposition to Roosevelt. A small number of World War I veterans, the Khaki Shirts led by Art Smith, hoped to reactivate the BEF (Bonus Expeditionary Force) to march on Washington not only to demand their bonus, but also to abolish representative government and to establish a dictatorship. Seward Collins and Lawrence Dennis, leaders of the American Fascist Party, were more sophisticated. Dennis spelled out his program in several books, of which *The Coming American Fascism* was the most widely read. An open admirer of Adolph Hitler in Germany and Benito Mussolini in Italy, Dennis advocated the abolition of democracy and constitutional government, and the creation, instead, of a dictatorship that could deal effectively with the economic crisis. The fascist appeal was always limited to a small number of Americans — less than 100,000 — but it revealed the profound questioning of American democratic values by a not insignificant minority.

FRINGE GROUPS

The frustrations and bewilderments felt by millions of Americans caught in the depression were reflected also in their tendency to join fringe groups. Among intellectuals and scientists, the Technocracy movement found thousands of adherents. Headed by a Columbia University engineer, Howard Scott, Technocracy proposed to apply engineering principles to the solution of economic problems. Specifically, Technocrats urged government control by engineers and by experts who could apply their specialized knowledge to depression problems. Even more esoteric was a group known as Mankind United, founded in 1934 by Arthur Bell. He promised his adherents that mysterious occult powers in his grasp enabled him to end poverty and war. His followers supported his demand for a guaranteed annual wage (of $3000), monthly pensions for the aged, and a guaranteed $25,000 home for everyone. This version of the Affluent Society was ahead of even the wildest dreams of the thirties, although in retrospect it seems far-sighted. More than 15,000 people joined Mankind United, to the great profit of its founder, who collected more than $100,000 in initiation fees. Even more numerous were the followers of the Ham and Eggs movement in California between 1933 and 1939. This was a pension scheme developed by two ambitious promoters in Hollywood, Willis and Lawrence Allen. Hoping to attract old people with their slogan, "Ham and Eggs," the Allen brothers suggested a comprehensive pension plan estimated to cost more than $1 billion annually, to be paid through the issuance of paper money. The scheme was placed on the ballot in California in 1938 and was defeated by a very narrow margin: there were 1.1 million votes for it, and 1.4 million ballots against. Thereafter, the "Ham and Eggs" crusade disappeared.

ALTERNATIVES TO NEW DEAL: SUMMARY

The numerous plans and programs emanating from the left, the right, and the fringe groups all reflected discontent with the New Deal and proposed alternate solutions to depression problems. In most cases they focused on areas of reform not emphasized in the Roosevelt programs. First, all of these programs envisaged the abolition of poverty and the eventual growth of an affluent society. Second, they focused on the need for increased economic planning in America, most likely under the auspices of the federal government. Third, they put forward measures to guarantee employment, minimum wages, and old-age security. Fourth, they proposed monetary and fiscal experimentation as a means of stimulating national recovery. By 1935, therefore, Roosevelt could ponder his own immediate course of action against the background of this multitude of reform proposals. As a master politician, his inclination was to find a consensus that would take into account the wide range of differing schemes and to steal their thunder by including a small portion of the supposed panaceas in his own program.

THE NEW DEAL AND THE INTELLECTUALS

The impact of the New Deal transcended political, social, and economic issues, and also left its influence on American culture. Essentially, it had a twofold effect. On the one hand, it led some intellectuals to reject American values (as some had already done in the twenties); on the other hand, the New Deal stimulated a reaffirmation of American values, which led to a revival of cultural nationalism. Those who were skeptical about American society included Communists, who rejected the entire system outright and proposed to substitute Marxism instead. A much larger number were Social Realists, however, critical of America during the depression, but unwilling to abandon everything in the American tradition. In addition to the critics the depression produced a group of intellectuals who were nationalists, as the sufferings wrought by the depression led them to re-examine — and to reaffirm — the ideas and institutions that had long been fundamental to life in the United States.

A small number of Communist writers in the thirties sought to signify their abandonment of the American system by creating a proletarian literature. Among them Meyer Gold was prominent, although his novel criticizing the values of capitalism, *Jews without Money,* enjoyed scant success. Far more skillful was the trilogy of John Dos Passos, *U.S.A.,* a Marxist condemnation of most things American. The works of Grace Lumpkin and Robert Cantwell were less artful. More interesting were the Communist literary critics, who viewed American literature as an extension of politics. Through the pages of the *New Masses* and the *Daily Worker* they examined most aspects of American life in a negative vein. Granville Hicks in *The Great Tradition* sought to describe the roots of American radicalism in literature, which he hoped would come to full fruition in his own time. V. F. Calverton's survey of American writing, *The Liberation of American Literature,* attempted to demonstrate how the "root factors in American culture . . . have determined the nature of our literature." Specifically, he wrote about the reflection of class conflict in United States culture, the pervasiveness of capitalist values in American writing, and the relation of social forces to literature. Calverton was a suggestive critic, which could not be said of Bernard Smith, another Communist literary figure. Although Communists constituted only a small group among American intellectuals, their criticisms of American society during the depression attracted attention beyond their own circle.

The Social Realists were far more numerous. The master craftsmen of this school included Ernest Hemingway, who artfully used *For Whom the Bell Tolls* to convey his hatred of war. William Faulkner in *The Sound and the Fury* and other works was not specifically concerned with the thirties but probed the destructive impact of crises on human personality, with clear implications for his own generation. Thomas Wolfe in his fictionalized self-chronicle, *You Can't Go Home Again,* vehemently condemned the crudities of American materialism, although he was as much a romantic as he was a Social Realist. James T. Farrell was more biting in his *Studs Lonigan* series, in which he portrayed the impact of the depression upon the disintegration of American (Chicago) youth. Equally caustic were John O'Hara in *Appointment in Samarra* and James M. Cain in *The Postman Always Rings Twice* as they described the terror and bewilderment of individuals under the impact of depression and decried the materialism of American life. But perhaps the novel of the thirties that most accurately caught the spirit of the American people was John Steinbeck's *Grapes of Wrath,* a saga of displaced farmers on the way to California to escape the blight of the depression. Steinbeck conveyed the mood of millions in the United States with a painter's brush.

The Social Realists were also active in the theater. Clifford Odets wrote *Waiting for Lefty,* a scathing indictment of American values, and Robert E. Sherwood in *Idiot's Delight* lampooned war. Maxwell Anderson in *Both Your Houses* castigated the indecision and lack of ideological commitment of the New Deal, as witnessed by the conflict of ideals versus realities among New Dealers.

This critical stance was also expressed by some of the leading painters in the United States. Charles Burchfield's paintings of farm houses dramatized the decline of agriculture, of rural America, and of its values. Edward Hopper dramatically portrayed city tenements in all their squalor, reflecting a way of life for millions of the urban masses. John Sloan concentrated on scenes from the low life of New York City, America's major metropolis and therefore a mirror for many of the problems and aspirations of an urban, industrial society.

Somewhat unexpectedly, the depression crisis also ushered in a decade of cultural nationalism as a significant group of intellectuals rose to the defense of fundamental American values. Among novelists Margaret Mitchell stood out; *Gone with the Wind,* her romanticization of the South during the Civil War and

Reconstruction, swept the hearts of millions of Americans in every section of the country. In the sphere of literary criticism Van Wyck Brooks re-emphasized the durability of American values in his very readable critical history of American literature, of which *The Flowering of New England* was an outstanding volume. Meanwhile, the WPA Writers' Project was giving birth to a significant series of guidebooks to the states, cities, and historic sites in the United States, which uncovered many historic American traditions. This urge to probe more deeply into the American past was often prompted by a search for precedents in other historical periods that could provide some guidance for Americans in the thirties. Burrowing into America's past also gave rise to a new literary genre—the documentary. This imaginative form of artistic expression combined a striking array of photographs depicting the impact of the depression on common folk, with dramatic text, in prose, ballad, or poetry. While starkly realistic in conveying the sufferings borne by poor people during the depression, documentaries also left their readers with a romantic reaffirmation of America and its human resources. James Agee's *Let Us Now Praise Famous Men* (about southern cotton farmers), Archibald MacLeish's *Land of the Free,* and Erskine Caldwell's *You Have Seen Their Faces* were some of the best examples of this type of literary effort.

The search for identity and roots in the national experience also fostered much activity in the field of United States history and biography during the thirties. Historians such as Charles M. Andrews in *The Colonial Period of American History,* Marcus Lee Hansen in *The Atlantic Migration,* and Ralph H. Gabriel in *The Course of American Democratic Thought* uncovered many facets of American life during previous crises. At the same time biographers delved into the lives of authentic American heroes of the past and produced a spate of outstanding biographies, including Carl Sandburg's *Abraham Lincoln,* Douglas Southall Freeman's *Robert E. Lee,* Allan Nevins' *Grover Cleveland, A Study in Courage,* Marquis James' *Andrew Jackson: Border Captain,* Claude Bowers' *Jefferson in Power,* and Carl Van Doren's *Benjamin Franklin.* The depression therefore stimulated an enormous and vital interest in America's past.

A vibrant group of American poets were also stimulated by the depression to make a ringing reaffirmation of democratic values. Carl Sandburg's "The People, Yes," Archibald MacLeish's "Panic," and Edna St. Vincent Millay's "Conversations at Midnight" all expressed a continued faith in the ideals that had made America great. They expressed confidence that these same ideals would continue to sustain the nation in its hour of crisis. Similar sentiments were voiced by some of the best musical composers of the decade as they concentrated on American themes. Deems Taylor in his opera *Peter Ibbetsen,* Douglas Moore in *The Devil and Daniel Webster,* and Aaron Copland in *Rodeo* celebrated rather than rejected various phases of American life in previous eras. And the sculptor Gutzon Borglum sought to perpetuate national heroes and the ideals they represented by carving images of the great presidents in natural rock at the Mount Rushmore Memorial in the Black Hills of South Dakota.

The revival of nationalism in the United States during the thirties was also seen in black American culture. The sufferings of black Americans during the depression spurred various individuals to undertake a closer examination of their roots and heritage. The Harlem Renaissance in the twenties had already begun such an examination, and it was carried further by several black short story writers and novelists such as Rudolph Fisher *(City of Refuge)*, Jean Toumer, and Bruce Nugent. Others wrote about the cultural past. Alain Locke, professor of philosophy at Howard University, produced *Negro Spirituals,* and his colleague at Howard University, Montgomery Gregory, authored *The Drama of Negro Life.* Jessie Fauset, literary editor of the National Association for the Advancement of Colored People's journal, *The Crisis,* commented on Negro humor in *The Gift of Laughter.* Meanwhile the well-known black historian William E. B. DuBois sought to recapture a segment of his people's experience in *Black Reconstruction,* and *The Philadelphia Negro.* Some black sociologists recorded still other phases of their people's cultural experiences, particularly E. Franklin Frazier (after 1934 at Howard University), who wrote *The Negro Middle Class* and *The Negro Family in the United States.*

The depression and the New Deal thus left their mark on the cultural life of the American people in the thirties. Intellectuals reacted to the crisis in various ways, but at least two major themes were dominant. One was the rejection of American values, both from a Marxist as well as from a non-Marxist orientation. Another action was the reaffirmation of American traditions, whether in literature, the arts, or music. The decade of the thirties was an agonizing period for Americans in many ways, but many of those who lived through it found also much intellectual vitality and stimulation.

THE IMPACT OF THE NEW DEAL

By 1939 as the New Deal drew to a close, Roosevelt became increasingly preoccupied with foreign problems. Inevitably Americans in all walks of life looked back upon the preceding six years to assess the impact of the New Deal upon the life of the nation. Invariably, they wondered about the Relief New Deal, the Recovery New Deal, and the Reform New Deal as they sought to formulate a general judgment of the age of Roosevelt.

On balance, the Relief New Deal achieved a limited success, with both gains and debits. Among the gains, Roosevelt's closing of the banks in March 1933 and his antihoarding campaign helped to restore confidence in the country's financial institutions. The Agricultural Adjustment Administration (AAA) constituted a second accomplishment, for it helped farmers to secure a larger share of the total national income. In 1932 total farm income was a mere $1.2 billion; by 1935 it had risen to $3 billion. Farm prices rose about thirty per cent during this same period. A third accomplishment was the improvement of labor conditions, prompted especially by Section No. 7A of the National Industrial Recovery Act. After only two years of its operation, labor organizations increased their membership from 2.8 million people to 3.8 million people. The number of strikes declined, wages improved slightly in many industries, and child labor was effectively diminished.

At the same time, critics of the Relief New Deal pointed to debits. First, they often questioned the wisdom of the National Recovery Administration, as its operation revealed at least three problems. Its effort to restrict production, rather than to expand it, contributed little to a business revival. Moreover, since the code-making procedure was hopelessly complicated, many NRA codes were not representative of the major interests in a particular industry, but primarily of the biggest companies, or trade associations. Smaller companies or associations were therefore often disgruntled because they could not make their voices heard. Enforcement of NRA codes was also cumbersome, and increasingly broke down. Actual administration of NRA regulations was frequently in the hands of industry representatives so that the regulators and the regulated were often the same person. Businessmen were virtually asked to apply regulations to themselves, and not all of them responded selflessly. Some aspects of the NRA experiment were more successful and were continued after 1935 when the United States Supreme Court declared the NRA unconstitutional as an unwarranted delegation of legislative powers (Schechter case). The Connally Hot Oil Act of 1935 continued one provision of the NRA's oil code, but most aspects of this experiment in business-government cooperation were abandoned. Very likely the NRA contributed little to the amelioration of the economic crisis. As for the temporary relief agencies such as the FERA and the CWA, they helped to relieve human suffering, but had little impact on economic activity.

The Recovery New Deal had few accomplishments to its credit because it failed to end the depression and to bring about fuller employment. Perhaps the most conspicuous failure of this aspect of the New Deal was the monetary experimentation, which failed to give rise to significant inflation. And the "bombshell message" to the London Economic Conference (July 1933) probably held back similar attempts at international economic cooperation. A second failure was in the realm of fiscal policy. The PWA spent its funds far too slowly and cautiously to have a fiscal impact on the economy. Indeed, Keynesian economists criticized the president for not spending sufficient money to reinvigorate economic activity. Roosevelt's policy was not one of wrongdoing, they argued, but one of doing too little and too late. Third, although the relief agencies such as the WPA, the CCC, and the NYA had many achievements to their credit, stimulating recovery was not among them. These agencies did help to rehabilitate thousands of individuals who had all but lost the discipline of work and a sense of human dignity. Direct relief also provided subsistence for millions who otherwise would have sunk into abject poverty and hunger; and it provided training for a large portion of the eligible labor force which offered an invaluable manpower pool to cope with the pressing labor needs of World War II. These significant results cannot be ignored by any means, but the hard fact remains that they did not do much to stimulate large-scale economic recovery.

Undoubtedly, the New Deal's greatest successes came in its Reform phase. Even though critics then and later charged that Roosevelt did either too much or too little, what was accomplished reflected Roosevelt's belief that it was more desirable to strive for objectives that were politically feasible than to aim for unattainable goals. What advantages were to be gained by the advocacy of reforms that would alienate a substantial proportion of the voters and erode the very foundations of political power for the administration? In charting his reform course, therefore, Roosevelt steered carefully between what seemed desirable and what appeared attainable. Keeping abreast of the demands of many diverse reformers, he sought to strike a consensus to which a large majority could subscribe. Most of the New Deal's reforms smacked of such consensus. This was true of banking and public utility regulation, the second AAA, and also the Wagner Act. In the realm of social reform the Social Security Act and the Housing Act of 1937 stole the thunder from many of Roosevelt's critics. In his judicial reform plans Roosevelt, for once, misjudged consensus and was forced to beat a hasty and precipitous retreat. Viewed in its entirety, however, the Reform New Deal accomplished substantial reforms in the economic, social, and political policies of the United States. Although the Relief New Deal enjoyed limited success, and the Recovery New Deal was a qualified failure, the Reform New Deal was the most substantial accomplishment of Roosevelt's first two administrations. The solid achievements in the elaboration of progressive reforms as well as in the development of innovative legislation rank the New Deal era as one of the outstanding periods in American reform.

THE IMPACT OF FRANKLIN D. ROOSEVELT

Over and beyond specific accomplishments, the broader achievements of Franklin D. Roosevelt must be noted. His influence was many sided, since he touched human, political, economic, social, and intellectual problems. No assessment can ignore his personal impact; the example of his own confidence, despite physical handicaps, proved to be inspirational to millions of people in whom he revived hope — hope in themselves and in the American democratic system. His resonant radio voice, his ebullient spirit, his confident stance, his jutting jaw, the very example of his own buoyant mood, invigorated a large portion of the nation. Roosevelt gave courage back to America when the nation seemed to be faltering under the cruel blows of depression.

As one of the most astute political leaders of the twentieth century, Roosevelt also hastened a political revolution that made the Democrats the majority party in the nation. Before 1932 the Republican Party had registered a majority of the electorate. Roosevelt brought about the great switch by fashioning the New Deal Coalition, a conglomeration of interest groups clustered mainly, but not exclusively, in the big cities. Included were black Americans, ethnic minorities and first generation Americans, laboring men, blue collar workers (particularly union members), the unemployed as well as many self-employed small business enterprisers, and also farmers. This powerful aggregation displaced the Republican Coalition, dominant before 1932, and composed of eastern financiers and midwestern farmers who had been the backbone of the Republican Party for over half a century. The rise of a new coalition of American voters constituted a veritable political revolution that sustained Roosevelt in the White House.

Perhaps Roosevelt's greatest contribution to American economic development was to save capitalism in the United States. At a time when many groups were questioning the viability of a democratic system confronted by an economic crisis, Roosevelt's faith in the mixed system of private and public enterprise that had developed in America remained unshaken. He conceived his own role as that of a doctor who had a responsibility to save the patient, i.e., American capitalism. Referring to himself as Dr. New Deal, he attempted to diagnose the ills of the country and then to experiment with various remedies designed to nurse the patient back to health. Despite mistakes, Roosevelt succeeded in achieving his main goal. By 1939 the faith of a majority of Americans in the nation's economic system had been restored, and if the United States had not fully recovered from its severe illness, at least it was still functioning. Roosevelt thus did not seek to transform or overturn America's economic system; rather, he sought to preserve it through a series of reforms.

In the realm of social policy Roosevelt's most significant

achievement was to improve the position of the American middle class. Roosevelt was not a revolutionary who sought to redistribute power drastically. He was not the champion of the dispossessed — of black Americans, tenant farmers, or the lowest 10 per cent of American wage earners. To be sure, these groups did benefit from many New Deal programs, but the prime thrust of the New Deal was to strengthen the position of the middle and lower middle classes in the United States. The regulation of Big Business, the encouragement of organized labor, and social welfare legislation not only diminished the decision-making power of corporations but also provided greater influence and security for millions of middle-class Americans. The New Deal did not undertake a radical shift of power in the United States, but it did foster a gradual redistribution.

Although Roosevelt himself was no intellectual, his optimism encouraged an entire generation of intellectuals in the thirties and stimulated vibrant cultural nationalism during the decade. Paradoxically, the pessimistic spirit of disillusionment that affected so many intellectuals during the prosperous twenties gave way to optimistic reaffirmation in the poverty-ridden thirties. Much of the credit for the changed orientation belongs to Roosevelt and his remarkable wife, Eleanor. For the first time in many years the White House showed a genuine interest in the creative arts, welcoming and even encouraging intellectuals. Mrs. Roosevelt's intervention in behalf of Marian Anderson constituted a symbolic gesture. Meanwhile, the WPA provided work, hope, and sustenance for thousands of unemployed writers, artists, actors, and musicians whose contributions to the country's cultural life were not insignificant. In a real sense, in the face of poverty and suffering, Roosevelt encouraged a cultural renaissance during the first eight years of his presidential tenure.

Roosevelt's impact on the life of the nation thus affected several different areas. He did much to revive hope among millions of Americans. He effected a political revolution that made the New Deal "urban coalition" dominant in American politics. He preserved the American economic system. He strengthened the power of the middle and lower middle classes. He encouraged a revival of cultural nationalism in the thirties. Altogether, his influence was considerable, and it was to persist for years after his death.

By 1939 the New Deal had ended. The implementation of

reforms, the growing opposition to Roosevelt even within his own party, and the worsening of the international situation all contributed to a shift of attention from domestic to foreign policy. But the preceding six years had been momentous. The Relief New Deal had mitigated the distress of millions; the Recovery New Deal had revealed the deep-seated pertinacity of the economic crisis; and the Reform New Deal had accomplished a wide range of changes in many phases of American life. The influence of the federal government in national life had been increased enormously. In addition, Roosevelt's personality had left an indelible imprint on American life. As later historians viewed Roosevelt and the New Deal in the broad perspective of the history of the Republic, they judged the man and the period as one of the most significant in the annals of the American experience.

FOR FURTHER READING

A fine one-volume biography of Franklin D. Roosevelt is by JAMES MCGREGOR BURNS, *Roosevelt: The Lion and the Fox* (New York: Harcourt, Brace, 1956). In addition to the standard multivolume study of FRANK FREIDEL, *Franklin D. Roosevelt* (Boston: Little, Brown, 1952), REXFORD G. TUGWELL, *The Democratic Roosevelt* (Garden City: Doubleday, 1957) is informative. A collection of contemporary as well as later appraisals of Roosevelt is in GERALD D. NASH, *Franklin Delano Roosevelt* (Englewood Cliffs, N.J.: Prentice-Hall, 1967). As an original member of the Brain Trust, REXFORD G. TUGWELL writes knowingly about it in *The Brains Trust* (New York: Viking Press, 1968). Other participants in the New Deal have written reminiscences, including FRANCES PERKINS, *The Roosevelt I Knew* (New York: Viking Press, 1946), RAYMOND MOLEY, *After Seven Years* (New York: Harper & Brothers, 1939), and ROBERT E. SHERWOOD, *Roosevelt and Hopkins: An Intimate History* (New York: Harper & Brothers, 1948). Good surveys of the New Deal include WILLIAM E. LEUCHTENBURG, *Franklin D. Roosevelt and the New Deal, 1932 – 1940* (New York: Harper & Row, 1963) and BASIL RAUCH, *The History of the New Deal, 1933 – 1938* (New York: Creative Age Press, 1944). A longer and magisterial account is by ARTHUR SCHLESINGER, JR., *The Age of Roosevelt*, 3 vols. (Boston: Houghton Mifflin, 1957), already a classic.

8

GATHERING WAR CLOUDS
United States Foreign Policy, 1929-1941

While Americans were preoccupied primarily with their domestic problems during the Great Depression, foreign problems grew increasingly more serious with each passing year of the decade. In 1929 the prospects for peace looked bright. The hopes of a whole generation were pinned on the recently concluded Kellogg-Briand Peace Pact. But by 1939 the world was once again at war. Americans could not isolate themselves from these currents, although they tried. Inexorably the pressures of world politics were moving United States foreign policy from an emphasis on isolationism toward greater internationalism, and a fuller participation in world affairs.

The shift from isolationism to greater internationalism did not come painlessly. Isolationist feelings ran strong from 1929 to 1937 as Americans seemed more determined than ever to remain aloof from the growing tensions in Europe, the Far East, and, to a lesser extent, Latin America. In the four years after 1937, however, American attitudes underwent a slow but persistent change as United States involvement appeared increasingly inevitable. By 1941, compared to the previous generation, a larger percentage of Americans favored cooperation with other nations to maintain world peace.

REASONS FOR SHIFT IN
UNITED STATES FOREIGN POLICY

What reasons account for these changing patterns in American diplomacy? First and foremost was the increasing danger to national security brought by the emergence of the Axis powers. In the West, Germany and Italy embarked on a series of aggressions that disrupted the balance of power in Europe and endangered United States interests there. After 1933, when Adolph Hitler became chancellor of Germany and established a totalitarian dictatorship, his German armies were on the move. By 1933 Germany left the League of Nations and undertook a massive rearmament; in 1935 German troops marched into the Rhineland in violation of the Treaty of Versailles, which stipulated its demilitarization. A year later Italy invaded Ethiopia in an effort to establish a new empire in Africa. Then, both Hitler and Mussolini intervened in the Spanish Revolution of 1936 by sending arms and volunteers to Spain to help General Franco overthrow the legitimately elected democratic Republican regime. And still the dictators continued their aggressions, creating crises that, they hoped, would facilitate their plans for world conquest. In 1938 Hitler's legions marched into Austria and made it possible for the Fuehrer to annex that country. In the same year German armies seized the Sudetenland from Czechoslovakia (where a minority of Germans lived), a prelude to their conquest of all of Czechoslovakia the next year. When the Germans invaded Poland in September 1939, they precipitated World War II, since England and France reluctantly went to aid the Polish cause. For the United States the German plans for world conquest bore an ominous message. With the defeat of the western democracies, Hitler intended to subdue the New World as well. Indeed, the gradual weakening of isolationism in American opinion was directly related to the increasing aggressiveness of German nationalism.

American security was also threatened from the Far East. There Japan was embarking on the establishment of a new order, a "greater co-prosperity sphere," which envisaged Japanese domination of most areas of Asia from Korea to all of China. The Japanese inaugurated their conquests with the invasion of Manchuria in 1931, violating the Open Door agreements, the Four Power and Nine Power treaties signed in Washington late in 1921, and also the Kellogg-Briand Pact of 1927. Six years later they launched a full-scale attack on China to subdue that great country. Japanese expansion posed a challenge to United States influence in the Pacific and created a real threat to the security of the Philippines and Hawaii. Certainly the United States could not view Japanese domination of the Far East with equanimity. Particularly in relation to German expansion in Europe, Japanese actions posed an imponderable danger to American security.

A second reason for the shift in American diplomacy was political. Americans were concerned with a seeming decline of democratic governments both in Europe and in the Far East, and their replacement by autocratic, totalitarian regimes. The rise of dictatorships and their aggressive antagonistic policies toward the democracies boded ill for the future of the United States and other republican regimes.

A third reason for the change from isolationism to internationalism was economic. The concerted drive of Germany, Italy, and Japan to increase their power was designed to lessen the influence of other nations, who were to play a role as economic tributaries of the master races. Thus, German plans for a "New Order" envisaged the economic dominance of Germany in Europe, and eventually elsewhere, characterized by the exploitation of other nations exclusively for Germany's economic welfare. In the Pacific the vision of Japanese leaders included the creation of a greater co-prosperity sphere in the Far East, with Japan as the dominant economic power and other nations in the area as subservient satellites. The implications of German and Japanese economic nationalism for the United States were clear. Either Americans would be willing to submit to the Axis rule and be content to play the part of a subordinate and inferior power; or Americans could join other nations struggling against Germany and Japan to prevent them from realizing their plans for world conquest.

Underlying the military, political, and economic considerations in the shift of American attitudes toward diplomacy was an intellectual repugnance to most of the principles underlying totalitarianism. In many ways the values of a democratic society such as the United States clashed with those of dictatorships like Germany and Japan. Democracy placed high value on the sanctity of human life; totalitarianism considered it worthless, even to the extent of glorifying systematic mass extermination of groups or individuals it considered undesirable. Democracy respected the dignity of the individual; totalitarianism rejected this ideal outright and instead emphasized the exclusive dignity of the state. Democracy encouraged diversity — in religion, ideas, and political activities; totalitarianism glorified enforced conformity, punishing those who deviated from officially established norms. Democracy encouraged freedom of action by individuals and groups; totalitarianism fostered restraints on such freedom, and ultimate repression. Democracy encouraged discussion, deliberation, dissent, and compromise in the development of domestic and foreign policies; totalitarianism favored obedience, repression, and submission.

The fundamental ideals of American society clashed directly with those of the totalitarian powers, therefore, and led many Americans slowly and subtly to favor international cooperation rather than isolation as an important principle of the nation's foreign policy.

THE HOOVER POLICIES

President Hoover, though an internationalist in his own outlook, reflected the feelings of a majority of Americans who, disillusioned by World War I, favored a foreign policy based on isolation. His diplomacy thus embodied a mixture of internationalism and isolationism. Toward Europe, the United States continued a stance of aloofness as reflected in insistence on full payment of reparations; but President Hoover, a professing Quaker, made special efforts to secure international disarmament. In the Far East, the Japanese invasion of Manchuria elicited no strong response from the United States. Desperately afraid of American involvement in a shooting war in Asia, Hoover, was determined to keep the United States out of hostilities at any price. As for Latin America, Hoover's disdain for European and Far Eastern entanglements encouraged him to seek closer and friendlier relations with nations of the Western Hemisphere.

EUROPEAN POLICY

During the Hoover years America's attitude toward cooperation with European countries to alleviate the international depression was decidedly isolationist. As one by one the economies of western nations collapsed under the weight of depression, their ability to continue World War I debt payments and reparations to the United States diminished. Some internationalists such as Secretary of State Henry Stimson urged cancellation of all such obligations because they were incurred in a common cause. But President Hoover and a majority of Americans continued to make a crass distinction between American and European interests, as revealed in the Congressional Resolution of December 23, 1931, which expressed opposition to any kind of debt cancellation.

Caught between the realities of the European economic collapse and the strong force of American public opinion, Hoover's policy sought a compromise with the issuance of the moratorium of 1931. This executive order suspended all debt and reparations payments by foreign nations to the United States for a period of one year. Thereafter they were to resume their obligations although, in fact, all except Finland defaulted.

Strong isolationist opinions prevented Hoover from involving the United States in international agreements to alleviate the world economic crisis. In 1931 he hoped to work out agreements for currency stabilization and the lessening of trade barriers with both France and Italy. First Premier Laval of France came to visit him in the White House in November 1931; then Foreign Minister Granziani of Italy. In neither case was Hoover able to promise significant concessions by the United States in view of strong isolationist views in Congress, so these meetings failed. Hoover subsequently planned American participation at a World Economic Conference to be held in London during June 1933 to deliberate on international monetary stabilization, but he could not be sure at all how far American isolationist sentiments would allow him to collaborate with other countries to improve the financial situation. An isolationist stance on the part of Congress was also revealed in the Smoot-Hawley Tariff of 1930, which was the highest tariff ever enacted and erected impenetrable trade barriers just when they needed to be lowered. Although 1000 economists sent a petition to President Hoover urging him to veto the measure, he stubbornly refused and, instead, endorsed the tariff. With domestic markets in the United States already shrinking under the impact of depression and unemployment, the placement of impediments on overseas trade contributed to economic disaster.

But American emotions concerning isolation were so strong that the Smoot-Hawley Tariff was widely hailed as an act of statesmanship.

Only in the realm of disarmament could Hoover find expression for his internationalist sympathies, but his accomplishments in this sphere were meager. His efforts resulted in the London Naval Conference of 1930, including the United States, Great Britain, and Japan. Largely because of the insistence of the Japanese for naval equality with the western powers, this conference broke up amid bitter disagreements. Meanwhile, American consultants to disarmament committees of the League of Nations worked on various proposals, which the president crystallized in the Hoover Plan of 1932. This envisaged complete disarmament, including the scrapping of planes, artillery, and chemical warfare equipment, and reduction of armed forces by at least one-third of their existing strength. It is doubtful whether this program was ever more than a dream. But whatever chances of success it might have had were shattered in January 1933 when Adolph Hitler became chancellor of Germany and soon withdrew German representatives from the League and disarmament negotiations.

Hoover's European diplomacy, then, leaned heavily toward isolationism. In his opposition to the cancellation of war debts, his support of the high Smoot-Hawley Tariff, and his unwillingness to join other nations in seeking remedies for the depression, he accurately reflected the views of a majority of the American people. Only in his highly developed pacifism did the president seek close collaboration with other nations.

FAR EAST POLICY

Hoover's tendency toward isolationism was even more strongly evident in policies in the Pacific, despite the appearance of new problems there for American diplomats. When Japan began its invasion and conquest of Manchuria in 1931, it created a whole range of difficulties for the United States. The Japanese attack created legal issues, for it violated the Open Door agreements, the Nine Power and Kellogg-Briand treaties, as well as the League of Nations Covenant. It also created military problems by posing a new threat to the Philippines. It created economic problems, since the Japanese proposed to exclude trade with other nations, including the United States, in areas under their influence. It also presented moral questions, particularly for an idealist like Hoover, since the imposition of a totalitarian government on Manchuria was repugnant to American ideals of representative democracy. The Japanese invasion of Manchuria, therefore, appeared to call for immediate and forceful action by the United States.

Yet the isolationist sentiment was still so strong in the United States that it paralyzed any serious effort to interfere with Japanese aggression. Logically, the United States should have used force to protect its interests, and to hold the Japanese to their treaty commitments. But Americans were emotionally unprepared for such action and, instead, desired peace at any price. President Hoover reflected these feelings in opposing Secretary of State Stimson's arguments for military action, or at least economic sanctions. Instead, he was unwilling to agree to more than a verbal moral condemnation. Reviving former Secretary of State William Jennings Bryan's policy of non-recognition (1913 – 1915), he supported the Stimson Doctrine (January 7, 1932), which stipulated nonrecognition by the United States of any territories acquired by force or by violation of treaties as in the case of the Japanese occupation of Manchuria. The League of Nations endorsed the Stimson Doctrine (March 11, 1932), for neither England nor France was willing to use military force to stop Japan without the United States. But the Japanese refused to heed the demand for withdrawal by either the United States or the League; instead they left the world organization. Hoover's moral suasion yielded no fruit and, in fact, laid the basis for future Japanese-American antagonisms. In his fear of involvement, however, Hoover accurately mirrored the feelings of millions of Americans.

LATIN AMERICAN DIPLOMACY

In Latin American affairs Hoover showed an urge toward greater collaboration, prompted in part by his desire to steer clear of European and Far Eastern involvements and to cement bonds between New World powers. In 1928 Hoover embarked on a good will trip to South America in which he stressed the American desire for closer and improved relations. Then, in the next year, Under-Secretary of State Reuben Clark issued the "Clark Memorandum," which was merely a policy declaration by the State

Department to the effect that it repudiated the doctrine of intervention as contained in the Roosevelt corollary (1905) to the Monroe Doctrine. Henceforth the United States would seek to settle its differences with Latin American nations by means other than intervention, Clark declared. The memorandum mollified some Latin Americans and laid the basis for improved relations between the United States and Latin America in the ensuing decade. From one point of view it was a gesture toward greater international collaboration; from another, it was a culmination of isolationist sentiment that sought to unify the New World in its stand against the old.

President Hoover thus accurately reflected the isolationist mood of America in the first four years of the Great Depression. United States policy in Europe was to remain as aloof as possible, and not to seek collaboration on issues other than disarmament. In the Far East, he withheld effective American interference, despite provocation. And he sought closer ties with Latin America as a means of consolidating the New World against the old.

ROOSEVELT'S DIPLOMACY OF ISOLATION, 1933 – 1937

The advent of Franklin Delano Roosevelt to the White House brought no great changes in American diplomacy. Whatever Roosevelt's own inclinations might have been, he kept his ears finely attuned to the public groundswell, which definitely directed him to a policy of isolation. Roosevelt's European diplomacy thus included the rejection of international collaboration to achieve currency stabilization, tacit agreement with the report of the Nye Committee investigating the causes of America's entry into World War I, and the approval of neutrality acts by Congress designed to keep the United States out of foreign embroilments. Roosevelt's only gesture toward international collaboration was his recognition of Soviet Russia in 1933, intended to dampen the aggressiveness of the new Hitler regime in Germany. Roosevelt also made no appreciable changes in the Far Eastern policy of the United States during the years between 1933 and 1937 other than maintaining the ineffectual Stimson Doctrine. In addition, he encouraged the eventual granting of independence for the Philippines, the Achilles heel of United States diplomacy. As for Latin America, Roosevelt enthusiastically carried on Hoover's policy of consolidating ties among nations in the Western Hemisphere and, indeed, glamorized it with his memorable phrase, the "Good Neighbor" policy. The contours of American diplomacy during the first Roosevelt Administration, therefore, were primarily isolationist.

EUROPEAN POLICY

Isolationism was reflected in Roosevelt's actions in international currency stabilization. The president himself was not unfavorably inclined toward United States participation in the world-wide efforts to combat the depression. He thought that agreements could be worked out at the London Economic Conference to meet in June 1933. But Roosevelt let himself be persuaded by Raymond Moley that success of his domestic recovery efforts absolutely required aloofness from international programs. Thus, he sent the "bombshell message" (July 5, 1933) to the conference, expressing America's determination to follow its own course in dealing with financial instability. While criticized for his precipitate action, Roosevelt undoubtedly reflected the feelings of many Americans who hoped to shun new international commitments.

Isolationist sentiment was clearly expressed in Congress with the report of the Nye Committee (1934). Created to investigate the causes of America's entry into World War I, the committee held exhaustive hearings, only to conclude that the United States had entered the war under the influence of rapacious munitions makers. Senator Nye had no direct evidence to document his conclusion, but his mood mirrored the disillusionment, the pacifism, and the isolationism of many Americans. The implications of the Nye Committee's conclusions for New Deal diplomacy were clear. The United States must not again make the mistake of becoming embroiled in European problems. To emphasize that determination, in 1934 Congress hastily passed the Johnson Act, prohibiting American loans to nations that had defaulted on their war debt and reparation payments.

Another result of the Nye investigation, and perhaps the clearest expression of isolationist sentiment during the Great Depression, came in three successive phases of congressional neutrality legislation. In the face of German occupation of the Rhine-land, the Italian attack on Ethiopia, and German-Italian interven-tion in the Spanish Civil War, Congress endorsed the Pitman Resolution in 1935. This prohibited the export of arms to areas where there was armed conflict, forbad United States ships to carry munitions to such places, and warned American travelers not to enter zones of active fighting. The Neutrality Act of 1936 also prohibited loans to belligerents and gave the president discre-tion to declare an area to be in a state of war. Somewhat unex-pectedly, the aggressor nations tended to benefit from these laws, which made it difficult for those attacked to secure arms and other aid for self-defense. Congress thus made some slight changes in the Neutrality Act of 1937. It provided for an arms embargo but included a "cash and carry" amendment that allowed individuals or nations to buy arms if they paid cash and carried them in their own vessels. The significance of the Neutrality Acts of these years was that they accurately reflected a deep-rooted fear of most Americans about another involvement in European wars.

Only in his recognition of Soviet Russia did Roosevelt re-flect a concern for collective security in the face of German rearmament. On October 10, 1933, the United States and Russia concluded an agreement under which the Russians agreed to com-pensate Americans whose property had been confiscated in Russia during the preceding decade. In addition, they promised to restrict Communist propaganda in return for formal recognition by the United States. Unfortunately, the Soviet government in succeeding years failed to live up fully to these stipulations.

FAR EAST POLICIES

Isolationism was also characteristic of Roosevelt's Far Eastern policies between 1933 and 1937. Certainly it was one motive that led Congress to pass the Tydings-McDuffie Act of 1934, which provided for the attainment of Philippine independence at the end of a ten-year period. To be sure, American beet sugar producers were also looking forward to independence because it would bring the imposition of tariff duties on competing Philippine sugar. But without isolationist sentiments they could not have achieved their goal. Meanwhile, in 1937 Roosevelt was confronted with a dilemma, not unlike the Manchurian crisis of 1931, when the Japanese launched a large-scale invasion of China. In their offensive they also sank the *Panay,* an American gunboat off Shanghai. What was the United States to do? A Gallup poll of the period reported that 70 per cent of Americans interrogated favored the withdrawal of American influence from China. Congress opposed the imposition of possible sanctions, economic or otherwise, by a majority of more than two to one. Thus, Roosevelt confined himself to no more than a moral protest, contained in a series of State Department notes to the Japanese. His efforts to rally western nations in joint protest at a conference in Brussels resulted in failure. The United States accepted a Japanese apology, and payment for the loss of the *Panay.* Thus, the United States demonstrated once again, as in 1931, that despite treaties and policy declarations, it was not inclined to implement these forcefully in the Far East; instead, it followed a policy of abstention and isolation.

LATIN AMERICAN POLICIES

Although perhaps not the originator of the Good Neighbor policy toward Latin America, Roosevelt did more than any other chief executive to change the tone of American relations with other Western Hemisphere nations. Lingering hostility of Latin Americans toward the United States, hoped-for increases in inter-American trade, and the desirability of consolidating Latin American nations in the interest of United States as well as hemispheric security, all prompted Roosevelt to cultivate the friendship of his neighbors to the south. His efforts resulted in formulating new treaty obligations and in promoting commercial expansion. As for the former, Roosevelt repudiated the doctrine of intervention used by the United States in the early twentieth century. At the seventh Inter-American Conference in Montevideo, Uruguay (1933), the United States pledged itself to non-intervention by accepting the responsibility of extending *de facto* recognition to new governments. Then, in 1934 the United States abrogated the Platt Amendment and renounced its right to intervene in the internal affairs of Cuba; at the same time, United States Marines withdrew from Haiti. When the treaty with Panama came up for renewal in 1936, the United States also gave up its right to intervene. In that year, at the Inter-American Conference in Buenos

Aires (Argentina) the United States, along with other nations, signed a protocol on non-intervention that stilled some of the lingering fears of many Latin Americans. From the active interference in Western Hemisphere affairs during the Progressive era, the United States moved to a policy of non-involvement during the Roosevelt period.

Meanwhile, self-interest and logic dictated closer economic relations between the United States and Latin America. Secretary of State Cordell Hull, a free trader, was especially avid in seeking closer commercial ties. His first accomplishment was the Reciprocal Trade Agreements Act of 1933, which gave the president authority to reduce tariff rates by as much as 50 per cent where such a lowering of trade barriers resulted in equivalent reductions by another nation. Within seven years more than twenty countries had concluded such agreements with the United States and had helped to boost American commerce by as much as 15 per cent over 1933 levels. In the next year Roosevelt and Hull secured establishment of the Export-Import Bank, which made loans to Latin American nations desiring to stabilize their currencies or to expand trade. And instead of intervention, the United States exercised great restraint in negotiating with the Mexican government concerning the compensation of Americans who had lost their properties by confiscation and nationalization. By 1941, after long negotiations, the United States and Mexico signed a mutually satisfactory agreement.

DOUBTS ABOUT ISOLATIONISM

The increasing number of international crises provoked by Germany, Italy, and Japan by 1937 gave Roosevelt doubts about the wisdom of emphasizing isolationism as a principle of American diplomacy. To be sure, in view of strong public sentiment in favor of American non-involvement in the affairs of Europe and Asia, he could not undertake a sudden or drastic reversal of United States foreign policy. But after 1937 he began a concerted effort to acquaint the American people with the dangers that totalitarian aggressions ultimately had for national security. In the period between 1937 and 1941 Roosevelt took a series of steps that moved American diplomacy from isolationism to international cooperation in order to lessen the military threats posed by Germany and Japan.

In retrospect, these measures also constituted stepping stones that ultimately led the United States into World War II.

ROOSEVELT'S DIPLOMACY AND COLLABORATION, 1937 – 1941

QUARANTINE SPEECH

The turning point in Roosevelt's diplomacy, signifying the gradual shift from isolation to cooperation, was his "quarantine" speech of October 5, 1937, in Chicago. Here, in the midst of public concern over the Japanese invasion of China, Roosevelt proposed that the democratic nations of the world combine to "quarantine the aggressors," lest the disease of totalitarian aggression spread to all corners of the globe. "The people of the United States must, for the sake of their own future . . . give thought to the rest of the world," Roosevelt noted. "The present reign of terror and international lawlessness," he cried, "has now reached a stage where the very foundations of civilization are seriously threatened. The peace, the freedom, the security of 90 per cent of the population of the world is being jeopardized by the remaining 10 per cent." While reiterating the desire of the United States to remain at peace, he urged common measures by peace-loving nations that would discourage further aggression by the dictator states. Roosevelt was purposely very general, both in his condemnations and in his proposals for remedial action; but his warning that isolationism might no longer serve American interests marked a subtle change in American diplomacy.

Roosevelt's task in reorienting United States foreign policy from isolation to collaboration was not easy, since isolationist feelings in 1937 were still running strong. In the Senate, Gerald P. Nye led a strong minority who espoused isolationist views, while in the House, Congressman Hamilton Fish was another outspoken isolationist. Meanwhile, Charles A. Lindbergh became a prominent speaker for the American First Committee, an organization of influential people committed to non-involvement in foreign affairs, as well as hatred of Roosevelt. Other anti–New Deal groups such as the American Liberty League, Father Coughlin's Christian Front, and the American Communist Party also actively opposed the president's program for increased national defense and international collaboration.

EUROPEAN POLICIES

The shift of United States diplomacy from isolation to collaboration thus was not sudden, but gradual. Indeed, between 1937 and 1941 the Roosevelt policies toward Europe went through three stages. The period of neutrality was prominent from 1938 to 1939; it was followed by a period of non-belligerency between September 1939 and June 1941; then Roosevelt led the United States into a third phase consisting of armed neutrality (July to December 1941). The Japanese attack on Pearl Harbor on December 7, 1941, ended any illusion that isolationists still harbored about the possibility of American non-involvement in World War II. As in a Greek tragedy, events seemed to catapult the American people into war, despite their great reluctance.

Neutrality
In the two years after the quarantine speech, Roosevelt embarked on a series of measures designed to improve American defenses in Europe and in the Pacific. His immediate concern over Hitler's aggressions was reflected in his program to maintain American neutrality through rearmament in the National Defense Act of 1938. Congress appropriated more than $1 billion for rearmament, including expansion of the army and the navy, and the boosting of the fledgling air force. America's defense effort was strengthened in the following year when Roosevelt prevailed upon Congress to repeal portions of the Neutrality Acts prohibiting arms shipments overseas (November 1939), thereby allowing more effective American aid to peoples opposing German and Italian aggression.

Non-belligerency
In the face of Axis victories from 1939 to 1940, and the German occupation of the Scandinavian countries, and France, Holland, and Belgium, Roosevelt moved to strengthen the national defense by assuming a stance of non-belligerency. In 1939 he persuaded Congress to authorize a peacetime draft program for one year, but one limiting the service of these draftees to the West-

ern Hemisphere. By the slim margin of one vote in the House, the Selective Service Act was renewed in 1940.

That was the year of the Battle of Britain, when the German Air Force sought to demolish England in preparation for a land invasion. In this dire predicament it became clear to Roosevelt and many Americans that Great Britain was America's first line of defense. Thus, Roosevelt tried to tie the United States closer to the British cause.

The change in Roosevelt's policy was well crystallized in an address the president made at the University of Virginia on June 10, 1940. In this speech Roosevelt flatly rejected isolationism as a guide for United States diplomacy as he said:

> Some indeed still hold to the now somewhat obvious delusion that we of the United States can safely permit the United States to become a lone island, a lone island in a world dominated by the philosophy of force.
>
> Such an island may be the dream of those who still talk and vote as isolationists. Such an island represents to me a helpless nightmare.
>
> Overwhelmingly we — as a nation — are convinced that military and naval victory for the gods of force and hate would endanger the institutions of democracy in the western world, and that equally, therefore, the whole of our sympathies lies with those nations that are giving their life blood in combat against these forces.
>
> We will extend to the opponents of force the material resources of this nation, and we will harness and speed up the use of those resources in order that we ourselves may have equipment and training equal to the task of any emergency and every defense.[1]

The destroyer deal was one such effort to achieve this goal. Executed under presidential authority, this deal provided for the transfer of fifty over-age (World War I vintage) American destroyers to the British, who desperately needed them for convoy duty. In return, the British made air and land bases available to the United States in Canada, Newfoundland, and the West Indies.

During this period of non-belligerency the development of lend-lease policy became significant. With the German occupation of France in June 1940, Germany stepped up air attacks on the British Isles, creating a precarious situation. Whether the English

[1] *New York Times,* June 11, 1940.

could survive the "blitz" of 1940 was an open question. In this emergency Prime Minister Winston Churchill came to Washington in December 1940 to plead for immediate large-scale aid lest Great Britain fall, and leave the United States to face Germany alone. The British had virtually exhausted their cash resources and needed credit. Faced with this dilemma, Roosevelt formulated a Lend-Lease policy designed to bolster England. On January 6, 1941, Congress authorized the president to sell the British more than $1 billion worth of goods and supplies in return for long-term leases in Canada and the West Indies for American military bases. By March 1941 Congress authorized more than $7 billion for Lend-Lease, as it became obvious that such aid was crucial in allowing England to ward off German might.

Roosevelt strongly defended his action. He noted that Great Britain was the best defense of the United States, and that munitions and war supplies could perform a greater service in England than in American warehouses. He was merely trying to eliminate the "foolish old dollar sign," he said.[2]

Armed Neutrality

As the United States committed its vast resources to defeat the Axis and moved farther away from isolation, Roosevelt took the nation into a period of armed neutrality in June 1941. Three steps taken by the president signified the new emphasis of American foreign policy. In the first place, he authorized extensive naval action to maintain the flow of American supplies to England. This included the furnishing of American merchant ships with armed escorts, the extension of the United States Navy's Neutrality Patrol to the west coast of Africa, and the opening of American ports to British ships in need of repairs. In July 1941 he also authorized the occupation of Iceland by American troops to prevent this stepping stone across the Atlantic from falling into the hands of the Germans, who were already occupying Denmark. Finally, in August 1941, Roosevelt brought the United States into an informal alliance with Great Britain when he met Prime Minister Winston Churchill on the U.S.S. *Augusta* in the Atlantic to formulate the Atlantic Charter. This was a mutual agreement on postwar policies proclaiming Anglo-American desires for self-determination of all peoples, economic cooperation, and

[2] *New York Times,* December 30, 1940.

political democracy. Roosevelt was still unwilling to make a military commitment to the Allied cause, but he did tie the United States closely to it. By September 1941, American vessels found themselves in a shooting war as German submarines attacked the *Greer,* an American destroyer. Thereafter, every United States vessel was provided with a naval escort.

FAR EASTERN POLICIES

Meanwhile, isolationism as a principle in American Far Eastern policy was also weakening. Roosevelt's thinking concerning the Japanese was considerably affected by the intransigence and inflexibility of Secretary of State Cordell Hull, who opposed any concessions to Japan by the United States. Indeed, Hull seemed willing to defy American public opinion favoring isolation between 1937 and 1940 by risking direct United States involvement to contain Japan by force.

Economic Sanctions

In contrast to Hoover's policies in the Manchurian crisis of 1931, and his own isolationist stance in late 1937, President Roosevelt increasingly sought to exert United States influence in the Pacific to stem Japanese expansion after 1939. Between 1939 and 1940 he took three measures designed to exert economic pressure on Japan. On July 26, 1939, just two days after the British signed a treaty with the Japanese recognizing their new conquests, the president undertook to limit trade between the United States and Japan. He gave the required six months notice to abrogate a commercial treaty under which the United States would restrict steel and oil exports to Japan, desperately needed by the Japanese for their war machine. The Japanese were angered rather than intimidated, and they signed a military alliance with Germany and Italy to create a tripartite Axis. Roosevelt moved cautiously, and in 1940 he declared an embargo on the shipment of scrap metals, gasoline, and tools to Japan. In the twelve months after June 1940, the president gradually extended this boycott to cover most vital war materials. At the same time he authorized United States loans to the Nationalist Chinese to bolster their ability to repel invading Japanese armies. But the Japanese were heartened by German victories in Europe and responded to the economic boycott with increased intransigence.

Diplomatic Negotiations

During the spring and summer of 1941 Roosevelt made several attempts at serious diplomatic negotiations designed to reconcile the principle of the Open Door, upheld by the United States, with that of the Closed Door advocated by Japan. First came the Nomura-Hull conversation in April 1941, between the Japanese Ambassador in Washington and Secretary of State Hull. Although the Japanese were willing to make concessions, they were not prepared to accept Hull's unconditional demand for their absolute adherence to the Open Door policy and Chinese independence. Another abortive move came a month later when Japanese Foreign Minister Matsuoka made a proposal to Hull for a Japanese-American neutrality pact. But Secretary Hull contemptuously rejected it. Soon thereafter the Japanese invaded French Indochina, in further violation of their treaty commitments. Their action only strengthened Hull's belief that the United States should be unyielding in its insistence on the Open Door, a position he made clear in the Hull-Nomura conversations of July 1941. His attitude narrowed the range of options available to the Japanese. They could yield or they could fight.

The Japanese doves still hoped to avert a war, however, and prompted another effort to settle Japanese-American differences. On August 28, 1941, Roosevelt received the Konoye proposal, reflecting Japanese willingness to withdraw from parts of China and advocating a high-level conference. Roosevelt was eager to attend such a meeting, but Secretary Hull prevailed upon him to demand recognition of the Open Door before going to a projected meeting. Hull's inflexible pose brought diplomatic negotiations to a halt and helped to bring Admiral Tojo and the war party to power in Japan. To the Japanese it appeared that they could maintain their national dignity only by resorting to war; otherwise, they would be surrendering weakly before the rigid demands of the United States.

Stalemate and War

The American rejection of the Konoye proposal led Roosevelt into a period of diplomatic stalemate (September-December, 1941). With both sides unwilling to compromise, open warfare appeared to be a distinct possibility. While the new Tojo government in Japan was making preparations for an armed attack on American possessions, it also sent a special emissary, Saburu Kurusu, to

Washington to continue negotiations. Throughout November, Hull, Saburu Kurusu, and Nomura (Japanese Ambassador to the United States) continued their fruitless conversations, with both sides aware that a compromise appeared unlikely. These talks were abruptly ended on December 7, 1941, when the Japanese undertook a surprise attack by bombing the large American naval base at Pearl Harbor in Hawaii. The United States and Japan were now at war.

EVE OF UNITED STATES ENTRY INTO WORLD WAR II

PEARL HARBOR

Pearl Harbor was one of the most serious military disasters ever experienced by the United States. On a dark dim Sunday morning at 7:55 A.M. and at 8:50 A.M., on December 7, 1941,

Pearl Harbor. Crew of sinking battleship U.S.S. California *abandoning vessel hit by Japanese bombs. (Wide World Photos)*

360 Japanese bombers and fighter planes swooped down on the Hawaiian Islands. Inexplicably, the United States had no air patrol or other effective means for detecting a massive enemy attack. Thus, the Japanese also benefited from the element of surprise. As they neared the large American naval base at Pearl Harbor, they found a substantial portion of the United States Navy's Pacific squadron sprawling before them, and hundreds of aircraft spread out on the huge landing fields like so many waiting ducks. The rain of bombs let loose by the Japanese was swift and terrible. More than 2000 Americans were killed, and the enemy attack disabled or sank all of the eight major battleships there, three cruisers, three destroyers, and hundreds of lesser craft. Meanwhile, the Japanese unleashed equally ferocious attacks on American forces in the Philippines, Guam, Wake, and Midway Islands, and upon the British possessions in Hong Kong.

On December 8, 1941, President Roosevelt somberly went before Congress to ask for a war declaration against Japan. "Yesterday, December 7, 1941," he said, "a date which will live in infamy, the United States of America was suddenly and deliberately attacked by naval and air forces of the Empire of Japan. . . . No matter how long it may take us to overcome this premeditated invasion, the American people in their righteous might will win through to absolute victory. . . . Hostilities exist. There is no blinking at the fact that our people, our territory and our interests are in grave danger." By a vote of 388 to 1 in the House, and 96 to 0 in the Senate, Congress gave overwhelming support to the president by passing a joint resolution declaring a state of war between the United States and Japan. Three days later Germany and Italy came to the aid of the Japanese by declaring war on the United States. As in World War I, international events seemed to involve the United States in armed conflict despite overwhelming efforts by the American people to remain aloof. In four short years the nation had moved from isolation to close international cooperation with other nations in a common effort to subject and repel the Axis powers.

Reasons for Vulnerability

Possible explanations have been offered for Japan's ability to inflict such a great military disaster on the United States at Pearl

Harbor. One factor, at least in the minds of many members of Congress, was the apparent failure of American commanders in the Pacific to prepare for enemy attacks, especially Admiral Husband E. Kimmel (in charge of naval activities in Hawaii) and General Walter Short. This happened despite months of rumors that the Japanese were contemplating some kind of military action. Since for some months the State Department had broken the Japanese secret code, Americans might have been in a better state of preparedness. It is true, however, that throughout the fall of 1941 American military men in Hawaii had been alerted at various times when diplomatic negotiations seemed near a breakdown, and they had become inured to warnings of attack. Nevertheless, carelessness on the part of American military leaders was one factor in the Pearl Harbor disaster.

More important, however, was bureaucratic bungling, the inefficiency and confusion that characterized various departments and agencies in Washington. To a large extent the Pearl Harbor debacle was due to a failure of communications. The War, Navy, and State Departments, as well as dozens of other agencies receiving and decoding secret messages, lacked a clearinghouse for the interchange of vital information. Although some government officials read about hints of an impending Japanese attack in dispatches, there was no centralized communications center into which they could channel their knowledge. Even worse, American military and naval commanders were not kept informed of the most recent information received by one or another federal agency. Thus, although Washington intercepted a message from Tokyo to the Japanese ambassador in the United States indicating that a major event could be expected on December 7, 1941, this communication was not decoded until 3 A.M. Sunday morning (Washington time). But no government official in the United States thought of telephoning authorities in Hawaii or other American possessions in the Pacific. The lack of a clearly defined communications system thus was a major factor in contributing to the surprise which the Japanese used to make their attack on Pearl Harbor more effective.

Once the initial shock of Pearl Harbor had abated, many Americans wondered about the reasons for United States entry into another world war. Despite divergent views, two major interpretations were widely held. Orthodox historians and their readers often defended the course of United States foreign policy since 1929; revisionists frequently condemned it.

The defenders of American diplomacy between 1929 and 1941 stressed four major points. First and foremost, they underscored the Axis military threat to American security, which really gave the United States little choice but to resist, unless it was willing to become a vassal state. A German and Japanese victory would clearly constitute a threat to American democracy, to American commerce, and to international peace. Isolationism no longer promised to protect the national interest. As the United States grew to become one of the strongest powers in a world bound together by transportation and communications, it could not protect its vital interests unless it assumed leadership in cooperating with other nations. Second, the United States entered World War II to protect its economic interests. German plans for a "New Order" and Japanese establishment of a co-prosperity sphere in Asia constituted direct threats to the commercial expansion of the United States. A third reason for United States entry into the war was political and ideological. It seemed clear that democratic institutions would not long survive in a world dominated by totalitarian regimes that were loath to tolerate other forms of government. Moreover, since totalitarian ideologies of force and repression were so totally opposed to the democratic emphasis on compromise and freedom, it was unlikely that the two could exist peaceably. Finally, the defenders of Roosevelt's diplomacy argued that he had little choice but to resort to war, since he had skillfully exhausted all diplomatic means at his disposal to protect American interests. The United States thus entered World War II because of military, economic, political, ideological, and diplomatic considerations.

The revisionist historians seriously attacked the record of American diplomacy. They questioned the threat to American security posed by the Axis powers. Instead, they emphasized the dangers of Soviet Communism. If Roosevelt sought to maintain national security, they argued, he went to war with the wrong powers. They also stressed the inflexibility of Roosevelt's diplomacy, which provoked war with Germany and Japan. American insistence on the Open Door, containment of Japanese expansion, and insistence on maintaining the status quo in the Pacific gave the Japanese little choice but to resort to war as a means of preserving their self-respect. American aggressiveness provoked the Axis powers, as Roosevelt's arming of merchant ships in the Atlantic clearly indicated. They also charged Roosevelt and his advisors with ignorance and bungling that led the nation into a needless war. Finally, they claimed that a conspiracy led the United States into conflict — a conspiracy of pro-Communist and pro-British interventionists who brought the United States into a war that was not in its best interests. The revisionists played down any Axis danger to American economic growth, and minimized differences between democratic and totalitarian institutions and ideologies.

REASONS FOR ENTRY INTO WORLD WAR II: SUMMARY

The United States clearly entered World War II for its own self-preservation. In Europe, Nazi ideology and aims spelled a clear danger for the future welfare of the United States. German designs menaced the political system of the United States, its economic interests, and its military security. American leaders really had little choice but to resist.

In the Far East the situation was not as clear. A substantial number of Japanese leaders hoped for an accommodation which the inflexibility of Secretary Hull increasingly prevented. It was apparent that Hull and his supporters expected the United States to be the dominant power in the Pacific. Whether or not such a role was in America's national interest, however, was not at all certain, neither then nor in retrospect. Perhaps the United States entered the Pacific war because of diplomatic bungling.

FROM ISOLATIONISM TO COLLABORATION: REVIEW

Whatever the reasons for American entry into World War II, observers of American diplomacy between 1929 and 1941 agreed that the nation's foreign policy underwent a profound transformation, shifting from isolationism to international cooperation. Few could fail to note the overwhelming public feeling in favor of isolation during the Hoover era and the first Roosevelt administration. Then Americans had raised high tariff walls, and had refused to cancel war debts owed by Europeans or to participate in attempts to secure international monetary stabilization. Nor had Americans shown an inclination to send aid to victims of aggression. They had openly turned their backs on Japanese expansion in Manchuria while seeking closer ties with their hemispheric neighbors. But by the time of the second Roosevelt administration, as the danger of Axis expansion became more apparent, the mood of many Americans began to change in favor of greater international collaboration. Between 1937 and 1941 President Roosevelt clearly sought closer cooperation with the western democracies, although he hoped to keep the United States out of war. Successive phases in American foreign policy revealed the stepwise transformation of diplomacy under Roosevelt: from emphasis on neutrality to non-belligerency, armed neutrality, and, finally, war. When the United States at last entered the conflict, it moved toward closer collaboration with other nations fighting the Axis powers. World War II largely ended isolation as a major premise of American diplomacy and ushered in a new era of international cooperation.

FOR FURTHER READING

A brief narrative of diplomatic events during this period is in ALLAN NEVINS, *The New Deal and World Affairs* (New Haven: Yale University Press, 1950). ROBERT A. DIVINE, *The Reluctant Belligerent: American Entry into the Second World War* (New York: Wiley, 1965), and *The Age of Insecurity: America, 1920 – 1945* (New York: A-W, 1968) are more detailed accounts. ROBERT H. FERRELL, *American Diplomacy in the Great Depression* (New Haven: Yale University Press, 1957) and HERBERT FEIS, *Diplomacy of the Dollar, 1919 – 1932*, rev. ed. (Hamden, Conn.: Archon Books, 1965) are very valuable analyses. See also HERBERT FEIS, *Nineteen Thirty-Three: Characters in Crisis* (Boston: Little, Brown, 1966) for incisive appraisals of contemporary policy makers. The isolationist theme in depression diplomacy is discussed in SELIG ADLER, *The Isolationist Impulse: Its Twentieth Century Reaction* (New York: Free Press, 1966), and in two other works, WALTER JOHNSON, *The Battle Against Isolation* (Chicago: University of Chicago Press, 1944) and WAYNE S. COLE, *America First: The Battle Against Isolation* (Madison: University of Wisconsin Press, 1953). The shift to internationalism in Roosevelt's policies is described in WILLIAM

L. LANGER and EVERETT S. GLEASON, *The Challenge to Isolation, 1937 – 1940* (New York: Harper, 1952), and *The Undeclared War, 1940 – 1941* (New York: Harper, 1953). EDGAR B. NIXON (ed.), *Franklin D. Roosevelt and Foreign Affairs,* 3 vols. (Cambridge: Harvard University Press, Belknap Press, 1968) is an outstanding collection of documents that highlight the President's internationalist leanings. Shorter works include DONALD F. DRUMMOND, *The Passing of American Neutrality, 1937 – 1941* (Ann Arbor: University of Michigan Press, 1955) and the defense of administration policies made by BASIL RAUCH in *Roosevelt: From Munich to Pearl Harbor* (New York: Creative Age Press, 1950). CORDELL HULL, *The Memoirs of Cordell Hull,* 2 vols. (New York: Macmillan, 1948) and HENRY L. STIMSON and MCGEORGE BUNDY, *On Active Service in Peace and War* (New York: Harper, 1948) convey the impressions of insiders.

II

THE TECHNOLOGICAL SOCIETY
1941 - 1970

9

THE UNITED STATES
IN WORLD WAR II

The entrance of the United States into World War II presented a whole new range of problems for the American people, some military and diplomatic, others primarily domestic. Uppermost in the minds of President Roosevelt and his advisors was ending the Axis threat by a military victory. Such an objective demanded decisive action in Europe, the Middle East, and the Pacific. Closely related problems concerned necessary cooperation between the United States and the United Nations, and coordination to achieve the common goal of victory. These military and diplomatic issues were compounded by the need for imaginative policies in the domestic sphere. Mobilization of the economy and of most aspects of life in the interests of the wartime effort was a herculean task that absorbed the best energies of millions of Americans. The war also had a profound impact on the domestic life of Americans, whether on politics, economy, society, race relations, or cultural trends. Like most armed conflicts, World War II did not initiate radical new departures in America, but it accelerated the pace of change. In virtually every phase, the war revealed an enormous flexibility on the part of most Americans who adapted to new and often unfamiliar problems, and revealed previously hidden potentials. At the conclusion of the conflict, many Americans seemed transformed. The depression-wracked generation of 1941 had been glum, cautious, and pessimistic; but by 1945, with a job well done, many Americans felt a sense of exhilaration, self-confi-

303

dence, and optimism. In the broad context of the American experience, World War II was a bridge between two distinct eras, between a nation preoccupied with depression and one characterized by an affluent society. It marked the end of the period of industrialism (1877 – 1940) and inaugurated a new stage in American development with the emergence of a technological society (1941 – 1970).

WARTIME PROBLEMS

Among the most immediate concerns of the president was the development of broad military strategy for successful prosecution of the conflict. As Theodore Roosevelt had feared early in the century, the United States now was engaged in a two-front war. The question facing Franklin Roosevelt therefore was whether to devote prime emphasis to a victory in Europe and the Mediterranean or to concentrate on the defeat of Japan in the Pacific. In addition, he had to fashion a network of formal and informal diplomatic contacts between the United States and its Allies to coordinate their joint wartime efforts and to facilitate close cooperation. With Great Britain this task seemed relatively easy, for Roosevelt and British Prime Minister Winston S. Churchill were on good personal terms. With scores of smaller nations the situation was similar; but with the Soviet Union's Premier Joseph Stalin, a ruthless and suspicious dictator, close mutual relations were more difficult to establish. After Hitler invaded Russia in June 1941 and embarked on a bitter war, the Soviets and the Americans became Allies by circumstance, and not by choice.

The problems created by the war at home were no less staggering. The entire economy had to be geared to wartime goals, including the supply and allocation of raw materials, industrial production, distribution, and prices. Manpower (and womanpower) had to be mobilized for the armed forces as well as for industry and agriculture. In addition, the nation's best scientific minds had to be harnessed for the overall victory effort. Understandably, such total mobilization affected the lives of most Americans and required their adjustment. It shaped their political behavior, their jobs, often determined their location, affected relations with their families as well as with scores of strangers with whom they were now thrown together in the armed forces or on the home front, and influenced their intellectual interests and their thinking. In no other conflict were Americans of all ages and from every conceivable background so profoundly involved in the wartime effort. To harness the energies of 150 million Americans at home and abroad proved to be a task of enormous magnitude.

ROOSEVELT'S MILITARY POLICIES

Early in the war Roosevelt made the far-reaching decision that the defeat of Germany should have first priority and that the Pacific theater should receive secondary attention. Within two weeks after Pearl Harbor, British Prime Minister Churchill journeyed to Washington to plan grand strategy with the American president. They agreed to emphasize the defeat of Germany while holding the Japanese at bay in the Pacific. They also agreed on close collaboration in the conduct of the war by the pooling of American and British war material, and the creation of a combined chiefs of staff and joint commands for selected areas. Naturally, only the future would tell how the grand design would be worked out in detail. As Allied military policy developed, it channeled war operations through three stages. The first period of United States participation was the era of Allied defense (December 1941 to October 1942). By 1942 Allied progress transformed this period into an era of Allied offense (October 1942 to June 1944) as the Axis powers virtually everywhere were in full retreat. The final phase of American participation in the conflict constituted an era of Allied victory (June 1944 to August 1945) when the United Nations accomplished the military victories that brought a successful conclusion to the war. As in World War I, the military contribution of the United States proved to be a vital element in the defeat of Germany and its allies.

ALLIED DEFENSE

In December of 1941 the military position of the United States was gloomy. In the Atlantic and in the European theater of war, Axis forces were exacting a frightful toll in the destruc-

tion of property and lives. Russia was reeling under the powerful blows of the Wehrmacht (German Army forces) deep inside
the Soviet Union. And German agents in the Western Hemisphere were active throughout South America stirring up hostility
against the United States.

Throughout the Pacific area during 1942 United States forces
were in retreat. After their effective attack on Pearl Harbor, the
Japanese swept into the Philippines with a large invading army.
General Douglas MacArthur commanded a small American and
Philippine Army there which held out for several months. When
MacArthur was ordered to Australia in March 1942, General
Jonathan Wainwright took over what was a hopeless cause and
surrendered to the Japanese in May of 1942. Meanwhile, the
Japanese also captured Guam and Wake islands while launching
a powerful attack against British possessions in the Far East,
capturing Hong Kong, Singapore, Burma, New Guinea, and the
Dutch East Indies. In the Battle of the Java Sea during March
of 1942, the Japanese destroyed an American and Allied naval
squadron with the exception of four United States destroyers,
which limped to Australia. The once vaunted Anglo-American
naval supremacy in the Far East suddenly seemed to have reached
an inglorious end.

By the middle of 1942, however, two major naval engagements revealed that the Allies were able to stand by their defense
positions. In the Battle of the Coral Sea of May 1942, American
aircraft from the carriers *Lexington* and *Yorktown* successfully
prevented a Japanese fleet from helping to expand Japanese power
in New Guinea. This engagement foreshadowed the great Battle
of Midway in July 1942, when Admiral Chester Nimitz's United
States naval air squadrons successfully blasted more than half a
dozen of the Japanese ships out of the water. After Midway the
Japanese navy never regained its earlier initiative.

At the same time, Allied forces found themselves on the
defensive in the Atlantic, in Africa, and in Russia. In the Atlantic, German submarines — often prowling in "wolf packs" of
more than a dozen — exacted a costly toll from Allied shipping.
During 1941 they sank at least 1000 ships, and in early 1942
they destroyed as much as 400,000 tons monthly. Gradually, the
United States Navy learned to cope with the menace. It developed
small but highly effective escort or convoy vessels; it stimulated

radar research to improve submarine detection; it converted all kinds of private vessels such as yachts into a "Hooligan Navy" to serve as a submarine patrol; and it encouraged the construction of "submarine chasers" that proved increasingly effective in hunting down Admiral Karl Doenitz's underwater raiders.

As the Germans penetrated more than 1000 miles into Russia, Premier Stalin appealed to President Roosevelt, not only for massive aid in war material, but also for the opening of a second front in western Europe to relieve German pressure on the hard-pressed Red Armies. Roosevelt did dispatch more than $1 billion worth of Lend-Lease aid to Russia in 1942 in the form of valuable supplies. But Prime Minister Churchill of Great Britain counseled the president not to agree to a second front in Europe. Instead, he urged immediate American military assistance for the British in Africa, where the German Afrika Korps under General Erwin Rommel threatened to break through weary British lines and to seize the Suez Canal. For the moment Roosevelt sided with Churchill and concentrated American aid on stopping the German advance in Africa. General Rommel began his forward thrust into Libya in late May 1942. In this crisis the United States rushed all available aid to the British, who, under General Montgomery, stopped Rommel at El Alamein by July, and defeated him there in October 1942. Meanwhile in July and August 1942, American military commanders including Generals George Marshall and Dwight D. Eisenhower and Admiral Ernest J. King counseled Roosevelt to sanction an invasion of France (Operation Sledgehammer) as the Russians were demanding. But British military leaders were adamantly and resolutely opposed to any such project. Roosevelt therefore temporarily laid aside the plan for a second front in the West and counseled joint British-American offensive operations in Africa (Operation Torch), a plan to which Prime Minister Churchill gladly agreed, while Russian Premier Stalin sulked angrily.

During the first nine months of 1942, therefore, the United States and its Allies were on the defensive. In the Pacific, the United States was driven from its possessions; and the navy lost its superiority and so left the way open for temporary Japanese hegemony. In the Atlantic, American ships ferrying men and supplies to England were vulnerable to attacks by German submarines. During most of 1942 German armies seemed on the verge of crushing Russia. In the Middle East it seemed that only a miracle could prevent the Germans from capturing the Suez Canal, thereby cutting off vital British oil supplies. For the United States, therefore, the first phase of World War II was very grim indeed.

ALLIED OFFENSE

By the fall of 1942 the tide began to turn as the strenuous efforts of the American and Allied forces inaugurated a second phase in the conduct of the war — the period of Allied offense (October 1942 to June 1944). During these months the United States largely cleared the Germans from the Atlantic; meanwhile, the Russian victory at Stalingrad turned into an attack that led to a gradual German retreat. In Africa the British decisively defeated and forced back the once threatening German forces and carried their attack forward with the invasion of Italy. At the same time the United States Navy mounted an increasingly effective offensive against the Japanese in the Northern Pacific, the Central Pacific, and the South Pacific, driving the foe back to home bases. By the middle of 1944 it became clear that the Allied offensive would result in an eventual full-fledged victory over the Axis. The former mood of apprehension felt by millions of Americans in 1942 changed to one of exuberance and hope during 1943.

The success of American efforts to combat the U-boat menace in the Atlantic was particularly striking during this period. By the middle of 1943 the aggressive and imaginative strategy of the United States Navy had virtually eliminated sinkings of American ships by roving German submarines. The extraordinary development of radar and other detecting devices, as well as large-scale construction of submarine chasers, reduced Allied shipping losses to less than 150,000 tons monthly in late 1943, and to no more than 30,000 tons monthly in the spring of 1944. By then the Allies had rendered the German submarines virtually useless as effective military weapons.

In the European theater of war, one event overshadowed all others — the Battle of Stalingrad (September 1942 to February 1943). It marked the beginning of the Russian offensive, which eventually drove the Germans out of the Soviet Union. Acting directly under Hitler's directives, German commanders were ordered to capture this strategic city at any price. Again and again the German battalions threw themselves against the stubborn Russian defenders holed up in the ruined houses of a once proud city. But the Russians were determined not to let the Germans pass. Aided by the ferocious Russian winter and by devising brilliant military strategy, Soviet General Vasili Chuikov gradually whittled the strength of the Nazi forces. Early in 1943 (February 7, 1943) the Russians turned defeat of the Germans into a rout as they captured a large German army under General Friedrich Paulus and ended the myth of German invincibility. Throughout 1943 and during the first half of 1944, the Russians began a systematic advance against the retreating Germans and virtually cleared them from Soviet territory. Militarily and psychologically the Russians became imbued with victory at the same time that the German mood turned somberly to pessimism and contemplation of possible defeat.

The Allied offensive also put the Germans to rout in Africa and in Italy. By January 1943, British and American forces captured the strategic North African port of Tripoli. American forces under Generals Dwight D. Eisenhower and Omar Bradley acquitted themselves unusually well in beating back General Rommel's strong attacks, and in the next five months drove all German and Italian forces out of North Africa. The Battle of Tunis (May 12, 1943) signified a heartening victory for combined American, British, and French armies, since it resulted in their complete mastery of this theater of the war. Coming at the same time as the great Russian victory at Stalingrad, these successes greatly bolstered the spirits and hopes of the Allies.

Hardly had the Germans and Italians been expelled from Africa when Allied military leaders began to lay plans for an invasion of Italy and the mainland of Europe. Treading warily step by step, the United States and British Expeditionary Forces moved cautiously from North Africa to Sicily, which they captured between June and August of 1943. From this island the supreme commander, General Dwight Eisenhower, planned to direct the invasion of Italy. By September 1943, King Victor Emanuel III forced Benito Mussolini to resign and appointed

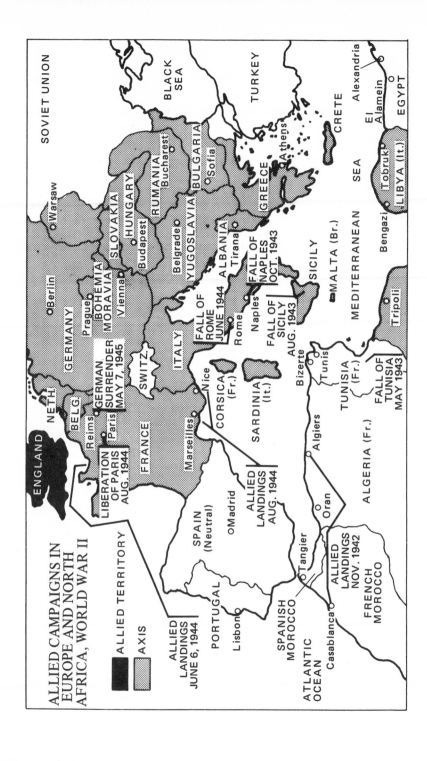

ALLIED CAMPAIGNS IN
EUROPE AND NORTH
AFRICA, WORLD WAR II

ALLIED TERRITORY

AXIS

Marshal Pietro Badoglio as Premier to negotiate an armistice with the Allies. On September 8, 1943, he concluded an agreement with General Eisenhower that took Italy out of the war. A month later Italy declared war on Germany, its former partner. This allowed the Allies to proceed with their attack on the mainland. In September and October 1943, British General Montgomery landed his troops at the toe of Italy while United States General Mark Clark advanced on Naples farther to the north. On the west coast of Italy, the Allied strategy was to detain as many German troops as possible while a major attack on Germany through a projected western front was in the planning stage. Throughout the winter of 1943, American troops encountered hard fighting and tough resistance from the Germans, especially at Monte Cassino and at the Anzio beachhead. Not until May 1944 did the Allied armies finally drive the Germans backward in sustained retreat. Perhaps the culmination of the American effort came with the capture of Rome on June 4, 1944. Although some German soldiers continued to operate in northern Italy, Allied domination of the peninsula seemed secure by that time.

Although the Allied effort to crush Germany had priority over the war in the Pacific, nevertheless the United States achieved significant victories in the Far East during 1943 and 1944. Methodically, American commanders moved to clear the Japanese from the North Pacific, the Central Pacific, and the South Pacific. In the north, where the Japanese had occupied several unimportant islands in the Aleutian chain near Alaska, American forces maneuvered skillfully so that by August 1943, the enemy troops were forced to complete withdrawal. The task of the United States in the Central Pacific was more difficult. American naval operations here centered on the Gilbert and Marshall islands. After a one-year lull in military activities, Rear Admiral Marc A. Mitscher in November 1943 led his famous Task Force 58 to attack Makin and Tarawa in the Gilbert Islands. Despite strong resistance from Japanese suicide squads, American Marines conquered the islands while United States aircraft demolished large segments of the enemy fleet in the area. The next object of attack was Kwajalein (near the Marshall Islands), which American forces seized by February 8, 1944, followed (in March) by the capture of Eniwetok, the largest of the west-

World War II in the Pacific: United States Marines landing at Guadalcanal, 1943. (UPI Newspictures. Photo by Sherman Montrose)

ern Marshall Islands. At the same time, in conjunction with Australians and New Zealanders, the Americans launched an offensive in the South Pacific. This began as early as August 1942 when a large American invasion fleet steamed on Guadalcanal near New Guinea to destroy Japanese air and naval bases. The amphibious operation was a great success, but it took more than six months of hard fighting to wrest the Japanese from some of the atolls on which they had entrenched themselves, determined to hold on or to die. At the same time, General Douglas Mac-Arthur launched an attack on the Japanese in New Guinea and in the Solomon Islands. Operations in these dense, humid jungles were exceedingly difficult; United States forces spent all of 1943 island-hopping and leapfrogging, engaging in thousands of difficult operations to drive the enemy from this area.

At the same time the United States and Great Britain unleashed a furious aerial assault on Germany that was designed to destroy its war industries and to dampen the morale of its people. By late 1942 massive fleets of as many as 1000 planes left England to let loose a veritable torrent of bombs on strategic targets and on major German cities. Between October 1942 and June 1944 Allied bombers made more than 1.5 million raids, seriously dislocating the German aircraft industry and destroying the morale of civilians; more than 300,000 Germans were killed. This "softening up" process paved the way for the ultimate defeat of Germany.

Allied operations in Europe, Africa, and the Pacific between October 1942 and June 1944 definitely placed Axis forces on the defensive. The initiative that Germany, Italy, and Japan had grasped in the early stages of the war was theirs no longer. Italy had deserted to the Allied cause. By the middle of 1944 the final outcome of the war no longer seemed doubtful, although much difficult fighting still lay ahead.

"I shall return." General Douglas MacArthur wading ashore in the Philippines, 1944. (U.S. Army photo)

VICTORY

The months between June 1944 and September 1945 saw the development of that final phase of victory for which millions of people in the Allied nations had been yearning. German submarines were virtually eliminated from the Atlantic; the Russians drove increasingly demoralized German armies beyond the boundaries of the Soviet Union; while the United States, Great Britain, and France finally opened the long-awaited second front in France. In the Far East, American forces hoped to utilize their newly won positions to strike directly at Japan and its surrounding territories. Everywhere among the Allies the smell of victory seemed in the air in 1944 and 1945, although that long-desired goal came neither easily nor cheaply.

To all intents and purposes, after June 1944 the Allies almost completely eliminated the German submarine menace in the Atlantic and concentrated on Operation Overlord (the opening of a second front). During those same months the United States suffered no shipping losses whatsoever on the sea lanes to England and the Continent. Meanwhile, early in 1944 President Roosevelt and Prime Minister Churchill agreed to appoint General Dwight D. Eisenhower as Supreme Commander of the Allied Expeditionary Forces to deliver a direct and final blow to Germany and her armed forces. After months of intensive and detailed planning, on June 6, 1944, a mighty invasion force left England for the coast of Normandy in France. With superb coordination Allied aircraft savagely pounded German installations in the area. Parachute troops landed behind the German lines while the main invasion army, soon numbering 1 million, clambered up heavily fortified beaches. This initial thrust was a great success, but much heavy fighting was still required until September, when the Allies finally drove the Germans out of France and reached the borders of the Fatherland. At the same time, in June 1944 the Russians began a massive offensive on the eastern front that left the Germans reeling. In August 1944 the Soviet armies reached the Baltic and poured into Polish territory. During the early months of 1945 they penetrated deep into Germany, with advance units just an hour from Berlin itself. Their sweep also resulted in the expulsion of Nazi forces from Bulgaria, Rumania, and Yugoslavia. The combined Soviet and Allied pincer

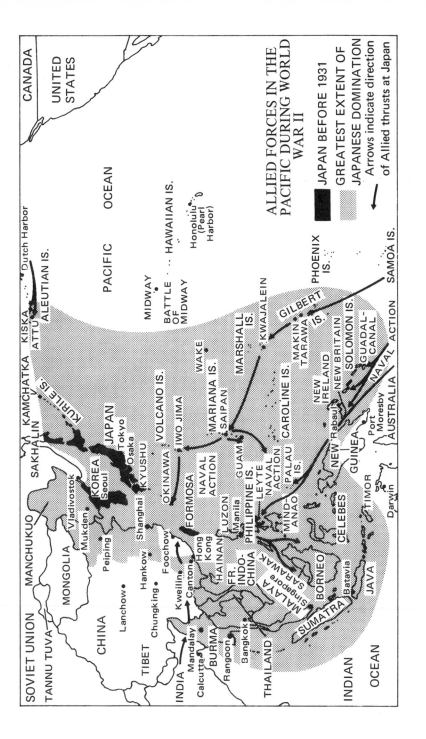

ALLIED FORCES IN THE
PACIFIC DURING WORLD
WAR II

■ JAPAN BEFORE 1931

GREATEST EXTENT OF
JAPANESE DOMINATION

Arrows indicate direction
of Allied thrusts at Japan

CANADA

UNITED
STATES

PACIFIC   OCEAN

Dutch Harbor
KISKA
ATTU
ALEUTIAN IS.

MIDWAY
BATTLE
OF
MIDWAY

HAWAIIAN IS.

Honolulu
(Pearl
Harbor)

PHOENIX
IS.

SAMOA IS.

GILBERT
IS.
MAKIN
TARAWA

KWAJALEIN

MARSHALL
IS.

WAKE

NAVAL ACTION

GUADAL-
CANAL

SOLOMON IS.

NEW BRITAIN
Rabaul
NEW
IRELAND

CAROLINE IS.

PALAU
IS.

MARIANA IS.
SAIPAN
GUAM

NAVAL
ACTION

VOLCANO IS.
IWO JIMA

OKINAWA

NAVAL
ACTION

FORMOSA

KYUSHU
Osaka
Tokyo
JAPAN

KURILE IS.

KAMCHATKA
SAKHALIN

SOVIET UNION

TANNU TUVA

MONGOLIA

MANCHUKUO

Vladivostok
Mukden
Peiping
KOREA
Seoul
Shanghai
Hankow
Foochow
CHINA
Lanchow
Chungking
TIBET
Kweiling
Canton
Hong Kong
HAINAN
FR.
INDO-
CHINA
Bangkok
THAILAND
Rangoon
BURMA
Mandalay
Calcutta
INDIA

MALAYA
Singapore
SARAWAK
BORNEO
SUMATRA
Batavia
JAVA
CELEBES
TIMOR
Darwin

NEW
GUINEA
Port
Moresby

LEYTE
PHILIPPINE IS.
Manila
LUZON
MIND-
ANAO

NAVAL
ACTION

AUSTRALIA

NAVAL ACTION

INDIAN
OCEAN

movement from the east and west effectively doomed Hitler's dream of a "Thousand Year Reich."

By the summer of 1944, United States forces in the Pacific were also girding for what they hoped would be their final drive to crush Japan. To make way for the eventual recapture of the Philippines, American commanders in the Central Pacific massed their strength to produce a great victory in the first Battle of the Philippine Sea (June 19, 1944), in which the Japanese lost 400 of their 500 attacking aircraft. Even more disastrous for the Japanese was the Battle for Leyte Gulf (October 24 – 25, 1944), where Americans destroyed most of their remaining fleet. Thus, the time was ripe for a major victory in the South Pacific, a direct invasion of the Philippines under the leadership of General Douglas MacArthur, which commenced in January 1945. More than six months of hard and bitter fighting was required before major Japanese forces could be rooted out of the difficult terrain. Late in 1944 the United States Air Force also began massive bombing raids by Super Fortresses against Japan itself, concentrating on the destruction of industrial areas as well as on large population centers. The American capture of Iwo Jima and Okinawa, two islands close to the Japanese mainland, during the first half of 1945 only intensified the terror and destruction wrought by the United States.

Americans thus lived to witness three major phases of World War II. Perhaps the grimmest was the period of defense, when Axis forces everywhere were advancing. Allied hopes were bolstered in the eighteen months after October 1942, as the period of Allied offensives presaged an eventual Allied victory. The actual accomplishment of this elusive goal came after June of 1944, when the period of Allied victory finally materialized.

ROOSEVELT'S DIPLOMATIC POLICIES

World War II further propelled the United States on the road to internationalism as military and diplomatic necessities brought an accelerated decline of isolationism as an element of United States diplomacy. President Roosevelt remembered well the debacle of Wilson at Versailles in 1919, resulting in part from his failure during the conflict to secure agreement among

Casualties of the Normandy Invasion. (Official U.S. Navy photo)

the Allies concerning postwar peace plans. He was determined not to repeat earlier mistakes as he formulated postwar policies. Yet, even with such precautions, numerous decisions made by Roosevelt as commander in chief were to come in for questioning and agonizing reappraisal.

ALLIES

Since the prime aim of the United States was to win the war, the president focused on close diplomatic collaboration with other nations, formulating two goals to attain this major objective. First, with the Allies, he sought to promote close cooperation not only in the conduct of the war, but also in planning for peace. As for the neutral nations, Roosevelt never lost sight of his major objective of victory, but sought to maintain their status as non-belligerents. During World War II, therefore, American foreign policy moved further from isolationism to international cooperation.

United States cooperation with its allies was implemented through a succession of joint agencies as well as by a series of notable international conferences. To secure military cooperation, the United States agreed with its allies to the establishment of the Combined Chiefs of Staff. This group worked out needed compromises in the formulation of military strategy and also determined the allocation of military equipment; other agencies coordinated supply. Special boards with representatives from each of the Allied powers allocated scarce raw materials, munitions, and food, and supervised merchant shipping. A third form of cooperation was developed in the Lend-Lease Program, which required representatives of the United States to work closely with those of a recipient nation.

In contrast to World War I, the United States during the Second World War fashioned close diplomatic ties with its allies. Within weeks after Pearl Harbor, America joined Great Britain, France, Russia, and four other countries in the Declaration of the United Nations (January 1, 1942), which constituted a statement of joint war aims. These included endorsement of the Atlantic Charter, a pledge to devote full military resources to the defeat of the Axis, and a promise not to enter into any possible separate peace arrangements. But Roosevelt usually pre-

ferred personal diplomacy to secure his major foreign policy
objectives and sought to knit close ties through a series of international conferences. His friendship with British Prime Minister
Churchill and his efforts to woo the steely Premier Joseph Stalin
of the Soviet Union were prime ingredients in the forging of the
Grand Alliance.

United States cooperation with its allies was facilitated by
six major conferences. The first of these was the Washington
Conference of December 22, 1941, referred to in codes as
ARCADIA, when Prime Minister Churchill came to the capital
to work out areas of Anglo-American agreement. The five points
of discussion included projection of industrial production quotas
and creation of the Combined Chiefs of Staff to coordinate and
unify joint war strategy. They also agreed to give the defeat of
Germany priority over the defeat of Japan, to work for an independent China, and agreed on independence of colonies after
the war.

A second conference came as the Allied war effort shifted
to an offensive phase in 1943, creating new problems that required diplomatic consultation. As the North African campaign
was being pressed to a successful conclusion, the Allies had to
plan the next steps in their operations. Thus, President Roosevelt and his chiefs of staff (Generals George C. Marshall and
Hap Arnold, and Admiral E. J. King) met with Prime Minister
Churchill and his military chiefs in January 1943 at the Casablanca (Algeria) Conference. Here the two world leaders agreed
to strive for domination of the Mediterranean by focusing on a
projected invasion of Sicily (and eventually Italy itself). They
deferred a second front in France, which Stalin as well as most
American leaders desired, to a later time. A second important
decision of the Casablanca Conference was insistence on unconditional surrender by the Axis. In unmistakable language, Roosevelt declared:

> The elimination of German, Japanese, and Italian war power
> means the unconditional surrender by Germany, Italy and Ja-
> pan. That means a reasonable assurance of future world peace.
> It does not mean the destruction of the population of Germany,
> Italy or Japan, but it does mean the destruction of the philoso-
> phies in those countries which are based on conquest and the
> subjugation of other people.

Generals George C. Marshall and Dwight D. Eisenhower conferring with British Prime Minister Winston Churchill in North Africa during World War II. (Courtesy British Information Services)

Roosevelt and Churchill were keenly aware that Hitler's rise to power in Germany was facilitated in part by his dubious claim that in World War I Germany had not really been defeated, but betrayed. They were determined not to let such claims rise again. Later critics of Roosevelt's diplomacy were to charge that this decision prolonged the war by stiffening Axis resistance. This meeting was followed by further discussion between Roosevelt and Churchill at the Washington Conference of March 1943, at which they agreed to support creation of another world organization, the United Nations. They also hoped to work for postwar disarmament, and decided not to oppose Russian domination of the Baltic.

Three additional conferences were planned because the greatest strains in the Grand Alliance were between the United States and Russia. This became evident especially at the Moscow Conference of Foreign Ministers in October 1943. By then, troops of the western Allies found themselves in the Italian campaign, while Premier Stalin was becoming increasingly impatient about the opening of a second front in western Europe. Only a personal meeting at the highest level could resolve outstanding issues. Under these circumstances, Roosevelt and Churchill met in Cairo in November 1943 and also invited Chinese Nationalist leader Chiang Kai-shek to join in their deliberations. Together they issued the Cairo Declaration (December 1, 1943), in which they promised the return of Manchuria and Formosa to China. Roosevelt had long wished to meet Premier Stalin, but the Russian leader had been reluctant to leave the confines of the Soviet Union. Under much urging, he finally agreed to journey to Teheran (in Iran), where on November 27, 1943, he was met by Roosevelt and Churchill. Together, the Big Three made several important diplomatic and military decisions. First, they agreed that a defeated Germany should be divided under joint Allied occupation for a time. Second, they sketched out general boundaries of Poland to include portions of East Germany. Third, they agreed that Russia would eventually enter the Pacific war against Japan. Above all, what the Russians wanted most, they got: a promise from Roosevelt to open a second front in western Europe in 1944 to relieve them of the pressures by German armies. The friendly cooperative spirit displayed by the Russians at Teheran persuaded Roosevelt that his famous personal charm could overpower even the stolid Stalin. In future months he came to rely more heavily on his personal brand of diplomacy.

NEUTRAL NATIONS

In regard to the neutral nations, too, Roosevelt developed a policy leading to closer coordination and cooperation. His prime objective was to keep them from joining the Axis powers or from impeding the Allied war effort. Thus, to the great dismay of General Charles DeGaulle, leader of the Free French (in exile), Roosevelt granted United States diplomatic recognition to the Vichy regime in France, a government headed by Marshal Henry Pétain, who collaborated with the Germans. Roosevelt hoped that this action would prevent use of the French fleet against Allied forces and would lessen possible French resistance to British and American occupation of French North Africa. But General DeGaulle, whom Roosevelt never liked, did not forget what he considered to be an affront to the Free French, and some observers felt that his anti-American sentiments during the postwar era had their source in World War II American diplomacy.

Toward Spain the United States also displayed a conciliatory attitude, although its dictator-leader, General Franco, was sympathetic to the Axis. Roosevelt hoped, however, that appeasement might prevent a Spanish attack on Gibraltar, the key to Allied shipping in the Mediterranean. Thus, the United States bought a large portion of Spanish tungsten exports while sending badly needed petroleum to Spain. Taking advantage of Spanish dependency, the United States was able to prevent it from falling into the Axis camp. With each successive phase of the war, the opportunist Franco government became more friendly to the Allied cause. In general, then, American policy of developing closer ties with neutral nations during World War II benefited the Allied war effort.

ROOSEVELT'S DOMESTIC POLICIES

Though the war focused attention on military and diplomatic events, it also made a profound impact on the American domestic scene, on life in the United States. Politically it furthered federal centralization, i.e., the growth of big government. The powers of the presidency expanded especially in time of war. To cope with the multitude of military supply problems, the Roosevelt administration created dozens of new federal executive agencies, whose task it was to harness the nation's resources for the war effort. The war created other political problems, especially those involving civil liberties of Japanese-Americans and the right of dissent. The economic impact of national mobilization also should not be underestimated, since the war decisively affected patterns of production and distribution. Social changes wrought by the conflict were understandably diverse. The war increased the mobility of millions, promised a greater measure of equality for minorities and women, and brought renewed questioning of prevailing American values. World War II also affected the intellectual life of the nation, including literature, journalism and drama, education, social sciences, and perhaps most visibly, technology and science. In one way or another, the war influenced the everyday lives of most Americans.

POLITICAL DEVELOPMENTS

Global conflict left its imprint on American politics. As Americans of various beliefs strove for the common national goal of victory, sharp party divisions were muted by necessity. The complex problems generated by the war also bred a distinct reluctance on the part of many Americans for a change in presidential leadership and led them to elect Franklin D. Roosevelt to an unprecedented fourth term. As Roosevelt noted, he was assuming the role of "Dr. Win-the-War," and was temporarily abandoning that of "Dr. New Deal."

The enormous increase of presidential powers during the war helped to bolster the president's prestige. In the congressional elections of 1942, the Republicans had made substantial gains and won forty-seven new seats in the House and nine in the Senate, leaving the Democrats with a very slim majority. Thus, the president was not at all sure of congressional support in the ensuing two years except in matters of national defense. Meanwhile, the Republicans looked forward to 1944 when they hoped to capture the White House with their new leader, Governor Thomas E. Dewey of New York. A tired President Roosevelt reluctantly agreed to run for an unprecedented fourth term to see the war effort to a successful conclusion. "All that is within me," he lamented, "cries out to go back to my home on the Hudson River."

Because Roosevelt's health was visibly waning, the party bosses were determined to dictate the selection of his vice-presidential running mate, since Henry A. Wallace was anathema to them. Their choice was Senator Harry S. Truman, chairman of the successful Senate Committee to Investigate War Expenditures and the National Defense program. Together with the president, Truman waged a vigorous, successful campaign.

During World War II political divisions were far less bitter than a generation earlier during the Wilson administration. The attitude of Wendell Willkie, the Republican presidential candidate of 1940, was symbolic. Not only did he fully support most of Roosevelt's wartime measures, but also after a trip around the globe in 1943 he wrote a moving appeal for internationalism in United States diplomacy entitled *One World*. A best-seller during the war — with more than a million copies in print — Willkie's plea for national and international harmony evoked an emotional response of approval from millions of Americans in both parties.

World War II witnessed little disloyalty and did not produce the extreme type of anti-German hysteria that had been generated in 1917. The Office of War Information under Elmer Davis, in contrast to its predecessor in World War I, the Committee for Public Information (CPI) under George Creel, used extraordinary prudence and moderation in censoring the news. And the Justice Department used similar caution in applying the provisions of the Espionage Act (1917) and the Smith Anti-Sedition Act (1940). In July 1941 the attorney general secured selection of a grand jury to investigate Nazi and fascist groups in the United States which resulted in thirty indictments against American fascists under the Smith Act. Trials were held during 1944, but two years later they were dismissed as a violation of the constitutional rights of the accused. Efforts to apply the Espionage Act to twenty-four leaders of the German-American Bund, a Nazi organization, were also fruitless, as the United States Supreme Court in 1944, in *Hartzel* v. *United States* (322 U.S. 688), decided that the attorney general would have to prove their specific intent to obstruct war activities before seeking conviction. In general, extremist groups represented few major problems during World War II. During the war the Communists and other left-wing groups suspended their opposition to the administration since the Soviet Union was an American ally. As for Nazis and Nazi sympathizers, the FBI kept a close watch on their activities, including enemy aliens who were required to register with the federal government.

Perhaps the only exception to the prudence that characterized the Roosevelt administration's campaign to secure national unity was the evacuation of Japanese-Americans from the Pacific Coast. In a wave of fear just after Pearl Harbor, Roosevelt ordered about 110,000 Japanese-Americans rounded up to be placed in internment camps in the interior. Many of them were later released but urged to resettle east of the Mississippi River. Most of these individuals were loyal, and Roosevelt incurred much criticism from civil rights advocates. But in 1944 the United States Supreme Court in *Korematsu v. United States* (323 U.S. 214) upheld the president's action.

The mobilization required by wartime necessities did much to expand the powers of the federal government. The most pressing was mobilization of manpower, which became an immediate need. With American entrance into the war, the Roosevelt administration greatly extended the Selective Service System to include men between the ages of eighteen and forty-four. About 10 million were inducted, constituting two-thirds of the total number of men and women in the armed forces.

Mobilization of the economy was even more complex and was the result of trial and error rather than of intensive planning. Strangely, many World War I experiences were not directly utilized. As early as 1939, President Roosevelt appointed a War Resources Board (WRB) composed of business executives who were to advise the War Department on plans for industrial mobilization. Two years later he created the Office of Production Management (OPM) under William S. Knudsen to assign priorities for scarce materials. To protect consumers against inflation and rising prices, in January 1942 Roosevelt established the Office of Price Administration (OPA) to impose rationing of scarce materials and to implement price control. Knudsen's success was less than anticipated, however; so the president hoped to clear up much prevailing confusion by creating a new agency in 1943 to mobilize industry, the War Production Board (WPB) headed by Donald Nelson.

The staggering task of coordinating allocation and distribution of goods was not easy without increased federal powers. Thus, Roosevelt delegated much of his own broad wartime authority to former United States Supreme Court Justice James F. Byrnes, who became director of the Office of Economic Stabilization (OES). Byrnes greatly improved coordination of federal agencies and achieved the reduction of conflicts within the wartime government organization. But the president continued to seek even greater centralization of war production and in 1944 created a super-agency, the Office of War Mobilization (OWM) under Fred Vinson, which had complete control over most phases of production and distribution in the United States. Meanwhile, wartime labor disputes and shortages were handled by the War Labor Board (WLB) and the War Manpower Commission (WMC). Scientific research was supervised and coordinated by the Office of Scientific Research and Development (OSRD), which also encouraged the atomic bomb project as well as scores of other significant war-directed scientific activities. Although the domestic mobilization program had its difficulties and often faced knotty problems, on the whole it achieved its primary objectives.

ECONOMIC CHANGES

The influence of the war upon the economy was far-reaching. It stimulated the creation of an affluent society that was characteristic of the postwar era. Industrial production reached new heights; agriculture finally enjoyed prosperity; new means of public finance were developed; and labor achieved the full employment and high wages of which it had often dreamed, but had found elusive throughout the depression.

Industrial Production

American production records skyrocketed in wartime. The GNP (Gross National Product) almost tripled between 1940 and 1945 as it rose from $90 billion in 1940 to $260 billion in 1945. Many individual industries such as aluminum had an even faster rate of growth. Other industries were virtually newly created, such as the manufacture of synthetic rubber. In almost every phase of the economy, American business was breaking new production records. In part, American businessmen were able to achieve these records because of innovation with new manufacturing techniques. One of the most daring innovators was the industrialist Henry J. Kaiser, who applied mass production techniques to shipbuilding, an industry in which he had had little experience. By prefabricating many parts, Kaiser was able to reduce the time needed to build a 10,000-ton freighter from 200 days to less than 17 days. Other companies and individuals used new methods of motivating their workers to increase their output, including financial incentives, recognition of individual achievements, and congenial work conditions. The Cleveland aircraft parts manufacturer, Jack and Heintz, became famous for such pioneering. Wartime pressures in many instances also furthered industrial efficiency. The cost of producing bombers, for example, declined by 30 per cent in 1943 compared to the preceding year; in the case of guns the decline was twice as great.

Taxation

The war also revealed the unsuspected potency of federal taxing and fiscal powers. In the first place, wartime experience underscored the efficacy of federal pump priming to achieve a high rate of economic growth. If the Roosevelt administration had not been able to bring the country out of depression between 1933 and 1939, this was largely because it spent too little and too late. Between 1941 and 1945, however, the federal government spent a great deal, and very rapidly. It poured out more than $320 billion in funds, which invigorated and stimulated the entire economy. The war also opened up hitherto unrecognized dimensions of federal taxing and borrowing powers. Between 1941 and 1945, the administration was able to raise more than $130 billion (40 per cent of war costs) from income, corporation, and excess profit taxes. The Bureau of Internal Revenue collected much of this by a new and extraordinarily effective method, the payroll deduction withholding tax. The Treasury secured the remainder by borrowing, partly through the sale of millions of war bonds. Never before had the financial powers of the federal government been displayed on such a vast scale. The war also underscored the power of government economic controls. Through price fixing and rationing, the Office of Price Administration was remarkably effective in restricting large-scale inflation. Between 1941 and 1945, real prices rose by no more than approximately 20 per cent, less than during any other war in which the United States had been engaged. World War II therefore underscored the enormous potency of deficit spending, federal taxation, and debt management and controls to restrict inflation. All of these experiences were fully utilized in the postwar years.

Agriculture

American farmers were also affected by the conflict. The war years ended the agricultural depression. Farm production in the period increased by 30 per cent as pressing new demands encouraged farmers to maximum efforts. Farm prices rose appreciably, so that total farm income more than doubled. The war encouraged greater efficiency, secured in part through mechanization, as rubber-tired tractors, corn huskers, combines, harvesters, and pick-up cotton balers helped farmers to meet unprecedented high production goals despite shortages of farm labor. In fact, increasing mechanization led to a further decline of farm population. Approximately 4 million individuals left the farms during the war years without returning, usually moving to towns and cities. In the ten years after 1940, one-half of the nation's 6 million farmers moved out of agriculture. As farming became more highly commercial, farms became increasingly bigger (by about 10 per cent in the war years) and fewer. World War II therefore accelerated many changes to which American agriculture had been subjected before 1939, especially mechanization and the flow of rural population to urban centers.

Labor

These years also witnessed great improvements in the position of the American worker. The war years demonstrated the possibilities of full employment. World War II — and pump priming — accomplished what the New Deal had been unable to achieve. Henry Wallace's dream of 60 million jobs in America — for which he had been widely ridiculed — was coming close to realization between 1941 and 1945 as employment rose from 46 million people to 53 million people. The shortage of labor proved a boon to unionization; labor organizations increased their membership from 10 million in 1941 to 15 million in 1945. The war also resulted in a rising standard of living for workers, whose real wages increased by approximately 40 per cent in the four years after 1941. Wartime conditions created greater equality and job opportunities for women and members of minority groups, who flocked to war industries in large numbers. No wonder that few strikes occurred amid such prosperity. Soon after Pearl Harbor union leaders issued a "no strike" pledge, which they and the rank and file honored more often than not. Less than 1 per cent of working time was lost as a result of strikes during the war. Labor thus achieved many of its aims in the context of the domestic mobilization program.

Review of Economic Effects

World War II was a watershed which gave rise to the affluent society that grew in America during the second half of the twentieth century. It stimulated American production records to new highs in industry and agriculture and for the first time assured virtual full employment for labor. These achievements were due in part to large-scale federal intervention in the economy on a hitherto unprecedented scale. Through deficit finance, taxation, debt management, and direct economic controls, the federal government was able to stimulate economic growth to a degree not believed possible before 1941. The lessons derived from this experience would have far-flung implications for postwar America. During World War II, Americans cast off their depression mood and viewed their future economic problems with unbounded confidence and optimism.

Science and Technology

Much of the economic prosperity between 1941 and 1945 was due to exciting developments in science and technology. Enormous achievements were noted in medicine and the development of new drugs. Ninety per cent of Americans wounded in World War II were returned to active duty — a remarkable record, since only one-third as many survived during World War I. American medical researchers made enormous strides in creating new antimalaria drugs such as atabrine compounds, and in making possible long-term storage of blood, plasma, and other blood constituents. Jungle warfare in the Pacific especially stimulated the manufacture of new and startlingly effective insecticides such as DDT (dichlor diphenyl trichloroethane). Perhaps the most remarkable new drugs produced during World War II were sulfonamides and penicillin, among the first to cure (rather than to control) infectious diseases.

Technological progress was no less spectacular. Headed by Vannevar Bush of the Carnegie Institution, the Office of Scientific Research and Development (OSRD) stimulated the improvement of weapons useful in wartime including radar, radio detection and ranging, rockets, and, of course, nuclear fission, resulting in the atomic bomb. In the effort to develop an effective weapon, President Roosevelt created the "Manhattan Project" in 1943 to coordinate the manifold activities involved in its manufacture. Hundreds of scientists worked secretly in the remote mountain area of Los Alamos, New Mexico, to develop such a device. After innumerable problems in splitting atoms and achieving nuclear fission, on July 16, 1945, they successfully exploded the first atomic bomb at Alamogordo, New Mexico, opening a new era in world history.

AMERICAN SOCIETY DURING THE WAR

Such vast technological and economic changes were bound to have a significant effect on American society. They accelerated the growth of urban America by encouraging inhabitants of rural communities to move to larger metropolitan centers. Often a direct consequence was the disintegration of family cohesion and family structure in the United States. At the same time that wartime conditions were challenging traditional social values and institutions, they tended to promote greater equality, ethnic and racial, as Americans from all walks of life were temporarily united by common goals. The civil rights movement, especially, received a boost from the surge of wartime patriotism. Thus, the war accelerated important trends in American society that had been gathering momentum even before 1941.

URBAN LIFE

World War II hastened the growth of metropolitan areas in the United States. The development of war work stimulated mobility of men and women in every section of the nation as they moved from the country to metropolitan areas, greatly swelling the number of urban dwellers. Decay of the central city — of the downtown areas — visibly grew in World War II. Three-fourths of new war plants were located in metropolitan areas with populations over 100,000 (e.g., Detroit, Washington, Chicago, Los Angeles, St. Louis, San Diego, and San Francisco). Serious shortages of men and supplies for maintenance work and physical improvement, and intensified use of downtown neighborhoods accelerated their deterioration. The influx of large numbers of war workers understandably created great strains on housing, as well as on social and community services everywhere. Higher federal taxes led to a corresponding decline of public revenues in the cities and worsened their financial situation, just as their various problems were mounting. Clashes between established residents and newcomers, the latter usually economically underprivileged and not accustomed to urban industrial life, resulted in new tensions and hostilities. The pattern was similar in most sections of the nation. But the Gulf Coast and the West proved to be unusual magnets as new opportunities in shipyards and aircraft factories rapidly opened millions of new jobs and opportunities for those who had found themselves stymied by the depression. Texas, Florida, and the West Coast states experienced an extraordinary influx of newcomers, who frequently remained there in the postwar years. Many of these people moved into suburbs. In 1940 one out of six Americans lived there; in 1945 three out of six resided in suburbia. Though World War II did not create metropolitan areas in the United States, it did a great deal to stimulate their rapid growth and exacerbate their problems.

The war accelerated changes already taking place in the American family. Whereas a tight-knit, large, patriarchal family group had been characteristic of rural areas, the urban family became a loose democratic unit in which each member contributed to the making of decisions. The service of men in the armed forces and the large-scale entry of women into war work had a direct influence on weakening the structure of the American family. Neglect of small children was reported in every part of the country, which resulted in an increase of juvenile delinquency. Expansion of day nurseries was a significant consequence of domestic mobilization, transferring an intrinsic family function outside the home. Related agencies concerned with social work, legal aid, and psychological counseling helped to assume family responsibilities in a period of changing family organization.

The war further boosted the status of women and strengthened their economic independence. The number of women in the labor force rose from 10.5 million in 1940 to 15 million in 1942. Women took over many jobs previously held only by men and served as bus or taxi drivers, welders, and factory workers.

RACE PROBLEMS

Wars — it is well known — have often acted as social equalizers. So also did World War II, which mixed America's population either in the armed forces or in moves to wartime jobs. Midwestern industrial centers and cities on the Gulf and Pacific coasts suddenly became polyglot.

Perhaps no single racial or ethnic group benefited as greatly from the movement for equality fostered by World War II as the nation's black Americans. Burgeoning war production opened new job opportunities for blacks although they did not always find it easy to secure equal treatment. Until 1941 only small numbers of black men and women found positions in defense industries. Essentially it was A. Philip Randolph who took the initiative in seeking effective action to open the doors of industry for members of his race. In January 1941 he threatened President Roosevelt with a march of 100,000 blacks on Washington to demand federal action to ensure the hiring of black people in defense plants. Under this pressure the chief executive issued his well-known Executive Order 8802 (June 25, 1941), which prohibited racial or religious discrimination in government agencies or in industries with federal contracts. He also created a Committee on Fair Employment Practices to hear complaints about violation of the order. This action had an encouraging effect in removing some — but by no means all — discriminatory practices in hiring. By 1945 almost every major industry had hired black Americans by the thousands (2 million in southern war plants alone) where they had employed but few before the war.

Although the war often heightened racial tensions, it did much to further the black American's fight for racial equality in the United States. As millions of blacks from southern rural areas migrated to the Northeast, Middle West, and West Coast to jobs in war industries, they precipitated new clashes. New York, Detroit, Cleveland, Chicago, Los Angeles, Portland, and Seattle suddenly found themselves with vastly increased black populations competing with other new arrivals for jobs and housing. The most serious race riots took place in Detroit (June 20, 1943), where twenty-five blacks and nine whites were killed before 6000 troops quelled the disorders. New York and Los Angeles had lesser disturbances.

Tension was sometimes high in the armed forces as well. In many army camps, clashes between blacks and whites broke out over discriminatory treatment. At Fort Bragg (N.C.) and Fort Dix (N.J.) serious riots ensued. At Freeman Field 100 black officers were arrested for seeking to enter a white officers' club. The rapid readjustment of racial attitudes of whites and blacks as they confronted each other in unfamiliar situations was bound to generate new tensions and anxieties.

In the armed forces segregation was still common. Although the Selective Service Act of 1940 contained a clause prohibiting discrimination in the drafting and training of men, many draft boards refused to accept black Americans. Black leaders like Walter White (secretary of the NAACP) and A. Philip Randolph (president of the Brotherhood of Sleeping Car Porters) vehemently protested to President Roosevelt and demanded equal training for blacks as for whites, as well as integration of officers. They also urged the navy and air force to abandon their rigid policies of excluding blacks. Not all of these demands were met by the administration. Black Americans were organized into separate units, usually with white officers. But the War Department organized ROTC units at five black colleges, and Benjamin O. Davies was appointed the first black man to be a brigadier general.

By 1945, 700,000 black men and women found themselves in the army, and 160,000 in the navy. They served in many branches of the armed forces and in the CB's (construction battalions). Only toward the end of the war, however, during the German campaign, did the army first integrate whites and blacks.

That the color question was arousing greater interest was reflected in the reading habits of white Americans. In 1943 Lillian Smith's *Strange Fruit,* the story of a white man's love for a black girl in a Georgia town, was extremely popular and a great success. At the same time, Richard Wright's *Black Boy,* an account of the black author's childhood in Mississippi and Tennessee, enjoyed a wide audience. Three other works with a serious analysis of race problems were also notable. Gunnar Myrdal's *American Dilemma* quickly took on the dimensions of a classic, and Charles S. Johnson's *Patterns of Negro Segregation* and Otto Klineberg's *Characteristics of the American Negro* pointed out the complexities of racism.

In fact, World War II squarely confronted most Americans with the race question. As the United States became a member of the United Nations, which included countries with many colored peoples, white Americans were brusquely confronted with their own race problems. The emphasis on national unity required by the war effort also tended to lessen racial and ethnic differences and to emphasize equality. In addition, it appeared incongruous for the United States to devote all of its resources to the defeat of Nazi Germany — guided as the Reich was by stark racist ideology — and to practice active racism at home. Nor were these factors lost among black Americans, who found a new pride along with new economic opportunities. Membership in the NAACP shot up from 100,000 in 1941 to 500,000 in 1944. Altogether, the egalitarian forces stimulated by World War II gave an enormous impetus to the movement for civil rights and racial equality.

CULTURAL DEVELOPMENTS

United States participation in World War II also left its mark on America's churches and schools. American education was never quite the same after the wartime experience. Literature and the stage, on the other hand, were not significantly affected by the momentous events of four years of conflict.

Churches

American churches bent many of their energies to support the war effort. While pacifist views were muted, ministers, pastors, and rabbis exhorted their flocks to give their best energies to the mobilization effort. In community centers most churches and synagogues were active in a variety of patriotic activities, such as conducting scrap metal drives or air raid drills. Many also threw open their doors to servicemen and expanded their recreational programming in order to serve members of the armed forces. In contrast to the Korean imbroglio of 1950 and the war in Vietnam after 1965, when many churchmen vigorously opposed the nation's foreign policies and military commitments, in World War II the clergy with very few exceptions was virtually united in its enthusiasm for the Allied cause.

Education

The war brought a significant change in education. Quite understandably, enrollment in the nation's colleges and universities dropped precipitously as only women and those rejected by the armed forces were able to pursue college studies. On campus after campus, therefore, course offerings were restricted to a minimum. Many of the faculty who were not in the armed forces sought to contribute to the war effort. Scientists, social scientists, and specialists in other fields worked on government projects, taught special classes for the army, navy, or air force, and developed new techniques of education. Those innovations affecting accelerated language training were most striking. Developments in teaching foreign languages (e.g., by use of tapes and recordings) were stimulated by the armed forces' need to train men and women in several dozen new tongues with which Americans now came into contact. The armed services also applied mass production methods of education, particularly in teaching large numbers of men with the aid of machines, or audiovisual technical equipment, such as movies. Psychological tests used by the army for classification of intelligence, vocational guidance, or jobs often had such merit that schools, colleges, and corporations used them widely in succeeding years.

In the nation's high schools the war prompted efforts by educators to make their curriculum more relevant to young people by allowing them greater choice in course selection and by emphasizing a world view rather than a parochial national outlook. The emphasis on relevance and immediate usefulness also led to the introduction of new courses, such as preflight aeronautics and home nursing. Even so, high school enrollments declined, largely because more than 3 million youngsters between the ages of 14 and 18 chose to work at well-paying jobs (compared to 800,000 in 1940). Educators then sought to make the schools even more relevant to the community life around them by developing work-study programs with nearby factories.

Perhaps it was in the nature of modern warfare that it affected even the lives of little preadolescent children. Many of these were left virtually parentless, as their fathers served in the armed forces while their mothers spent much of the day (or night) with wartime jobs. Thus, millions of children did not receive the care or security previously found in the close circle of a peacetime family. In response to this problem, many communities and agencies greatly increased the number of child care centers in the country as a large number of young mothers took jobs in war factories and elsewhere. With the loosening of family cohesiveness between 1941 and 1945, such nursery schools became an important adjunct of primary education in the United States.

Literature and Drama

As the war became an increasing preoccupation of millions of Americans, their reading habits changed accordingly. Intense interest in various phases of military and diplomatic aspects led to a great popularity of reportorial accounts. In quality these were usually far superior to the novels of the war years, most of which were undistinguished.

Americans gained different perspectives of the war by reading a wide range of non-fiction. During 1941 one of America's outstanding foreign correspondents, William L. Shirer, gave his dramatic first-hand impressions of the Nazis and their aims in his best-seller, *Berlin Diary*. No less popular was Joseph E. Davies' *Mission to Moscow,* a personal and revealing account of a former American ambassador's experiences in the Soviet Union. By 1943 the great popularity of Wendell Willkie's *One World* reflected the further abandonment of isolationism by Americans. As the United States became more intimately embroiled in the military war, reading tastes followed accordingly. Millions of people avidly read Major Alexander de Seversky's *Victory through Air Power,* a somewhat overenthusiastic plea for reliance on air power as the key to victory. They alternately laughed and cried over Private Marion Hargrove's intimate account of army life as American youths saw it in his *See Here, Private Hargrove,* which sold almost 3 million copies. Eyewitness accounts of Americans in battle were also read loyally by the civilians at home. William L. White's *They Were Expendable* chronicled the exploits of American P-T boats in the Philippines; Richard Tregaskis's *Guadalcanal Diary* recorded the first American victories in the Pacific. But the writer who best captured the imagination of millions by focusing on the daily life of the average American G.I. fighting man was a shy, small, self-effacing correspondent, Ernie Pyle. More than any other writer at the battlefront, he brought the drama as well as the drudgery of war into American homes, rich and poor. Among soldiers themselves, no one captured their mood more effectively in text and sketches than Sergeant Bill Mauldin in his cartoons for the Army Journal *Yank* and his book *Up Front.* Accounts such as these provided human, personal glimpses of the war for most Americans who stayed at home.

World War II did not produce great novelists. Some of the best fiction writers of the decade — Ernest Hemingway, John Dos Passos, William Saroyan, Theodore Dreiser, and Pearl Buck — either served as correspondents in the armed forces or were silent. John Steinbeck's *The Moon Is Down* was severely criticized for its mild-mannered attitude toward the Germans. Perhaps the most skillful war novel was *A Bell for Adano,* John Hersey's sensitively told story about the American occupation of an Italian town.

United States soldiers in World War II themselves were probably better read than any Americans in previous conflicts. The Armed Service Editions of hundreds of books made reading materials available for G.I.'s everywhere. More than 100 million copies were sent overseas (1943 – 1945), even to the most remote outposts. Few realized at the time that the army was inaugurating the paperback revolution that was to sweep the United States in the postwar years.

In their theaters, too, Americans focused on wartime situations. One of the sprightliest and most popular musicals about the war was Irving Berlin's *This Is the Army,* with an all-army cast, which opened in New York on July 4, 1942. Through song and dance, it well conveyed the average man's mixed feelings and emotions about the armed services and the willingness of most Americans to take the bitter with the sweet. Far less successful was Moss Hart's *Winged Victory,* which was frequently oversentimental in seeking to convey its patriotic message. Very few serious plays about the war had any great success, and no one wrote or produced an outstanding drama. Among the lesser productions, *Tomorrow the World* enjoyed some popularity (later as a movie). It chronicled the re-education of a young Nazi boy in an American home. Maxwell Anderson's *Eve of St. Mark* (1943) told the story of a rural New York farm boy who became an army hero in the Philippines. In 1944 *Jacobowski and the Colonel* played to full houses. Its plot involved a shrewd Jewish refugee and a Polish colonel, both fleeing before the Nazis. Lillian Hellman's *Searching Wind* was an indictment of appeasement, a play in which the message was more defensible than the plot. On the whole, the American stage produced little of merit during World War II (with the exception of Irving Berlin's musical) and captured few of the emotions or morals generated by the war.

In. part, perhaps, this record was due to the vividness that moving pictures brought to the public. In 1942 *Mrs. Miniver* sentimentally acquainted American audiences with wartime conditions in England during the Blitz. Later in the year when the United States was fighting in Guadalcanal, *Wake Island* brought Americans face to face with the nature of war in faraway Pacific islands. Meanwhile, the classic *Casablanca* focused on North African intrigues in that newly emerging theater of conflict. Patriotic sentiments were stirred by Warner Brothers' *Air Force* and *Guadalcanal Diary,* realistic portrayals of American fighting men in action. *Mission to Moscow,* the movie version of Ambassador Davies' book, sought to present favorable impressions of the Soviet Union. The image of the war that Hollywood presented to the American public was not always starkly realistic, but it did convey some sense of the complexity of global conflict to civilians. The documentary films were grimmer, however. By 1944 *With the Marines at Tarawa* unabashedly showed just how much ferocious fighting was necessary to conquer Japanese outposts; *The Battle for the Marianas* and *The Memphis Belle,* an account of United States bombing missions over Germany, were also extremely well produced. More than the theater, moving pictures provided a major means for communicating the realities of war to the folks back home.

EFFECTS OF WAR ON DOMESTIC LIFE: SUMMARY

Few aspects of life in the United States between 1941 and 1945, therefore, were left unaffected by the epic struggle in which the United States was engaged. Domestic mobilization stimulated the growth of bureaucracy and the federal government and temporarily muted party differences. The economy was jolted out of depression to achieve new heights of production and mass distribution. Prosperity led to a consequent change of mood — from gloom and pessimism to anticipation and optimism. American society was thrown into a maelstrom of turmoil as millions moved to large urban centers where they often changed their ways of life. Perhaps this transition was more marked among black Americans than among whites, since wartime conditions whetted their desire for equality. To a degree these momentous changes in American life were mirrored in cultural activities such as religion, education, literature, and drama. In World War II, not only soldiers, but also civilians became intimately involved in the massive effort to achieve victory.

WORLD WAR II — THE FINAL PHASE

By the spring of 1945 the Allies saw their goal of military victory in sight and were beginning postwar preparations. American, British, and Russian armies were rapidly closing in on Germany from the west and east in Europe, slowly but surely crushing the once vaunted German war machine. German surrender, on VE day, came on May 7, 1945, to the jubilation of Allied capitals throughout the world. Next, the United States turned its full might on Japan. Much heavy fighting was expected, but detonation of the first atomic bombs over Hiroshima and Nagasaki cut short a possible prolonged conflict. On the diplomatic front, Allied leaders hastened plans for the creation of a functioning United Nations organization and for another high level meeting to deal with the rapidly changing situation.

YALTA CONFERENCE

As early as 1945 the military successes of the Allies presaged a victory; these created new and pressing problems within the Alliance, which required another meeting of the Big Three leaders. The immediate political future of Poland and Germany, as well as of Italy and Greece, called for decisions at the highest level. In addition, Roosevelt hoped to make the United Nations (UN) a functioning organization, for he was well aware of Wilson's debacle with the League of Nations just after World War I. At the Dumbarton Oaks Conference (in Washington, D.C.) in September 1944, the United States had clashed with Russia concerning voting procedures, and this new controversy required an early resolution. Although extremely tired after the grueling presidential campaign of 1944, President Roosevelt felt sure that a face to face encounter with Premier Stalin would allow him to resolve most issues. The Russian leader was unwilling to stray far from his homeland, however, for he felt himself to be indispensable to the Russian war effort. Thus, the Big Three leaders ultimately agreed to meet early in February 1945 at the seaside resort of Yalta in the Crimea (Russia). There they gathered to deal with some of their most pressing problems.

At the Yalta Conference the Big Three Allied leaders deliberated about three major problems concerning the postwar map of Europe. After considerable wrangling, they developed a compromise regarding Germany. First, they agreed to the creation of four occupation zones (United States, Russia, Great Britain, and France) to be administered by an Inter-Allied Control Commission. Second, they agreed on the desirability of keeping Germany divided, although specific details of such a plan were left to future negotiations. A third issue concerned reparations. Roosevelt and Churchill opposed Stalin's demand for $20 billion from Germany and managed to secure his agreement to the establishment of a Reparations Commission to determine a specific sum. In a cordial atmosphere, these compromise agreements appeared to foretell close Allied cooperation.

The second major problem, relating to the re-establishment of an independent Poland, was more difficult. The Big Three worked out boundaries according to which the Soviet Union was to receive portions of east Poland, while Poland was to secure parts of east Germany. Compromise on the establishment of a government for Poland occasioned some dispute. Stalin favored recognition of the Lublin regime, a pro-Communist Polish government installed by the Red Army in Lublin. On the other hand, Roosevelt and Churchill urged recognition of the London government, a pro-western group of Polish leaders in exile who had functioned in London throughout the war. Much haggling led to a Yalta Compromise, according to which the Lublin government was to be reorganized to include non-Communists. For this purpose the Russians promised to allow free elections in Poland — a promise they did not keep.

The Big Three at Yalta also settled some of their differences over the United Nations. After some discussion the Russians agreed to an American proposal to include all countries in the United Nations who were at war with Germany, thus providing the United States with a sizeable group of supporters. The Russians gave up their claim to sixteen votes in the Assembly (based on sixteen states in the Soviet federation) and yielded on some technical points concerning use of the veto power by members of the Security Council.

Some knotty controversial problems regarding the Far East also required the attention of the Big Three at Yalta. Stalin demanded Japan's return to the Soviet Union of the Kurile Islands, which Russia had lost in 1905. He also demanded American recognition of Russian interests in Outer Mongolia and in Manchuria. Stalin was willing to sign a treaty of friendship with Nationalist China and to recognize its sovereignty over Manchuria. He promised to bring Russia into the Pacific War against Japan soon after the European fighting ceased. As critics soon pointed out, Roosevelt had no right to bargain away Chinese possessions and was offering much while receiving little in return. But Roosevelt was convinced that he had won the good will of the Soviet dictator, and was laying a firm foundation for close Soviet-American friendship in the postwar era. This he deemed necessary for the welfare of the United States and, indeed, the entire world.

EUROPE

Meanwhile, during the early months of 1945 the final drama of the war in Europe was to take place in Germany and Poland. Under General Eisenhower American armies had driven forward rapidly through France since their landings in June of 1944 until they encountered surprising stiff German resistance in December 1944. Then they had to fight for their lives at the Battle of the Bulge but ultimately they bested the Germans and continued their drive eastward, reaching the borders of Germany in March 1945. Meanwhile, Soviet armies in the east had broken German lines by early 1945 and were rapidly pouring into Bulgaria, Poland, Hungary, Rumania, Yugoslavia, Czechoslovakia, and Austria. At almost the same time that American forces reached the German borders in the west (March 1945), the Russian armies had swept through Poland to reach Germany's boundaries in the east. As Americans and Russians seemed poised for a race to Berlin, General Eisenhower issued a fateful order to the armies under his command to halt at the Elbe River. The American general was concerned about the overextension of his supply lines and about capturing Hitler's retreat at Berchtesgaden near the Austrian border. Thus, although United States troops could have been the first to enter Berlin, this symbolic triumph was left to the Russians. In addition, in the face of very strong Russian demands, General Eisenhower restrained his dynamic General George S. Patton, Commander of the Third United States Army, from moving his men with lightning speed into Czechoslovakia, and into its capital, Prague. Not all Allied leaders were aware of the political consequences of these decisions, nor were they apparent to many individuals at the time. But Winston Churchill clearly saw the implications of Soviet domination of central and eastern Europe. Perhaps his warnings would have been heeded at this crucial moment if President Roosevelt had not succumbed to a coronary thrombosis on April 12, 1945, just when these fateful problems required decisions.

The fall of Berlin was but a prelude to the final surrender of Germany. On April 16, 1945, the Russians launched a violent attack on the German capital, which fell on May 2, 1945. During these weeks most Nazi leaders left Berlin, but Hitler remained in his underground bunker there, seeking to rally the forces of his crumbling Reich and exhorting Germans to fight to the bitter end. On April 23, Field Marshall Hermann Goering, heir designate to the Fuehrer, announced that he would take charge of the German government — an act which Hitler considered treasonable. Instead, he designated Admiral Karl Doenitz, commander of the German Navy, as his successor, and vowed that he would not be captured. On April 30, 1945, together with his long-time friend Eva Braun, Hitler committed suicide in his secret bunker, where the Russians later found his charred remains. Representatives of the Doenitz regime immediately approached the Allies about surrender. General Eisenhower was firm in demanding capitulation on all fronts. On May 7, 1945, German General Alfred Jodl signed the articles of unconditional surrender at General Eisenhower's headquarters in Reims and so made the Allied defeat of Germany official. Occupied by United States, British, French, and Russian troops, Hitler's vaunted "Thousand Year Reich" lay prostrate.

FAR EAST

The surrender of Germany allowed the United States to turn all of its awesome might against Japan. American plans for the conquest of Japan were methodical and effective. After securing control of the sea lanes to the Philippines in the Central and South Pacific, American commanders planned the recapture of the Philippine Islands and further island-hopping, to culminate in a direct invasion of Japan. On October 20, 1944, American troops under General Douglas MacArthur landed on Leyte in the Philippines. They were covered by strong naval forces under Admirals Thomas C. Kincaid and William F. Halsey, who destroyed a large Japanese fleet in the Battle of Leyte Gulf (October 25, 1944). Although the conquest of the entire archipelago was to take more than six months, American occupation allowed the establishment of new air bases close to Japan. In November 1944 the United States Air Force began a systematic campaign to destroy aircraft and other munitions factories on the Japanese mainland with its B-29 Super Fortresses. In March 1945 the B-29's dropped their new type of potent firebombs, which wreaked great havoc among the civilian population in large cities, where more than 300,000 lost their lives. Meanwhile, the American push to Japan inexorably continued. In February 1945 United States Marines fought savage battles on the tiny isle of Iwo Jima to oust Japanese defenders and gained possession of the island and its airfields at great cost. Six weeks later (April 1) American forces swarmed over Okinawa, an island only a little more than 300 miles from Japan itself. Because of Japanese suicide tactics — as exemplified by Kamikaze planes — Okinawa was not secured until the last week of June. The desperate efforts of Japanese defenders and the high toll of American lives they exacted, despite their awareness of impending doom, chastened the essential optimism of American commanders in the Pacific.

The great question in the minds of American leaders during the spring of 1945 was whether a full-scale United States invasion of Japan would be required to force unconditional surrender. Within Japan, army generals favored a fight to the death, whereas the emperor and many of his followers hoped for an early peace. Appealing to Russia to act as a mediator, in May 1945, the emperor openly gave voice to his desire for peace, but in succeeding months was unable to control the war hawks. Under these circumstances President Harry Truman made the fateful decision to use the atomic bomb, the terrible new weapon that American scientists had just made operational. On August 6, 1945, a B-29 dropped the first A-bomb in history on Hiroshima, killing more than 80,000 people and exposing many more to the lethal effects of radiation. On August 9 an American plane dropped another A-bomb on Nagasaki, where it caused similar destruction. The emperor asked for peace on the following day. On September 2, emissaries of the Japanese government signed the articles of surrender on board the battleship *Missouri* anchored in Tokyo Bay as General Douglas MacArthur, supreme commander of the Allied powers in the Pacific, looked on. At last, V-J day had arrived to bring World War II to its formal end.

WORLD WAR II STRATEGY — THE GREAT DEBATE

Inevitably some of the momentous decisions made by Roosevelt and the Allied leaders came in for criticism during the war and after. Four issues in regard to the European theater of war were most frequently discussed. First, was the decision to demand unconditional surrender of the Axis wise? Second, was Roosevelt's attitude toward the Russians naive? Third, was the opening of a second front in the west a mistake? Fourth, did Allied military policies contribute to Communist domination of central Europe? Certainly, Roosevelt and the Allies had many difficult issues to resolve and the broad ramifications of so many of Roosevelt's decisions laid them open to careful scrutiny and examination.

Nagging doubts about Roosevelt's Far Eastern policies also concerned many observers. Was America's China policy realistic? Was it wrong for the United States to encourage Russian participation in the war against Japan? Perhaps the greatest single question concerned American use of the atomic bomb. Was this really necessary? One theme ran through a whole range of questions such as these. Roosevelt's policies seemed to be guided primarily by short-range military objectives rather than by long-range political goals. Indeed, this was a fatal characteristic weakness of United States diplomacy during World War II.

UNCONDITIONAL SURRENDER OF THE AXIS

Roosevelt's decision to demand unconditional surrender from the Axis was controversial. Critics argued that this policy may have strengthened Axis determination to resist, and thus lengthened the war. Defenders of the administration's stand often noted, however, that Roosevelt consciously sought to avoid Wilson's mistakes in World War I. The conditional surrender of Germany in 1918 led Hitler to claim during the inter-war years that Germany had not really been defeated, but stabbed in the back and betrayed. A second point made by the critics was that insistence on unconditional surrender unified the Germans and the Japanese and discouraged internal dissent. To this many advocates of Allied unity replied that insistence on unconditional surrender was a psychological necessity to keep Allied powers unified, especially since Russia was wary of a possible separate Allied peace with Germany. A third stricture of Roosevelt's policy was that the complete destruction of the German government created a political vacuum which the Soviets were only too eager to fill. And yet, could the Allies compromise with thousands of Nazi officials, who, with great enthusiasm, had proudly murdered and gassed more than 6 million innocent civilians?

ROOSEVELT AND RUSSIA

It has been charged that Roosevelt's attitude toward the Russians was based on an idealism that harbored misconceptions. On the other hand, Stalin's views concerning the United States were founded on stark realism, and the use of power politics. A strong believer in personalized diplomacy, Roosevelt felt sure that his much vaunted charm could win over the supposedly icy Soviet dictator. Yet, Stalin was moved less by personal considerations than by long-range and impersonal Russian objectives. Roosevelt also thought that the Communists had definitely abandoned their long-time goal of world revolution, when, in fact, the Soviet leaders only suspended it during the war.

A SECOND FRONT

Another questionable decision was the American preference for the opening of a second front in France, a step of which the British, led by Prime Minister Churchill, were extremely dubious. Roosevelt and his chief advisors, Generals George C. Marshall, Dwight D. Eisenhower, and Secretary of War Henry Stimson, believed that an Allied invasion of France would shorten the time needed to crush Germany, that it would relieve the hard-pressed Russians by forcing the Germans to scatter their forces, and that it had geographical advantages since primarily it entailed a land war. Such reasoning emcompassed a short-range emphasis on a quick end to the military conflict. British opposition to the plan was based on long-range political considerations, however. Churchill felt that an Allied invasion of Mediterranean areas, particularly the Balkans, was more desirable. Not only would it entail naval operations, which promised to be less costly in toll of human lives, but also it would place Allied armies in the Balkans, where the Russians would otherwise seek to increase their influence through exertion of their military power. Thus, a Balkan invasion would accomplish two objectives. It would divert the Germans from their rear where they were weak. At the same time, it would provide a barrier to Russian Communist expansion in the Balkans. Perhaps it was for this reason that Premier Stalin strenuously opposed the British position and argued avidly for the American plan envisaging an Allied invasion of the west.

ALLIED MILITARY POLICIES

Finally, the American decision in April 1945 to refrain from capturing Berlin and Prague — and instead to let the Russians have the first opportunity to occupy these crucial cities — has often been seriously questioned. Primary responsibility for issuing the specific orders belong to General Eisenhower, who was swayed by military rather than by political considerations. Always cautious, General Eisenhower feared the possibility of a strong German attack, especially since he was concerned about the overextension of his supply lines. In addition he was anxious to avoid a direct confrontation between large American and Soviet armies, lest an incident provoke violence between the two unsteady allies. Moreover, the Russians had strongly intimated that they considered Czechoslovakia to be in their sphere of influence and would not tolerate a United States army of occupation there. But that experienced and worldly statesman, Winston Churchill, loudly lamented General Eisenhower's failure to capture Berlin and Prague before the Russians. Not only would such an action have provided an enormous boost to American prestige throughout the world, but it would have given the Allies some voice in the reconstruction of central and eastern Europe instead of leaving this area almost entirely under Soviet domination. Churchill's pleas to Eisenhower, and to the ailing president, were to no avail. Thus, the United States let slip a unique opportunity to play a strong role in the stabilization of Europe in the postwar era.

Roosevelt's Far Eastern policy continued to come in for heavy criticism. The president himself believed that a direct United States attack on Japan would exact a heavy cost in American lives, if resistance on the Pacific islands was an indication. A simultaneous Russian attack would divide Japanese energies and make a final blow easier and quicker to administer. Opponents of his view charged that the president was acting on outdated intelligence information regarding the real strength of Japanese forces and that Soviet aid — secured by concessions which constituted a heavy price — was unnecessary. Indeed, it tilted the balance of power in the Far East in favor of the Communists.

Even more stringent were the critics of American policy toward China. Throughout the war, Roosevelt sent supplies and advisors to General Chiang Kai-shek, leader of Nationalist China, to help him combat both the Japanese and the Chinese Communists. By this action, Roosevelt hoped to help in the creation of an independent democratic Chinese state. But American aid was too little and too late, the critics charged, and United States efforts to mediate between the Nationalists and the Communists, through the missions of Patrick Hurley (1943) and General George C. Marshall (1945), were fruitless. In fact, such straddling only strengthened the hands of the Chinese Communists.

Possibly the most far-reaching decision during World War II was President Harry S. Truman's order for use of the atomic bomb against Japan. Truman acted on the best advice available to him. His informants counseled this action because they were sure that it would hasten the end of the war, and that it would save an untold number of American lives. Opponents charged that by August 1945, Japan was already militarily defeated and that the bomb did little to hurry the war's conclusion. Much was also made of the moral issue in loosing such a terrible weapon upon humanity. Finally, some observers questioned the diplomatic wisdom of the step. With Japan so utterly defeated, a power vacuum was created in the Pacific which the Soviets were eager to fill. A prostrate Japan, many argued, eased Communist expansion in the area.

Thus, the far-reaching military and diplomatic decisions made by Presidents Roosevelt and Truman during World War II came in for close scrutiny. Many of the critics felt that American policy had emphasized short-range military considerations rather than long-range diplomatic factors, thereby laying the groundwork for innumerable new problems of the postwar period. The decision to strike at Germany through France, rather than through the Balkans, and General Eisenhower's command to American troops to halt at the Elbe served as examples. In the Pacific, the administration's unrealistic stance toward China and its eagerness to bring Soviet Russia into the fight against Japan were further examples of mistakes. A seasoned statesman such as

Churchill was well aware of the limitations of United States policy. But Roosevelt and many American leaders were pragmatists and therefore were most immediately concerned with a successful conclusion of the war.

IMPACT OF WORLD WAR II

Though World War II did not produce revolutionary changes in American life, it had a profound impact on the United States and set the stage for the postwar world. It gave the military establishment a more prominent place in public affairs than it had ever had before. It further weaned American diplomacy from isolationist impulses and made international cooperation one of its major premises. And at home the war strengthened the tendencies toward Big Government and bureaucracy, toward a highly centralized, sophisticated, industrial and technological economy, toward greater social and racial equality, and toward new levels of scientific and cultural achievements. World War II served as a link between depression America and the affluent society of the postwar world. By accelerating the pace of change in the United States, it phased out the industrial society while ushering in the new technological society characteristic of America during the second half of the twentieth century.

FOR FURTHER READING

Summary descriptions of military and diplomatic events of the period can be found in ROGER W. SHUGG and HARVEY DeWEERD, *World War II: A Concise History* (Washington: The Infantry Journal, 1946) and LOUIS L. SNYDER, *The War: A Concise History, 1939 – 1945* (New York: J. Messner, 1960). An interesting pictorial record is *Life's Picture History of World War II* (New York, 1950). Critical appraisals of American military and diplomatic policies are in HANSON W. BALDWIN, *Great Mistakes of World War II* (New York: Harper, 1950) and KENT R. GREENFIELD (ed.), *Command Decisions* (Washington: U.S. Department of the Army, Office of Military History, 1960). The voice of the New Left is represented by GABRIEL KOLKO, *The Politics of War: The World and U.S. Foreign Policy, 1943 – 1945* (New York: Random House, 1968). The classic narrative of the conflict is WINSTON S. CHURCHILL, *The Second World War*, 6 vols. (Boston: Houghton Mifflin, 1948 – 1953). A stimulating analysis that defends the Roosevelt policies is HERBERT FEIS, *Churchill-Roosevelt-Stalin: The War They Waged and the Peace They Sought* (Princeton, N.J.: Princeton University Press, 1957). Historians have as yet written little about the impact of the Second World War on domestic life. Brief surveys of mobilization include ELIOT JANEWAY, *The Struggle for Survival* (New Haven: Yale University Press, 1951) and BRUCE CATTON, *The War Lords of Washington* (New York: Harcourt, Brace, 1948). JAMES PHINNEY BAXTER III, *Scientists Against Time* (Boston: Little, Brown, 1946) surveys wartime scientific research. Some of the workings of the military-industrial complex are detailed in RAY S. CLINE, *Washington Command Post: The Operations Division* (Washington: Department of the Army, Office of Military History, 1951). A contemporary estimate of social and cultural trends is JACK GOODMAN (ed.), *While You Were Gone: A Report on Wartime Life in the United States* (New York: Simon & Schuster, 1946). ARNOLD M. ROSE, *The Negro in America* (New York: Harper & Brothers, 1948) is an abridgment of GUNNAR MYRDAL'S classic study, *An American Dilemma,* 2 vols. (New York: Harper & Brothers, 1944). Social tensions are touched upon in FRANCIS E. MERRILL, *Social Problems on the Home Front* (New York: Harper & Brothers, 1948). Some aspects of black American economic problems are treated in ROBERT C. WEAVER, *Negro Labor* (New York: Harcourt, Brace, 1946). MORTON GRODZINS, *Americans Betrayed* (Chicago: University of Chicago Press, 1949) tells the story of Japanese-Americans in wartime. A glimpse of educational problems is obtained through I. L. KANDEL, *The Impact of War upon American Education* (Chapel Hill: University of North Carolina Press, 1948).

10

THE AGE OF REVOLUTION
The United States, 1945-1970

The period between 1945 and 1970 witnessed a veritable revolution in American life. This era saw not only the opening of the atomic age, but also another major transformation of American civilization. Prior to the war Americans had looked back to the experiences of the preceding half century for guidance; after 1945 they looked forward and sought to adjust ideas and institutions to six major revolutions. Pre-eminent was the technological revolution as reflected in the development of automation and computers. In turn, it ushered in an economic revolution that resulted in creating the affluent society. Economic change also prompted a social revolution that tended to further egalitarianism and to make this period an age of the common man. Partly out of this transition came a powerful black revolution as black Americans aggressively demanded full equality. Most of these far-reaching transformations were taking place in the nation's metropolitan areas, stimulating what amounted to an urban revolution. A large majority of the American people (nine out of ten) now came to be urban and suburban rather than rural dwellers. As never before, the problems of the city came to be the problems of America itself. Since urban areas were also the centers of cultural life in the United States, the throbbing pulse of change also triggered a cultural revolution, dominated by the rise of mass culture. No wonder that the sixties witnessed a wide generation gap, since middle-aged Americans were puzzled by a contemporary America that differed so much from the America of their own youth in the thirties. The United States had been transformed by six revolutions.

TECHNOLOGICAL REVOLUTION

If the technological revolution that swept America in the twenty-five years after World War II was neither new nor sudden, the speed with which it engulfed American society was unprecedented. In addition, its impact on various aspects of American life was more profound than at any previous time. Two products of the technological revolution which seemed especially important were automation and mass produced computers.

Perhaps the harnessing of atomic energy was no less significant, but its non-military uses between 1945 and 1970 were restricted, and its widespread application as a source of power lay in the future.

AUTOMATION AND COMPUTERS

Automation burst upon the American scene during World War II as it accelerated the development of mechanical devices as substitutes for human effort. In its simplest form between 1945 and 1970 automation involved the use of machines to operate other machines. It resulted from the invention of mechanisms and electronic devices to control machines or conveyors, feedback systems, and computers. The latter machines, designed to simulate the human mind, were used during the war to provide automatic control of aircraft, turrets, missiles, and torpedoes. After 1945 engineers and scientists developed automation in a more highly sophisticated form and applied it to complex manufacturing operations, attaining new standards of quality, precision, and efficiency.

The principles that underlay automation included mechanization, the use of continuous processes, automatic feedback controls, and the rationalization and integration of diverse processes. Mechanization involved the use of machines rather than human labor for the performance of work tasks. The use of continuous processes was particularly marked in various phases of mass production in which the application of assembly line techniques operating in connected sequences had a striking effect in boosting the quantity as well as quality of goods. Automatic controls operated on a feedback principle, so that the input of a machine could be regulated by its output. The rationalization of processes required the application of appropriate scientific or engineering knowledge to fit particular social needs.

The growth of automation in the postwar period was rapid. In 1955 there were perhaps no more than fifty computer systems in the United States. Five years later more than 11,000 computers were in use, and by 1965 more than 20,000 were busily at work. At least 8000 of these machines were engaged in the solution of scientific or engineering problems; the others accomplished innumerable administrative or clerical chores.

Application of automation to production processes revolutionized the speed, the quality, and the quantity of goods produced in the United States during the second half of the twentieth century. Three types of factory automation became common: automatic production machines such as lathes; automatic process control machines, used to replace human operators (as in oil refineries or chemical plants); and automatic materials handling equipment that transported finished or semifinished products from one place or machine to another. Most of these forms of automation were increasingly operated by electronic computers using magnetic tapes, punched cards, or automatic sensing devices like photoelectric cells that simulated human sight, hearing, or feeling. In Ford's Cleveland engine plant, for example, one man operated a transfer machine that performed over 500 operations. Before the computer age, thirty-five to seventy men had been required for the task. And in the same factory, by 1968, forty-eight men with automated machinery made one engine block in twenty minutes, whereas ten years earlier it took 100 men twice as long. Similarly, in a Chicago radio plant in 1960 two men assembled 1000 radios daily, a chore performed by 200 men before automation. Automation thus made possible large-volume mass production.

Automation also revolutionized American offices — and the white-collar workers in them. Both analog and digital computers were introduced during this period. Analog computers translated problems and consequent solutions into mathematical terms; digital computers solved problems by counting at lightning speed, much like adding machines. By 1960 the Bank of America possessed a computer capable of 237,000 additions and subtractions per minute. This machine serviced almost 200,000 loans daily and provided accurate reports about them for management. Several hundred clerks had been required to perform the same job before the computer age. The United States Treasury — which issued 350 million checks in 1960 — also replaced 450 clerks with a computer to provide for an accurate accounting of its expenditures. A large corporation such as the Sylvania Electric Products Company was able to process its payroll for 26,000 persons by operating a computer for less than half an hour weekly. Similarly, the Chesapeake and Ohio Railroad used one of its computers one hour weekly to prepare 90,000 quarterly dividend checks for stockholders. Most large companies and government offices computerized their inventory control systems. By 1970 almost all of the 500 largest corporations in the United States had automated data processing, and thousands of smaller companies were engaged in the process of automating at least a portion of their operations.

ECONOMIC IMPACT OF AUTOMATION

The economic impact of automation on the American economy was considerable. Most obviously, it increased productivity and output per man-hour. This varied greatly in different types of operations, ranging from a modest 5 per cent increase in some fields to a thousandfold increase in others. Whatever the variations, however, automation greatly boosted productivity in most fields of enterprise. Automation also resulted in greater quality and uniformity in goods produced, thereby improving productive efficiency. It caused less waste and breakage and required less handling than manual operations. Many factories reported that the adoption of automation resulted in a declining proportion of imperfect products, from 25 per cent to 5 per cent. Automation also tended to centralize management and decision-making in most businesses since coordination of many diverse mechanical processes required greater integration, centralized direction, and control.

SOCIAL IMPACT OF AUTOMATION

Hardly less significant was the social impact of automation. Sometimes it led to temporary unemployment as machines replaced scores of unskilled or semiskilled workers, many of whom required guidance and training before they could enter some other occupation. Automation also widened the gap between top management

Automated factory, 1963. (Wide World Photos)

and labor, whether white- or blue-collar workers. The distance between executives and employees in the hierarchical administrative structure of large organizations was as great in private corporations as in governmental agencies. The small creative group of decision-makers who occupied the leading positions in large enterprises comprised an elite quite separate from the technicians and routine administrators who filled posts in middle management and workers in offices, or on the assembly line. More than ever, the gulf between them widened as technical knowledge and creativity of the highest order were required for the supervision of complicated automatic processes.

The consequences of automation for individuals were far-reaching. With the further reduction of hours in the working week, mechanization increased the amount of leisure time available to most people. By 1970 this proved to be a mixed blessing because many Americans were ill prepared to make constructive use of the increased amount of time at their disposal. For some it created a crisis in spiritual values. After all, the Puritan ethic had dominated American values for centuries. And the Puritan ethic related morality to hard work, frugality, and thrift, characteristics which automation seemingly made obsolete. Automation often increased monotony for millions of workers on production lines or in offices, perhaps leading them to seek outlets for their frustrations in drugs or drink. Performance of a purely mechanical operation on the job stifled creativity of individuals. Machines often pre-empted outlets for even modest forms of self-expression, leaving workers frustrated, bored, and unhappy. They sometimes left individuals without a sense of status, self-respect, human dignity, or identity. Automation, therefore, tended to heighten personal conflicts and tensions, and at times even forms of mental illness. The effects of automation clearly transcended purely economic considerations and reached into the everyday lives of most Americans, altering interpersonal relationships.

ECONOMIC REVOLUTION

In the quarter century after World War II the United States entered upon a period of unprecedented economic prosperity. During the Great Depression of the thirties most Americans had been preoccupied with economic stagnation and scarcity; after 1945, rapid economic growth brought affluence to a majority of Americans, at the same time spotlighting the poverty of a significant minority. The gross national product rose from approximately $275 billion in 1945 to almost $1000 billion in 1970 (allowing for inflation of the dollar). These were decades of relatively full employment, with an average of 5 per cent or less unemployed each year. Consequently, per capita income rose from $1350 per person in 1945 to $1845 per person in 1960, and to more than $2000 per person in 1970. Enormous increases in national consumption of consumer goods reflected the material well-being of the majority of Americans. In 1950 they had spent $191 billion for such goods; by 1967, they spent $492 billion.[1] For the first time in world history, a civilization appeared to be capable of satisfying many of the material wants of its citizens.

THE AFFLUENT SOCIETY

What factors brought about this abundance? Above all, the technological revolution played a major part in creating affluence in the United States. Scientists and engineers, often themselves

[1] *The World Almanac and Book of Facts, 1969* (Garden City: Doubleday, 1969), p. 124.

conservative by nature, ironically wrought revolutionary changes through their discoveries and improvements. Mechanization of manifold processes in production and distribution made an unprecedented volume of material goods available to large numbers of Americans. Among the innovations that contributed to this material well-being were the rapid development of automation feedback techniques, data processing by means of computers, and a variety of new electronic devices. Such means increased output per man-hour by more than 50 per cent between 1945 and 1970. Other reasons for affluence included organizational and technical skills of businessmen and corporate managers, and a highly efficient labor force. Nor should the influence of government be ignored. It is doubtful whether America's rate of economic development between 1945 and 1970 would have been as striking if it had not been for large-scale federal spending. In fact, between 1945 and 1970 the percentage of federal expenditures in relation to the GNP more than doubled, providing a major stimulus to economic growth. That some of these outlays were prompted by foreign crises and military involvements did not lessen their impact on the domestic economy. Industrial expansion was also stimulated by the absolute growth of the nation's population after World War II, from 140 million people in 1945 to 210 million people in 1970. In this truly remarkable era, Americans achieved a level of material abundance that was only a remote dream to most other peoples of the world.

Businessmen, farmers, and organized labor especially profited from more than two decades of prosperity in post – World War II America. Corporate profits almost doubled in this period as corporations paid larger dividends to an increasing number of stockholders (totaling as many as 25 million people). Farmers shared in the prosperity, though to a lesser extent. Those with medium-sized or large properties made the greatest profits, but improvement of the standard of living also affected many smaller operators. During these years more than 90 per cent of the nation's farms were supplied with electricity, refrigerators, and automobiles. Workers, too, made substantial gains. Union membership grew from 14 million in 1945 to 20 million in 1970 as labor organizations secured higher wages, job security, pension plans, and medical benefits for their members. For a majority of Americans, then, the two post – World War II decades brought unprecedented affluence.

Problems of the Affluent Society

The affluent society was not without its problems, however. Among its consequences was persistent as well as precarious inflation, a growing concentration of economic power in the hands of a few giant corporations, and an increasing imbalance between expenditures in the private and in the public sectors of the economy. Inflation became chronic, partly as a result of the large expenditures that Americans made for consumer goods. This outlay increased at a rate twice as rapid as incomes. Almost one-half of all consumer expenditures were made on the installment plan, thereby creating one important source of economic uncertainty, and promoting spiraling prices as demand outreached supply. And few politicians during these years were willing to sanction drastic tax or income redistribution plans to reduce demand.

Another possible source of economic instability in the two decades after 1945 was the continued growth of oligopoly. Technological advances and automation often tended to foster bigness in business. The years between 1945 and 1970 witnessed more than 3000 corporation mergers involving companies whose assets exceeded $10 million. By 1970 the 200 largest corporations in the United States secured 30 per cent of all corporate profits; and of twenty-six major industries surveyed, one-half were dominated by one, two, or three giant companies. Such concentration led to a decline in competition and the increased practice of "administered prices," which introduced another potentially unstable element in the national economy.

A third problem of affluence concerned the imbalance between private and public goods. In the two decades after 1945 Americans spent their increased incomes primarily for more consumer goods, including TV sets, automobiles, and scores of appliances. This investment in material goods was in part made at the expense of services designed to improve the quality of human life. Meanwhile, poor housing, polluted air and streams, inadequate health services, congested roads and streets, and increased crime were lessening the enjoyment of living by millions of Americans. Economist John Kenneth Galbraith first pointed to the paradox between material opulence in the United States, on the one hand, and increasing dissatisfaction or unhappiness on the other. This was due partly to an uneven emphasis on expenditures for consumer items and a consequent neglect of spending for the improvement of society. The question which he posed was profound: Did Americans wish to invest their wealth in material things or in human beings, in luxuries and gadgets or in the improvement of individuals? Could they strike a better balance than they did in the two decades after World War II?

Perhaps the most glaring problem of the affluent society was its seeming insularization of poverty. In addition to the affluent America, which included as many as two-thirds of the nation, there was another America composed of poor people — possibly as many as 50 million people. Not that poverty was new. But in earlier years, as in the Great Depression, poverty had affected a wide cross section of the nation and was starkly familiar in every portion of the country. In an affluent society, however, poverty appeared to be more insulated. While an increasing majority of affluent Americans moved to the suburbs after World War II, poor people came to concentrate in urban ghettos, in remote rural areas, and in depressed regions such as Appalachia. Poverty thus became less visible but not less serious. Indeed, individuals caught in the culture of poverty who became enmeshed in its vicious cycle found that to escape it in a highly technological society was far more difficult than in a less complex economy a generation earlier.

So affluent America in the fifties and sixties had a choice: it could spend its wealth on still more consumer goods, or it could use a portion of it for the improvement of the individuals caught in the throes of poverty in the hope of making them happier and more productive citizens.

POVERTY

Who were the poor, the inhabitants of that other America? A large proportion of America's aged, those people over sixty-five years old, found themselves among the poor, numbering as many as 8 million people. Poverty also affected the young, however. At least 11 million children (under eighteen years) were caught in the poverty cycle with little hope of breaking out into the world of affluence. Also swelling the ranks of America's poor were the technologically unemployed, often men over forty years old whose jobs had been taken over by machines or, as in the case of coal miners, rendered obsolete by technological advances. A similar predicament was faced by the rural poor as the mechanization of agriculture placed small farmers and tenants into an increasingly precarious financial situation. Finally, a substantial portion of the poor belonged to racial or ethnic minorities, particularly black Americans.

The Aged

After 1945 the United States had an increasing proportion of citizens over sixty-five years of age, many of whom were forced to live in poverty. As medical advances lengthened life expectancy (for males from 60.8 years in 1940 to 66.7 years in 1956 and an expected 70 in 1970, and for females from 65.2 years in 1940 to 73 years in 1956 and an expected 77 in 1970), the percentage of older people grew, so that in 1970 they constituted almost 12 per cent of the total population, compared to 4.1 per cent in 1900, or 2.5 per cent in 1850.[2] In the rural agricultural society of nine-teenth-century America, many older people had lived out their last years in the circle of their families. There they found them-selves among children and grandchildren who afforded them a measure of security and companionship. But in the urban civil-ization of the twentieth century, older persons frequently had no homes, no money, no friends or relatives. Even their grown children were often scattered from one end of the country to the other. In a nation that venerated youth, their reward after a lifetime of toil often was to achieve the status of an outcast. Loneliness, isolation, illness, and economic want were the major burdens of more than 9 million Americans in this group. A congressional report in 1960 noted that "at least one-half of the aged cannot afford today decent housing, proper nutrition, adequate medical care, preventive or acute, or necessary recreation." In 1958 almost 60 per cent of the aged had annual incomes of less than $1000, well below the $1500 required for minimum subsistence. Only one-half of those over sixty-five qualified for some form of social security payments, and those who did in 1960 averaged no more than $900 yearly. Some of the poor had been poor all their lives,

[2]See the interesting tables in U. S. Bureau of the Census, *Historical Statistics of the United States — Colonial Times to 1957* (Washington: U. S. Government Printing Office, 1960), p. 25.

and unable to save for their last years; others had known greater prosperity during their working years, but were forced to part with their savings because of illness. Persons with incomes near or below the poverty line had four times as many sicknesses as the well-to-do.

It has been argued, however, that the number of aged poor in the United States increases if displaced workers over fifty years old are included in the group. Unskilled or semiskilled farm or industrial workers over fifty who lost their jobs due to technological progress or obsolescence rarely found comparable employment thereafter. To all intents and purposes, American society had little use for their labor, and many were condemned to spend their remaining years in idleness or in low-paying jobs. No wonder that they often had strong feelings of inadequacy and rejection.

Young People

Along with the aged, children constituted another portion of the other America. Most of them were sons and daughters of the poor. Their numbers grew because of the high birth rate prevalent among poverty-stricken people, the lower rate of infant mortality, and the inducements to large families offered by an irrational public welfare system. Consequently, between 1945 and 1970 persons under eighteen comprised roughly one-third of the poor. Starting life with inherited poverty, a significant percentage of this group was likely to remain entrapped in the culture of poverty and to perpetuate it. In addition to their lack of aspiration stemming from their parents or from broken homes, they faced the employment market of a highly complex technological society that demanded increasingly higher educational requirements for most jobs. And most poor youngsters failed to take advantage of such educational opportunities as were available to them. But often educational facilities within their reach were inferior to those serving more affluent Americans. Children of the poor also grew up with less medical and dental care than children of parents with higher incomes. This was another disadvantage that tended to perpetuate their life in poverty. By 1970, therefore, the United States contained a significant concentration of young people who seemed destined to succumb to hereditary poverty. Their background, measured against the needs of a technological society, appeared only to perpetuate their status.

Technologically Unemployed

Another segment of the poor were the technologically unemployed. These included miners in Pennsylvania, West Virginia, and Kentucky, for example, whose jobs were abolished by machines or a declining demand for coal. Unfortunately, their skills were not transferable to other occupations. Some found opportunities in other industries or were retrained. But many of those over forty years of age could not find new employment, or secured unskilled jobs at very low wages. Still others stayed at home while their women went to work. Such situations often led to increased family tensions, as well as crushed pride and gloomy spirits. In addition to coal miners, workers in some mass production industries that were automated between 1950 and 1970 had similar experiences. The proportion of blue-collar workers in the labor force declined from 59 per cent in 1929 to 45 per cent in 1960. Between 1953 and 1959 alone, automation eliminated more than 1.5 million blue-collar jobs. Many of these displaced workers did not move to other areas because they lacked job skills which were in demand, or because of personal ties to their locality. In this manner "depressed areas" such as Appalachia came into being. But whether or not they moved elsewhere, they came to constitute a sizeable component of the American poor.

Rural Poor

That a highly urbanized society would concern itself largely with urban problems and neglect the rural poor was understandable. Not easily visible to city dwellers, the rural poor included migratory workers, farm tenants, and small independent farm owners in low-yield areas like Appalachia, some portions of the South, the Rocky Mountain states, and the Pacific Northwest. Farmers with little capital found it increasingly difficult to compete successfully with larger and more efficient agricultural units. In 1954, 32.2 per cent of the nation's commercial farms — about 1 million — were low-income properties. Of the poor farm families 50 per cent had insufficient diets or suffered from an infant mortality rate well above the national average. They also had less access to adequate educational opportunities and health care than slum dwellers in the cities. Possibly the plight of migrant farm workers was most serious. Numbering about 200,-000, they included not only native white Americans, but also

Mexicans, Mexican-Americans, Filipinos, and black Americans. Many of them were concentrated in California's vast fruit and vegetable fields, whose enormous need for seasonal agricultural labor exceeded that of any other state. But field hands could also be found toiling in the eastern states. Wherever they were, however, they worked for pitiable wages, lived in substandard shacks on insufficient diets, and were rarely able to send their children to good schools (if they went at all). And when these children sought to break out of the vicious pattern of rural poverty by moving to the cities, they found that their inadequate educational training made them ineligible for most available jobs, so that they quickly sank into the lowest strata of the urban poor.

Minorities

A substantial number of the poor — about one-fourth — were black Americans. Whatever the reasons for their poverty, racial prejudices of whites were a contributing factor. Until 1960 new economic opportunities for blacks were far more limited than those for whites. And the heritage of poverty made it difficult for blacks to compete even where the racial barriers were few. In the 1950's, wages of black workers were about three-fifths of those of whites; they held only 4 per cent of professional positions, and only 9 per cent of skilled industrial jobs. But almost one-half of black males occupied semiskilled or laborer's jobs, twice as great a percentage as the whites. Forty-three per cent of nonwhite families lived in poverty, contrasted to 16 per cent of whites; 9 per cent of the black population had incomes totaling less than $1000 annually, compared to only 3 per cent for the whites.[3] Concentration of black Americans in southern agriculture only made the extent of poverty among them deeper.

Thus, by 1970 the richest nation in the world was squarely confronted with large-scale poverty within its own borders. Between 1945 and 1970 Americans combined automation with managerial skills to create mass production industries on an unprecedented scale. For the first time in history, the United States found itself with the capacity to abolish poverty and want. But mere plenitude did not necessarily lead to equitable distribution of wealth. Among

[3] A good discussion of black poverty can be found in Michael Harrington, *The Other America* (New York: The Macmillan Co., 1962), pp. 72 – 82.

those who did not share in the affluence were many of the aged and the young, displaced workers in town and country, and many black Americans. The challenge of America in 1970 was to bring the benefits of material abundance to these disadvantaged groups.

THE BLACK REVOLUTION

Among the poor, black Americans proved to be the most vocal in seeking to better their position in American society during this period. Their efforts resulted in the movement for racial equality after 1945, which represented one of the most profound social upheavals in the American experience. Until 1865 blacks were slaves; between 1865 and 1945 they endured a status as second-class citizens; after 1945 they strove aggressively for full equality with white Americans. This revolutionary surge was not accidental. Rather, it was a product of new conditions and influences both at home and abroad. Like most revolutions, this one evolved in stages, with some of the results not yet apparent. But one fact was clear to white America in 1970 — in the future black Americans would be loath to accept the subordinate role that had been assigned to them before the outbreak of World War II.

REASONS FOR THE BLACK REVOLUTION

The reasons for the black revolution were varied and revealed domestic as well as foreign influences. On the international scene, the ousting of colonial powers from the Dark Continent, and the emergence of native independent states in Africa, had a profound impact on black Americans, giving them a new sense of racial pride. If native Africans could throw off the yoke of their white oppressors, why could not dark Americans? Moreover, why should they not determine their own destinies instead of deferring to whites? In addition, the ideological conflict between the United States and Communist powers in the postwar world placed racial relations in an altered context. If Americans were sincere in supporting democracy and freedom, as opposed to Communist totalitarianism and oppression, then it was time for them to practice what they preached at home.

In addition to these international influences, the black revolution was fired by profound changes on the American domestic scene. The impact of technology on the American economy was fundamental as mechanization of agriculture in the South eliminated millions of farm jobs once performed by rural blacks in the region. Unemployed and uprooted, these masses migrated to the great industrial cities of the Northeast, Middle West, and Pacific slope where burgeoning industries promised greater job opportunities. Sometimes high hopes for economic improvement were met, but often they only led to unattainable aspirations or disappointments. Yet in little more than a generation the technological revolution transformed a predominately southern rural proletariat into a nationally distributed urban proletariat. Consequently, black Americans found themselves concentrated in the cities of the East, Middle West, South, and West in large numbers. Those who held good jobs suddenly found they could wield economic power as a group, which they hoped to turn to their advantage. Even those without means, or on the public welfare rolls, discovered that they could at least exert political power to implement many of their demands. In either case, urban blacks of the post – World War II era were able to assert themselves more effectively, either as individuals or in groups, than poor disfranchised rural southern black Americans had ever been able to do before 1939.

Other forces also stimulated the black revolution. World War II, which greatly accelerated the influence of technology, created many new jobs in wartime industries that proved to be magnets for black Americans in the South. Wartime service also tended to bolster the self-confidence of many black people as they acquitted themselves well in responsible positions in and out of the armed forces. Those who had tasted a measure of equality while in uniform were loath to surrender it upon returning to civilian life.

The black revolution was also encouraged by federal and state laws designed to lessen discrimination. The Fair Employment Practices Commission created by President Roosevelt in 1941 prompted thousands of employers to hire black men and women when otherwise they would have been reluctant; and by 1960 twenty-two states had established similar agencies. Housing discrimination was often lessened when military authorities placed pressures on communities to further integration. Of vital importance was the attitude of federal and state courts in lessening discrimination. In various southern states and localities, federal judges ordered white election officials to enter black Americans on the voting rolls — a right that had been denied them for many decades.

Perhaps the most important judicial landmark in lessening racial discrimination during the two decades after World War II was the United States Supreme Court's decision in *Brown* v. *Topeka* (1954), which ordered gradual racial integration of all of the nation's public schools. Commenting on the issue, Chief Justice Earl Warren declared:

> In approaching this problem, we cannot turn the clock back to 1868 when the [Fourteenth] Amendment was adopted, or even to 1896 when *Plessy* v. *Ferguson* was written. We must consider public education in the light of its full development and its present place in American life throughout the Nation. Only in this way can it be determined if segregation in public schools deprives these plaintiffs of the equal protection of the laws.
>
> Today, education is perhaps the most important function of state and local governments. . . . Today it is a principal instrument in awakening the child to cultural values, in preparing him for later professional training, and in helping him to adjust normally to his environment. In these days it is doubtful that any child may reasonably be expected to succeed in life if he is denied the opportunity of education. Such an opportunity where the state has undertaken to provide it, is a right which must be made available to all on equal terms.
>
> We come then to the question presented: Does segregation of children in public schools solely on the basis of race, even though the physical facilities and other "tangible" factors may be equal, deprive the children of the minority group of equal educational opportunities? We believe that it does.[4]

Altogether, the technological changes resulting in the mechanization of agriculture and further expansion of industry (accelerated by World War II), growing racial pride and awareness by black Americans themselves, and the gradual commitment of federal and state governments to the lessening of racial discrimination gave impetus to a black revolution of increasing intensity.

[4]From Brown v. Topeka, 347 U. S. 483 (1954), 492–3.

Stages of the Black Revolution

Between 1945 and 1970 the black revolution evolved through three stages. In the decade after World War II, the United States witnessed the blossoming of a civil rights movement that emphasized legal action through courts and legislators to achieve integration. Shortly after the *Brown* v. *Topeka* (1954) decision many blacks and their white supporters embarked on the second phase of the black revolution, which focused on nonviolent resistance. Led by the dynamic Reverend Martin Luther King, they aroused the sympathy of millions of white Americans. After 1964, however, another shift in the drive for equality became discernible with the emergence of a black power movement. Many of its leaders rejected integration as a goal, instead advocating separatism and, at times, also violence. If there was one trend that characterized these diverse stages of the black revolution in the quarter of a century after 1945, it was increasing militancy, the ultimate result of which in 1970 was still uncertain.

Civil Rights Movement

The civil rights movement was led by several well-established black leaders and organizations. In the forefront were the National Association for the Advancement of Colored People (NAACP) led by Roy Wilkins, the Brotherhood of Sleeping Car Porters headed by A. Philip Randolph, and the National Urban League under Whitney Young. The prime emphasis of these leaders — and the organizations they represented — was integration through legal means. They encouraged lawsuits to secure full-fledged voting rights, to bar discrimination in employment, housing, or in the use of public facilities, and above all, in public education. The high point of their campaign came in the United States Supreme Court's decision in *Brown* v. *Topeka*. Using the findings of social science research, Chief Justice Earl Warren, speaking for the majority on the Supreme Court, declared that segregation had harmful effects on personality development; separate educational facilities therefore could never be equal. The Court left it to lower tribunals to work out detailed schedules for the actual accomplishment of school desegregation in the South and elsewhere over a period of years.

Nonviolent Resistance

The second phase of the black revolution — the period of nonviolent resistance — was characterized by a change of leadership and program. Although the NAACP did not cease its efforts in the courts, newspaper headlines during these years were increasingly captured by other organizations and their leaders. Most

Martin Luther King. (Wide World Photos)

prominent was the Southern Christian Leadership Conference led by the Reverend Martin Luther King of Birmingham, Alabama, and the new Congress of Racial Equality (CORE) headed by James Farmer. They advocated nonviolent resistance as a prime means for attaining their demands, which included the complete integration of public facilities and equality of treatment elsewhere. King, in particular, developed new modes of nonviolent protest and passive resistance such as boycotts, sit-ins, mass picketing, and freedom rides. In 1955 he organized the Montgomery (Alabama) Improvement Association to carry out a one-year boycott by the city's black community against the local bus company to secure integration. Within a year, as paying passengers declined by more than 40 per cent, the bus company agreed to integrate seating on its vehicles. Another new tactic was the sit-in, first utilized by King at lunch counters in Greensboro, North Carolina. His followers sat in eating establishments for hours and even days, disrupting normal business, until the owners agreed to serve blacks as equally as whites. This tactic was widely used in restaurants, hotels, parks, and swimming pools throughout the nation. It succeeded in desegregating many facilities that had previously refused service to black Americans. Another method used was the freedom ride, which gained popularity for about three years after 1961. College students especially were attracted by this form of protest, which saw thousands of civil rights advocates from all sections of the nation, both white and black, converge upon the southern countryside, and into towns or cities. Their prime purpose was to integrate segregated facilities through sit-ins, picketing, and protest marches. During summers many of the freedom riders also actively engaged in the registration of black voters. Such efforts by whites and blacks were fired by a spirit of moral fervor and enthusiasm which reached its apogee in the great civil rights march on Washington in the summer of 1963. More than 100,000 supporters gathered in the capital in July 1963 to march in unison to the Lincoln Memorial to dramatize their support of the civil rights bill then pending in Congress.

Black Power Movement

The third stage of the black revolution came after 1964 with the rise of the movement for Black Power. The success of the civil rights advocates in achieving greater legal equality for black Americans, as well as the limitations of civil rights laws in achieving immediate improvements in the everyday lives of urban ghetto dwellers, were some of the factors behind the shifting emphasis. Another was increased black racial consciousness and pride. They sought to rely less on whites and to assume prime responsibility themselves for gaining true equality in the United States. Perhaps the rise of Black Power was also due to frustrated expectations, as the visions of immediate wealth and power held by millions of black citizens were not realized by the mid-sixties. And the abandonment by urban black Americans of the old Negro subculture developed in the nineteenth-century South, in which black churches had played a dominant role, left a vacuum that Black Power advocates sought to fill.

The rise of Black Power was characterized by the emergence of new leaders. To be sure, many of the civil rights advocates of the fifties, men like Martin Luther King, Roy Wilkins, and Whitney Young, continued to be active, but the imagination of many of the younger black generation was clearly captured by young, revolutionary, activist firebrands. Already in the 1950's the Black Muslims, a small group of black racists who rejected integration in favor of separatism, had won an increasing number of followers. Led by their dynamic chief, Malcolm X, they focused on arousing an intense black nationalism and hatred of whites among black Americans. Malcolm X was assassinated by one of his own followers in 1965, but the seeds of racial consciousness which he sowed were taken up by others.

After 1960 the Black Power movement revealed two distinct factions — one wing advocating violence, the other nonviolence. Among the former the inaptly named Student Non-Violent Coordinating Committee (SNCC) led by Stokely Carmichael (a West Indian) and H. Rap Brown was prominent between 1964 and 1968. These revolutionaries preached the need for violence as the best means for achieving black power and influence in America. After 1968, as SNCC influence waned, a similar program was carried on by the militant Black Panther movement headed by Eldridge Cleaver, author of the best-seller *Soul on Ice.* Among the nonviolent Black Nationalists, intellectuals like Harold Cruse, author of *The Crisis of the Negro Intellectuals,* were prominent. Unlike the activists who urged rioting and insurrection,

Cruse and his followers advocated the formulation of ideologies and goals that would aid black people to improve their status.

Although the programs of the various activist Black Power groups differed in detail, they shared several common assumptions. Unlike the civil rights organizations of the fifties that sought integration, the prime goal of the Black Power advocates was separatism. They eschewed mixing with whites but espoused black nationalism to embrace cultural, economic, political, and social activities. Second, many (not all) Black Power leaders preached direct action and counseled the use of violence. Whereas civil rights leaders urged action within the framework of American institutions, Carmichael, Brown, and Cleaver admired revolutionaries like Fidel Castro, Ernesto ("Che") Guevara, and Mao Tsetung, and openly advocated the destruction and overthrow of the entire framework of American society. In the third place, Black Power proponents rejected what they considered to be the hypocritical values and beliefs of democracy. Instead, they advocated a vague authoritarian totalitarianism which to them embodied ideals of what they considered to be a true participatory democracy.

On the other hand, Black Nationalists like Harold Cruse had somewhat different aims. Their purpose was to provide a coherent philosophy for black Americans that would enable them to realize their full potentials within the context of American society. In particular, Cruse urged three immediate goals. He urged black Americans to form new political parties to promote their special interests; he proposed the formation of new self-help organizations by black Americans such as consumer cooperatives, tenants' unions, and educational groups; and finally, he hoped that black Americans would develop cultural nationalism to give expression to various talents and aspirations. Black Nationalists of Cruse's persuasion therefore did not advocate the destruction of existing American institutions, but rather the creation of new ones to allow fuller expression by the nation's 20 million blacks.

RESULTS OF THE BLACK REVOLUTION

Each phase of the black revolution left its own distinctive mark on American life. The primary achievement of the civil rights movement was to secure legal action by the courts, legislatures, and executives, which provided a springboard for further advances in succeeding decades. Such legal action included favorable court decisions, not only the landmark case of *Brown* v. *Topeka* (1954) but also decisions in the lower courts that effectively ruled denial of voting rights, segregation in schools and in public facilities, and racial discrimination by private employers to be illegal. The civil rights advocates also lobbied effectively in Congress and state legislatures for laws to lessen discrimination. By 1960, twenty states had created Fair Employment Practices Commissions, and more than forty states had laws to prohibit discrimination in housing or other public facilities. The NAACP also kept up its pressure on Congress and the White House. Despite the recommendations of President Truman's Committee on Civil Rights for stronger civil rights legislation (1949), the conservative Republican-Democratic coalition in Congress was loath to act. In 1951 President Truman himself took the initiative of issuing an executive order to end segregation in the armed forces, a significant step in the movement to abolish racial barriers.

During the period of nonviolent resistance the pace of change quickened. Between 1955 and 1964 most public accommodations such as hotels, restaurants, and amusement areas in many areas of the South and elsewhere abandoned discriminatory practices against black Americans. At the same time, private employers, especially the large corporations, made special efforts to recruit black Americans, particularly for white-collar jobs. Whereas Jackie Robinson had been the first black player in major league baseball in 1950, ten years later there was not a single team in the American or National League that did not have black Americans on its roster. Nonviolent resistance also appeared to speed the pace of legal action. The Civil Rights Act of 1957 helped to increase the number of black voters in the South, especially after black and white activists conducted concerted voter registration drives. Perhaps the high point of this phase of the black revolution came with congressional passage of the Civil Rights Act of 1964.

The results of the Black Power movement between 1964 and 1970 were not as readily discernible. That it greatly stimulated racial consciousness and pride among black Americans is indisputable. "Black is beautiful" became a common slogan that was reflected in various manifestations of behavior. Black Americans began to wear their hair "natural" rather than to tame it in order to approximate that of whites. They often wore African dress and jewelry, and expressed interest in African languages as well as songs and dances. Increasingly, younger black Americans evinced great curiosity about their origins and their history. Almost everywhere, in public schools as well as in universities, they demanded black American history courses, which became more common toward the close of the decade. At the same time, many black Americans professed a preference for "soul food," the staples of the South's poorest economic class, such as chitterlings, pig's knuckles, corn pone, and fried chicken. After 1964, an utter fascination with their own unique cultural history and background gripped millions of black Americans, many of whom had once considered themselves only a dim and inferior shadow of white society.

In its more violent manifestations, black racial consciousness — fueled by white racism and other frustrations of ghetto dwellers — reflected itself in urban riots, which came with increasing frequency and intensity. In 1964 racial tensions in New York City's Harlem erupted in looting, arson, and widespread attacks on whites. Similar disturbances, such as in the Watts area of Los Angeles (1965), often spearheaded by young men and adolescents, were more serious. Twenty-five people were killed, and more than $2 million in property was destroyed in Watts. If nothing else, this riot focused the attention of Americans everywhere on some of the problems facing black slum dwellers.

In succeeding years the "long, hot summers" were marked by even greater violence. Amid cries of "kill whitey" and "burn, baby, burn" Detroit in July of 1967 erupted in one of the worst racial disorders within memory. As hundreds of buildings were set ablaze by enraged black Americans, thousands poured into the streets to loot and pillage all kinds of stores. Governor George Romney called out the National Guard to quell the disturbances in which scores of blacks and whites were killed or injured. Similar riots, although on a smaller scale, rocked more than 100 other cities in July and August of 1967, making it a year of urban insurrections.

From a minority protest movement in 1945, the black revolution had evolved to confront white America with one of its major problems by 1970. Generated by forces within and without the United States, the revolution successively focused on civil rights, nonviolent resistance, and black power. During these years its cumulative impact was considerable. In 1945 most black Americans believed themselves to be politically impotent; they felt excluded from most white-collar jobs and the professions; they experienced daily discrimination in public facilities; and they were formally segregated in many areas of the nation. Though they did not attain full equality by 1970, they had made considerable progress toward this goal. Their political power constituted a potent balance in many states and cities. A variety of jobs and job-training programs were now available to them, and discrimination by most public places had been abandoned. The road to equality was long and hard, but between 1945 and 1970 black Americans traveled on it for a considerable distance.

THE SOCIAL REVOLUTION

Social unrest was not confined to black people, however, but also manifested itself in white society. Between 1945 and 1970 many Americans could see and feel that the nation was undergoing a veritable social revolution. Everyday relationships between people in the United States were obviously changing. The causes for this shift are not hard to find. The impact of automation, the expansion of big corporations, new styles of urban and suburban living, the growth of black militancy, and the influence of the mass media all fostered a vast social transformation. It was reflected in a growing emphasis on egalitarianism, and a de-emphasis on ethnic, social, or economic distinctions. Related to this tendency was a growing trend toward conformity in many phases of American life. Another distinctive social characteristic was the age distribution during this period as America's population came to contain an increasing percentage of young and old people. Finally, these years saw the rise of deep-seated rebelliousness among a minority of American youth who rejected contemporary American values and institutions. While eager to destroy the prevailing system, they lacked a clear conception of what to substitute in its place.

EQUALITY

An emphasis on egalitarianism was characteristic of the twenty-five years after 1945, encompassing economic, social, and political equality. During this period the standard of living among families with incomes over $3000 annually tended to be more similar than in previous years. Whether they lived on $10,000 or $40,000 yearly, their homes tended to be in the suburbs. They were equipped with radios and television sets, with appliances such as refrigerators, freezers, washing machines, toasters, and a variety of gadgets. The garage invariably contained one or two family cars. Backyard swimming pools could be found in moderate income areas as well as among the rich. These families very likely ate the same frozen foods purchased in a large supermarket at a modern shopping center. Their clothing was usually ready-made. Their sources of entertainment were not very different. When not viewing television or attending mass sports events, movies, or concerts, they spent leisure hours in the home, or in country clubs — once the preserves of the wealthy, but now available to many. Affluence thus brought a measure of uniformity into the life styles of a majority of Americans, more so than during any previous period.

The quarter century after World War II also witnessed a significant effort by many Americans to bring social equality into everyday life. Informality in manners as in dress was widely practiced, while formality was eschewed. More than ever, status in American society was determined not by birth, but by wealth or achievement. In politics the first and second generations of sons and daughters of former immigrants rose to high office, including John F. Kennedy, Michael V. DiSalle (mayor of Toledo), and Arthur Goldberg (secretary of labor). In business and the professions similar trends could be observed. Education also served as a great social equalizer. The average length of schooling in the United States increased from about nine years in 1945 to more than twelve years in 1970, resulting in more equal speech patterns among Americans, and fewer disparities in educational backgrounds.

Egalitarian trends also affected politics during this period. A larger percentage of Americans took advantage of their right to vote than in previous years. In many parts of the South, where for many years black Americans had been unable to exercise their privilege of voting, changing public opinion as well as federal laws enabled millions to exercise their franchise for the first time in the twentieth century. Moreover, officeholders in local, state, and federal governments revealed a very broad spectrum of diverse backgrounds, partly as a result of the equalizing effects of the civil service system. In many aspects of American life, therefore, egalitarianism emerged as a dominant trend in the post – World War II era.

CONFORMITY

Invariably the drive for equality in many walks of life also created pressures for conformity. The impact of automation and the mass media tended to lessen individualism and creativity. This became apparent in the housing, dress, and appearance of Americans, and more significantly in their behavior and their thought. In fact, soon after World War II various observers of American society began to note this trend. Perhaps the classic exposition was made by Harvard sociologist David Riesman in his book, *The Lonely Crowd*. Riesman observed that most of his fellow Americans tended to be outer-directed, having few values of their own, but modeling their behavior on what they thought was the will of the majority. Only a minority, Riesman found, were inner-directed, or behaved in accordance with stable and strongly held inner values. Without a clear sense of goals or values, the outer-directed individual in the crowd felt an abiding sense of loneliness because of an inner spiritual vacuum. This was the human condition of most Americans, Riesman noted, as he warned of the perils of the new conformity.

CHANGES IN AGE DISTRIBUTION OF POPULATION

During these years the United States population came to include a significantly larger number of young and old. Medical advances accounted for the increased percentage of the population under thirty years of age and also for the larger proportion of citizens over sixty-five. Youth comprised 50 per cent of the population in 1946, and about the same in 1967, although appreciable increases were forecast for the years thereafter. On the other hand, the percentage of aged rose quickly. In 1945 approximately 8 per cent of the population was over sixty-five; in 1970, it was almost 11 per cent, and rapidly rising. The significance of these statistics was evident. A veritable cult of youth swept many spheres of American life. It was reflected not only in clothing, amusements, and in the appearance of automobiles and consumer goods, but also in the demands of young people for increased power, whether in educational systems, corporations, or politics. At the same time, the rising number of aged presented unique problems of another kind. The plight of the old in the United States — a nation obsessed with youth — was not easy. They lacked facilities for adequate medical care or incomes sufficient for a decent life. Many who were still capable of a good day's work felt rejected when retirement was forced upon them. Above all, perhaps the most serious problem of the aged was an abiding sense of loneliness in a highly urbanized and mobile society in which family ties were becoming looser, and in which old people usually lived apart from their children, relatives, and friends. Increasing efforts to provide Medicare, nursing homes, and locally sponsored activities for senior citizens between 1945 and 1970 represented fledgling efforts to deal with the special problems of a growing minority of Americans.

SOCIAL PROTEST

Though American society had never been placid, the rebelliousness of some Americans between 1945 and 1970 became unusually vehement. Many young people became protesters who rejected most aspects of American life, and seriously doubted whether the American system was worth preserving. During the 1950's some of these rebels called themselves the "beat generation." The movement soon floundered, however, and was succeeded by the rise of hippies after 1960. At the same time a small band of student radicals followed the lead of philosopher Herbert Marcuse, who advocated creation of a totalitarian society. Organized as the Students for a Democratic Society (SDS), their prime purpose was to transform and sometimes to disrupt and destroy existing American institutions. Between 1965 and 1970 they concentrated their efforts mainly on colleges and universities.

Why did youth rebel? The sources of discontent were deep, rooted to a considerable extent in the urbanized technological and affluent society that was developing in the United States. Idealistic youth was prone to revolt against the extraordinary emphasis on material goods and success in America, with its accompanying spiritual vacuum. Moreover, urban and suburban life led to the loss of community, bringing with it a sense of alienation, loneliness, and isolation. The visibility of crowds seemed to make such loneliness more intense. In addition, the replacement of human labor by machines narrowed the outlets for individuality and creativity that average men and women had once found in their daily work. Now, meaningful self-expression by ordinary individuals appeared to be more restricted than ever, experienced only by a relatively small number of people belonging to the intellectual or managerial elite. Without a doubt, exposure to television dulled the creative senses of many of these youths, who were unaccustomed to drawing upon their inner resources and often dependent on outside stimuli and crowds for so many of their needs. A combination of these factors resulted in creating an enormous spiritual vacuum among a significant minority of American youth, which expressed itself in a rebelliousness against the entire system.

Beatniks

The beatniks of the 1950's were critical mainly of what they considered to be the crass materialism of American civilization. Advocating an extension of bohemianism, many beatniks claimed to be beatific. Although the beat movement began as a literary effort fostered by writers like Jack Kerouac and poet Allan Ginsberg, it produced little of lasting value and was soon transformed by younger people into a vehicle for social protest. The beatniks often went without shoes, wore ragged clothing, beards, or bizarre hair styles, refused to work, and disdained most conventions of polite society. Such outer manifestations of rebellion were a reflection of beat beliefs. These people rejected the concern with material wealth, which was a major preoccupation of their fellows. They looked askance at much of the hypocrisy and dishonesty that accompanied striving for success in a market-oriented society. Instead, hoping to escape from a phony to a genuine existence, they advocated passivity as a response to the hostile, competitive world around them, and the fullest expression of individualism. Thus they repudiated most of the conventions and aims of American society, including rules and restrictions on sexual activities. Disdaining marriage or chastity, the beatniks advocated untrammeled and uninhibited behavior in this as in other spheres. Although they were to be found in every section of the country, their main communities were in San Francisco (North Beach) and New York (Greenwich Village). By 1960 the beat movement began to decline — a victim of conformity among its own adherents. Although the criticism of American life by beatniks undoubtedly was valid, their failure to offer constructive and creative alternatives had much to do with their demise.

Hippies

A not dissimilar form of protest was carried on after 1960 by self-styled hippies. Although they did not think of themselves as descendants of the beatniks, they shared many of their habits and beliefs. The appeal of hippie life was greatest for adolescents and young adults (thirteen to twenty-one), many of whom were seeking freedom from parental and social restraints. In appearance they resembled beatniks. But if the beats were un-intellectual, hippies were anti-intellectual. They too rejected the materialism of American society, but in addition they condemned war and preached (in theory) love for one's fellow creatures. More passive than the beatniks, they also strove for uninhibited expressions of individualism. Urging every person to "do his thing" (to find some form of individual expression), the hippies found special pleasure in childlike games. Rejecting virtually all prevailing customs concerning sexual behavior, they often encountered difficulties with local authorities. More than the beatniks, hippies sought an escape (through widespread use of drugs) from what they considered to be a corrupt civilization. Beatniks usually had done no more than experiment with marijuana; but most hippies indulged in very potent narcotics such as heroin, "speed," and LSD. Unfortunately, continued use of such drugs often led their users to violent crimes (sometimes to secure money for more drugs), undermining the peaceful aims of former "flower children." Most American towns and cities had at least some hippies, but between 1963 and 1968 the largest communities were to be found in San Francisco (Haight-Ashbury district) and New York (East Village).

New Left

After 1965, the rebelliousness of white American youth found another outlet in the "New Left" movement. Various groups constituted the New Left, including the Students for a Democratic Society (SDS), the Yippies, and the Third World Liberation Front. Having virtually no ties with the Old Left of the 1930's or with Communism, the New Left attracted aggressive young intellectuals, dissatisfied high school and college students, as well as unintellectual drifters and misfits. Eschewing a clear or positive statement of goals or purposes, the New Left concentrated its energies on criticizing the failures of the American system, which they considered so corrupt as to be beyond redemption. Their criticisms often were a popularized version of Professor Herbert Marcuse's influential book, *One Dimensional Man,* in which this noted philosopher pointed to the conformity and oppressiveness imposed on the individual by a technological society. Except for the vague promise of a "participatory democracy," the New Left offered few alternatives to the prevailing American system, which they hoped to destroy through violence and revolution. Some critics of the New Left — such as the eminent philosopher Sidney Hook — considered it to be an anarchist or perhaps nihilist movement. Between 1965 and 1970 the New Left directed its main energies toward encouraging young men to evade the military draft and toward disrupting academic life on the nation's campuses.

SUMMARY OF SOCIAL CHANGES

The post – World War II years thus witnessed great social changes in America, the product of an increasingly technological society. The standardization which it fostered was reflected in growing egalitarianism and conformity, and a consequent reaction of dissent. At the same time it produced an increasing percentage of youths as well as aged who left their own distinctive imprint on the period. In many ways, the years between 1945 and 1970 constituted an era of turbulent social change.

THE URBAN REVOLUTION

Much of the social turmoil took place in the nation's cities. In fact, since 1890 America had undergone two great changes in its living patterns, experiencing an urban revolution after 1890, and a suburban revolution after World War II. At the turn of the century rural Americans and immigrants moved to the city; after 1945 they and their descendents moved from the city to the suburbs. In 1890 the cities were centers of industrial and commercial activity, and workers and managers lived close to hubs. But the metropolitan areas that mushroomed after 1945 created a new community with constantly shifting and expanding boundaries. A new kind of society emerged — usually containing people with higher than average incomes, with new tastes in living standards, and with an independent mobility gained largely through widespread ownership of automobiles. The growth of the suburbs between 1945 and 1970 and the attendant deterioration of the central cities revolutionized the life styles of most Americans and contributed to some of the major problems facing American society, whether economic, social, or environmental.

The expansion of metropolitan areas was particularly rapid in the two decades after World War II. Not only did the number of metropolitan areas increase, but also the population that lived there grew as well. Metropolitan areas, containing a central city of over 50,000 people, almost doubled between 1945 and 1960, totaling 192 in 1960. Their population growth was twice as great as for rural areas, many of which stagnated or lost population. Suburbs grew four times as rapidly as the inner city and accounted for more than one-half of the total population growth in the United States.

SUBURBAN GROWTH

The reasons for suburban growth were varied. One underlying factor was automation, which so dramatically reduced the number of hours in the work week for most wage earners. Unless the average individual worker spent forty hours or less weekly on his job, he could not have spared commuting time, nor would he have had the weekend free to enjoy advantages offered by the suburbs. To a considerable extent, therefore, the suburb was the child of a technological society. Certainly, the expansion of transportation facilities had fostered satellite areas since the turn of the century. But after 1945 the extension of subways and bus lines into outlying areas was especially rapid. Yet it was the enormous increase in automobiles and the construction of highways leading

Levittown—suburbia in the 1950's. (Wide World Photos)

into the business centers of the inner city which acted as special catalysts in promoting a mass movement of population to the suburbs between 1945 and 1970. Another factor in suburban growth was "industrial suburbanization," as large industries often sought to decentralize their operations to effect lower operating costs. Increasingly they preferred to move to "satellite" cities near large urban areas. Their motivation was understandable. As a highway and transportation network brought workers and management from distant areas closer, such moves became feasible. They also looked for areas where land for large industrial sites was still relatively cheap, and where taxes were lower than in the inner city. Other reasons for the tremendous expansion of the rim areas in metropolitan centers were environmental. The suburbs simply provided a more pleasant living environment than many of the old neighborhoods near downtown areas. Ample space, clean air, greenery and trees contrasted vividly with congestion and over-crowding, polluted air and water, and faceless miles of concrete streets and sidewalks of the inner cities. In addition, many former urban dwellers escaped to the suburbs hoping to leave most of the city's social problems behind them, including crime, deteriorating schools, prostitution, and various health hazards. Finally, it is doubtful whether or not the suburbs would have grown as rapidly as they did had it not been for federal policies that directly stimulated that growth. The Federal Housing Administration (FHA) provided low-cost loans to individual home owners and government-guaranteed mortgages, thus encouraging individuals to own their houses, rather than to rent apartments.

To some extent, racism also played a part in fostering the amazing growth of suburban areas. The greater majority of new suburbanites were whites who frequently were prompted in their move by the large-scale influx of black Americans or Puerto Ricans into the core areas of most large cities. Between 1945 and 1970 the exodus of black Americans from the South, which had begun early in the century, gathered momentum.

In fact, racial minorities who moved into the inner city often took the place of the ex-urbanites who had moved to the suburbs. Perhaps as many as 8 million black Americans migrated from

Los Angeles freeways, 1966. (Wide World Photos)

the rural South to industrial cities throughout the nation between 1945 and 1970. In 1910, 89 per cent of black Americans still lived south of the Mason-Dixon line; in 1950, 55 per cent; in 1970, 30 per cent; and demographers estimated that by 1980 perhaps only 10 to 15 per cent would reside in the South. Invariably the destination of most of these migrants was the city. They poured into the great urban centers of the Northeast, the Middle West, and the Far West. During this period the black population of cities over 100,000 increased until it was estimated that by 1980 more than 60 per cent of the population in major cities such as New York, Chicago, Cleveland, St. Louis, and Detroit would be black. Already by 1970 the nation's capital had a population of which less than 30 per cent was white. This tendency was viewed with alarm both by white and by black advocates of integration, for such population movements were creating metropolitan areas bifurcated along racial lines. Before 1900 the typical American city allowed people of all classes to mingle together, especially since most of them lived near their place of work. But the typical American city in the second half of the twentieth century contained a black inner city and white suburbs.

URBAN PROBLEMS

Such great population movements understandably created many urban problems. Most central cities became boom towns during the day and ghost towns at night. They experienced extra-ordinary pressures on public service facilities (such as transporta-tion, electricity, telephone, water) because their daytime population often was 50 per cent greater than their residential users. Between 1945 and 1965 many cities vastly increased the expressways leading to the core areas and added to the availability of parking space. But they fought a losing battle as traffic congestion worsened. The utilization of the few remaining vacant spaces in the city for parking, rather than for parks, added to the general ugliness. After 1965 some cities like Washington, D.C., and San Francisco began to plan new rapid transit systems to avoid the choking of almost every artery of their transportation network. But in the years be-tween 1945 and 1970 the physical frustrations of urban living increased greatly both for the inner city dweller as well as for the suburban commuter.

Environmental problems affected American urban dwellers between 1945 and 1970 with a suddenness that found many unprepared. Air pollution — due to industrial waste and heavy automobile traffic — became increasingly serious after 1950. Los Angeles and New York vied for the dubious distinction of being the smog capital of the United States. But to a greater or lesser extent, most metropolitan areas struggled with the same problem. A related by-product of urban industry was water pollution, which affected thousands of streams and rivers, killing wildlife and vegetation, while endangering the water supply systems of many cities. Since the growth of most metropolitan areas was unplanned, many of their newer neighborhoods became commercial ribbon-developments — composed of unsightly billboards, gasoline stations, hamburger drive-ins, and motels. The richest nation in the world was building some of the ugliest cities in memory.

ECONOMIC PROBLEMS

The mushrooming of the suburbs also created severe economic problems for the cities. The recovery of large inner-city areas from blight and obsolescence proved to be a task of such great magnitude that most city governments felt helpless and looked appealingly to the federal government for help. At the same time they found their tax base shrinking as high- and middle-income groups, in addition to scores of manufacturing corporations, retail stores, and research organizations, moved to the suburbs. The low-income migrants in the inner city not only contributed less in taxes, but also placed unprecedented strains on public and social services offered by the city. By 1970 all of the large cities (over 100,000) in the United States experienced severe financial problems.

SOCIAL PROBLEMS

Like a cancer in the body politic the social problems of the inner city affected Americans everywhere. Noticeably on the rise in 1945, by 1970 these problems increased at alarming rates, as increases in the use of drugs and alcohol, riots and arson, prostitution, public health problems, fragmentation of families, and many characteristics of the "culture of poverty" thrived in large cities and became serious urban and national problems.

CRIME PROBLEMS

Both organized and unorganized crime became a major public issue. A special United States Senate Committee investigating crime, headed by Senator Estes Kefauver in 1951, revealed that organized racketeering in big cities under the aegis of mobs such as the Mafia was flourishing. The situation had not changed nearly twenty years later; instead, crime rates soared far above predictions in these two ensuing decades. Between 1945 and 1967 the number of serious crimes committed in the United States (murder, robbery, assaults) more than doubled. Even allowing for a population increase of about 20 per cent in these years, the statistics alarmed many Americans. In 1946, the number of serious crimes committed was 1.685 million, the largest number until that time. Ten years later this total had risen to 2.5 million, an appreciable although not dramatic increase. But between 1956 and 1967 a veritable crime wave swept the United States, in big cities especially, as the FBI reported 3.8 million serious crimes in 1967. Inner city dwellers, both rich and poor, often lived in fear, afraid to leave their homes after dark, subject to assaults and muggings. Crime was not restricted to the streets, however. Burglaries and car thefts also multiplied during the decade. In 1968 Congress enacted a "Crime in the Streets" law designed to provide federal aid to local law enforcement agencies in an effort to stem the tide.

To a considerable extent, the increase of crime was only an index to a variety of other serious social ills plaguing the nation's cities. One of these was the widespread use of drugs, which frustrated many state and local authorities seeking to cope with the increase of narcotics addicts, who numbered perhaps as many as 5 million people. Feeling oppressed by the impersonality of urban and suburban life, by a seeming decline of individualism with the rise of a mass society, and often frustrated and bored amid material abundance, young people in particular sought an escape through marijuana, heroin, LSD, or other drugs. The relationship between criminal activities and drug use was often very close.

Among black Americans the frustrations of city life erupted in riots, arson, and looting in scores of cities, including New York (1964), Los Angeles (Watts, 1965), and Detroit (1967). The sense of loneliness and alienation felt by many urban dwellers, black and white, was due partly to the breakdown of communities and neighborhoods within the cities, and partly to the disruption of family life, so important to a stable social order. As a consequence, public welfare rolls soared between 1960 and 1970, at a time when the nation was near full employment. Total federal, state, and local welfare payments rose from $1.8 billion in 1960 to more than $6 billion in 1968, threatening to disrupt the financial solvency of most cities.

URBAN DILEMMA

By 1970 America's cities were in deep trouble. And since the urban-suburban communities had become the hub of American civilization, their problems were the nation's problems. The challenge posed by the urban crisis was profound. Was the urban-suburban way of life as it had developed in the United States by 1970 compatible with the material and spiritual well-being of men and women? Was it a satisfying way of life for citizens of the most affluent society in the history of mankind? American cities seemed to be so out of touch with the needs of human beings, and urban problems seemed so complex and insoluble, that some experts advocated abandoning the cities and building new communities more in tune with the needs of a technological society. A major task of Americans in the last three decades of the twentieth century therefore would be to recreate that sense of community disrupted by the growth of cities in the twenty-five years after World War II.

THE CULTURAL REVOLUTION

That the post – World War II era was one of turmoil and rapid change was partly due to a veritable cultural revolution in America. The two decades after 1945 witnessed a knowledge explosion that had an impact on many levels of cultural activity. One striking characteristic of this cultural revolution was the enormous expansion of mass culture as the unprecedented increase of educational facilities and of the mass media made millions of people conscious of cultural activities. To be sure, dissemination to the masses often required dilution and popularization. More often than not it was derivative rather than creative. At the same time, the explosion of knowledge also brought great advances in creative work, usually performed under the auspices of universities and thus related to an emerging academic culture. The cultural revolution thus proceeded on two levels — it took place in the realm of mass culture and in the sphere of academic culture.

MASS CULTURE

The reasons for the expansion of mass culture are not obscure. In fact, they were closely related to the technological and economic revolutions that were sweeping America. Technological innovations really made possible the large-scale dissemination of knowledge. Automation and mechanical devices created more leisure time for the average individual as they shortened the working day and so allowed time for other activities. For some this resulted in boredom, but others used their spare time to good advantage in some form of creative endeavor. A majority of Americans sought to pass the time as spectators in various forms of diversion, leading to the boom in mass culture. If technology made available this new-found leisure, it also created the instruments for its use through the mass media, especially motion pictures, radio, and television. At the same time, the affluence and wealth created by American industry provided new opportunities for extending educational training to the masses. Indeed, a technological society such as the United States between 1945 and 1970 required increasingly fewer unskilled workers, but had a great need for skilled and professional personnel. New opportunities for skilled individuals understandably generated widespread demands for the extension of educational and technical training just as the new leisure time allowed millions of others to take advantage of new educational opportunities. The technological and economic revolutions were therefore major factors in fomenting the cultural revolution of this period. They were reinforced by the urbanization of the nation, for cultural activities are almost always concentrated in towns and cities. In addition, the social revolution witnessed a renewed emphasis on equality and conformity, which also found expression in cultural activities. In sum, the technological and economic revolutions in America, reinforced by the urban and social revolutions, had a direct impact in bringing about the emergence of mass culture.

Television

Mass culture manifested itself in a variety of ways. Many Americans became utterly absorbed with television and spent a large part of their nonworking hours before a picture tube. Popular sports, music, and literature engaged the energies of many others. Art became a pastime of millions. Even religion did not escape the sweep of mass culture.

Unlike any other communication medium, however, television captured the minds and hearts of Americans between 1945 and 1970. Developed on a small scale in the years just preceding World War II, in the ensuing period it revolutionized the electronics industry, if not also everyday life in America. In 1945 television factories turned out no more than 2000 sets; by 1952 this had increased to 6 million; by 1960, more than 55 million sets were in use; and by 1967, 92 million sets had been manufactured (including 12.7 million color TV sets). Sixteen of seventeen American homes had at least one television set. This widespread ownership was more than matched by the rapid multiplication of television stations — from 100 in 1950 to 655 by 1968.[5] The enormous influence of this new means of communication was profound, for it reached 96 per cent of the population. Unfortunately, the hopes of some of the early boosters that television would serve as a major tool to raise the cultural level of Americans were not realized. To be sure, television programs brought university courses, serious drama, music, and discussion of political issues into living rooms across the nation. But increasing commercialization after 1955 led advertisers to cater to the lowest possible common denominator among the public. Thereafter, television fare was primarily composed of programs of a trivial and superficial nature, including musical variety and comedy, a proliferation of soap operas and western dramas, quiz and give-away programs, mystery and detective dramas, and sports. A large proportion of television programs emphasized physical violence and brutality, indeed to such an extent that Congress and the Federal Communications Commis-

[5]One estimate concerning television sets can be found in *The World Almanac and Book of Facts, 1970* (Garden City: Doubleday, 1970), p. 896.

sion inaugurated an investigation of the television broadcasters in 1968.

Literature

It was often charged that popular culture culminated in the vulgarization of literature, music, and art. As publishers came to print an increasing number of paperbacks, they themselves inaugurated a revolution resulting in the mass distribution of hundreds of millions of inexpensive works. The proliferation of "book clubs," which distributed large quantities of low-cost hard cover books opened additional new markets. Between 1945 and 1970 about ninety of these clubs sold more than 900 million volumes, a staggering total. Indeed, the dissemination of books on such a large scale to a large segment of the American people was one of the most significant developments in the growth of mass culture. Books bought by Americans covered every conceivable subject and appealed to various levels of the intellect. Whether or not the level of reading was higher or lower during the period would be difficult to determine. But one striking aspect of the paperback revolution was the special popularity of detective fiction — of mystery stories by such best-selling writers as Erle Stanley Gardner, Mickey Spillane, and Dorothy L. Sayers — which seemed to satisfy a deep-seated need for escape by millions of their readers. Magazines also revealed popular tastes. *Readers Digest, Life, Look,* and for a time the *Saturday Evening Post* each reached as many as 25 million readers with a bland diet of stories often pretending to pseudo-sophistication.

Comic books and cartoon strips — although intended for the young — found a large audience of adult readers. It has been estimated that four out of five Americans read these comic strips regularly, providing a painless avenue of escape from the everyday frustrations of modern American life. The adventures of Blondie, Dick Tracy, L'il Abner, Orphan Annie, Pogo, and Peanuts concerned life situations that millions of Americans found meaningful.

Music

Popular music found a wider audience than at any previous time, through radios, recordings, tapes, and television. Popular ballads — often expressing the yearnings, disappointments, and frustrations of the average individual — continued in vogue during the years between 1945 and 1970. Frank Sinatra, Perry Como, and Vic Damone were among the most popular vocalists in this genre. At the same time these years saw a revival of jazz and the blues, especially by black Americans and self-professed nonconformists who sought individuality. Duke Ellington, Dizzie Gillespie, and Louie Armstrong represented the older jazz, while the Dave Brubeck Quartet developed the "smooth" jazz of the Jet Age. After 1960, and the success of the Beatles in England, rock and roll music — utilizing electronic instruments — came into vogue, particularly with those under thirty years of age. A smaller number, often found on the nation's campuses, were devotees of folk music, stimulated by popular artists such as Joan Baez, Bob Dylan, and Peter, Paul, and Mary.

Education

The influence of mass tastes was also felt in the field of education. Between 1945 and 1970 colleges and universities were expected to do more than to engage in teaching and research. They were asked to render various services to the community, such as providing comprehensive cultural and entertainment programs, in addition to large-scale athletic events like football and basketball. Demands arose for greater relevance of their educational offerings to everyday affairs as the number of undergraduates grew. Students also desired a greater voice in the selection of faculty, curriculum, and administration. Many of the disturbances on campuses between 1964 and 1970 supposedly were designed to achieve these goals. In 1945 only 30 per cent of all high school graduates went on to college; by 1970 almost 60 per cent of high school seniors planned to extend their education. In the first year after the war, there were approximately 1.5 million students in college; the estimate for 1970 was about 5 million. An increasing proportion of young people entered the newer "community college" (or junior college) as more than 300 such institutions sprang up from California to New York. They offered two-year college programs, often including vocational training. Meanwhile, the nation's public schools braced themselves for burgeoning enrollments, which soared from 25 million in 1945 to 40 million in 1970. Such a large increase placed an enormous strain on physical facilities, teachers, curricula, and school finances. In addition, the challenge of educating a large number of children from minority groups with disadvantaged backgrounds posed special problems. In many large cities black American parents became especially concerned with the slowness of public school integration in slum areas and demanded control over the schools by special community boards. In New York City such demands provoked a city-wide school strike during 1968 which paralyzed that education system, and which touched off violence and disorder in scores of other schools. Elsewhere, the demand for local control over schools created equivalent tensions. As with many other aspects of the nation's culture, education was profoundly affected by the desire of the masses to turn colleges and schools to popularly controlled needs and desires.

Appraisal of Mass Culture

Popular culture has been attacked as well as defended. The appeal of the popular arts stemmed from an ability to express the fantasies, longings, and suppressed impulses of people living in a chaotic world. To lives burdened by frustrations and monotony, the popular arts brought temporary release. Heroes and heroines did everything of which the average person dreamed. Critics argued that such gratification was dangerous: it catered to the lowest common denominator of an audience and discouraged more wholesome or creative activities, and it turned listeners, learners, or viewers away from reality — away from confrontation with real life problems. With increasing frequency some aspects of popular culture stimulated antisocial and aggressive impulses. Defenders believed, however, that the popular arts satisfied the psychic needs of their audiences and aided them in making personal adjustments. In fact, they supposedly provided a harmless outlet for impulses that otherwise might have been more antisocial. Whatever appraisal of popular culture is made, though, it represents one of the striking developments in American society after World War II.

ACADEMIC CULTURE

Although popular culture seemed to predominate in the United States between 1945 and 1970, academic culture also thrived. In fact, technological developments and affluence combined to increase the volume of books written, the number of musical performances and recordings made, the number of paintings completed by artists, and daring research in the social sciences. But whether or not the increased quantity of products in academic culture was accompanied by rising levels of quality was a question that critics were often prone to ask.

Literature

American literature in the post – World War II era reflected the deep-seated fear of many writers that a technological society such as that emerging in the United States was undermining many human values, particularly individualism. In one way or another this message was forcefully conveyed by James Jones in *From Here to Eternity* (1951), by James G. Cozzens in *By Love Possessed* (1957), and by Truman Capote in *The Grass Harp* (1951). John O'Hara in *Ten North Frederick* (1955) and Nelson Algren in *Man with the Golden Arm* (1964) further elaborated on the theme and helped to buttress it with extreme frankness in explicit discussion of sexual matters — often in colorful colloquial language as if to assert man's humanity in the face of a seemingly impersonal and chaotic world. J. D. Salinger's *Catcher in the Rye* (1951), Saul Bellow's *Adventures of Augie March* (1953) and *Herzog* (1961), and John Updike's *Poorhouse Fair* (1959) further examined the irrationality of modern American society. On the stage, Tennessee Williams in *A Streetcar Named Desire* and Arthur Miller in *Death of a Salesman* traced the disintegrating impact of modern industrial life on human personality. Leading poets during this decade reflected a similar disenchantment with their contemporary society, including W. H. Auden, Karl Shapiro, Richard Eberhart, Conrad Aiken, and Marianne Moore.

Art

Some American artists of these years were also dissatisfied with various aspects of contemporary life around them. One group of Romantic Realists revealed a decided nostalgia for the past in their works. This group included Charles Burchfield, Edward Hopper, and Andrew Wyeth, who focused on the loneliness and desolation of the modern world. Another school of artists, known as Social Protesters, attempted to reassert human values in a seemingly inhuman technological society. George Grosz, William

Gropper, Jack Levine, Peter Bloom, and Ben Shahn used their canvasses to make searing indictments of numerous phases of contemporary American life. A third important form of artistic expression came at the hands of the Abstractionists, whose aim often was emphatically to assert human individualism, amid the confusions of mass society. Stuart Davis, Jackson Pollock, Mark Rothko, Robert Motherwell, William De Kooning, William Bazcotes, and Adolph Gottlieb were among the leading exponents of abstractionism. Of far lesser artistic merit were more superficial Pop artists of the 1960's like Andy Warhol and Jasper Johns, who attacked not only the obscurity of abstract art but also the excessive emphasis on materialism in American life. Whatever their vehicle of expression, however, American artists tended to be critical of the complex technological society that was developing before their eyes.

Social Sciences

The quarter century after World War II witnessed striking advances in the social sciences. Indeed, the use of computers and highly sophisticated mathematical techniques virtually transformed many academic fields. Psychology, sociology, and economics, not to mention political science and anthropology, became behaviorist in orientation. This meant that researchers stressed the construction of abstract models and theories, which they sought to prove by the use of experimentation with quantitative or qualitative data (according to the dictates of scientific method). Many hoped to replace the humanistic emphasis of the older generation of scholars with what they considered to be the more precise, scientific doctrines of behaviorism.

REVIEW OF CULTURAL REVOLUTION

Thus, the revolution in popular as well as academic culture reflected the profound technological and economic changes sweeping the United States. Not only was the volume of cultural activity greater than at any previous period in American life, but also the fruits of varied cultural activities reached a larger number of individuals than ever before, as a result of new technological devices. At the same time, cultural standards did not appear to rise appreciably as efforts to appeal to mass audiences often led to a search for a common denominator. The hope of many reformers that the masses would use their leisure time in various efforts to seek self-improvement was not realized during these years. Nor did relief from back-breaking labor or long working hours necessarily result in greater happiness for individuals. Leisure for the many often led them to boredom, frustration, and a search for excitement and entertainment. On the other hand, academic culture was stimulated as an increasingly larger number of creative artists, scientists, and scholars found that technology often relieved them of drudgery and allowed them to move forward more rapidly in broadening the frontiers of knowledge.

AGE OF REVOLUTION: SUMMARY

The quarter century after World War II, then, witnessed extraordinary changes in American civilization, and constituted a new era in the nation's development. During these years most phases of life in the United States were drastically transformed by a series of revolutions that set off chain reactions. The most fundamental was the technological revolution, which spawned an age of affluence, which in turn stimulated profound social turmoil in the form of the black revolution, the social revolution, and the urban revolution. From these a cultural revolution also took form. Whether or not the United States could withstand the impact of these upheavals and continue to adhere to the traditional values and institutions upon which it had been founded was a serious question in 1970. And the gravity of these problems was compounded by the political and international crises to which the nation was subjected in the years stretching from the administration of Harry S. Truman to that of Richard M. Nixon.

FOR FURTHER READING

A very broad, readable, and sweeping survey of the post–World War II era is by JOHN BROOKS, *The Greap Leap* (New York: Harper & Row, 1966). For automation see WALTER S. BUCKINGHAM, *Automation and Society* (New York: Harper & Row, 1962). One of the finest introductions to the world of computers is NORBERT P. WIENER, *Cybernetics,* 2d ed. (Cambridge: M.I.T. Press, 1961) and also *The Human Use of Human Beings* (Garden City: Doubleday, 1954). Economic causes and effects of affluence are ably discussed by JOHN K. GALBRAITH, *The Affluent Society,* 2d ed. (Boston: Houghton Mifflin, 1969). A striking indictment of advertising men who generate new and often dubious wants is in VANCE O. PACKARD, *The Hidden Persuaders* (New York: D. McKay Co., 1957). One of the best popular, short introductions to the problems of poverty in the United States is MICHAEL HARRINGTON, *The Other America* (New York: Macmillan, 1962). See also DAVID HAMILTON, *A Primer on the Economics of Poverty* (New York: Random House, 1968) for a brief analysis by an economist. Indispensable to an understanding of modern urban problems are the works of LEWIS MUMFORD, including *The City in History* (New York: Harcourt, Brace & World, 1961) and *The Urban Prospect* (New York: Harcourt, Brace & World, 1968). JANE JACOBS, *The Death and Life of Great American Cities* (New York: Random House, 1961) is a provocative critique of twentieth-century American urban culture. The black revolution can be followed in RICHARD BARDOLPH, *The Negro Vanguard* (New York: Rinehart, 1959), HAROLD CRUSE, *The Crisis of the Negro Intellectual* (New York: Marrow, 1967) and *The Autobiography of Malcolm X* (New York: Grove Press, 1965), and ELDRIDGE CLEAVER, *Soul on Ice* (New York: McGraw-Hill, 1968). The social effects of affluence are touched upon in DAVID RIESMAN, *The Lonely Crowd* (New Haven: Yale University Press, 1950) and WILLIAM H. WHYTE, *The Organization Man* (New York: Simon and Schuster, 1956). A sampling of "beat" literature can be found in SEYMOUR KRIM (ed.), *The Beats: A Gold Medal Anthology* (Greenwich, Conn.: Fawcett Publications, 1960). JACK KEROUAC, *On the Road* (New York: Viking Press, 1957) and LAWRENCE LIPTON, *The Holy Barbarians* (New York: J. Messner, 1959) help toward an understanding of the "beat" phenomenon. Hippies are dealt with in HENRY GROSS, *The Flower People* (New York: Ballantine, 1968) and in LEONARD WOLF, *Voices from the Love Generation* (Boston: Little, Brown, 1968). The revolt of youth is discussed sympathetically by KENNETH KENISTON, *Uncommitted: Alienated Youth in American Society* (New York: Harcourt, Brace & World, 1965), and more critically by LEWIS FEUER, *The Conflict of Generations* (New York: Basic Books, 1968). Profound changes in American education of the sixties are covered in DAVID RIESMAN and CHRISTOPHER JENCKS, *The Academic Revolution* (Garden City: Doubleday, 1968). On the mass media see ERIK BARNOUW, *Mass Communication: Television, Radio, Film and Press* (New York: Rinehart, 1956) and the more caustic analysis by GILBERT SELDES, *The New Mass Media: Challenge to a Free*

Society (Washington: Public Affairs Press, 1957). For popular culture consult STUART HALL and PADDY WHANNEL, *The Popular Arts* (New York: Pantheon Books, 1965) and the excellent collection in BERNARD ROSENBERG and D. M. WHITE (eds.), *Mass Culture: The Popular Arts in America* (Glencoe, Ill: The Free Press, 1965). A critique of post – World War II literature can be found in MAXWELL GEISMAR, *American Moderns* (New York: Hill and Wang, 1958).

11

RECONSTRUCTION
AND NORMALCY
Politics and Diplomacy
under Truman and Eisenhower
1945-1960

The revolutions transforming American society after World War II were not always clearly apparent to contemporaries of the period, nor did many people in the United States readily grasp their full implications. In the seven years after V-J Day, many Americans were concerned with reconverting national life from a wartime to a peacetime basis. And under the presidency of Dwight D. Eisenhower the revolutionary phases of change in the United States seemed to be muted and not too visible. Outwardly, a placid calm characterized American civilization as President Eisenhower emphasized normalcy — a time of consolidation and stock-taking, rather than rapid change. But this superficial tranquility appeared only on the surface. Meanwhile, men, movements, and machines were working feverishly for change, which erupted violently and passionately in the troublesome sixties.

TRUMAN AND DOMESTIC POLICIES

Reconstruction of domestic and foreign policies was to become a major preoccupation of the administration of Harry S.

Truman. At home, the multitudinous problems of guiding the nation from war to peace preoccupied the president and left him little opportunity to effect other changes. Abroad, the shift in the postwar balance of power that made the United States and Russia the two strongest nations in the world — and Great Britain and France less significant — required President Truman to innovate a new diplomacy. That he was able to deal with such major issues in the relatively short time at his disposal created an admiration for him among many Americans, who expressed their approval by re-electing him to another term in the White House.

At the end of the war, few men expected great things of Harry Truman, who was still little known to the average voter.

Harry S. Truman. (Wide World Photos)

Born on a Missouri farm in 1884, Truman was nevertheless an urban dweller, since he grew up in Kansas City, Missouri, and its suburb of Independence. His ambition to attend West Point was frustrated by poor eyesight. After graduating from high school in 1901, he worked in a variety of jobs, both as a farmer and as a bank clerk. During World War I he served as a major of an artillery company. Something of a late bloomer, by 1919 he had not found his place in life. Between 1919 and 1922 he operated a haberdashery shop in Kansas City, which foundered in the postwar depression. It was then that Harry Truman turned to his true vocation of politics. As a faithful worker in the Democratic party machine of Kansas City, headed by Boss Tom Pendergast, he secured election as a county judge (on the county commission) in 1922 and remained in office for two years, when he was defeated for re-election because of his opposition to the Ku Klux Klan. Between 1927 and 1934 he served as a judge in Independence, impressing his neighbors with his homely integrity as well as his shrewd political sagacity. These qualities endeared him to Boss Pendergast, who rewarded him with the Democratic nomination for the United States Senate in 1934, a post to which Truman subsequently won election. In his first term as a United States senator he was an unspectacular New Dealer. After re-election in 1940 he gradually won some national prominence as chairman of the Truman Committee, a senatorial group investigating federal expenditures for the war effort.

Though the Democratic party bosses in 1944 balked at the renomination of Henry A. Wallace for the vice-presidency, they viewed Truman's candidacy with satisfaction. He was a Middle Westerner, a big-city politician, a faithful party follower, personable, and he had the appearance of a simple and dignified rural American. These assets stood him in good stead when on April 12, 1945, he succeeded Franklin D. Roosevelt to the presidency.

Truman had a colorful personality. His simplicity and undoubted personal charm seemed to embody many traditional American virtues of the homespun variety. Both he and his wife, Bess, were unpretentious and appeared to be not much different from millions of other Americans. His personal honesty and integrity were rarely questioned, nor his loyalty to former friends. One of his outstanding virtues was his decisiveness, for he rarely shrank from making difficult decisions. To remind himself of his responsibilities as the nation's chief executive, he liked to keep a replica of a wooden bucket on his desk with the inscription, "The buck stops right here" — an injunction he usually obeyed. His grasp of public issues was often trenchant and realistic. A hard worker, Truman was also an especially effective stump speaker who was able to communicate well with average men and women. Not everyone liked the president, however. On occasion he revealed pettiness and vindictiveness, as critics of his daughter's musical ability soon discovered. His impulsiveness and sharp tongue often involved him in unnecessary difficulties. And sometimes he displayed weaknesses as a judge of human character when he placed trust in persons of dubious integrity. An outspoken individual, Truman aroused both antipathies as well as loyalties. As one observer noted, he was an ordinary-looking man with extraordinary political ability.

POSTWAR RECONSTRUCTION

In 1945, problems of postwar reconversion preoccupied the new president. Pressures for demobilization of the armed forces and of federal wartime agencies were intense. Control and development of atomic energy was another issue. Third, the recent World War II experiences strongly suggested the need for some form of unification for the various branches of the military establishment. A similar need existed for coordination of many disparate federal agencies. Meanwhile, President Truman's ascent to the White House focused much attention on the revision of procedures for such presidential succession. To the surprise of many, in dealing with these problems President Truman showed considerably more skill and sagacity than Woodrow Wilson had revealed under similar circumstances twenty-six years earlier. Indeed, his record in leading the nation from war to peace compared most favorably with that of other presidents before him who had sought to deal with postwar reconstruction.

Demobilization

Soon after V-J Day the administration was subjected to intense popular demand for a dismantling of most wartime measures. "Bring the boys back home" was as popular a slogan in 1945 as it had been in 1919. The demobilization of the armed services was achieved almost overnight. In less than two months, more than 10 million men and women were returned to civilian life and only 1.5 million remained in uniform. To ease the influx of such large numbers into the labor force, and to reward them for loyal service, Congress enacted the G.I. Bill, under which veterans seeking to continue their education were paid regular stipends for living expenses and tuition. More than 4 million took advantage of this opportunity in what came to be one of the federal government's most successful programs.

The president also abolished hundreds of wartime executive agencies that had been involved in the task of mobilization. These included such key offices as the Office of Defense Mobilization and Reconversion, the Office of Strategic Services (OSS), and the Office of Scientific Research and Development. By the summer of 1946 virtually all had ceased their operations and disbanded.

Congress was far more impatient than President Truman in seeking a rapid end to most wartime policies. During 1945 it refused to enact any form of legislation to provide for universal military service and placed a $13 billion limitation on defense expenditures. In the following year the Republicans won control of both houses of the Eightieth Congress on a promise to end most vestiges of wartime organization. Jealous of the expansion of presidential powers, the legislators fought a running battle with President Truman to end all federal economic controls whether of prices, scarce raw materials, or consumer goods. Already in June 1946 Congress allowed the Office of Price Administration (OPA) to go out of existence. In the succeeding two years most other economic regulations were left to expire. Congressional will also prevailed in the Revenue Act of 1946, which undertook drastic tax reductions (more than $6 billion) in the face of the president's protestations that this would encourage inflation. At the same time, the lawmakers abolished most wartime excise and excess profit levies, and reduced corporate and individual income taxes, possibly contributing to a rise in price levels during the period from 1946 to 1948.

Atomic Energy

Another postwar issue was the harnessing of atomic energy, which aroused a diversity of views. That this potent source of

The atomic age: hydrogen bomb explosion, 1952. (U.S. Army photo)

energy should be under government control was rarely disputed. But who was to exercise direct supervision? The question aroused a far-ranging debate in Congress, from which two differing viewpoints gradually crystallized. One position was upheld by Senator Arthur H. Vandenberg (Michigan), who believed in complete control of nuclear materials by the nation's military establishment. On the other hand, Senator Brian McMahon (Connecticut) eloquently argued for control by a civilian agency, since potential uses of atomic energy encompassed not only destructive weapons but also many peacetime uses. Eventually Congress worked out a compromise embodying both of these suggestions in the Atomic Energy Act of 1946. This provided for the establishment of a civilian agency, the Atomic Energy Commission, which was to sponsor and administer all nuclear research in the United States in its own laboratories, and through contracts. But all authority to order the use of atomic weapons was lodged in the president — acting as commander in chief of the armed forces. Thus, civilian control and military supervision were combined. The Atomic Energy Act of 1946 laid down fundamental guidelines for national management of nuclear resources over the next twenty-five years.

Military Unification

A third problem that emerged fully blown from recent World War II experiences was the lack of coordination among the various branches of the armed forces. Between 1941 and 1945 no formal agency existed to unify divergent goals and policies of the services, despite an apparent need. Pearl Harbor had served as a bitter lesson about the consequences of confusion. Both the president and congressional leaders therefore made proposals for unification of the armed services, many of which aroused jealousy and fear among military leaders. Much deliberation ultimately led to a compromise embodied in the National Security Act of 1947, which Congress passed by an overwhelming vote. Like the legislation dealing with atomic energy, this law created a framework that was not seriously altered over the next twenty-four years. It provided, first, for the creation of a Department of Defense composed of the army, navy, and air force as coordinate divisions. Secondly, the law established a new committee comprised by joint chiefs of staff, who were to meet regularly to coordinate their respective policies. A third innovation of the act was creation of the Central Intelligence Agency (CIA), whose task it was to engage in intelligence and espionage activities, and to coordinate vital information concerning national defense received by scores of other federal agencies. A fourth provision of the act was creation of the National Security Council to unify civilian and military policies. The group was to consist not only of the joint chiefs of staff but also of various civilian leaders including the president, vice-president, secretary of defense, and director of the Central Intelligence Agency (CIA). Finally, the law provided for a National Security Resources Board, which was to engage in plans for domestic mobilization needed to make any national defense effort effective. The National Security Act broke tradition by providing the United States with a comprehensive system of defense agencies while the nation was at peace.

Presidential Succession and Government Reorganization

Just as the war had prompted reorganization of the military forces, so it pointed to certain weaknesses in the federal government. In order to make succession to the presidency more democratic in 1947 Congress enacted the Presidential Succession Act. It provided that the speaker of the House of Representatives and the president pro-tem of the Senate were to succeed the vice-president in case of the president's and vice-president's death, and thereafter members of the cabinet. Prior to this law the speaker and the president pro-tem had not been considered for presidential succession, and this new law was an effort to give elected rather than appointed officials an opportunity to serve. At the same time, since the war had given birth to a proliferation of federal agencies, President Truman sought their more effective coordination. For this task he called upon ex-President Herbert Hoover to head a commission that was to recommend reorganization of the national bureaucracy. The Hoover Commission and its staff labored long and hard. Not all of its suggestions were implemented by Congress, but a substantial number of federal agencies were reorganized between 1947 and 1951 to avoid overlapping functions.

The Red Scare

Perhaps one of the most difficult tasks of reconstruction was the calming of wartime emotions, of fears and hatreds that found an outlet in the Second Red Scare. An outburst of hatred — often leading to suppression — had been characteristic after every war in which the United States had been engaged. It had cropped up in persecution of the Loyalists after 1783; in southern reconstruction after 1865; and in the Red Scare of A. Mitchell Palmer after World War I. Between 1945 and 1953 many Americans experienced a similar case of jitters, primarily due to fears of a Communist conspiracy.

At least half a dozen incidents heightened these fears. They were triggered in 1945 by the *Amerasia* case, which revealed that Philip Jaffe, editor of a left-wing magazine, *Amerasia,* during the war had secured important secret documents from the files of the Office of Strategic Services (OSS). At the same time, the Canadian government exposed the existence of a vast Communist spy network there which had channeled military secrets to the Soviet Union. Soon thereafter American newspaper readers were startled to read about the Klaus Fuchs case. Fuchs, a British physicist who had worked on atomic bomb projects in the United States between 1943 and 1947, had been passing vital scientific information to Russia, where he absconded after the disclosures. Even more unsettling was the trial of Alger Hiss, president of the Carnegie Endowment for Peace and a former State Department official, who had also been present at the Yalta Conference. He was accused by Whittaker Chambers, a former friend, of having been a Soviet spy during the New Deal era. When Chambers repeated his charges before the House Un-American Activities Committee, Hiss sued him for libel, although the courts eventually (1950) convicted him of perjury. This celebrated case was followed by that involving Judith Coplon, an obscure Department of Justice employee who confessed to passing secret information to a Soviet agent. Year after year these disclosures fed passions that heightened the anti-red hysteria.

But the most sensational charges concerning alleged Communist influence in America were made by Republican Senator Joseph McCarthy of Wisconsin. He began his red-baiting campaign in 1950 when he claimed that he had the names of fifty-seven known Communists who were working for the Department of State. As was to become characteristic of his technique, however, McCarthy never provided evidence to substantiate his accusations, but contented himself with repeating them at every opportunity. In succeeding months he charged a large number of individuals as being Communists or Communist sympathizers, including United States Ambassador to the United Nations Philip Jessup and Generals George C. Marshall and Dwight D. Eisenhower. McCarthy was also instrumental in bringing about the defeat for re-election of conservative Democratic Senator Joseph E. Tydings of Maryland in 1950 on trumped-up charges of Communism. As the Wisconsin senator's accusations became increasingly irresponsible, the United States Senate in 1953 cast a vote of censure on him which effectively ended a campaign that had stirred up significant numbers of Americans.

President Truman sought to deal more soberly with feelings aroused by the Second Red Scare by inaugurating a many-sided federal loyalty and internal security program. One of his first actions was the issuance of a presidential executive order on March 22, 1947, ordering the investigation of the loyalty of all federal employees by the United States Civil Service Commission and the Federal Bureau of Investigation. Altogether, 3 million civil servants were cleared of possible Communist taint, and only 212 resigned because they felt themselves to be under possible suspicion. In another executive order of August 1950,

President Truman provided for a revision of dismissal procedures, allowing department heads to dismiss federal employees whom they considered to be questionable security risks.

Meanwhile, the Department of Justice and Congress, too, moved to fashion an internal security program. The attorney general brought suit against eleven leaders of the Communist party of the United States under the Smith Act of 1940, which prohibited advocacy of the violent overthrow of the United States government. In 1951 the United States Supreme Court in *Dennis* v. *United States* (341 U.S. 494) upheld their conviction. At the same time the Justice Department brought similar and successful suits against forty state and regional Communist party leaders.

Congress appeared even more concerned about Communist influences and approved two acts to deal with them, both passed over President Truman's veto. The McCarran Internal Security Act of 1950 provided for the registration of all Communist organizations with the United States attorney general, prohibited the issuance of passports to American Communists or the immigration of foreign Communists to the United States, and forbad activities designed to create a totalitarian dictatorship. A new Subversive Activities Control Board was created to publicize many of the subversive activities prohibited by this law. The McCarran-Walter Immigration Act of 1952 was further designed to combat Communist influences by providing procedures for the deportation of undesirable aliens. Thus, the president, the courts, and Congress all combined their efforts to lessen possible Communist influences in American life.

THE FAIR DEAL AND REFORM

Although reconstruction problems and policies consumed a major share of President Truman's energies during his first three years, he did not wholly neglect what he considered to be an urgent need for domestic reform. A staunch follower of the New Deal — which had been suspended because of wartime necessities — Truman sought to revitalize it soon after the cessation of hostilities. Labeling his own extension of New Deal reforms as the Fair Deal, Truman first offered his program in 1945 to a Congress preoccupied with postwar demobilization. The president urged economic measures to provide for the maintenance of controls on inflation, regional resource development on the model of the TVA, government support of farm prices at 90 per cent of parity, and liberalization of laws affecting labor. More daring were his proposals for social reforms, including the extension of social security, a rise in minimum wage levels, a massive federally sponsored housing program, more federal aid to education, and adoption of national health insurance. He also called attention to the need for civil rights legislation.

After the Republicans captured both houses in the 1946 elections, Congress was inclined neither to follow presidential leadership nor to extend the New Deal. It simply refused to act on the president's recommendations. Only on the issue of full employment was there some genuine consensus as the legislators and the president agreed on the Employment Act of 1946 — a landmark in American public policy. With this law the federal government officially assumed responsibility for maintaining full employment in the United States — a responsibility once considered to belong exclusively to private individuals. The act also created the President's Council of Economic Advisers, composed of a group of professional economists who were to maintain a constant watch on the nation's economic trends. Their task was to recommend to the chief executive ways and means of maintaining full employment. Congress overrode Truman's veto of the Taft-Hartley Act of 1947, which defined and prohibited a number of unfair labor practices by unions and forbad the closed shop (making union membership a prerequisite to employment in a particular job). The lawmakers also did not heed the chief executive's warnings on inflation and during 1947 and 1948 insisted on further tax reductions. The Fair Deal, therefore, received short shrift from Congress, as the lawmakers refused to act on most of Truman's proposals.

THE ELECTION OF 1948

Many Americans expected the dispute between the president and Congress to be settled by the 1948 elections. Republicans were hopeful that the apparent unpopularity of President Truman would lead them to capture the White House with relative ease. In choosing Governor Thomas E. Dewey of New York as their presidential candidate, the Republicans hoped to unify the conservative and liberal wings of their party. Their sense of victory was whetted further by deep divisions among the Democrats, many of whom hoped to substitute another standard-bearer in place of Truman. Only with very great reluctance did the Democratic convention renominate Truman for another term. Indeed, Southerners were so agitated over Truman's civil rights proposals that they formed a third party, the States Rights Democratic party, popularly known as the Dixiecrats. With Governor Strom Thurmond of South Carolina as their presidential candidate they hoped to win sufficient votes to throw the election into the House of Representatives. Meanwhile, disaffected and sulking liberals, who felt that Truman had not fought hard enough for the Fair Deal, were determined to oppose his re-election with a fourth party, the Progressives. Headed by former Vice-President Henry A. Wallace, this new party also attracted some Communists and their sympathizers. No wonder, therefore, that most public opinion polls predicted a Republican sweep of perhaps unprecedented proportions. The prospects for President Truman's re-election appeared dim, indeed.

But the election of 1948 developed as one of the most surprising in American history. Harry Truman himself refused to indulge in the prevailing Democratic mood of pessimism and despair and campaigned instead like a winner. Making effective use of a special campaign train, he conducted a 60,000-mile whistle stop tour in which he shook the hands of thousands of voters, and delivered more than 351 speeches to more than 12 million people. He delighted them with his own special brand of "give 'em hell" oratory and mercilessly lashed at his opponents. His audiences in small towns as well as in the large cities seemed appreciative of his style, at the same time expressing a traditional American sympathy for the underdog. Meanwhile, he called the Republican Congress into special session on July 26, 1948, to enact the pledges made in the Republican platform — to the obvious discomfiture of the GOP. The session was barren of accomplishment. An overconfident Governor Thomas E. Dewey, however, seemed not to be perturbed and continued to deliver smooth, polished — though colorless — speeches to large gatherings. On election day, when the votes were counted, to almost everyone's surprise — except his own — President Truman had achieved a startling upset victory. Capturing ballots in large cities as well as in the middle western farm states, he garnered 24 million popular votes, compared to 21 million for Dewey, and only 1 million each for Thurmond and Wallace. In addition the voters elected a Democratic Congress. Truman's triumph was one of the most remarkable in the annals of American politics.

In view of this stunning political victory the barren record of the second Truman administration proved to be disappointing. Largely because of a coalition of Republicans and conservative southern Democrats in Congress, President Truman was unable to implement most of the proposals in his Fair Deal program. In the realm of economic policy he was able to secure no more than increased appropriations for the TVA and western reclamation projects; Congress flatly refused to authorize a Missouri Valley Authority or any other new regional development agency. Few of the president's suggestions concerning social legislation were enacted. Congress liberalized the immigration laws with the Displaced Persons Act of 1950, which increased annual immigration quotas from 205,000 to 415,000. A Democratic-Republican coalition also approved the moderate National Housing Act of 1949 which authorized federal subsidies for 800,000 new low-cost housing units; but it refused support for federal aid to education or for a national health program. Similarly the congressional majority refused to enact civil rights legislation although in 1949 the President's Committee on Civil Rights made specific recommendations for securing greater racial equality. When segregation in the armed forces was abolished in 1951, this was done by an executive order from the president's office. In short, Truman's brilliant electoral victory of 1948 was eclipsed by four years of meager accomplishments in domestic policy.

TRUMAN AND FOREIGN POLICIES

In addition to the many domestic policy issues that Harry Truman faced when he was swept suddenly into the White House, he encountered the enormous task of adjusting American diplomacy from wartime to peacetime needs. This was particularly difficult because the end of World War II witnessed a diplomatic revolution in which the United States and the Soviet Union decisively displaced Great Britain and France as major world pow-

ers. An agonizing reappraisal of American foreign policy therefore took place during the Truman era among political leaders of
various persuasions. The result came to be called Cold War
diplomacy — concerned primarily with the containment of Communism, and applied by President Truman in Europe, the Far
East, and Latin America. Whether or not this was the wisest
course which American policy makers could have adopted came
to be an object of heated debate in ensuing years, revolving
around the origins of the Cold War. This dispute only underscored the fact that few presidents ever faced such momentous
decisions in foreign affairs as Harry Truman did after World
War II.

Truman's diplomatic problems in 1945 were threefold. First,
since the prewar collective security system in Europe had been
shattered, the reconstruction of American alliances in Europe to
preserve a new balance of power there was imperative for American security. Germany was crushed, England and France were
exhausted, and in this power vacuum Soviet hegemony seemed
virtually unchallenged. Second, the organization of the United
Nations required immediate attention. The United States was
expected to play a leading role in putting it in operation. A third
immediate problem was the rebuilding of many war-ravaged
areas in Europe, a task that could be accomplished only if the
United States assumed major responsibility.

To meet these new challenges to American diplomacy President Truman and his advisors — especially Secretaries of State
George C. Marshall and Dean Acheson — and counselor to the
State Department, George Kennan, worked out new policies that
came to constitute the Truman design for American diplomacy.
In order to build a new network of alliances in Europe, to contain Communist expansion, and to aid European recovery, the
Truman administration offered three major policies. It emphasized close collaboration — political, military, and economic —
with the nations of western Europe. It focused on containment
of Communist influence, seeking not to destroy it, but to prevent
its further expansion. Finally, in the shadow of the hydrogen
bomb the administration developed the controversial doctrine of
limited war, for total war appeared too horrible to comprehend
in the atomic era. Instead, President Truman sought to fight limited wars to contain Communist influence where no means other

than force seemed feasible. This amalgam of policies constituted a consensus drawn from divergent alternatives, including General Douglas MacArthur's recommendations for total war, and former President Hoover's and Senator Robert Taft's pleading for some form of isolation. Between 1945 and 1952 the Truman design was applied to world problems in Europe, the Far East, and Latin America.

COLLABORATION WITH WESTERN EUROPEAN NATIONS

United States support for international collaboration was reflected in various ways. In order to build a new collective security system, the United States worked closely with its wartime allies to make the United Nations operational. In April 1945 an international conference met in San Francisco to map the specific provisions for the charter of the new world organization. Despite increasing Soviet opposition, the United States had great influence on the final draft. In its formal organizational structure the United Nations clearly reflected American influences, for it had an executive branch (Secretary-General), a legislative branch (General Assembly and Security Council), and a judicial branch (International Court of Justice).

Europe's suffering and destitution also prompted Congress between 1945 and 1947 to appropriate more than $7 billion for a direct relief program. American forces in Europe spent additional sums, which bolstered the economies of the war-weary continent. Heavy United States contributions to the United Nations Relief and Recovery Administration (UNRRA) further improved the condition of millions of suffering Europeans.

Meanwhile, President Truman soon found himself faced with increasing Russian-American friction, which contrasted with the cooperative spirit between the two new world powers during the recent war. The strain was revealed at the Potsdam (Germany) Conference in August 1945, where the new president met with Churchill and Stalin to deliberate on immediate postwar plans. There the Russians insisted on maintaining Communist governments in Poland and Rumania despite their earlier promises at Yalta to allow free elections. Stalin also opposed the United States position for creating a demilitarized but united Germany, insisting instead on a divided German nation, part of which would be occupied indefinitely by Soviet troops. The United States was able to sign peace treaties with Hungary, Bulgaria, Rumania, and Italy at Potsdam. But the conference heralded the end of close Soviet-American wartime cooperation and inaugurated an era of strained relations between the two superpowers. Indeed, some felt that it marked the beginning of the Cold War.

The growing tension was also revealed in attempts to provide international control of atomic energy. By 1946 the Russians had created what Winston Churchill (in a speech at Westminster College in Fulton, Missouri) aptly termed an Iron Curtain across eastern Europe which Westerners found difficult to penetrate. When the United States therefore presented the Baruch Plan in the United Nations to provide for the international control of nuclear materials, the Soviets opposed it. They objected to foreign inspection of atomic materials within their borders. Rather, they argued for policing by each nation, a proposal rejected by the United States because of its profound distrust of Russia. Mutual recriminations, hostilities, and fears, therefore, led to a deadlock on the issue.

CONTAINMENT

The Truman Doctrine

United States policy toward Europe was also characterized by an effort to knit closer ties of cooperation and to contain the expansion of Communism, a policy prompted by a concern for American security.

The first of three major decisions by President Truman delineating his new pattern of American diplomacy was the Truman Doctrine, announced in April 1947 in response to threatened Communist domination of Greece. As the British, pressed by their serious financial problems, prepared to withdraw economic and military aid from the pro-western government in Greece, the Soviets hoped to fill this vacuum by supporting a Communist regime in the country. They intended to extend their influence throughout the Mediterranean. The United States considered such possible Russian domination of Turkey, as well as southern and eastern Europe, a threat to its own security. Consequently, on March 12, 1947, the president announced the Truman Doctrine, embodying two major premises. He promised that to contain the spread of Communism, the United States would extend large-scale economic aid ($700 million) to the tottering democratic Greek government; and in addition the United States would provide military supplies to enable the Greek regime to suppress Communist revolutionaries within its own borders. This program aroused considerable controversy. Its critics charged that it sharpened the tensions between the United States and Russia and intensified the Cold War; its defenders praised its efficacy in preventing the spread of Communist power in Greece, where the last Communist resistance was ended by 1949. The extension of American economic and military aid to nations threatened by Communism to enable them to contain Communist influence added a new dimension to diplomacy.

The Marshall Plan

In succeeding months the Truman administration inaugurated two additional programs that extended the containment policy to most of the European continent. In a famous commencement address at Harvard University on June 5, 1947, Secretary of State George C. Marshall enunciated what came to be known as the Marshall Plan. He explained the reasons for the policy as follows:

> The truth of the matter is that Europe's requirements for the next three or four years of foreign food and other essential products — principally from America — are so much greater than her present ability to pay that she must have substantial additional help or face economic, social, and political deterioration of a very grave character. . . .
>
> Aside from the demoralizing effect on the world at large and the possibilities of disturbances arising as a result of the desperation of the people concerned, the consequences to the economy of the United States should be apparent to all. It is logical that the United States should do whatever it is able to do to assist in the return of normal economic health in the world, without which there can be no political stability and no assured peace. Our policy is directed not against any country or doctrine but against hunger, poverty, desperation, and chaos. Its purpose should be the revival of a working economy in the world so as to permit the emergence of political and social conditions in which free institutions can exist.[1]

[1] *New York Times,* June 6, 1947.

In line with these goals he announced a huge American economic aid program for all European nations — east and west — to assist them in reconstructing their war-torn economies. Marshall promised more than $22 billion for the program, designed to strengthen their economies so as to make them less prone to Communist domination. Although European powers were to allocate and administer the funds themselves through an Economic Cooperation Administration, later the European Economic Council (EEC), the countries in the Soviet bloc did not participate. In the ensuing five years western European nations embraced the plan with enthusiasm, with the result that it became one of the most successful American foreign aid programs. The gross national product of western Europe rose by 25 per cent by 1952, and industrial and farm production increased by 64 per cent and 74 per cent, respectively. By strengthening the economies of European democracies, the Marshall Plan played a significant role in containing the spread of Soviet influence.

NATO

In addition, President Truman and his advisors sought to strengthen western Europe's military power so as to withstand Russian pressures. That these pressures were real was demonstrated by the Soviet blockade of Berlin in 1948 (in protest against the formation of a new West German government), which was only broken by a massive United States airlift of supplies. As a result of American initiatives, western European nations formed the Council of Europe for closer military and economic cooperation. They also joined their military resources in a pact known as the North Atlantic Treaty Organization (NATO). And in 1948 the United States signed a military alliance with these countries — its first since the Franco-American treaty of 1778. This allowed American military bases in NATO countries, provided for the stationing of American troops within their borders, promised the delivery of American arms and equipment to bolster their own forces, and stipulated joint maneuvers and military action in case any NATO members were attacked by another power. Just how effective the Marshall Plan and NATO were in preventing the spread of Soviet Communism in Europe cannot be measured precisely, but it is true that after

1949 Soviet pressures on Western Europe lessened. Altogether, the Truman Doctrine, the Marshall Plan, and NATO comprised the major components of American containment policy.

LATIN AMERICAN DIPLOMACY

Although in theory United States diplomacy in Latin America was also designed to emphasize cooperation and containment, in practice it proved ineffective because of the Truman Administration's undue concern with European problems. American Ambassador Spruille Braden's clumsy attempts to interfere in internal Argentine politics in 1946 only resulted in the election of a totalitarian regime under Juan Peron. It is true that at the Inter-American Conference at Bogota, Colombia, in 1948 the United States succeeded in securing the creation of the Organization of American States (OAS) to facilitate closer economic cooperation in the Western Hemisphere. But Congress failed to provide sufficient funds to implement the program, to the great disappointment and frustration of many Latin Americans. As a result, the decade after 1945 witnessed few significant reforms in Latin America, and a consequent increase in Communist influence in most South American nations.

ASIAN DIPLOMACY

Truman's containment policy also proved itself ineffective in Asia. Certainly it was a desire to contain Communist influence in the Far East that led the United States to sign a very conciliatory peace treaty with Japan in 1951, in an effort to woo Japanese support for American diplomacy. The treaty required only minimal reparations from Japan, gave it the explicit right of rearmament, and deprived it only of colonies gained by conquest. In 1954 it led the Eisenhower administration to initiate the formation of a new alliance bloc of seven Far Eastern nations, the Southeast Asia Treaty Organization (SEATO), a Pacific equivalent to NATO in the Atlantic area. The SEATO treaties gave the United States the right to establish military bases, provided for the stationing of American troops within borders of allied nations, arranged for the delivery of American arms and equipment, and contained provisions for mutual military aid in case of attack by other nations. Whether the formation of a new group of American allies in the Pacific actually deterred Communist activities in that area was widely debated at the time, and in succeeding years.

China

The effort to contain Communist expansion by closer economic and military collaboration failed in China and Korea. For years the United States had sought closer ties with Nationalist China under General Chiang Kai-shek. Between 1941 and 1945 the Roosevelt administration spent more than $300 million for economic aid, and supplied military weapons and advisors. Within China, however, the Communist Chinese steadily continued to win ground. In 1944 President Roosevelt had assigned General Patrick Hurley to China as an emissary to urge Chiang to establish a coalition with the Communists. But he met only rebuffs. Then in December of 1945 President Truman sent General George C. Marshall on a similar mission, which also proved fruitless. Probably only direct American intervention could have prevented Communist domination of all of China, and neither Truman nor a majority of Americans were prepared to make such a sweeping commitment. Consequently, by 1949 the Chinese Communists dominated their entire mainland, forcing the Nationalists to take refuge in Formosa. United States policy in China seemed a total failure.

Korea

Cooperation also failed to stem the tide of Communist expansion in Korea. After liberating the country from the Japanese, Russia and the United States occupied it between 1945 and 1949, dividing it into respective northern and southern zones divided at the thirty-eighth parallel. Then, in 1949 the United States withdrew its troops, leading to the creation of a Communist-controlled North Korea above the thirty-eighth meridian and democratic South Korea below that line. In 1950, however, the North Koreans launched a large-scale invasion of the south in an effort to control the entire country. As thousands of North Koreans poured into the south — with tacit and open support by the Soviet Union and Communist China — the United Nations Security Council condemned the action as unwarranted aggression and ordered United Nations members to dispatch military forces to repel them. While many nations contributed arms and men for this action, the major burden was borne by the United States.

The conflict raged through four phases over the next three weary years. The months between June and September 1950 were marked by the North Korean offensive; September and October of 1950 witnessed a United Nations attack; November 1950 to January 1951 saw a powerful invasion by Chinese forces bolstering the North Koreans; and for the next two years a tense stalemate characterized the position of United Nations and Communist armies. When the two sides agreed to an armistice at Panmunjon in July of 1953, delimiting North and South Korea at the thirty-eighth parallel, neither gained more than an inconclusive, tentative, and uneasy truce.

Doctrine of Limited War

Communist expansion into South Korea required an agonizing reappraisal of American diplomacy and led the Truman administration to develop the doctrine of limited war. Clearly, containment of Communism by close economic and military cooperation with American allies did not always restrain Communist influences as the case of Korea revealed clearly. But what was to be done? One group of critics, led by ex-President Herbert Hoover and Senator Robert A. Taft of Ohio, proposed a neoisolationist course advocating United States withdrawal from most areas of the world. They suggested that American interests extended only to Great Britain in the West and Japan in the east, and did not extend beyond. At the other extreme, General Douglas MacArthur and other leaders urged total offensive war to destroy Communist power in Korea and wherever else it appeared. Indeed, MacArthur's advocacy of massive American bombing of China in December 1950 in direct defiance of the administration's more limited policy led President Truman to remove him as commander in the Pacific during April of the following year. President Truman and his advisors gradually decided to follow a course somewhere midway between the views of Hoover and Taft on the one hand, and those of MacArthur and his followers on the other. Their position came to be embodied in the doctrine of limited war. To contain Communism, the United States would have to use direct force — with non-nuclear weapons — but not to win victories that would result in the extermination of Communist influence. Rather, the nation would engage in holding actions, or limited wars, that would merely contain Communism's further spread. The Korean War was a prime example of the doctrine. Such a limited goal did not find widespread appeal, especially among military men, but it was realistically designed to achieve containment without plunging the world into a nuclear holocaust.

APPRAISAL OF TRUMAN'S FOREIGN POLICIES

The results of Truman's foreign policies were varied. To some contemporaries it appeared that they were successful in preventing the further expansion of Communist power, especially in Europe and the Far East. But they also provoked another reappraisal of American diplomacy as critics pointed to weaknesses and flaws. Containment could be viewed as a static policy, since it was dedicated to maintaining the status quo and did not aim for long-range elimination of the menace posed by Communism. At the same time, the cost of the Truman policies in men and money was enormous. In Korea alone 25,000 Americans lost their lives, and more than 100,000 were wounded. The total monetary cost of economic and military aid policies between 1945 and 1951 was well over $50 billion. The question many Americans came to ask was, "Was it worth it?" During the presidential election of 1952 foreign affairs were to become a vital issue.

Over and beyond the specific strengths and weaknesses of Truman's foreign policies contemporaries and later critics engaged in a great debate which focused on responsibility for the outbreak of the Cold War between the United States and Russia. Two major views stood out in this debate — between traditionalists, defending United States policies, and revisionists, who attacked them. To reverse the English poet Alexander Pope's dictum, whatever was, was not necessarily right.

The defenders of Truman and Eisenhower's diplomacy, often known as traditionalists, argued that the Cold War was begun by the Soviet Union. They included well-known writers such as Herbert Feis, *Churchill, Roosevelt, Stalin;* diplomat

George F. Kennan, *American Diplomacy, 1900 – 1950;* and historian Norman Graebner, *Cold War Diplomacy*. Their defense revolved around three arguments. Communist expansion and aggression required an appropriate response by the United States. Russian hostility to the United States was inherent in Communist doctrines and goals of world revolution, no matter how conciliatory American policy might be; and Russian treaty violations — such as the failure to hold free elections in Poland as Stalin had promised at Yalta — clearly showed the bad faith of the Soviets.

But these views were vigorously challenged by a group of radical revisionists. Among them Gar Alperovitz, *Atomic Diplomacy;* William Appleman Williams, *The Tragedy of American Diplomacy;* D. F. Fleming, *The Cold War and Its Origins;* and David Horowitz, *Free World Colossus* were widely read. According to their interpretation, the United States and not Russia inaugurated the Cold War. Why? First, because United States foreign policy was devoted to maintenance of the status quo, to opposition to revolutions, even revolutions designed to throw off the yoke of colonialism. The reactionary leaders of American capitalism were therefore determined to destroy the Soviet system. In fact, a conspiracy existed in the Truman administration to use the atomic bomb to force Russia to submit to American demands. Nuclear bombs over Hiroshima and Nagasaki were used mainly not to defeat the Japanese, but to intimidate the Russians. Truman's refusal to uphold idealism in American diplomacy after 1945 brought about the collapse of the close Russo-American alliance of World War II and replaced good will and cooperation with fear and suspicion. Though the revisionists frequently overstated their case, they brought a realistic note to an understanding of United States diplomacy in the Cold War. On many occasions, American policies may have been a response to Soviet aggression, but there were times when American actions contributed to mutual hostility and distrust.

EISENHOWER ADMINISTRATION, 1952 – 1960

Inevitably, the foreign and domestic policies of the Truman administration came to be issues in the election of 1952. Yet, to a remarkable extent, the succeeding Eisenhower administration maintained the framework of the Truman policies in both the domestic and the foreign sphere. These were years of consolidation rather than of innovation or retrenchment, and seeming placidity despite many pressing problems.

THE ELECTION OF 1952

The election of 1952 tended to revolve as much around personalities as issues. President Truman was determined to retire and ultimately threw his support to Adlai E. Stevenson, the former governor of Illinois, who promised to continue the Truman programs. Considerable excitement attended the Republican convention where isolationists, under the banner of Senator Robert A. Taft of Ohio, battled to a draw with internationalists supporting the candidacy of Thomas E. Dewey. In view of these divisions the party leaders eagerly sought a candidate who could unify the divergent factions. Their obvious choice was General of the Army Dwight D. Eisenhower, who spoke in vague generalities that were designed to cause little controversy or offense. Moreover, he was undeniably one of the most popular personalities in American public life. The results of the election were a foregone conclusion despite Stevenson's brilliant discussions of the major issues. More than 34 million Americans cast votes that supported the "I Like Ike" slogan compared to 27 million for his Democratic opponent.

The new chief executive came to the presidency from a long and distinguished military career. He was born in Denison, Texas, in 1890, but after 1892 grew up in Abilene, Kansas, where his father struggled on a small income to maintain his seven sons. Between 1907 and 1909 Dwight Eisenhower attended the local high school, at the same time working to help support his family. Because he was too old in 1911 to meet the age requirements of the United States Naval Academy at Annapolis, he entered the United States Military Academy at West Point, from which he graduated in 1915 in the upper third of his class. Then followed more than twenty years in the peacetime army, and special training at the General Staff School at Fort Leavenworth, Kansas, and the Army War College in Washington, D.C. By 1939 Eisenhower was a lieutenant colonel, and after that his rise was rapid. In 1942 President Roosevelt appointed him commanding general for the European theater of war and commander in chief of forces in

North Africa. Two years later Roosevelt chose him as supreme commander of the Allied Expeditionary Force for invasion of the Continent, in which role he supervised and coordinated the complex operations before and after D-Day. He closed his distinguished military career as chief of staff and general of the army, before retiring in 1948 to become president of Columbia University. Two years later President Truman temporarily recalled him to organize NATO forces, a task which he accomplished with dispatch.

Many Americans in the 1950's proudly sported their "I Like Ike" buttons. And indeed, even those who did not vote for him found it difficult not to like Ike. His personal charm and simplicity, his genuine friendliness and warmth, and his even-tempered personality added to his charismatic quality. Characteristics such as these made him one of the most popular chief executives ever to occupy the White House. But his tenure as president also revealed limitations. Seeking relaxation at the conclusion of a distinguished military career, he often sought to escape the arduous work load of the presidency by indulging in his favorite pastime of golf, meanwhile leaving crucial executive decisions to subordinates. Consequently, he often failed to display a sure grasp of public issues. Moreover, considering himself to be above the wiles of partisan politics, he did not provide sure and firm leadership for the Republican party, for Congress, and for the executive departments. Even his closest followers were often distressed by his great admiration for big business executives, to the exclusion of men of achievement in other spheres. But the glow of President Eisenhower's personality tended to obscure many of these personal shortcomings during his lifetime.

EISENHOWER'S DOMESTIC POLICIES

Having spent a lifetime in the military forces, President Eisenhower was a stranger to the ways and means of politics. Where possible, he sought to stand above political conflicts in accord with three major ideas he had about government. In the first place, he believed in delegating the authority of the presidency through a chain of command including a chief of staff, and scores of new committees. His own chief of staff was former Governor Sherman Adams of New Hampshire, who made many top-level executive decisions and was so powerful during the Eisenhower administration that he was informally known as assistant president. A second belief was a literal interpretation of the separation of powers doctrine. As he understood the Constitution, Congress made laws, the courts interpreted them, and the president simply executed them. Thus he disdained strong leadership, but confined himself to a passive role as a general custodian of executive agencies. A third characteristic was Eisenhower's professed sympathy for states' rights. Distrustful of the powers of the federal government, he preferred to locate governmental powers at the state rather than at the national level where possible. Between 1952 and 1960 politicians of both major parties frequently noted that in practice a strong president would find it difficult to delegate unique presidential functions, that the separation of powers was more real in theory than in practice, and that the states were not inherently better administrators than the federal government. However, President Eisenhower governed not by effective use of executive authority but by the overwhelming popular appeal of his personality.

In domestic as in foreign policy President Eisenhower preferred to play a passive role, which emphasized his moderation. He had no wish to undo the work of the New Deal or the Fair Deal, most of which was left untouched. Hence some observers dubbed his policies as representing "Modern Republicanism." His economic advisors did urge him to abolish federal economic controls, to balance the federal budget, and to reduce individual and corporation taxes under the Revenue Act of 1954. Whether the nation entered a recession in 1954 as a result of these policies was widely debated. Congress did approve a massive new federal interstate highway program in 1956 at a cost of $40 billion to improve the domestic communications system, to bolster national defense, and to keep up a high level of federal public works expenditures. But the chief executive also encouraged private over public power development as revealed in his approval of the Dixon-Yates contract in 1954, which allowed private interests rather than the TVA to construct a power plant for the city of Memphis. It was also seen in his desire to end federal participation in the Hell's Canyon power project in Idaho. In addition Eisenhower favored a slight lowering of federal price supports for agriculture, from 90 per cent to 82.5 per cent of parity. A believer in states' rights, President Eisenhower approved the grant of offshore oil tidelands to the states (1953) instead of to the federal government.

Moderation also characterized social policies of the Eisenhower years. Eisenhower approved the extension of social security to 10 million additional persons, although he used his influence to defeat proposals for federal aid to education or a national health program. Congress also enacted a limited federal housing law authorizing 45,000 new units annually. In the field of civil rights President Eisenhower's nominee for chief justice of the United States Supreme Court, Earl Warren, wrote the landmark school decision in *Brown* v. *Topeka*. The Civil Rights Act of 1957 furthered the cause of integration by extending federal protection to voters — designed to encourage the black electorate in southern states. The president sent federal troops to Little Rock, Arkansas, in 1957 to maintain order while a local high school was integrated. "Mob rule cannot be allowed to override the decisions of our courts," he declared. Some critics charged, however, that Eisenhower's action lacked decisiveness and vigor.

The Eisenhower era, then, seemed placid and undramatic. In temperament and outlook it was a middle-aged man's government — a period of consolidation and stocktaking, and of attempted normalcy. Few major New Deal measures were abolished, nor many new programs initiated. Yet the outward calm presented by American life in the 1950's was illusory, for revolutionary forces were at work transforming America, although their disruptive impact did not become apparent until the 1960's. In foreign relations, however, increasing turbulence characterized even the Eisenhower years, and defied satisfactory solutions.

EISENHOWER AND FOREIGN POLICIES

Since the president preferred to delegate major decisions to his associates throughout most of his administration, he did not take personal charge of American diplomacy but left this vital responsibility to John Foster Dulles, his trusted secretary of state. Few men enjoyed the president's trust to the degree that Dulles did. Hence, until his death in 1959 he was the undisputed leader of United States foreign policy. Increasingly, however, the gap between Dulles' professed aims and his accomplishments in Europe, the Middle East, and Latin America widened, with the result that by the end of the decade, the international prestige of the United States had deteriorated sadly. Such was the force of Dulles' personality, however, that for good or ill he left his stamp on American diplomacy of the decade.

By dint of background, upbringing, and experience, John Foster Dulles was no stranger to American foreign policy. Born in 1888 of well-to-do, distinguished New England forebears, he grew up in the shadow of his uncle, John W. Foster, who served as secretary of state (1897 – 1899) under President McKinley. A graduate of Princeton and the George Washington University Law School, he practiced law with the well-known firm of Sullivan and Cromwell. Meanwhile, he served in a variety of diplomatic posts: In 1907 he was an American delegate to the International Disarmament Conference at the Hague; and in 1919 he was an advisor to the United States delegation at Versailles. Then, at the end of World War II he was a United States delegate to the San Francisco Conference of 1945 which drafted the charter of the United Nations. Two years later he became counselor to the Department of State; and during the last years of the Truman administration he was primarily responsible for organizing the SEATO alliance in the Pacific.

In outlook and in personality, Dulles appeared on the stage of American diplomacy as a latter-day Woodrow Wilson. A devout Presbyterian, he was at the same time a high-minded idealist as well as a hard-headed realist. His idealism focused on three concepts derived from his Puritan heritage. He was a convinced moralist and a believer in the force of moral precepts in everyday affairs. He was also conscious of a sense of mission, not only of individuals like himself, but also of nations such as the United States, whose responsibility it was to bring doctrines of righteousness to the less fortunate peoples of the world. He was convinced, too, of the doctrine of predestination, believing that men and nations who trod the path of righteousness would ultimately win victory and salvation no matter how many temporary obstacles might be placed in their path. His passionate devotion to such ideals often made it difficult for him to compromise on particular issues since general principles guided so many of his actions. Yet, he was not impractical. As a skilled diplomat, he relied as often on patient persuasion as on the naked threat of military force. Not unlike Woodrow Wilson, he presented a glorious vision to the world, which in turn often found him frustrating to deal with on specific issues.

DULLES' POLICY

Like many Americans in 1953, Dulles appeared dissatisfied with the seemingly static quality of Truman's design for American diplomacy and hoped to develop a more dynamic policy. Instead of containment of Communism, Dulles proposed that the United States undertake its destruction wherever it existed. While not completely rejecting cooperation and limited wars as instruments of United States foreign policy, Dulles proposed what he considered to be a more effective means — massive retaliation. Not only did the United States fail to win decisive victories in limited wars; but also such conflicts were enormously expensive and anathema to an administration devoted to economy and a balanced budget. Thus, Dulles advocated that, instead, the United States should resort to the use of ballistic missiles and nuclear weapons to deal crushing and decisive blows to Communist nations guilty of aggression. As he conceived it, he would renovate American foreign policy to give it a more modern, dynamic, and attractive look.

In practice, however, the Dulles policies between 1953 and 1959 closely followed patterns developed in the Truman era. In Europe, the Middle East, the Pacific, and Latin America, American policies emphasized containment of Communism by military and economic aid and by limited war. President Eisenhower himself seemed unwilling to utilize massive retaliation, since it would have involved the United States in a large-scale nuclear war; the cure might be more fatal than the disease. As a matter of fact, critics soon found many weaknesses in the Dulles theory that prevented its application. Moreover, American threats of nuclear warfare seemed particularly impotent in local situations. There conventional arms seemed far more effective — especially where American reluctance to use nuclear weapons was evident because of fear of plunging the world into a large-scale war. An atomic bomb designed to destroy the Communists of a given area might at the same time destroy all non-Communists as well, in addition to demolishing and contaminating entire areas and regions. However attractive in theory, the Dulles views did not prove particularly effective in minimizing Communist influence in practice.

To some critics (Herman Kahn, Henry Kissinger, Adlai Stevenson) Dulles' ideals were self-contradictory. Without denying his high moral purpose, they wondered how the morality of nuclear war could be defended; without questioning his sense of mission, they wondered whether it was desirable, feasible, or possible for the United States to impose its will on the rest of the world by force; without rejecting his confidence in predestination they wondered whether the United States should not follow a more flexible and pragmatic course; and in addition to questioning his theory, they also underscored the impracticality of the Dulles views.

Europe

After initial failures, the Dulles theories gave way to reliance on the Truman design, which continued to guide American policies toward Europe. One of the first tests for the doctrine came in 1953 with a German revolt against the Communist regime in East Berlin. Contrary to the expectations of the East Berliners, however, the United States did not come to their aid, and East German Communist forces ruthlessly crushed the rebellion, undeterred by the Dulles threat of massive retaliation. After all, was the United States likely to plunge into a major nuclear war with Russia over a local uprising in East Germany? The impracticality of the Dulles theory became even more evident during the Hungarian Revolt of 1956 when a group of Hungarian youths attacked Soviet tanks and armored vehicles in a vain attempt to drive Russian occupation troops from the country. Once again American aid was not forthcoming, as the Russians savagely suppressed the dissidents and reasserted their iron rule. Again the United States shrank from the use of nuclear weapons against the Russians in view of the dangers of a possible world war or Soviet retaliation with their own H-bombs against the West. However attractive massive retaliation might appear in rhetoric or theory, therefore, it showed itself to be largely unworkable in practice.

Instead, Dulles was forced to rely more extensively on military, economic, and diplomatic collaboration. Thus, the United States continued to provide extensive military support for NATO, expending more than $3 billion annually for arms, now also including West Germany. The State Department also supported the efforts of the thirteen continental nations in 1959 to form an economic union, known as the European Common Market. Among the functions of this European economic community were the removal of tariff barriers and the pooling of loan funds for industrial development. A united Europe was therefore emerging as a third power between the United States and Russia. In addition, the Eisenhower administration continued to place great emphasis on diplomatic collaboration. The Summit Conference of 1955 in Geneva, Switzerland, witnessed a personal meeting between President Eisenhower and Soviet Premier Khrushchev, which created a more friendly atmosphere between the two nations although it did not result in any settlement of major issues. As the Russians undertook another blockade of West Berlin in 1959 in the hope of forcing American recognition of East Germany, Eisenhower and Khrushchev met again in Geneva without any firm resolution on the German problem. The United States hoped for a united German state; the Russians were adamant in keeping East Germany in the Communist orbit. In a gesture of mutual good will the Russian leader visited the United States at President Eisenhower's invitation in May 1960, but this good will was quickly dissipated by the U-2 incident. To the great discomfiture of the United States, the Russians shot down an American U-2 "spy plane" deep over Soviet territory and captured its pilot, Gary Powers, who was gathering intelligence. Suddenly, Russo-American relations became more strained than ever, while the Soviets displayed seeming American duplicity to all the world. Soviet Foreign Minister Andrei A. Gromyko angrily shouted in the United Nations:

> Here we must dwell on one important aspect of this whole matter: the perfidy displayed by the United States Government in relation to the Soviet Union. . . . Only a short time ago [1959] the President of the United States received the Head of the Soviet Government at Washington and Camp David [Maryland], entertained him cordially, and spoke of the need to strengthen mutual trust. Yet it turns out that at that very time the United States Air Force was engaged in carrying out a programme of aggression against the Soviet Union to which President Eisenhower had given his personal approval. . . .

This alone graphically reveals the nature of the present foreign policy of the United States. How is it possible after this to regard such a policy without mistrust? How is it possible after this to trust the statements of United States Government officials? . . .[2]

The Dulles policies in Europe, therefore, although bombastic in theory, failed to weaken Soviet Communism significantly in practice. And the wide gap between the grandiose objectives of massive retaliation and the modest accomplishments of collaboration and containment only served to damage the prestige of the United States in the international community.

Middle East

Nor did the Dulles policies succeed in containing Communist influences in the Middle East. As a major source of oil supply for NATO, the Middle East became increasingly important to American defense plans after World War II. Consequently, many of the political rivalries in the area directly affected American diplomacy. This was particularly true of the antagonisms between the Arab countries and Israel, ever since 1948 when the United Nations had authorized the creation of a Jewish state. Although the Israelis had defeated the Arabs in a short war of 1949, the Arabs were planning another conflict for revenge in 1955. The Arab countries were increasingly aided and abetted by the Soviet Union, which was rapidly consolidating its political, economic, and military influence in the region. Dulles' veiled threats between 1953 and 1955 of nuclear deterrence did little to prevent the spread of Communism in the Middle East, as thousands of Russian technicians and military advisors poured into every Arab country. The Soviets also sent large-scale economic aid and military equipment to the Arabs.

Under such circumstances the Eisenhower administration fell back on the Truman policies of containment and limited war, although Dulles did so with extraordinary clumsiness. He attempted to use economic pressures on the Egyptians to force them to cut their ties with Russia and Communist China. Thus, Dulles threatened to withhold a United States loan for the building of the Aswan Dam in Egypt, expected to become a regional power and multi-purpose development project like the TVA.

[2] *New York Times,* May 24, 1960.

The Egyptian leader General Abdul Nasser rejected the American demand, confident of Soviet aid. Then, to show his disdain of the Western powers, he nationalized the Suez Canal in July 1956, precipitating an invasion of Egypt by British, French, and Israeli forces. Aware of the need for lessening Arab antagonism toward the United States, Dulles now joined the Russians in condemning the British-French-Israeli action and insisted on their withdrawal. This was accomplished within a two-week period. Far from being grateful to the United States, however, General Nasser and other Arab leaders attributed their salvation to the Russians.

In a further attempt to win Arab friendship, the president extended them military and economic aid. Proclaiming the Eisenhower Doctrine of 1958, the chief executive and Congress announced that the United States would give military help and economic assistance to any nation in the Middle East whose independence was threatened by Communist influences, if the president considered its independence vital to American security. Under the Eisenhower Doctrine, Jordan, Iraq, and Lebanon in 1958 received military supplies and loans. At the same time the United States Navy (in Jordan) and United States Marines (in Lebanon) helped to maintain non-Communist regimes in power. American diplomacy in the Middle East, therefore, further revealed the impracticality of massive retaliation and reflected a not very skillful use of collaboration and containment and limited war as prime instruments of United States foreign policy in the region.

Latin America

The Dulles policies also enjoyed no spectacular successes in the Western Hemisphere. Threats of nuclear attack obviously did not deter Communists in Latin America, as the victory of Fidel Castro and his Communist sympathizers in Cuba during 1959 clearly revealed. Nor did the United States extend massive economic aid to its neighbors in the south as it did to Europe and the Middle East. Consequently, many Latin Americans were disgruntled as the Good Neighbor policy deteriorated from neglect. The State Department did initiate talks concerning a regional economic market in the hemisphere and negotiated export quota pacts to increase trade; and Congress authorized (1959) the re-establishment of the Inter-American Bank to provide $500 million worth of credit.

Latin American bitterness was increased by American policies toward Guatemala and Cuba. Dulles' intervention in Guatemalan affairs (June 1954) made many wonder whether the United States really did want to refrain from interfering in the affairs of its neighbors. When President Eisenhower entered the White House in 1953 many Communists and their sympathizers in Guatemala had already found high places in the regime of Jacabo Arbenz Guzman. Consequently, in March of 1954 Secretary of State Dulles secured passage of a resolution by the Organization of American States calling for consultation among its members to consider action against any Latin American state whose sovereignty was threatened by Communists. But both Dulles and the Central Intelligence Agency were impatient about the efficacy of such action. Instead, in June of 1954 they encouraged a counter-revolution in Guatemala against the Guzman regime by Colonel Carlos Castillo Armas, an avowed anti-Communist. After leading a successful invasion from Nicaragua and Honduras, Armas was installed as provisional president of Guatemala. Not surprisingly, many Latin Americans believed that Theodore Roosevelt's Big Stick diplomacy was being revived by Dulles and that henceforth the United States would unilaterally undermine governments to whose policies it was unsympathetic.

American policy toward Cuba also won few friends in the Western Hemisphere. The Eisenhower administration continued to give strong support to General Fulgencio Batista, the Cuban dictator, and even sent him arms. Secretary Dulles was rather dismayed by Batista's overthrow in 1958 at the hands of social reformer Fidel Castro. While not a Communist at the time, Castro was sympathetic to radical reform. Within a year after assuming control of the Cuban government, Castro embarked on large-scale executions of opponents and also expropriated American-owned properties. In response, the State Department sent vigorous notes of protest and sought to apply economic pressure to Cuba by cutting sugar import quotas. Meanwhile, Castro attempted with mixed success to export his brand of revolution into other parts of South America. Under United States prodding, in 1960 the Organization of American States approved the Declaration of San Jose, which condemned such intervention in the affairs of American republics. Castro remained unperturbed, however. In the same year he signed an important trade agreement with the Soviet Union, which obligated itself to buy large amounts of Cuban sugar and to extend loans. Thus, efforts by the United States to chastise Castro were largely ineffective. Many Latin Americans felt that the primary emphasis of American foreign policy was on Europe, the Middle East, and the Pacific, and tended to neglect the Western Hemisphere.

Far East

Indeed, a large portion of Secretary Dulles' active energies were devoted to Far Eastern problems, which provided an additional testing ground for his convictions. Flushed with the pride of his new cabinet office, Dulles liked to believe that the North Koreans had been persuaded to agree to the armistice at Panmunjon in July of 1953 by his threats of nuclear warfare. Later observers were not as sure, especially since the doctrine of massive retaliation did not actively contain Communist influence in other Far Eastern nations. In Vietnam, for example, the United States extended large-scale aid to the French, who were seeking to suppress a nationalist uprising led by Ho Chi Minh, supported by Soviet and Chinese Communists. When the French withdrew in defeat during 1954, the United States appeared impotent. Massive retaliation would have required an American nuclear attack on China, but President Eisenhower was unwilling to authorize such drastic action. Thus, Ho Chi Minh and his followers, including some Communists, extended their influence southward from their stronghold in North Vietnam. They effectively divided the country into two separate nations — Communist-oriented North Vietnam, and western-oriented South Vietnam, which received an increasing amount of American military and economic aid. Members of the SEATO alliance received similar help.

In respect to Formosa, too, American policy was characterized by collaboration and containment. When Communist China claimed Formosa in 1954, the last bastion of Chiang Kai-shek and the Nationalist Chinese, Congress gave President Eisenhower the authority to defend its offshore islands, Quemoy and Matsu, against a possible attack by the Chinese Communists. Such an attack did not materialize during the decade. But American policy was clear. The United States was seeking to maintain the status quo in the Far East, as in the Truman era, rather than to "roll back" existing Communist power, as Secretary Dulles had once promised.

APPRAISAL OF EISENHOWER POLICIES

American foreign policy during the Eisenhower administration thus did not differ sharply from the Truman-Acheson design of the preceding decade. Although in 1953 John Foster Dulles had proclaimed a new era in American foreign relations, the new age never materialized. The United States did not seek to destroy Communist governments where they existed, nor even to grant direct aid to uprisings against Communist rule. Despite much talk of massive retaliation with nuclear weapons, the course of United States policy was on a different track. In Europe, the Middle East, Latin America, and the Pacific, Eisenhower and Dulles followed a cautious policy, emphasizing international cooperation, containment, and limited war. Yet to the peoples of the world, and especially the Russians, the wide gap between the theory and the practice of American diplomacy became apparent. Before his death in 1959 John Foster Dulles was aware of the gap. Words and deeds, power and diplomacy, seemed uncoordinated under Dulles. Consequently, the prestige of the United States in international affairs plummeted during the last years of the Eisenhower administration.

The Eisenhower era was one of moderation and consolidation rather than of bold new innovation. Taking a cue from the cautious mood of President Eisenhower, Republican leaders made few dramatic changes in domestic policies, but worked to revise and refine existing programs. The president's effort to lessen executive powers by large-scale delegation and the appointment of scores of new committees had not proved itself effective before 1960 and was gradually abandoned. Few major changes were made in the nation's economic or social policies. The emphasis on a balanced budget and governmental economy did lead the president to search for a less expensive foreign policy. Secretary Dulles seemed to offer such an opportunity, but it proved to be far more attractive in theory than in practice. As in domestic affairs, the United States witnessed few drastic changes in its foreign policy.

SUMMARY: 1945 – 1960

The years between 1945 and 1960 saw the United States transformed into an affluent society. During the immediate postwar years Truman made major efforts to make a smooth transition from war to peace, to reconstruct many phases of national life. His attempt — when compared to other postwar reconstruction programs — was amazingly successful. Indeed, he implemented his reconstruction policies far more effectively than his reform proposals, most of which Congress rejected. This was due in large part to a cautious mood of Americans after 1948 as they strove for normalcy — with an emphasis on material comforts and a disinclination for participation in wars of domestic conflict and strife. President Eisenhower accurately represented the mood of millions of Americans who, in a period of general prosperity, were loath to "rock the boat." But if the emphasis on reconstruction and normalcy characterized the first fifteen years after the end of World War II, it was to be quickly displaced by dynamic and turbulent changes of the 1960's.

FOR FURTHER READING

A general survey of political events of this period is ERIC F. GOLDMAN, *The Crucial Decade and After: America, 1945 – 1960* (New York: Vintage Books, 1960). A fine summary of foreign affairs is JOHN W. SPANIER, *American Foreign Policy since World War II* (New York: Praeger, 1960). Informative also for the vagaries of the Presidency after the war is RICHARD E. NEUSTADT, *Presidential Power: The Politics of Leadership* (New York: Wiley, 1960). On the Truman years see BARTON J. BERNSTEIN and ALLEN MATUSOW (eds.), *The Truman Administration: A Documentary History* (New York: Harper & Row, 1966). CABELL PHILLIPS, *The Truman Presidency* (New York: Macmillan, 1966) is one of the best journalistic appraisals. Postwar diplomacy is reviewed in HERBERT FEIS, *The Atomic Bomb and the End of World War II*, Rev. ed. (Princeton: Princeton University Press, 1966) and NORMAN S. GRAEBNER, *Cold War Diplomacy: American Foreign Policy, 1945 – 1960* (New York: Van Nostrand, 1962). One of the best revisionist accounts embodying a New Left viewpoint is GAR ALPEROVITZ, *Atomic Diplomacy* (New York: Simon & Schuster, 1965). HARRY B. PRICE, *The Marshall Plan and Its Meaning* (Ithaca: Cornell University Press, 1955) and JOSEPH M. JONES, *The Fifteen Weeks (February 21 – June 5, 1947)* (New York: Viking Press, 1955) cover American economic aid to Europe very well, as does HUGH SETON-WATSON,

Neither War nor Peace: The Struggle for Power in the Post-War World (New York: Praeger, 1960). KLAUS KNORR (ed.), *NATO and American Security* (Princeton: Princeton University Press, 1959) focuses on military policies. The Eisenhower presidency is appraised in ROBERT J. DONOVAN, *Eisenhower: The Inside Story* (New York: Harper, 1956) and more critically by EMMET J. HUGHES, *The Ordeal of Power: A Political Memoir of the Eisenhower Years* (New York: Atheneum, 1963). ARTHUR LARSON, *Eisenhower: The President Nobody Knew* (New York: Scribner, 1968) is an astute critical appraisal by a former member of the inner Eisenhower circle. Senator Joseph McCarthy's activities called forth a spate of books. Among his defenders WILLIAM F. BUCKLEY, JR., and L. BRENT BOZELL, *McCarthy and His Enemies* (Chicago: H. Regnery Co., 1954) is among the most readable. RICHARD ROVERE, *Senator Joe McCarthy* (New York: Harcourt, Brace, 1959) is critical. McCarthyism is placed in historical context in REINHARD LUTHIN, *American Demagogues: Twentieth Century* (Boston: Beacon Press, 1954). On diplomacy of the Eisenhower era consult ROSCOE DRUMMOND and GASTON COBLENTZ, *Duel at the Brink* (Garden City: Doubleday, 1960) and the caustic appraisal of HERMAN S. FINER, *Dulles over Suez* (Chicago: Quadrangle, 1964). THOMAS G. SCHELLING and MORTON H. HALPERIN, *Strategy and Arms Control* (New York: Twentieth Century Fund, 1961) cover disarmament problems of the 1950's.

12

NEW FRONTIERS
OF THE GREAT SOCIETY

The United States in the Turbulent Sixties

Suddenly in the 1960's many Americans realized — as they had not before — that the post–World War II decades really heralded a new era in the development of the United States. World War II served as the dividing point between two distinct periods in which the quality of life in America changed markedly. Prewar America had looked largely to the past, particularly to the early twentieth century, and to the problems it had inherited. Postwar America looked primarily to the future as it struggled with new issues arising from revolutions at home and abroad. The tasks facing men of the sixties and seventies stemmed directly from the vast and disruptive changes introduced by a technological society that was transforming civilization in America. Their problem was to adjust inherited values, goals, and institutions of the industrial society to the vastly changed conditions of the new age. The perplexing problems encountered in this effort explain many of the anxieties and tensions that characterized the United States in the quarter century after World War II. Whether the American democracy was flexible enough to adapt itself to the revolutionary trends of the new age or whether it would itself be destroyed by them was a vexing question. But men of the 1960's resolutely turned to the great challenge before them as they sought to plan for a better America in the future. Thus John F. Kennedy captured the attention of the country when he pleaded

436

for new goals and policies in the shape of New Frontiers. In his brief lifetime he was able to do little more than to raise a vision and to stimulate the imagination of the country. His successor, Lyndon B. Johnson, sought to retain the momentum that Kennedy had aroused by proclaiming his intention of creating a Great Society. Just as he seemed on the verge of making progress toward this goal, the expanding scale of American involvement in the Vietnam war not only seriously disrupted domestic programs but also destroyed national unity by creating deep divisions among Americans. President Nixon, it was clear, eschewed broad and overambitious visions of the future, but instead sought efficient and businesslike solutions for immediate and pressing problems.

Whatever their differences, national leaders of the sixties agreed on certain goals, which constituted New Frontiers of the Great Society. They were concerned with maintaining the pace of scientific discovery and development. They were fully occupied with extending the benefits of affluence on the one hand, and with diminishing poverty on the other. They were confronted with a full-scale black revolution, and its demand for immediate improvement of conditions for all black Americans. They devoted increasing energies to the problems created by the urban revolution, including housing congestion, slums, traffic problems, pollution, crime, health hazards, and education, as the great majority of Americans came to reside in metropolitan areas. They also faced a social revolution led by a minority of the younger generation who became determined to transform most American values and institutions. And they had to ponder the state of the nation's cultural life, suffering from a dearth of money at the very time when Americans were spending unprecedented sums for material goods.

Hopefully, the New Frontiers of the Great Society would help Americans overcome some of their difficulties. The goals of the sixties came to constitute technological and scientific progress, sustained economic growth and the abolition of poverty, the improvement of conditions for blacks, the eradication of urban blight, the easing of social tensions, and the improvement of the quality of American culture. The dimensions of these problems were sweeping, and the difficulties attending their solution were tremendous. But the challenges were raised, and Americans

of the sixties attempted to adjust themselves to the revolutionary era in which they lived. In foreign relations the task was to
develop new goals and techniques to avoid nuclear war and to
maintain international peace.

JOHN F. KENNEDY AND NEW FRONTIERS AT HOME

Imbued with a sense of urgency, John F. Kennedy planned
to dedicate himself to dealing with current problems. His acces-
sion to the presidency brought a subtle change to American politics. Under the leadership of Dwight Eisenhower and his predominantly middle-aged advisors, Americans had been relatively
smug and self-content. Satisfied with the material achievements
of the decade, they conceived their task to be one of primarily
maintaining and consolidating existing progress. Kennedy, however, brought zest and youth to the White House and surrounded
himself with a large group of relatively young men (under forty)
to help him shape his policies. Kennedy was deeply concerned
over burgeoning issues created by the revolutionary trends that
were transforming the United States. He hoped to arouse and
to educate Americans about the new problems they would soon
be facing. As with Theodore Roosevelt, his rhetoric outreached
his accomplishments during the 1000 days that he was in office.
Nevertheless, in domestic as well as in foreign policies, the Kennedy administration was significant in changing the nation's
mood from placidity to active concern.

John F. Kennedy's rise to the highest office in the land was
meteoric. He was born in 1917, the second of nine children of
Joseph P. and Rose Kennedy. Both of his grandfathers were
Irish-born Roman Catholic politicians. His father was one of
America's most successful businessmen, and a powerful figure in
the Democratic party. The young Kennedy attended private
schools in New York and Boston and graduated from Groton, an
exclusive preparatory academy. From there he went on to Harvard, where in 1940 he received a bachelor's degree. His senior
thesis, "While England Slept," was published at the time, reflecting impressions gained while serving as secretary to his father,
then the United States ambassador to Great Britain. Upon American participation in World War II he joined the United States

John F. Kennedy accepting the Democratic presidential nomination in 1960. (Courtesy Democratic National Committee)

Navy and won citations for heroic action as skipper of a P-T boat in the Pacific; he returned from the war with a spinal injury. In 1945 he enrolled at Stanford University to obtain an M.A. degree in economics, but returned to Massachusetts in the following year to enter the race for the United States House of Representatives from the Eleventh District. His great energies were rewarded by success, and for the next six years he served ably in the House. He was elected to the United States Senate from Massachusetts in 1952 and re-elected to a second term. During these years he wrote a book about morality in politics, *Profiles in Courage,* which won him a Pulitzer Prize and great national acclaim. Meanwhile, together with his younger brothers, Robert and Edward, he conducted a very aggressive and effective campaign to win the Democratic presidential nomination in 1960, vanquishing such leading contenders as Hubert Humphrey, and also Lyndon B. Johnson, who reluctantly accepted the vice-presidential slot on the ticket. Kennedy focused upon the need to stimulate economic growth and welfare programs, explaining them with great effectiveness in a series of television debates with the Republican candidate, Richard M. Nixon. In a very close and heated contest (with a spread of only 100,000 votes), Kennedy and Johnson bested their Republican opponents, Richard M. Nixon and Henry Cabot Lodge, who had promised to continue the Eisenhower policies. Thus, Kennedy became the youngest man to be elected president and also the first Roman Catholic to hold the office.

Kennedy cut a dashing figure. His youth belied his maturity, sophistication, and a keen and quick intelligence. With an outgoing personality, he was able to win over Americans from every walk of life, but especially young people. At the same time he had an inner toughness and, indeed, ruthlessness, which surfaced on various occasions during his career. Like his father, he was out to win in everything he did and to best competitors or opponents. A pragmatist with ideals, Kennedy showed himself to be a consummate politician. Most Americans did not like Kennedy in the same easygoing way in which they "liked Ike," but they tended increasingly to respect and admire him as he grew to become a formidable leader.

THE NEW FRONTIER

To dramatize his dynamic approach to the nation's problems, the new chief executive called upon Americans to join him in developing new frontiers to achieve greatness. "Let the word go forth from this time and place, to friend and foe alike, that the torch has been passed to a new generation of Americans —

born in this century, tempered by war, disciplined by a hard and bitter peace, proud of our ancient heritage," he cried.[1]

Kennedy gathered around himself a lively group of young men and intellectuals who came to constitute a Brain Trust. His brother Robert became attorney general and perhaps his closest confidante. McGeorge Bundy, a former dean of Harvard College, served as one of the principal presidential assistants, in addition to former Professors W. W. Rostow of M. I. T., and Arthur M. Schlesinger, Jr., and Carl Kaysen of Harvard. Theodore Sorensen, a young lawyer from Nebraska, came to be one of the president's major speech writers. And Kenneth O'Donnell, an expert in practical politics, skillfully handled relations with Congress. Many of Kennedy's plans and projects emerged from the deliberations of this inner group.

But the president's achievements fell far short of his proclaimed goals. To a considerable extent this was due to congressional opposition, since a coalition of conservative Democrats and Republicans was able effectively to stymie his legislative program. It was also due to unforeseen international difficulties such as the Cuban crisis and the Vietnam war. Moreover, 1000 days did not give Kennedy sufficient time in which to accomplish his ambitious program. Part of the Kennedy myth in later years stemmed directly from speculation about the promises that were left unfulfilled.

More than his predecessor, President Kennedy was acutely aware of the revolutions that were transforming America. Still a young man, he looked hopefully to the future rather than to the past. In domestic policies his prime interest was to spur the nation's economic growth and to lessen poverty. This focus was related to social and urban reform in health, housing, and conservation. He was also greatly concerned with maintaining American leadership in the world of science and was a special booster of the space program. Perhaps no occupant of the White House since Theodore Roosevelt had as lively an interest in cultural events as the young president, who lent support and encouragement to a wide range of cultural activities. In addition, he developed close bonds with many of the nation's intellectuals. But

[1]*New York Times,* January 21, 1961.

if Kennedy was aware of the new forces affecting American life, he was also a highly skilled and consummate politician — an idealist without illusions. Impressed by the closeness of his election, he knew that he must first build a foundation of support for his far-ranging programs among the electorate and in Congress. Thus, he displayed extreme caution and deliberation in formulating policies that he hoped would deal effectively with the outstanding issues in American life of the 1960's and 1970's.

SPACE EXPLORATION

President Kennedy had a great passion for maintaining American leadership in space exploration. By 1961 many scientists believed that the American space program was two years behind that of the Russians. His fervent hope was that the United States could place a man on the moon by 1970. In relation to that objective the National Aeronautics and Space Administration (NASA) launched various satellites and made progress on studies of solar radiation, magnetic fields, and the topography of the moon and other planets. One result of these efforts was the sub-orbital flight of Commander Alan S. Shepard in Freedom 7 on May 5, 1961, more than three weeks after Russian cosmonaut Yuri Gagarin made a single orbit around the earth in his spaceship, Vostok I. In August 1961 another Russian, Gherman Titov, completed seventeen orbits, outdistancing Friendship 7, the American spacecraft piloted by Commander John H. Glenn on February 20, 1962. Then, in May 1963 Major L. Gordon Cooper circled the earth twenty-two times in his space vehicle. American programs continued to progress when on January 29, 1964, NASA placed a Saturn spacecraft into orbit with a one-ton load. In Congress the space program received bi-partisan support.

ECONOMIC REFORM

As expected, Kennedy placed a great emphasis on the stimulation of the country's economic growth. To his great disappointment, Congress ignored many of his proposals and acted only on a selected few. These included appropriations for the federal interstate highway program, an Area Development Program for depressed regions ($900 million), and the Tax Credits Act of 1962, under which businesses that invested in new equipment received a 7 per cent tax credit. In view of rising joblessness in the coal, textile, and automobile industries, and a total of about 5 million people unemployed, Congress reluctantly agreed to a temporary thirteen-week extension of unemployment compensation insurance. To increase international commerce, Congress agreed to the Trade Expansion Act of 1962, authorizing the president to adjust tariff rates to meet competitive conditions. President Kennedy himself sought to stem the rising trend of inflation, especially after labor contracts in the auto industry (1961) and the steel industry (1962) drove up wages. In fact, when the United States Steel Company increased its steel prices by $6 per ton (April 1962), Kennedy publicly condemned the move as dangerous and inflationary and ordered all federal contractors to shift their orders. Such pressure resulted in caution by other steel companies, who held the line on prices. As a further means of maintaining a measure of control over those businessmen whom Kennedy considered to be endangering the nation's economic stability, he fostered a federal antitrust campaign that resulted in Justice Department suits against conflicts of interest on the part of Chrysler Corporation executives, and price-fixing conspiracies by General Electric and Westinghouse. Otherwise, the economy-minded Congress was unwilling to follow Kennedy's leadership in undertaking large-scale tax cuts to spur investment or to appropriate large sums for depressed regions.

SOCIAL REFORM

The young president had little luck with his proposals for social reform legislation. His programs for Medicare, for large-scale federal aid to education, and aid to the nation's cities were largely ignored by an unsympathetic Congress. Of twenty-three proposals for reform sent to the House by Kennedy in 1961, the conservative Republican-Democratic coalition defeated sixteen. Instead, the lawmakers did undertake an expansion of federal aid to housing ($5 billion for four years) under the Housing Act of 1961. And Congress authorized extension of social security, and also of minimum wage provisions to about 3 million persons, while raising the minimum wage (1963) to $1.25 per hour. A very

restricted Manpower Training Bill also was enacted to provide
federal funds for retraining workers who were unemployed because of technological changes. Otherwise, the conservative coalition in Congress stalled the president's program.

In various ways Kennedy expressed his sympathy with the
civil rights movement. He continued the Federal Civil Rights
Commission for two years and appointed Vice-President Johnson
to head the Committee on Equal Employment Opportunities,
which soon secured anti-discrimination pledges from government
suppliers. Kennedy appointed two black Americans to federal
judgeships, and selected another black, Robert Weaver, to direct
the Federal Housing Agency. To enforce national laws against
segregation, the president sent federal troops to the University
of Mississippi in October of 1962 to protect James Meredith, a
black student who sought to earn a degree in this once strictly
segregated institution. And during the famous march on Washington during July of 1963 — when more than 100,000 white
and black civil rights advocates marched in orderly fashion in
the capital to dramatize their support for the pending civil rights
bill — President Kennedy provided federal troops to support the
marchers. In addition, the administration endorsed the Twenty-
third and Twenty-fourth Amendments to the Constitution, respectively conferring voting rights for citizens of the District of
Columbia (60 per cent black) and stipulating the abolition of
poll taxes as a requirement for voting.

POLITICAL REFORM

President Kennedy began the first serious efforts to extend
federal aid to the cities of the nation. In 1962 the United States
Supreme Court handed down its famous reapportionment decision requiring at least forty-four states to reapportion both their
state legislatures and congressional districts. Ever since the nineteenth century these had been controlled by men from rural
areas. The growth of metropolitan centers changed population
patterns everywhere in the United States. Yet lawmakers from
rural areas, though representing a minority of the population,
constituted a majority in many state legislatures where they wielded great and often decisive political power. Only in 1962 did the

federal courts require a very thoroughgoing reapportionment to give urban voters more equitable representation.

CULTURE AND THE ARTS

Kennedy believed firmly that a nation's greatness was shaped to a large extent by its cultural achievements. Consequently, he saw it as one of his major tasks to vitalize the arts in America. While the major burden of such accomplishments must obviously be borne by creative individuals, Kennedy felt that the federal government should play a direct as well as an indirect role in furthering such efforts. A free government, he once noted, was the reflection of a people's will and desire — and their taste. It was his hope that the federal government would encourage a wide array of cultural activities. Symbolically, he invited 155 leading cultural figures to his inauguration. During his years in the White House famous artists such as cellist Pablo Casals and the Bolshoi Ballet were frequently invited for guest appearances. Looking further into the future, in 1961 he supported the construction of a National Cultural Center in the nation's capital (renamed in 1963 as the John F. Kennedy Center for the Performing Arts). Chartered by Congress, which donated land for the site, the building was to be financed by private effort. In this series of concert halls and theaters, Kennedy hoped, the best symphony orchestras, opera, ballet, and theater companies in the world would perform, setting a cultural example for the entire nation and providing inspiration for all Americans. In addition, in 1963 he appointed a Federal Advisory Council on Arts (after Congress refused to enact appropriate legislation), which was to consider the financial needs of individual artists, symphony orchestras, and theater groups. To aid him in developing a comprehensive program, the president selected August Heckscher as a part-time White House cultural coordinator in 1962. Heckscher resigned after a year, disappointed by lack of support in Congress. Just before his death, Kennedy planned to appoint Richard N. Goodwin in his place. Kennedy's concern with the arts electrified the cultural community, who gave him enthusiastic support. In turn, the chief executive thought that one of his most fascinating challenges in the White House was to further the appreciation of culture among all the people, to increase respect for the creative individual, and to widen participation in the processes and fulfillments of art. Few chief executives had as keen an appreciation of the place of culture in a nation's accomplishments as did Kennedy, and few were able to convey the message with greater or more forthright eloquence.

ACHIEVEMENTS OF KENNEDY'S DOMESTIC POLICIES

In his domestic program, therefore, President Kennedy promised much but was able to accomplish relatively little. Most of his efforts were devoted to stimulating economic growth, but he was frequently stymied by a conservative Democratic-Republican coalition in Congress. His contributions to furthering civil rights were notable but not far-reaching. As for urban problems, he had barely begun to mobilize the vast resources of the federal establishment. Although his recommendations for social reforms were sweeping, they were effectively impeded by hostile legislators. Without doubt, federal support for the arts had the effect of boosting the morale of many craftsmen and intellectuals. Over and beyond these specific measures, however, President Kennedy was able to infuse the nation with a youthful, buoyant, zestful optimism which led many Americans to feel a forward movement. His was an optimism based not on romantic dreams of a world that never was or could be, but one based on a hard-headed realistic assessment of America's strengths and weaknesses. His vision of the future was not utopian, but sufficiently real to capture the imagination of millions in the United States and elsewhere who were seeking a better world. Perhaps this style was Kennedy's prime contribution to domestic policy. He illustrated what might be accomplished by a pragmatist with a sense of mission or, as his wife once noted, by an idealist without illusions.

JOHN F. KENNEDY AND NEW FRONTIERS ABROAD

President Kennedy's handling of the presidency impressed not only Americans at home but also other peoples throughout the world. As in domestic affairs, many of Kennedy's hopes and plans were left unfulfilled. He hoped for new frontiers in foreign relations, including a strengthening of the United Nations, gradual international control over nuclear weapons, a lessening of tensions between the United States and Russia, and a massive American foreign aid program to lessen poverty and ignorance in underdeveloped areas of the world such as Latin America, Africa, and Asia. But such dreams required time — time that was not to be at his disposal. Consequently, Kennedy's foreign policies were not strikingly different from those of his predecessors. But younger and more flexible than Eisenhower and Dulles, President Kennedy appeared far more willing to try a wider range of alternatives than they had sought. The thawing of the Cold War with Russia — as the Soviets experienced increasing tensions with Communist China — and abandonment of many of Dulles' ideas presented some new alternatives for American policy makers. But underlying problems of coexistence between Communist and non-Communist nations in a nuclear age did not change appreciably. Thus, the pattern of American diplomacy was not significantly altered, but continued to focus on collaboration, containment, and limited war.

When he took over the reins of government in 1961, Kennedy found the international prestige of the United States at a low ebb. Everywhere Communist expansion appeared on the increase and American influence was on the decline. In Europe, the North Atlantic Treaty Organization appeared visibly weakened; Communist forces in the Far East reached into India, Laos, and South Vietnam. Close to home, the Soviet presence in Cuba presented a growing threat; and increased left-wing revolutionary activities in Latin America were on the rise. United States foreign policy appeared in need of reinvigoration.

BAY OF PIGS

Kennedy's debut as the nation's chief foreign spokesman was marred by the Bay of Pigs fiasco in Cuba. Although John Foster Dulles had died in 1959, not all of his ideas died with him. In fact, a number of President Kennedy's closest advisors — in addition to the Central Intelligence Agency — firmly believed that wars of liberation would stem the tide of Communist influence. Thus in April 1961 the CIA planned an armed invasion of Cuba to overthrow the pro-Communist regime of Fidel Castro. Somewhat incredibly the president and his cabinet approved of this foolhardy enterprise. It called for an expedition of about 1500 men, many of whom were inexperienced and ill-equipped. This motley group attempted to land in the Bay of Pigs at the southern end of Cuba on April 17, 1961, where the Cubans promptly captured all those whom they did not kill. Many of the prisoners were later shot by the Castro regime. Instead of weakening Communist influence on the islands, the Bay of Pigs invasion strengthened it, since most world opinion became outraged at this brusque American attempt at direct intervention.

THE PEACE CORPS

In the hope of winning back some of the friends of the United States who had been alienated by the Bay of Pigs invasion, in September of 1961 President Kennedy created the Peace Corps, one of the most popular measures of his administration. The Peace Corps was composed of Americans of all ages who volunteered to work for token wages in virtually every nation outside the Communist bloc. Their task was to teach and to work with native citizens of the country in any way that would be of help. More than 3000 men and women, many of them idealistic young people, flocked to join the Peace Corps, which was directed by President Kennedy's brother-in-law, Sargent Shriver. Their work and that of thousands of additional volunteers elicited an almost uniformly favorable response throughout the world and contributed significantly to restoring American prestige on the international scene.

THE ALLIANCE FOR PROGRESS — LATIN AMERICA

Partly to assuage the wounded feelings of many Latin Americans, Kennedy attempted to win their confidence and friendship by emphasizing closer hemispheric cooperation. For over a decade they had felt neglected and he hoped to remedy that situation. In August 1961 the members of the Economic and Social Council of the OAS met in Punta del Este, Uruguay, to map out specific plans for collaboration. They developed the blueprint for an Alliance for Progress program, designed to provide a working cooperative relationship among the nations of the Western Hemisphere to raise standards of living and social welfare. The United States pledged $20 billion to aid the effort, and other Latin American countries promised smaller contributions. The Alliance for Progress was seen by Kennedy as a first step toward improving the image of the United States in Latin America. He hoped to do more in future years.

But Soviet power in Cuba grew so rapidly during 1962 that it presented Kennedy with his most urgent Latin American problem. By October of 1962 the Russians had sent more than 6000 technicians to Cuba, where they constructed numerous large missile sites representing an investment of almost $1 billion. These sites were designed to launch offensive weapons, aimed straight at the Panama Canal, Washington, D.C., and other strategic areas in the United States. Rarely had American security been so directly threatened.

In this crisis the young president had to think long and hard about alternative courses of action for his country. After agonizing deliberation with his brother Robert and other advisors, he fell back on a combination of Dulles' doctrine of massive retaliation and Truman's concept of limited war. He ordered a United States naval blockade of Cuba to stop the further flow of Soviet arms to the hostile Castro government and refused to abandon it in the face of United Nations protests. Meanwhile he alerted the Strategic Air Command and held 300,000 men in readiness for a possible invasion of the island. He made it clear to Russian Premier Khrushchev that he would resort to nuclear arms, if necessary, should the Soviets insist on a confrontation at America's doorstep in the Caribbean. Meanwhile, on October 23, 1962, the Organization of American States supported the American arms blockade against Cuba. With the development of a serious crisis, the Soviet government became wary of risking a nuclear conflict and retreated. On October 27, 1962, Premier Khrushchev agreed to the American demand for dismantlement of the missile sites if the United States would end its blockade and not invade Cuba. President Kennedy consented to these terms and this tense confrontation faded into history. American prestige in the world was bolstered by this dramatic episode as many people sympathized with the courageous young president in what was thought to be his most trying hour as chief executive.

EUROPE

Kennedy also succeeded in improving American prestige in Europe, as he skillfully utilized collaboration and containment to counter Communist influence. During the spring of 1961 Kennedy met a bellicose and blustering Khrushchev in Vienna who threatened to reimpose a Russian blockade of Berlin and to force the Allies out of the German city. And, as if to test the mettle of the new American leader, the East German government closed off its sector of Berlin by building an almost impenetrable brick wall to divide it from West Germany. At the same time, urged on by the Russians, they renewed their demand for American recognition.

In the face of this threat Kennedy stood firm. He increased the number of American troops in Germany (by two National Guard divisions), recommended that Congress increase military appropriations, and steadfastly refused recognition of East Germany or of Berlin as a free city. Kennedy also envisioned a grand design for an Atlantic community based on a strong United States and a united Europe. He hoped to increase the strength of NATO by urging the integration of NATO troops without reference to nationality, and the storage of American nuclear missile war heads in France. Although the French leader, General Charles De Gaulle, was far more sympathetic to Kennedy than to most other Americans, the French government showed itself increasingly reluctant to cooperate with the United States or NATO.

Meanwhile, busily at work in developing plans for eventual disarmament, the Arms Control and Disarmament Agency devised several plausible programs and presented them to the United Nations. A significant step in this direction was the Nuclear Test Ban Treaty of July 1963, between the United States and the Soviet Union, which severely restricted nuclear testing above ground. Negotiations for this treaty had begun in 1958 to prevent nuclear contamination of the atmosphere. Most major powers joined in this agreement although France, Cuba, and Communist China refused to sign the document. The Nuclear Test Ban Treaty raised hopes of future agreements on disarmament by all nations and raised Kennedy's stature as a statesman.

AFRICA

Kennedy also hoped to stabilize political conditions in the Congo (Africa) to prevent the spread of Soviet influence there. In 1961 various native factions were struggling for control of the central government then headed by Prime Minister Cyrille Adoula. His strongest rival was Moise Tshombe, head of the province of Katanga. The Soviet Union favored the breakup of the Congo into smaller states, a move opposed by the United States. Since the United Nations lacked funds to defend Adoula's regime, President Kennedy persuaded Congress to purchase $1 million worth of United Nations bonds so that political stability in the Congo — one of the largest states in Africa — could be maintained.

FAR EAST

An effort to promote collaboration also characterized Kennedy's diplomacy in the Far East. When India became involved with Communist China in 1962 over a boundary dispute along the Himalaya mountains, the United States sent military and economic aid to the Indians, which strengthened them sufficiently to negotiate a truce with the Chinese. More vexing was the civil war in Vietnam and Laos between the North Vietnamese under Ho Chi Minh (sympathetic to the Communists) and Bao Dai of South Vietnam (supported by the West). The United States had sent aid to South Vietnam since 1954 apparently without much effect, since Communist and North Vietnamese influence was definitely spreading throughout the area. Mindful of President Truman's intervention in Korea, President Kennedy therefore took cautious first steps toward a limited war and direct American intervention to stop the Communists. In 1962 he sent 5000 American troops to South Vietnam to act as advisors to the South Vietnamese Army and to strengthen its effectiveness as a fighting instrument. Little could Kennedy foresee the extent of United States involvement that his action helped to precipitate. His decision helped to propel the United States toward the longest war in its history.

EFFECT OF KENNEDY FOREIGN POLICIES

The Kennedy foreign policies, therefore, opened few new frontiers, but were developed within a framework of collaboration, containment, and limited war, as used by Truman and Eisenhower. In Latin America the United States continued to emphasize closer hemispheric cooperation, although President Kennedy took a greater interest in this area than any other president since Franklin D. Roosevelt. A staunch believer in the integrity of the North Atlantic community, Kennedy re-emphasized American determination to contain the spread of Communism in Europe, and to cooperate closely with European nations to attain that end. He was also eager to support American commitments to contain Communism in the Far East (SEATO), even to the extent of authorizing limited American intervention on the mainland of Asia. If American diplomacy under Kennedy seemed to have a new look, it was not because of great changes in ends or means. Rather, the youthful vigor of the new president, his buoyant optimism, his dedication, his grasp, and his idealism were attractive to peoples all over the world. In 1000 short days, despite mistakes, Kennedy did much to restore and rejuvenate the image of America in every corner of the globe.

END OF THE 1000 DAYS, AND LYNDON JOHNSON

Who is to say what new frontiers Kennedy might have been able to conquer both at home and abroad if he had been given the opportunity? No one would ever know, for on November 22, 1963, he was struck down by an assassin's bullet. Riding in an open motorcar in Dallas, where he was traveling on a speaking tour, President Kennedy was fatally wounded by several shots purportedly fired by a lone gunman, Lee Harvey Oswald. Perhaps a madman, the assassin's motives were not clearly explained at the time. Within twenty-four hours after he was taken into custody, Oswald himself — in the hands of Dallas Police Department officers — was shot by Jack Ruby, a Dallas night club operator who was enraged by the young president's murder. So, tragedy was compounded by tragedy. Kennedy's body was flown back to Washington for a solemn funeral while the entire nation

Lyndon B. Johnson. (Courtesy Democratic National Committee)

and, indeed, the world, stunned with grief, went into deep mourning.

But the wheels of government ground on as Vice-President Lyndon B. Johnson now assumed the highest office in the land. Taking his oath of office in Air Force One, the presidential jet, in Dallas before taking off for the capital, Johnson attempted to provide continuity and stability in the face of this unexpected crisis.

Suddenly the eyes of the entire nation were on Johnson. Although a well-known public figure, many Americans wondered what kind of man he was. Born near Stonewall, Texas, on August 27, 1908, in a farm family, he was a descendent of Central Texas pioneers. Five years later his parents moved to Johnson City, which his grandfather had founded, and he attended local schools. Working his way through Southwest Texas State College, he graduated in 1930 and for two years worked as a public school teacher in Houston. But his real vocation was politics. In 1935, a year after he married Claudia Taylor (Ladybird), he became secretary to United States Representative Richard M. Kleberg from Texas and was selected by President Roosevelt as Texas director of the National Youth Administration. Two years later he was nominated by the Democrats for a vacant House seat and won election and re-election to it until 1948. Throughout these years Johnson showed himself to be an exceptionally loyal follower of Franklin D. Roosevelt and the New Deal. In 1948 he narrowly won the Democratic primary nomination to the United States Senate (by eighty-seven votes out of a total of one million cast) and secured election in November. In the Senate he soon (1953) became the Democratic floor leader and showed himself to be unusually skillful in this capacity, with a special gift for working out compromises. He was re-elected to a second term as United States senator in 1954, and became one of the most powerful Senate leaders in history. Thus, in 1960 he was an avowed aspirant to the Democratic presidential nomination, which he lost to John F. Kennedy. But to the surprise of many, he was willing to accept a place as vice-president. In this capacity he showed a surprising ability to play a subordinate role. He shunned the limelight and carefully deferred to the chief executive.

LYNDON B. JOHNSON AND
THE GREAT SOCIETY AT HOME

Once entrusted with the powers of the presidency, Johnson showed great relish in assuming his responsibilities. In domestic affairs he soon displayed the sure hand of political mastery. During his first year in office, through adroit maneuvers and his extensive personal contacts, Johnson was able to secure legislative approval for most of the measures Kennedy had not been able to steer through Congress. But Johnson was not satisfied with merely completing the unfinished business of his predecessor. He devised his own program for a Great Society, a comprehensive set of proposals far more sweeping than Kennedy's plans for

New Frontiers. Indeed, his recommendations for reform were perhaps greater than any ever proposed in the United States. They included a war on poverty, plans for continued economic growth, improvement of conditions for blacks, an attack on urban problems, and a concerted drive to increase social security. Johnson's skills with Congress led to the enactment of many of his recommendations. Few could foresee in 1964, however, that the president's diplomatic difficulties would undermine his domestic programs and create such deep divisions in the nation as to vitiate his effectiveness as chief executive. More than any other single policy, Johnson's decision to resort to limited war to contain pro-Communist influences in Vietnam overshadowed his many constructive achievements.

ECONOMIC STABILITY

Lyndon Johnson was keenly aware of the federal government's responsibility to maintain economic stability. Thus his administration took varied measures to sustain the nation's prosperity. The president was extremely loath to authorize a tax increase and did not sanction the 10 per cent surtax on income levies until late in 1968. Meanwhile, Congress increased minimum wage levels from $1.25 per hour to $1.60 an hour and took long steps toward the lessening of unemployment. The Manpower Development and Training Act of 1964 was designed to train the unskilled or technologically displaced worker in new skills. A similar purpose was accomplished for young people by the Job Corps. Another measure toward economic stability was the Appalachian Development Program of 1965, which was designed to widen economic development and job opportunities in eleven states of Appalachia, designated as a depressed area.

A key element of Johnson's economic policies was the War on Poverty. Begun in the Economic Opportunity Act of 1964, this far-ranging program was based on three major phases. The first was a Youth Program, to be carried out by a Job Corps, by direct federal grants, and by a work-study program. The Job Corps was designed for young people between sixteen and twenty-one years of age who had dropped out of school, or who were without work. Brought together in training centers, about 100,-000 individuals each year received instruction in new skills that would enable them to hold a steady job. Federal grants were also made to private agencies that provided work or training for another 200,000 disadvantaged youths. Colleges and universities received federal aid to administer a work-study program that made part-time jobs available to students so that they could continue their education. A second phase of the War on Poverty included the urban and rural community action program. Federal monies were paid to private and public community agencies that were engaged in finding employment for young people, or in providing education, improvement of slum conditions, or health services. A third aspect of the drive on poverty was establishment of rural poverty projects, through which federal loans were authorized for low income farm families and migratory farm workers to improve their property, housing, health, and education. Congress created an Office of Economic Opportunity (OEO) to administer these various projects.

CIVIL RIGHTS

The president was passionately committed to the cause of civil rights and to many of the aims of the black revolution. Apart from expressing sympathy with the movement, Johnson wrung three important acts from Congress in this sphere. First came the Civil Rights Act of 1964, which symbolized the hopes of so many whites and blacks. It outlawed discrimination in hospitals, restaurants, hotels, and employment, and authorized the withholding of federal funds to secure compliance. The Voting Act of 1965 protected black Americans in the full exercise of their voting rights in national, state, and local elections, and proved especially effective in the South. In addition, the Housing Act of 1968 provided for the enforcement of fair, non-discriminatory practices in buildings constructed with federal aid and protected civil rights workers who sought to oppose racial discrimination in housing.

Despite these efforts and the administration's War on Poverty, racial unrest increased during the last three years of Johnson's presidency. To a large extent, the civil rights movement and the cause of integration became moribund as Black Power and separatist oratory captured the imagination of many black Americans, particularly the younger generation. To be sure, no single black leader could speak for his people as a whole, nor did black citizens unite on common goals or a common program. Malcolm X (until his death in 1965), Stokeley Carmichael of the Student Non-Violent Coordinating Committee (SNCC) in 1966 or H. Rap Brown in 1967, and the Reverend Martin Luther King all proved to be charismatic figures. However, they were unable to win the loyalty of a great majority of their people. Nevertheless, an increasingly larger minority of black Americans came to acquiesce in guerrilla warfare against whites, believing that somehow, in some way, this would improve their condition. Such tactics were reflected not only in spiralling crime statistics, but also in the racial conflagrations that broke out during the summer of 1967 in Detroit and Newark (July 1967), characterized by arson and mass looting. These uprisings were ultimately quelled only by large numbers of National Guardsmen. On July 27, 1967, President Johnson appointed a Special Advisory Commission on Civil Disorder headed by Governor Otto Kerner of Illinois to look into the causes of these upheavals. In a series of interim reports the commission recommended increased recruiting of black Americans for the National Guard and appealed to whites for an end to racism. Meanwhile, Cleveland, Ohio, and Gary, Indiana, elected their first black mayors, as Carl B. Stokes and Richard Hatcher (respectively) revealed the increased political power being wielded by black Americans.

URBAN PROBLEMS

Black Americans also benefited from Johnson's great awareness of problems of the cities. Conscious that the limited tax funds of metropolitan areas were inadequate to deal with their difficulties as three-fourths of the nation became urban, Johnson brought the federal government's vast financial resources into play. Five legislative measures were designed to help the cities. The War on Poverty as elaborated in the Economic Opportunity Act of 1964 focused on the lessening of one of the cities' major problems — the rapid increase of the urban poor whose ranks were multiplied as technology made unskilled individuals jobless while eliminating the need for farm labor. The provisions of the Economic Opportunity Act bore directly on urban poverty. A second group of measures included the Urban Mass Transportation Acts of 1964 and 1966, which provided for federal funds to help localities build new means of rapid transit, and also highways, to relieve the heavy traffic congestion that was choking the thoroughfares of most major metropolitan areas. A third step to provide urban aid was the Model Cities Act of 1966. This act stipulated payment of federal monies for the fight on urban problems and was specifically directed to slum areas to improve housing, health, education, job training, recreational facilities, welfare, and transportation. A fourth measure was the Rent Supplement Act of 1966, under which the Department of Health, Education and Welfare made grants to low-income families to supplement their rents in the hope of rapidly improving their housing. Finally, the Safe Streets and Crime Control Act of 1968 provided for federal grants to states and localities to aid them in improving law enforcement.

Related to the improvement of urban living conditions, but extending also to the countryside, were many of the conservation policies of the Johnson era. The Air Quality Acts of 1965 and 1967 made federal grants available to local agencies for fighting air pollution. The Water Quality Act of 1965, the Clean Water Restoration Act of 1966, and the Solid Waste Disposal Act of 1965 were all designed to provide for improved water purification and sewage treatment plants. Federal grants for creation of urban recreational areas and parks were also available. Under Johnson, the process of providing massive federal aid to the cities to enable them to cope with their pressing problems thus was well under way.

SOCIAL REFORMS

The social reform programs of President Johnson were also comprehensive. Never before had the federal government invested so heavily in education. The Elementary and Secondary School Acts of 1965 and 1966 allowed federal monies to be spent for books in private and in public schools, and for other aids to improve teaching and learning. The Higher Education Act of 1965 allowed for liberal loans and scholarships to aid college students, while making construction money available to college and university administrations. In 1965 Congress also authorized a Teacher Corps to improve the training of teachers and their placement in areas where they were needed. In addition, the Educational Opportunity Act of 1968 provided financial help for poor youths seeking a college education, and the Adult Education Act of 1968 had similar provisions for older people.

Another significant area of social reform during the Johnson era was federal support of health care, a long-time demand of reformers. In 1965 Congress authorized the establishment of Medicare, an insurance program for Americans over sixty-five years of age to cover hospital and doctor costs, administered under the Social Security program. Also related was the Medicaid program of 1965, which stipulated special funds to cover medical costs of the needy. Other laws like the Health Professions Act of 1963 sought to stimulate training of more doctors and nurses, and to establish more mental health centers. Few measures reflected President Johnson's humanitarian zeal better than the laws affecting health, education, and welfare.

Unfortunately, the preoccupation of the Johnson administration with its problems of foreign policy and the War on Poverty led it to neglect federal support for cultural programs. Since 1961, the National Council for the Arts had been making federal grants to symphony orchestras, drama groups, and artists to encourage their activities. In addition the Fulbright program sponsored visits by foreign students and scholars in the United States while enabling their American counterparts to go overseas. Partly because of the acrimony produced by the Vietnam war, President Johnson's relationship with the nation's intellectuals became increasingly strained during his presidential tenure. Certainly the financial pressures for economy exerted by the war led the chief executive and Congress to reduce expenditures for what they considered to be nonessential spheres. Support of cultural activities was one of these. In 1967 and 1968 funds for the National Council for the Arts and the Fulbright program were drastically reduced, amounting to no more than nominal appropriations. Federal support for the arts became one of the first casualties of the Vietnam war.

ACHIEVEMENTS OF JOHNSON'S DOMESTIC POLICIES

Despite setbacks and shortcomings, however, the domestic accomplishments of the Johnson administration were many. It maintained prosperity, reduced unemployment, and inaugurated a full-scale War on Poverty. It began an attack on urban blight as related to a whole range of problems besetting the big cities, and it fostered the conservation of natural resources. It expanded federal social welfare programs and extended them into education and health, and it significantly furthered many demands of black Americans. Yet Johnson's presidency constituted a paradox. John F. Kennedy had far fewer legislative accomplishments to his credit during his occupancy of the White House, but even before his assassination he was well on the way to capturing the imagination of a majority of the American people, who lent him their support for achievement of his hopes and dreams. Lyndon B. Johnson, on the other hand, secured more constructive laws and programs during his tenure as chief executive than most presidents; yet after 1965 a majority of Americans actively came to distrust and to dislike him. The reasons for this irony were twofold. As a master politician and manipulator, President Johnson was often less than candid with the American public and increasingly lost their confidence. And, in addition, many of his foreign policies, especially American intervention in Vietnam, detracted from his accomplishments in the domestic sphere.

LYNDON B. JOHNSON AND
THE GREAT SOCIETY ABROAD

Indeed, Johnson's prestige as president began to falter largely as a result of his diplomatic policies. Europeans became increasingly critical of the United States policies in Vietnam, and only grudgingly cooperated with NATO. American relations with Russia were less tense than a decade earlier, although Johnson could not find solutions for fundamental areas of disagreement. American support of the Congo government against a rebel faction was viewed by many Africans with disfavor. The failure of the Alliance for Progress in hastening large-scale economic and social change in Latin America was — rightly or wrongly — often blamed on the United States. Johnson's effort to retain a neutral stance during the Arab-Israeli War of June 1967 only earned him further hostility in the Arab world. But overshadowing all other problems of foreign policy during the Johnson era was American intervention in Vietnam. More than any other single issue it proved to be the undoing of a president.

Lyndon Johnson clarified his foreign policy aims during the

presidential campaign of 1964. Unlike his Republican opponent, Senator Barry Goldwater, Johnson urged a prudent course in the conduct of diplomatic negotiations in the Truman and Eisenhower manner. His goals, he noted, were to strengthen the United Nations and to reduce Cold War tensions. In addition, he hoped for large-scale American economic aid to poor and underdeveloped nations, and an expansion of world trade. He opposed use of nuclear weapons and counseled patience and moderation in dealing with international crises wherever they might occur. Most Americans in the presidential election of 1964 approved of such a stance and expected Johnson's deeds to follow his words.

EUROPEAN POLICY

Without doubt, President Johnson's preoccupation with the Vietnam war led him to neglect American interest in Europe. Somewhat inexplicably, he made no effort to maintain the good will toward the United States that President Kennedy had fostered and failed to make a personal trip to visit the various European powers. Consequently, the bonds between the United States and NATO weakened considerably in the Johnson era. American proposals for MLF (a nuclear-armed multi-lateral force) in 1964 aroused particular hostility from the French. American efforts to achieve full integration of NATO military and naval units met similar opposition, for many Europeans still feared the Germans and were apprehensive about Soviet opposition to these projects. A real blow to the effectiveness of NATO came in February 1966 when General De Gaulle ordered the withdrawal of all United States military forces and bases under NATO from France within a three-year period (by April 4, 1969). With some reluctance, but having little choice, the Johnson administration acquiesced.

Many of the controversies surrounding NATO stemmed directly from worsening relations between the United States and France. President De Gaulle not only had a personal dislike for Lyndon B. Johnson, but also was seeking to strengthen France's prestige as a great power, and hoped to unify western Europe under French rather than American leadership. Such motivation prompted De Gaulle's opposition to MLF. Moreover, the French government argued that NATO detracted from the effectiveness of the United Nations and was obsolete, suggesting that it should even be abandoned. At times De Gaulle threatened to take France out of NATO before the end of the decade, although he resigned as president of France (1969) without taking this drastic step.

THE UNITED STATES AND RUSSIA

If many Europeans between 1963 and 1969 showed less adherence to NATO than they had a decade earlier, this was partly due to a thawing of the Cold War in Europe and an improvement in the relations between the United States and Russia. In fact, some observers felt that the two superpowers had established a détente. Various events underscored the lessening of tensions already evidenced by the Nuclear Test Ban Treaty of 1963. In 1964 the two nations worked out agreements for closer cultural exchanges involving teachers, researchers, and artists. American and Soviet technicians also collaborated in a project for the desalination of sea water under a mutual agreement. Both countries signed a new consular treaty allowing for the opening of additional consular offices in each other's territories. Other agreements during 1964 included a joint understanding not to place nuclear war heads into orbit and to exchange weather information. The American public was perhaps most conscious of a new direct "hot line" established between Washington and Moscow to allow instant communication between government leaders of the two countries in the event of a crisis.

The improved tone in relations between the two great powers was also reflected in the United Nations. For a time, the United States had been insisting that Russia be deprived of its votes in the Assembly because of failure to pay United Nations dues in 1964 and 1965. But Ambassadors Adlai Stevenson (who died in 1965) and Arthur Goldberg agreed to a compromise allowing voluntary contributions to the world organization, a solution that averted a direct Soviet-American confrontation. And while the Soviets clearly supported the North Vietnamese in their struggle to drive Americans out of Asia, they used relative restraint in attacking United States policy. During the Arab-Israeli war of June 1967 the United States and Russia again found themselves in a clash with divergent interest, but both used caution in an effort to prevent the struggle from erupting into a major world-wide conflagration. As if to symbolize the lessening of Russo-American tensions, later that month (June 23 – 25, 1967) Soviet Premier Aleksei N. Kosygin personally met President Johnson at Glassboro, New Jersey, where they had amiable, if inconclusive, conversations.

LATIN AMERICA

In Latin America, United States foreign policy attempts to further collaboration and to contain Communism continued to falter. Throughout the Johnson era Fidel Castro strengthened his regime in Cuba and experienced moderate success in exporting his brand of revolution to various South American nations. In 1967 one of his most trusted confidants, Ernesto ("Che") Guevara, was killed in Bolivia as he led a guerrilla band in a vain hope of overthrowing the established government there. Meanwhile, the Alliance for Progress program moved at a snail's pace, largely because so many entrenched interest groups in respective South American countries were extremely wary of supporting significant social or economic changes.

Unfortunately much of the good will that Kennedy had been seeking to foster was lost by President Johnson through hasty United States military intervention in Santo Domingo during April 1965. That strife-torn island was plunged into turmoil by a revolution against its ruling military junta. According to some rumors, Fidel Castro and perhaps Communists were supporting the rebels. Consequently, on April 28, 1965, President Johnson sent a contingent of United States Marines to Santo Domingo to protect American property. But most Latin Americans interpreted the action as a move by the United States to support the ruling military junta and to maintain the status quo. Although American troops left the island in September 1966, and although President Johnson met with leaders of twenty Latin American countries in Punta del Este, Uruguay, in April 1967, this military intervention reinforced many long-standing fears of Latin Americans and placed new strains on their relations with the colossus to the north.

VIETNAM

Easily the overriding issue in the Johnson policies both at home and abroad, however, was the limited war being waged by the United States in Vietnam. This major problem was compounded by what many observers considered to be President Johnson's duplicity, his "credibility gap." There seemed to be an enormous difference between what he said and what he did, between his public statements and the policies he actually carried out. While speaking consistently of peace and de-escalation of the war, as commander in chief he continued to escalate the conflict to drive for a decisive military victory and to step up United States participation. Moreover, his policies in Vietnam brought no success. After five years of heavy fighting the North Vietnamese were stronger than ever. And the South Vietnamese government proved itself unable to rally a majority of the Vietnamese people to its side. By 1968 the United States was spending more than $30 billion in Vietnam annually, more than 30,000 young Americans had lost their lives, and yet Communist influence there had not been contained to any appreciable extent. No wonder that the issue of Vietnam came to be the Achilles heel of the Great Society.

Under Johnson the course of American intervention in North Vietnam closely paralleled the development of the Korean War in the days of Harry S. Truman. American involvement went through four stages. First came a period of American advisement (1961 – 1964); this was followed by a period emphasizing defense (1964 – 1965); as North Vietnamese incursions of the south continued, United States forces took an offensive stand (1965 – 1966); and as a clear-cut victory eluded American commanders, the war settled into a costly stalemate (1966 – 1970). Like Korea, the Vietnam intervention emphasized the frustrations and shortcomings of the limited war doctrine.

Advisement

As he moved into the White House, President Johnson hoped to continue his predecessor's policy concerning Vietnam. This required a severely limited direct United States involvement, emphasizing advisement for the Vietnamese. It also included economic support of the South Vietnamese government as a means of containing the spread of Communist influence in the area. But American policy failed to accomplish this goal.

Americans fighting in Vietnam. (U.S. Army photo)

Defense — Tonkin Gulf Resolution

As North Vietnamese attacks on the United States military advisors in the south and in the Gulf of Tonkin increased during 1963 and 1964, the president asked Congress for authorization to retaliate with force, inaugurating a period of defense. On August 28, 1964, Congress enacted the Gulf of Tonkin Resolution, supporting United States military reprisals against North Vietnamese aggression. Nevertheless, Johnson publicly urged the utmost restraint. His speeches during the presidential campaign in the fall of 1964 contrasted sharply with those of Senator Barry Goldwater, the Republican presidential candidate. Goldwater urged full-scale war, including American use of nuclear weapons in Vietnam, mass bombings of Northern Vietnam, and perhaps even of Communist China. He advocated a large-scale military effort by the United States to win a quick and decisive victory over Ho Chi Minh and the Viet Cong, the military arm of the North Vietnamese government. On the other hand, Johnson pleaded for a limited war with conventional weapons and avoidance of provocative air strikes, and he made explicit disclaimers about any great commitment of United States military forces. President Johnson's overwhelming electoral victory in November 1964 was interpreted by many as an endorsement of his stance emphasizing a minimum of direct American military involvement on the mainland of Asia by a majority of the American people.

Escalation

To the surprise of most Americans, however, by January 1965 Johnson seemed to have abandoned his moderate position on Vietnam, as he began large-scale escalation of the war and a period of offense. Perhaps he was prompted by the steadily deteriorating American and South Vietnamese military situation there; or perhaps he was coming to rely more heavily on his military advisors. In any case, he undertook two measures that led the United States into a full-fledged war. First, after the Viet Cong attacked the United States military base at Pleiku (South Vietnam) in February 1965, he ordered American bombing of North Vietnam, especially of the supply routes being used by the Viet Cong to infiltrate to the south. Then he ordered 50,000 additional American troops into the area to join the 23,000 military advisors already there.

Nevertheless, President Johnson insisted that he was seeking negotiations. In an important speech at Johns Hopkins University on April 7, 1965, he reiterated the American commitment to the independence of the South Vietnamese, but expressed his great desire to negotiate unconditionally with the North Vietnamese. He also offered $1 billion of United States economic aid to develop Southeast Asia once the fighting stopped. A few months later on June 25, 1965, when he addressed a United Nations Conference in San Francisco, the chief executive repeated his hopes for negotiations. But in late July of 1965 he ordered a significant increase of American troops in Vietnam — from 75,000 to 125,000 men.

Stalemate

Between 1966 and 1970 many observers agreed that the war in Vietnam had developed into a costly stalemate. On the one hand, the North Vietnamese obviously lacked the military power to drive the United States out of Southeast Asia. But the United States, despite its "search and destroy operations," could not stop Communist infiltration of the south nor exert sufficient force to bring them to enter into genuine negotiations. And the United States refrained from an actual invasion of the north partly because it feared a massive retaliatory attack by Communist China. Thus, the war became like a treadmill, alternating between peace efforts and escalated fighting.

In January 1966 President Johnson embarked on another diplomatic campaign to secure peace. Through foreign embassies he let it be known that the United States was willing to negotiate on the basis of the Geneva Agreement of 1954, under which the major powers (Great Britain, France, and Russia) had pledged themselves to support creation of an independent Vietnam. But American and North Vietnamese interpretations of the Geneva accords differed, and Johnson's efforts resulted in naught. In the following month the president made a dramatic flight to Honolulu, where he conferred with Premier Nguyen Kao Ky and other South Vietnamese leaders. Then, in October 1966, Johnson made a tour of the non-Communist Far East to rally support for the American presence in Vietnam, visiting South Korea, Australia, New Zealand, and the Philippines. Meanwhile, vicious ground fighting and American air raids over North Vietnam continued, and the president ordered 225,000 additional American troops into the area, bringing the total to over 400,000. By this time as many as 300 Americans were being killed weekly, with many more maimed or wounded.

Over the next two years the situation did not change appreciably. United States bombing of North Vietnam was intensified, including its capital Hanoi, which was previously off-limits. By 1968 the president had dispatched an additional 100,000 Americans to fight in the jungles of Vietnam, where by then more than 100,000 Americans had been killed or wounded. In October 1967 President Johnson again offered to stop all bombardment of North Vietnam if it would negotiate in good faith, but Ho Chi Minh, believing that time and world opinion were on his side, rejected the proposal. Instead, at Christmas time, 1967, the North Vietnamese launched the Tet offensive, which inflicted heavy losses on United States and South Vietnamese forces while endangering many American positions. In addition, it resulted in North Vietnamese gains in the countryside.

Negotiations

Indeed, by 1968 it had become clear to many Americans that escalation of military activities was unlikely to result in a viable political solution in Vietnam. Despite the presence of more than one-half million American troops in Vietnam, the possibility of a settlement was more remote than ever. Amid the increasing unpopularity of the Vietnam war in the United States and around the world, in March of 1968 President Johnson made a dramatic move. In a television address to the nation he announced that he would not be a candidate in the forthcoming presidential elections, and that he had ordered a unilateral temporary halt to American bombing of North Vietnam in the hope of initiating peace negotiations. This action evoked a favorable response in most non-Communist areas of the world. Perhaps conscious of world opinion, in April 1968 the North Vietnamese agreed to send representatives to Paris to meet with American delegates to discuss conditions concerning a possible armistice. These negotiations proceeded at an agonizingly slow pace as the North Vietnamese often appeared to use the weekly sessions mainly for purposes of propaganda. After almost a year of such discussions a definite agreement still was not forthcoming. Meanwhile the fighting raged with no lessening of intensity.

Both President Johnson's public statements as well as his executive actions provoked a great debate in the United States over the course of the nation's foreign policies. Among the many positions that were discussed, four stood out. Many members of the New Left, especially those belonging to the Students for a Democratic Society (SDS), advocated immediate American withdrawal and openly demonstrated on many college campuses in favor of a North Vietnamese victory. Claiming that the American presence in Vietnam was immoral, they also sent supplies to Communists and their sympathizers. During 1965 and 1966 one of their leaders, Professor Staughton Lynd, visited Hanoi to display his sympathy for the North Vietnamese. At the other extreme was a group of "hawks" urging immediate escalation of the war and possible use of nuclear weapons. Believing in the domino theory — that the fall of South Vietnam would trigger the collapse of other pro-western governments in Asia — Barry Goldwater and Senator Walter Russell of Georgia became spokesmen for this view, urging a quick and decisive victory. Between these poles two other segments of opinion crystallized. A large number of prominent figures urged stabilization of United States military activities in Vietnam, and a greater emphasis on negotiations. The most important critic of the Johnson policies was Senator J. William Fulbright, chairman of the United States Senate

Committee on Foreign Relations. Former Lieutenant-General James M. Gavin, Columnist Walter Lippmann, and Professor Hans Morgenthau of the University of Chicago were other vocal spokesmen for the position that the United States had no real interests in Vietnam. Finally, the supporters of President Johnson's policies became increasingly more vocal as the popularity of their cause lagged. They included Secretary of State Dean Rusk and presidential assistants McGeorge Bundy and W. W. Rostow, who felt that the United States was committed to contain Communist expansion in every quarter of the globe.

RESULTS OF JOHNSON'S POLICIES

The results of Johnson's diplomacy were far-reaching. Very likely, the debacle in Vietnam led the president to retire from the presidency voluntarily, for his loss of popularity was so great that his re-election was in doubt. Over and beyond the effect of Johnson's personal career were the divisions that United States intervention brought in American society. As no other issue, the Vietnam conflict created bitter tensions between many groups. In particular, the Johnson policies aroused the hostility of young adults on the nation's campuses. Draft card burning and protest meetings became more common. But opposition to the war also crystallized other student grievances. These erupted in riots and mass demonstrations at the University of California in Berkeley during April 1964, leading to the suspension of classes. In the ensuing years the pattern at Berkeley was repeated at scores of other colleges and universities, with one of the most serious disruptions at San Francisco State College in 1968. Students were demanding an end to government-sponsored university research related to the war effort and an end to on-campus recruiting by the CIA or large corporations. In some instances they demonstrated against racism or simply to secure power over all aspects of their education. Whatever the reason, opposition to the war served as a catalyst in stimulating their unrest.

The economic impact of the war was also significant. Federal expenditures for the armed forces in Asia averaged $30 billion annually, creating new inflationary pressures that affected the entire economy. Moreover, war industries were especially stimulated. Such economic effects could not fail to influence the administration's social programs, despite frequent denials by the president himself. Without question, many of President Johnson's Great Society programs faltered because of heavy American commitments in Vietnam. The War on Poverty, expansion of health services, and extended federal aid to education were only a few of the programs probably limited by war expenditures. And the Johnson administration's determination to cut all non-military expenses (such as federal aid for cultural activities) affected most phases of domestic life. Finally, the moral issues raised by American intervention in Vietnam led some administration critics to claim that the war brutalized many Americans, making them insensitive to traditional American ideals of democracy and self-determination.

In contrast to achievements of his domestic program, then, President Johnson experienced many frustrations in his foreign policies. None could equal the disappointment of American intervention in Vietnam, which profoundly affected so many diverse aspects of American life. But it also embittered public opinion against the United States in almost every portion of the globe and made effective American diplomacy more difficult. In Europe, NATO appeared to be dissolving while deep cleavages between the United States and Russia and its East European bloc continued. The achievements of the Alliance for Progress in Latin America were hardly encouraging. Arab hostility toward the United States was on the increase. And neither the goals nor the methods of American diplomacy seemed clearly defined during the Johnson administration. Foreign policies, together with disturbing domestic issues, left the nation more bitterly divided than it had been perhaps for a hundred years.

ELECTION OF 1968

Amid a gloomy atmosphere in 1968, preparations for the presidential election in the fall went forward. The first announced candidate for the Democratic presidential nomination was Senator Eugene McCarthy (Minnesota), who declared himself unalterably opposed to President Johnson's Vietnam policies. Favoring some form of negotiated settlement, McCarthy was the first major public figure who had the courage to speak out openly against United States policy in the Far East. Few took his candidacy seriously in early 1968, but his popularity proved to be astounding. Capturing the loyalty of many young people, his greatest triumph came in the New Hampshire Democratic presidential primaries during March 1968, when he received more votes than the president or Senator Robert Kennedy. In other state primaries (Oregon) he revealed considerable strength and suddenly emerged as a serious contender. Very likely his strong showing was a factor in leading President Johnson to announce his retirement. Certainly, it also prompted Senator Robert Kennedy to enter the presidential race. Hitherto unwilling to challenge what had been assumed to be President Johnson's impregnable political power, Kennedy declared himself a contender for the Democratic presidential nomination within a week after the New Hampshire primaries.

Kennedy's entry into the race had several results. It badly split the critics of Johnson's Vietnam policies, and at the same time it seemed to win the support of many black Americans who placed great trust in him. Their patience was particularly tried in May 1968 when an assassin, James Earl Ray (in Memphis, Tennessee), tragically killed Martin Luther King, the revered leader of the Southern Christian Leadership Conference and one of the outstanding black Americans in the world. While tensions mounted and sporadic violence erupted throughout the country, the black community maintained restraint. The entire nation mourned his death.

Yet the incident served to fan racial tensions and to improve the chances of a presidential aspirant such as Robert Kennedy, who inspired confidence among black people. Thus, in May 1968 Kennedy won a majority in the Oregon primaries and early in June repeated this feat in the important state of California. Celebrating his primary election victory on the evening of June 7, 1968, at the Hilton Hotel in Los Angeles, Kennedy was just leaving the hotel through a back door when he was suddenly attacked by an assassin who fired three times at short range. Senator Kennedy fell, bleeding profusely, mortally wounded. While his aides pounced upon his murderer, a stunned radio and television audience listened and watched with horror. The assailant proved to be Sirhan Sirhan, a Jordanian immigrant who reportedly hated Senator Kennedy for his sympathetic attitudes toward the state of Israel. As the Kennedy family mourned the death of another son, the nation lost another one of its most dynamic public figures.

The ensuing campaign for the presidency developed much as many political observers had predicted. Meeting in Miami Beach, Florida, in August 1968, the Republicans nominated Rich-

ard M. Nixon for the presidency on the first ballot, easily over-
coming Nelson Rockefeller and George Romney. To everyone's
surprise, Mr. Nixon picked Spiro Agnew, the little-known governor of Maryland, as his running mate. The Democratic National
Convention in Chicago during August 1968 proved to be much
more turbulent. To prevent disruption by various New Left
groups such as the Yippies, Mayor Daley of Chicago had taken
elaborate precautions to station extra police in the downtown and
convention areas, giving the city the appearance of an armed
camp. Despite several clashes between police and demonstrators,
the proceedings ran on much as planned. Senator Eugene Mc-
Carthy received less support than expected as the convention
nominated Vice-President Hubert H. Humphrey (Minnesota) for
the presidency, and Senator Edmund H. Muskie (Maine) for second place on the ticket.

*The fight over integration: Governor George Wallace confronts
Nicholas Katzenbach. (Wide World Photos)*

A third party also entered the field — the new American
Party organized by former Alabama Governor George M. Wallace, who became its presidential candidate. Wallace hoped to
win at least one-fifth of the nation's votes in the hope of creating

a tie between the major parties, thus leaving it to the House of Representatives to choose a president. Humphrey and Muskie campaigned hard in the ensuing months, while Richard Nixon conducted a well-organized campaign that steered away from specific promises on most issues. The results of the election were very close. Richard M. Nixon was the winner, with 31,770,237 votes, less than a 1 per cent majority over the 31,270,533 ballots received by Hubert Humphrey. Governor Wallace did not fare as well as expected, drawing 9 million votes (12 per cent of the total), most of which came from southern states. The contest proved to be one of personalities rather than of issues, and did not commit the United States to any great changes either in domestic or in foreign policies.

NIXON

In the ensuing months both Lyndon B. Johnson and Richard M. Nixon cooperated closely to effect an extraordinarily smooth transition. In Paris, the peace negotiations with the North Vietnamese languished, but in Washington the members of the new administration were striving for efficiency. President Nixon revived many of the intergovernmental committees that had fallen into disuse with the return of the Democrats under Kennedy, especially the National Security Council. Revealing a much greater desire than Lyndon Johnson to knit close ties between the United States and Europe, during the last week of February 1969 he toured the major western European capitals, where he received a warm reception. His initial approach to the problems of the presidency was characterized by prudence and caution, qualities that made a favorable impression on most Americans and many Europeans.

Americans of diverse political persuasions found a common ground for rejoicing in July of 1969 with the landing of Apollo 11 on the moon. This long voyage fulfilled the dream of John F. Kennedy, who had hoped that the United States could be the first nation to explore that planet before the end of the decade. In a dramatic flight characterized by near perfection in a multitude of technical and human operations, on July 20, 1969, the crew of Apollo 11 — consisting of Commander Neil Armstrong, Colonel

Edwin E. Aldrin, and Lieutenant-Colonel Michael Collins in the command module — effected a perfect landing on the Sea of Tranquility. Armstrong became the first man to walk on the moon, as he uttered words soon to become famous: "That's one small step for man, one giant leap for mankind." He and Aldren spent two hours and twenty-one minutes on the moon's surface, gathering dust and rocks for analysis by scientists on earth. President Nixon talked to the astronauts on the moon by telephone while perhaps more than 50 million Americans watched the entire operation on their television sets. Throughout the world the feat was hailed as one of the great scientific triumphs of the modern age.

But America's spectacular space explorations only diverted the minds of many individuals temporarily from the very pressing domestic and foreign problems faced by the Nixon administration. Among these, inflation was prominent. During 1969 the cost of living rose by more than 7 per cent to reach all-time highs. At the same time, interest rates rose more rapidly than in any previous period, as banks were demanding a 9 per cent rate for home mortgages, leading to a serious slump in the construction industry. Consequently, by April of 1969 President Nixon and his advisors began to map an anti-inflation program to halt spiraling prices. Masterminded by Arthur F. Burns, who became chairman of the Federal Reserve Board in February 1970, the administration's proposals centered on tax reforms. Nixon urged a plugging of tax loopholes, and revisions affecting large corporations and very wealthy individuals. But when Congress received the plan in April of 1969, it proceeded to emasculate the recommendations beyond recognition, as scores of special interest groups converged upon the capital. The tax reform bill enacted by Congress in December of 1969 was a bundle of compromises that pleased no one. It provided for a reduction of the surcharge on individual income taxes from 10 to 5 per cent, closed a few of the more glaring tax loopholes, and reduced the oil depletion allowance from 27.5 to 23 per cent. At the same time, it stipulated a small increase of personal income tax exemptions and authorized a rise in social security benefits. Whether in its final form the measure effectively combated inflation was questionable.

President Nixon's caution was also evident in his handling of welfare and civil rights problems during his first years in the

Richard M. Nixon. (Courtesy Republican National Committee)

White House. In August 1969 he took the initiative in recommending to Congress a significant revision of the nation's welfare programs. Perhaps the most striking feature of the chief executive's proposals was his plea for adoption of a minimum guaranteed income for every American family. In addition, he urged that persons on public welfare should be provided with incentives to seek suitable employment. Expansion of federal training programs would be designed to aid the accomplishment of these objectives. As for civil rights, various members of President Nixon's staff made public statements in 1969 in which they questioned the desirability of bussing children to integrated schools uniformly throughout the nation. Attorney General John Mitchell's policy of slowing the pace of school integration in the South especially angered significant segments of the black community.

It also aroused many whites, although President Nixon confidently declared in November of 1969 that he felt himself to have the support of the "silent majority" in the United States.

More than any other president since Herbert Hoover, Nixon experienced serious problems with the United States Senate in securing ratification of major appointments. To fill a United States Supreme Court vacancy occasioned by the resignation of Abe Fortas, because of conflict of interest, President Nixon nominated federal Circuit Court Judge Clement Haynesworth of South Carolina. The move was viewed by many as a special gesture to southern Republicans who had been of great help in the election of 1968. Haynesworth's record as a civil rights advocate was not impressive and his career was not free of blemish. Consequently, a furious debate broke out in the United States Senate, which in November of 1969 refused to provide the necessary confirmation. Thereupon President Nixon presented the name of Harold Carswell of North Carolina for the post, to be rebuffed again by the Senate just a few months later.

But perhaps the most controversial member of Nixon's circle was Vice-President Spiro Agnew. To the surprise of many, this once relatively unknown political figure emerged as an extremely outspoken advocate of the Nixon policies. In numerous speaking engagements throughout the country Agnew attacked dissident college students, extremist advocates of civil rights or welfare, and critics of United States involvement in Vietnam. Some of his sharpest barbs were aimed at the news media, however, whom he accused of seriously distorting the presentation of contemporary events. No less biting was his condemnation of "effete snobs," a term he used to describe American intellectuals who were vehement critics of the Nixon policies. Many Republicans rejoiced in Agnew's bluntness and his effort to "tell it as it is." To his opponents he was one of the most disliked spokesmen for the Nixon forces.

Certainly the most important single problem faced by President Nixon was American involvement in Vietnam. More than any other issue in domestic or foreign affairs, the question of Vietnam continued to divide the American people sharply. Little progress was made at the Paris negotiations between representatives of the United States and North Vietnam between 1968 and 1970. Meanwhile, in June of 1969 President Nixon sought to

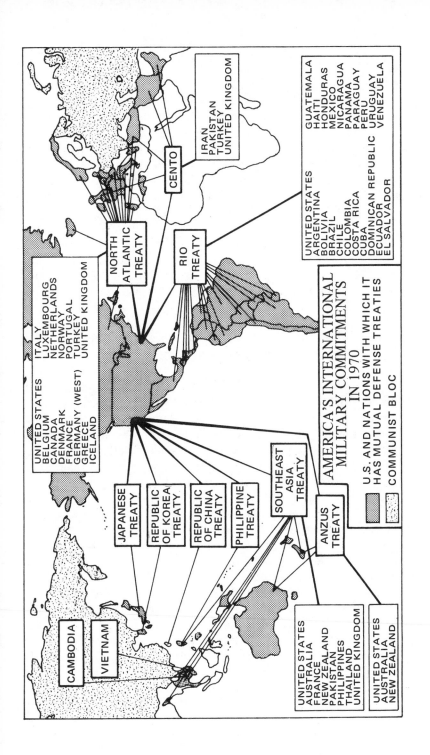

AMERICA'S INTERNATIONAL
MILITARY COMMITMENTS
IN 1970

U.S. AND NATIONS WITH WHICH IT
HAS MUTUAL DEFENSE TREATIES

COMMUNIST BLOC

NORTH ATLANTIC TREATY

UNITED STATES
BELGIUM
CANADA
DENMARK
FRANCE
GERMANY (WEST)
GREECE
ICELAND
ITALY
LUXEMBOURG
NETHERLANDS
NORWAY
PORTUGAL
TURKEY
UNITED KINGDOM

CENTO

IRAN
PAKISTAN
TURKEY
UNITED KINGDOM

RIO TREATY

UNITED STATES
ARGENTINA
BOLIVIA
BRAZIL
CHILE
COLOMBIA
COSTA RICA
CUBA
DOMINICAN REPUBLIC
ECUADOR
EL SALVADOR
GUATEMALA
HAITI
HONDURAS
MEXICO
NICARAGUA
PANAMA
PARAGUAY
PERU
URUGUAY
VENEZUELA

JAPANESE TREATY

REPUBLIC OF KOREA TREATY

REPUBLIC OF CHINA TREATY

PHILIPPINE TREATY

SOUTHEAST ASIA TREATY

ANZUS TREATY

CAMBODIA

VIETNAM

SOUTHEAST ASIA TREATY

UNITED STATES
AUSTRALIA
FRANCE
NEW ZEALAND
PAKISTAN
PHILIPPINES
THAILAND
UNITED KINGDOM

ANZUS TREATY

UNITED STATES
AUSTRALIA
NEW ZEALAND

take the initiative toward a gradual American withdrawal by announcing that 25,000 United States troops in Vietnam would be sent home (of approximately 600,000 there). This was to be the beginning of a long-range program designed to place the main burden of the war as well as pacification on the government of South Vietnam. If the president believed that his action would make the North Vietnamese negotiators in Paris more conciliatory, he was mistaken, for in ensuing months they remained as intractable as ever. Within the United States, however, his action appeared to soften the critics of the administration's Southeast Asia policies, especially when in December of 1969 he ordered the withdrawal of an additional 50,000 men from Vietnam. The moderation of anti-war critics was reflected in their national Vietnam Moratorium Day activities on November 15, 1969, not only on the nation's campuses but also in the peaceful march in Washington. Toward the close of 1969 it seemed as if the difficult problems of environmental imbalance were taking the place of Vietnam in the concerns of a large segment of America's youth.

During 1969 the administration's views also seemed to prevail in other aspects of the nation's defense policies, particularly the construction of an ABM missile defense system. The president strongly supported the creation of new weapons detection facilities early in 1969, to cost more than $3 billion. Nixon believed this to be a necessary step to keep up with the rapid progress of the Soviet Union in weapons development and to provide Americans with maximum security against attacks by foreign powers. Opponents of the ABM scheme were vociferous, however. They questioned the true effectiveness of the ABM plan in providing protection, and thought its cost to be prohibitive. Above all, they believed that adoption of the proposal would tend to disrupt disarmament talks just then beginning between the United States and the Soviet Union, and so would contribute to the heightening of international tensions. The debate on the ABM system ranged inside and outside of Congress. In early August 1969, by a narrow margin, the United States Senate approved the construction of a modified ABM plan, to be built during the seventies at a cost of at least $1 billion.

But the calm which President Nixon appeared to have brought the nation during his first year in office was rudely shattered by events during the spring of 1970. In late April and May of that year the country was plunged into violence and turmoil. The immediate occasion for strife was President Nixon's announcement on the last day of April that United States troops would enter Cambodia for a period of six weeks to destroy what was believed to be the headquarters of the North Vietnamese fighting in Vietnam. Top officials in the Pentagon for years had advocated such a course of action, and the president's decision was widely interpreted as a victory of military men over civilians in the shaping of American diplomacy. Reaction to the president's announcement was particularly violent on the nation's college campuses, of which more than 200 witnessed student disturbances and strikes during the first weeks of May. Governors in many states called out the National Guard to restore order. It was in the midst of one such confrontation at Kent State University in Ohio that National Guardsmen fatally shot four students on May 4, 1970. This action brought a widespread revulsion among large segments of the nation and resulted in the closing of many colleges and universities. By the summer of 1970, the nation appeared to be as divided as ever.

SUMMARY

By 1970 it was clear that the American people would face one of the most critical periods in their history as they sought to reach some of the New Frontiers of the Great Society. The years since World War II had witnessed far-reaching and accelerated changes — changes so great that they wrought a veritable transformation of American civilization. In 1960 John F. Kennedy — in advance of many of his contemporaries — caught a glimpse of the revolutionary era heralding the future. The goals he visualized in formulating his plans for new frontiers were to remain a dream for him — and nothing more — in view of his short lifetime. He envisioned unprecedented accomplishments in space, the abolition of poverty, an age of racial harmony, model cities, social welfare, rising levels of cultural life, and international cooperation and peace. Americans wished him well in his journey to achieve these ends, a journey he could not complete because of his untimely death. His successor, Lyndon B. Johnson, did not lose sight of the vision, and proved himself remarkably effective in implementing many goals of the New Frontier. His own program for a Great Society took long strides toward attaining some of John F. Kennedy's goals including technological progress in space travel, and federal programs to lessen poverty, racial injustice, urban blight, and social insecurity. But the difficulties President Johnson encountered in his foreign policies, above all the war in Vietnam, seriously vitiated his entire domestic program. And Richard Nixon experienced very similar problems. Obviously a bitterly divided nation could not proceed well on the path toward New Frontiers of the Great Society. Only a united people could weather the severe shocks in domestic and foreign affairs to which the United States was subjected. The achievement of such unity thus emerged as the greatest and most pressing task before the nation.

The experiences of John F. Kennedy, Lyndon B. Johnson, and Richard Nixon only underscored the extraordinary difficulties that Americans faced in seeking to adjust their values and institutions to the revolutionary currents loosed by the advent of a technological society. The technological revolution ushered in the age of mass production and the computer; the economic revolution created the affluent society and underlay the attack on poverty; the urban revolution moved the mainstream of American life from the country to the city; the social revolution stimulated the formation of an egalitarian society; the black revolution not only elevated the status of black Americans but also threatened to cause some disruption; and the cultural revolution brought recreation and amusements, once reserved for a select few, to the average man and the masses. In the 1960's these profound changes in American life were rapidly gathering momentum and effecting the transformation of the industrial America of 1890 to the technological America of 1970. Only the future could tell how well Americans in the last three decades of the twentieth century would deal with the many difficult and perplexing problems resulting from this great transition, one of the most remarkable in the long history of man.

FOR FURTHER READING

On the Kennedy years ARTHUR SCHLESINGER, JR., *The Thou-sand Days* (Boston: Houghton Mifflin, 1965) is an excellent, if highly sympathetic, appraisal by a historian who was also a participant. THEODORE C. SORENSEN, *Kennedy* (New York: Harper & Row, 1965) contains recollections by a close presidential assistant. A detailed balanced analysis of the Cuban crisis of 1961 is in ELIE ABEL, *The Missile Crisis* (Philadelphia: Lippincott, 1966). An indictment of American policy is MARIO LAZO, *Dagger in the Heart: American Policy Failures in Cuba* (New York: Funk & Wagnall's, 1968); an insider's view is by ROBERT KENNEDY, *Thirteen Days: A Memoir of the Cuban Missile Crisis* (New York: Norton, 1969). Source materials are in DAVID L. LARSON (ed.), *The Cuban Crisis of 1962* (Boston: Houghton Mifflin, 1963). A moving, if controversial, account of President Kennedy's assassination is in WILLIAM S. MANCHESTER, *The Death of a President* (New York: Harper & Row, 1967). Less satisfactory is Jim Bishop, *The Day Kennedy Was Shot* (New York: Funk & Wagnall's, 1968). On Lyndon B. Johnson see ALFRED STEINBERG, *Sam Johnson's Boy* (New York: Macmillan, 1968); a somewhat caustic and interesting collection of material is in *The Great Society Reader* edited by M. E. GETTLEMAN and DAVID MERMELSTEIN (New York: Random House, 1967). ERIC F. GOLDMAN, *The Tragedy of Lyndon Johnson* (New York: Knopf, 1969) is an abrasive estimate by a disillusioned presidential assistant. The most incisive appraisal of the Vietnam embroglio is in the books of BERNARD B. FALL, *Viet-Nam Witness, 1953 – 66* (New York: Praeger, 1966), and *Hell in a Very Small Place* (Philadelphia: Lippincott, 1966).

INDEX

485

486

487

Cather, Willa, novelist, *190*
Catholics, *16, 30, 39, 178, 181, 182, 183, 204, 438, 440*
Censorship in World War I:
by British, *114*
in U.S., *129-130*
Central Intelligence Agency (CIA), *404, 431, 447, 448, 469*
Central Pacific in World War II, *307, 311-312, 316*
Central Powers in World War I, *120, 145*
Chain stores, *176*
Chambers, Whittaker, ex-Communist, and Alger Hiss case, *258-259, 406*
Chateau-Thierry, U.S. troops at, *132*
Chautauquas, *31*
Chemical industry, *175, 177*
Chesapeake and Ohio Railroad, *354*
Chiang Kai-shek, *321, 348, 417, 432*
Chicago, *10, 17, 35, 36, 42, 46, 47, 64, 161, 184, 192, 213, 223, 287, 331, 333, 353, 384, 472*
Chicago Federation of Churches, *47*
Chicago race riot of 1919, *155*
Chicago *Tribune*, *182*
Chicanos, *363*
Child care centers, *336*
Child labor:
as issue, *36, 55-56, 68, 169*
prohibition, *250*
Children:
in World War II, *331-332*
1945-1960, *359-360*
Children's Bureau, *68*
Chile, *107*
China, *81, 93, 101, 109, 112, 145, 198, 215, 276, 277, 280-281, 285, 287, 291, 319, 321, 341, 345, 348, 417, 418, 429, 432, 447, 450, 451, 465, 467*
Chrysler, *207, 443*
Chuikov, Vasili, defender of Stalingrad, *309*
Churches:
in early twentieth century, *29-30*
in 1920's, *185-186*
in World War II, *334-335*
Churchill, Winston, and U.S. policy in World War II, *290, 304, 305, 307, 314, 340, 341, 342, 346, 347, 412-413*
CIA, *404, 431, 447, 448, 469*
Cincinnati, Ohio, *47, 65*
Cities, *33*
in Progressive era, *44-51*
in 1920's, *159, 160, 177*
in depression, *223-224, 246*
in World War II, *330-332*
1945-1960, *351*
urban problems, *381-387, 443, 457-458, 479*
City government in Progressive era, *44-46*

City problems in early twentieth century, *25*
City-manager plan, *46*
Civil Aeronautics Act of 1938, *247*
Civil Aeronautics Board, *247*
Civil liberties:
in World War I, *129-130*
in World War II, *323*
Civil rights:
in New Deal, *259*
in World War II, *330*
1945-1970, *408, 409, 444, 446, 456-457, 475-476*
Civil Rights Acts:
of 1957, *372, 424*
of 1964, *372, 456*
Civil rights legislation, *256-257, 372, 424, 456*
Civil Rights March of 1963 (Washington), *369*
Civil rights movement, *367, 371, 372, 374*
Civil service, *23, 64*
Civil Works Administration (CWA), *240, 243, 270*
Civilian Conservation Corps (CCC), *240, 256, 270*
Clark, Champ, and Democratic Convention of 1912, *70*
Clark, Mark, U.S. military commander, *311*
Clark Memorandum, *281*
Clark, Reuben, *281-282*
Clark, Sue Ainslee, muckraking journalist, *35*
Class conflict in U.S., *265*
Clayton Act of 1914, *76, 77*
Clayton-Bulwer Treaty, *97-98*
Clean Water Restoration Act of 1966, *458*
Cleaver, Eldridge, Black power advocate, *370, 371*
Clemenceau, Georges, French statesman, *138, 141, 142-146*
Cleveland, Ohio, *16, 17, 43, 46, 47, 333, 384, 457*
Closed Door policy of Japan, *292*
Closed shop, *408*
Coal, *4, 125, 206, 362*
conservation, *63*
Coal industry, *173, 177*
Coal miners and poverty, *359-360, 362*
Coal strikes:
1902, *65*
1919, *154-155*
Codification of statutes, in states, *53*
Cohan, George M., composer, *132*
Cold War diplomacy, *411, 412-414*
debate over origins, *419-420, 447, 461, 462*
Collaboration:
U.S. and international, *281, 282, 287-293, 297-298*

489

Corruption, political:
  in early twentieth century, *22-23,
    24, 35, 36, 45*
  in 1920's, *164-166*
  and Harry S. Truman, *401*
Cosmopolitan, 35
Costigan, Edward, and anti-lynching
  bill, *256*
Cotton:
  1919, *153*
  in 1920's, *172*
  in 1930's, *238*
Cotton States Exposition, *41*
Coughlin, Charles E., radio priest,
  225, 244, 251, 258, 260, 287
Council of Europe, *415*
Council of Four, *141*
Council of National Defense, *125*
Council of Ten, *141*
Court packing plan, *254*
Cox, James M., Democratic presi-
  dential candidate in 1920, *161*
Cozzens, James G., writer, *393*
CPI (*see* Committee on Public
  Information)
Crane, Stephen, writer, *29*
Credibility gap of Lyndon B.
  Johnson, *464*
Creel, George, *129-130, 324*
Crime:
  in early twentieth century, *18, 35,
    46*
  in 1920's, *184*
  in depression, *214, 219*
  1945-1970, *358-359, 379, 382,
    386-387, 458*
"Crime in the Streets" law (1968),
  386
Crimea, *340*
Crisis, *42*
Crisis of 1919, *147-156*
  domestic, *152-157*
  economic crisis, *153-154*
  foreign, *147-151*
  political crisis, *152-153*
  social crisis, *154-156*
Crissinger, Daniel R., and Federal
  Reserve Board, *163*
Cruse, Harold, Black Power advocate,
  370, 371
Cuba, U.S. policy and:
  in early twentieth century, *87-89,
    90-92, 97*
  in 1930's, *285*
  1945-1970, *431, 432, 441, 448-449*
Cuban missile crisis, *448-449, 450*
Cullen, Countee, poet, *187*
Cultural life:
  in early twentieth century, *3, 7, 18,
    25-31*
  in 1920's, *189-195*
  in 1930's, *265-269*
  in World War II, *334-339*

1945-1970, *387-399, 445-446, 470,
  479*
Cultural revolution, 1945-1970, *351,
  387-395, 437, 441, 480*
Cummins, Albert, governor of Iowa in
  Progressive era, *43, 44*
Currency stabilization, international,
  Hoover and, *279*
Curriculum in schools during World
  War II, *335*
Czechoslovakia, *143, 148, 276, 342,
  347*

Daily Worker, 265
Dallas, Texas, *452, 453*
Damone, Vic, vocalist, *391*
Damrosch, Walter, conductor, *192*
Danzig, *146*
Dardanelles, *138*
Darrow, Charles, and Scopes trial, *185*
Darwin, Charles, influence in U.S., *26,
  27, 29, 185, 193*
Daugherty, Harry, *161, 163, 164, 165*
Davies, Benjamin E., first black U.S.
  Army general, *333*
Davies, Joseph E., diplomat, *336*
Davis, Elmer, and Office of War
  Information, *324*
Davis, Stuart, painter, *394*
Dawes Commission, *196*
Day, William R., diplomat, *90*
Dayton, Ohio, *46*
Dayton, Tennessee, *185*
D-Day, *314, 422*
DDT (dichlor diphenyl trichlorethane),
  329
Dearborn Independent, 182
DeA. Reid, Ira, in Black Cabinet, *255*
Debs, Eugene, *71, 72*
  in World War I, *129-130, 167*
Debtors, protection, *219*
Debts, international, *279*
Declaration of the United Nations,
  318
Defense, Department of, *404*
Deficit financing, in New Deal, *242-
  243*
DeForest, Lee, inventor, *175*
De Gaulle, Charles, *450*
  in World War II, *322, 450, 461-462*
De Kooning, William, painter, *394*
De Lesseps, Ferdinand, engineer, *98*
De Lome, Dupuy, Spanish diplomat,
  88
De Lome Letter, *88-89*
Demobilization:
  after World War I, *151, 157*
  after World War II, *401-402*
Democracy, *123, 277-278*
Democrats, *22, 23, 24, 52, 70, 139,
  147, 148, 150, 151, 225, 226, 232,
  233, 262, 400, 409, 410, 421, 438,*

490

Democrats—cont'd
440, 441, 443, 446, 454, 471-473
in 1920's, *161*
Denmark, and Virgin Islands, *97, 290*
Dennis, Lawrence, American Fascist, *263*
Dennis v. *United States,* sedition trial, *407*
Denver, Colorado, *47*
Department of Agriculture, *7, 63, 64, 235*
Department of Commerce, *255*
Department of Commerce and Labor, *61*
Department of Defense, *404*
Department of Health, Education and Welfare, *458*
Department of the Interior, *235, 255*
Department of Justice, *165, 166, 167, 169, 185, 324, 407, 443*
Department of Labor, *68, 235, 255*
Department of the Navy, *295*
Department of State, *235, 295, 425*
Department of War, *235, 240, 295, 333*
Depressed regions, *360, 362, 455*
Depression, *31, 304, 423*
of 1921, *167*
and Herbert Hoover, *212-215*
in 1930's, *231-274*
Des Moines idea, *45*
Destroyer deal of Franklin D. Roosevelt, *289*
Detective stories and popular culture, *390*
Detroit, Michigan, *43, 47, 155, 223, 260, 331, 333, 373, 384, 386, 457*
Detroit Bar Association, *48*
Dewey, George, commands U.S. fleet in Philippines, *89*
Dewey, John, philosopher, *39*
Dewey, Thomas E., Republican presidential candidate, *323, 408, 409, 410, 421*
De Wolfe, Florence, President Harding's wife, *163*
Diaz, Porfirio, Mexican ruler, *106*
Dietary habits in U.S., *172*
Digital computers, *353*
Diplomacy, New:
aims and methods, *86-87*
framers, *84-86*
reasons for, *80-83*
Diplomacy, U.S.:
in early twentieth century, *80-111*
reasons for, *80-83*
U.S. and Europe, *82, 86, 87*
U.S. and Far East, *86, 87, 90*
U.S. and Latin America, *81, 82*
in 1920's, *195-200*
U.S. and Europe, *196-197*
U.S. and Far East, *197-199*
U.S. and Latin America, *199-200*

in 1930's, *275-299*
U.S. and Europe, *278-280, 283-284, 288-291*
U.S. and Far East, *280-281, 284-285, 291-297*
U.S. and Latin America, *281-282, 285-286*
in World War II, *303-322, 339-349*
1945-1970, *410-420*
U.S. and Europe, *412-416, 427-429, 450, 461-463*
U.S. and Far East, *416-419, 432, 451-464, 469, 476-478*
U.S. and Latin America, *416, 430-432, 447-449, 463*
Middle East, *429-430*
Africa, *451*
Diplomatic warnings, *116*
Direct election of U.S. senators, *24, 52, 68*
Direct primary in states, *52*
Di Salle, Michael, politician, *375*
Disarmament:
in 1907, *100*
in 1920's, *197, 198*
and Herbert Hoover, *223, 278-279, 280*
Discrimination, racial, *366, 367, 372, 450*
Disease control, *56*
Disillusionment after World War I, *195-200, 283*
Displaced Persons Act of 1950, *410*
Dissent:
in New Deal, *257-264*
in World War II, *324*
District of Columbia, *221, 222, 444*
Disunity in U.S., *469, 470, 476, 479, 480*
Division in American society, *469, 470, 476, 479, 480*
Divorces, *214*
Dixiecrats, *409*
Dixon-Yates contract, *423*
Documentaries, *267*
Doenitz, Karl, German admiral, *307, 342-343*
Doheny, Edward L., *165-166*
Dollar diplomacy, formulated under W. H. Taft, *103*
Domino theory on Vietnam, *468*
Dos Passos, John, writer, *191, 265, 337*
Douglas, Paul, economist, *251*
Draft, military:
in World War I, *129, 131*
in World War II, *288-289, 380*
draft protests, *469*
Drama:
in 1920's, *191-192*
in 1930's, *266*
in World War II, *337-338*
1945-1970, *393*

491

Dreiser, Theodore, writer, *29, 337*
Drought of 1930, *220-221*
Drugs and medicines in World War II, *329*
Drugs, use of, *355, 378-379, 385, 386*
"Drys," *183-184*
Du Bois, William E. B., publicist and historian, *41, 189, 269*
Dulles, John Foster:
life, *425, 447, 449*
as Secretary of State, *424-433*
Dumbarton Oaks Conference, *340*
Dumbbell tenement, *46*
Du Pont, E. I., *175*
Du Pont family, *262*
Dust Bowl, *221*
Dutch East Indies, *306*
Dylan, Bob, singer, *391*

East Berlin, *427*
East Germany, *427, 428*
building of Berlin Wall, *450*
East Saint Louis, Illinois, race riot (1919), *155*
East Village (New York City), *379*
Eastman, George, and cloth cutting machines, *11*
Eastman, George, developer of Kodak camera, *14*
Eastman, Joseph, transportation expert, *239*
Eberhart, Richard, poet, *393*
Economic aid, by U.S. to Europe, 1945-1970, *414-415*
Economic changes, *3*
Economic changes in World War II, *326-329*
Economic controls in post-World War II era, *402*
Economic Cooperation Administration, *415*
Economic crisis after World War I, *153-154*
Economic depression, *153-154*
Economic growth:
in early twentieth century, *3-8*
in 1920's, *170-177*
in 1930's, *236-252, 257-258*
in World War II, *325-329*
1945-1970, *440, 442-443, 446, 455-456*
Economic interests, U.S., *123, 124, 296*
Economic Opportunity Act of 1964, *455, 457-458*
Economic revolution, 1945-1970, *351, 356-364, 388, 480*
Economics, as a discipline in early twentieth century, *39*
Education:
in early twentieth century, *30-31, 56-57, 65*

in 1920's, *219*
in New Deal, *244*
in World War II, *335-336*
1945-1970, *366, 367, 382, 387, 388, 391, 392, 402*
federal aid, *408, 410, 424, 443, 458-459, 470*
Educational opportunities, *17, 361, 362*
Educational Opportunity Act of 1968, *458-459*
"Effete snobs," Vice-President Spiro Agnew and, *476*
Efficiency, in Government, *53*
Egalitarianism, *374, 375-376*
Egypt, *429, 430*
Eighteenth Amendment, *184*
Eight-hour day, in World War I, *128, 167*
Eightieth Congress, *402*
Einstein, Albert, physicist, *194*
Eisenhower, Dwight David, *307, 309, 310, 314*
in World War II, *341-343, 346, 347*
election of 1952, *420-422*
life, *421-422*
domestic policies, *422-424*
foreign policies, *406, 416, 424-433, 438, 447, 461*
Eisenhower Doctrine, *430*
El Alamein, *307*
Elbe River, *342, 348*
Elderly Americans, *359-360, 364, 376-377* (*see also* Aged)
Elections:
1900, *90*
1912, *69-72*
1916, *120*
1918, *139*
1920, *152, 160-162*
1928, *203-204*
1932, *226-228*
1936, *244*
1948, *408-410*
1952, *419-422*
1964, *461, 465, 466*
1968, *470-473*
Electric appliances in 1920's, *174-175*
Electric power, *9*
Electronic computers, *353*
Elementary and Secondary School Acts of 1965 and 1966, *458*
Eliot, T. S., poet, *190*
Elk Hills, California, oil reserve, *166*
Elkins, William W., *12*
Elkins Act (1903), *38, 62*
Ellington, Duke, musician, *391*
Ely, Richard, economist, *39*
Embargoes, U.S. against Japan, *291*
Emergency Committee for Employment, *218*
Employment Act of 1946, *408*
Employment Service, *218*

492

494

495

497

Kahn, Herman, *427*
Kaiser, German, *113, 114, 132, 136, 143*
Kaiser, Henry J., *326-327*
Kamikaze planes, *344*
Kansas, *421*
Kansas City, *10, 400*
Katanga, *451*
Katsura, Taro, Japanese diplomat, *101*
Kaysen, Carl, and Kennedy administration, *441*
Keating-Owen Child Labor Bill, *77*
Kefauver, Estes, politician, *386*
Kelley, Florence, social worker, *36*
Kellogg-Briand Pact, *197, 275, 277, 280*
Kelly, William, iron manufacturer, *11*
Kennan, George F., *411, 420*
Kennedy, Edward, *440*
Kennedy, John F., *375, 436*
  administration of, *438-454*
  life, *438-440*
  and space exploration, *442*
  economic reforms, *442-443*
  social reforms, *443-444*
  political reforms, *444-445*
  and culture, *445-446*
  foreign policies, *446-452*
    Bay of Pigs, *447-448*
    Peace Corps, *448*
    Latin America, *448-449*
    Europe, *450*
    Africa, *451*
    Far East, *451-452*
  assassination, *452-453, 454, 460, 461, 473, 479, 480*
Kennedy, Joseph P., *438*
Kennedy, Robert, *440, 441, 449, 471*
Kennedy, Rose, *438*
Kent, Rockwell, artist, *193*
Kent State University, *479*
Kentucky, *362*
Kerner, Otto H., politician, *457*
Kerouac, Jack, beat writer, *378-379*
Keynes, John Maynard, *243, 270*
Khaki Shirts, *263*
Kimmel, Husband E., at Pearl Harbor, *295*
Kincaid, Thomas C., and Pacific fleet, *343*
King, Ernest J., U.S. naval leader, *307, 319*
King, Martin Luther, civil rights leader, *367, 369, 370, 457, 471*
Kipling, Rudyard, writer, *83*
Kissinger, Henry, and nuclear strategy, *427*
Kleberg, Richard M., and Lyndon B. Johnson, *454*
Klineberg, Otto, social psychologist, *334*
Knights of Labor, *8*
Knox, Philander C., *61-62, 103, 148*

Knoxville (Tenn.), *155*
Knudsen, William S., *325*
Kodak camera, *14*
Konoye, Fumimaro, Japanese diplomat, *292*
Korea, *101, 276, 335, 417, 418, 432, 451*
Korean War, *417-419, 464*
Korematsu v. *United States,* and civil liberties, *325*
Kosygin, Aleksei N., Soviet Premier, *463*
Krushchev, Nikita, Soviet leader, *428, 449, 450*
Ku Klux Klan, *181-182, 400*
Kurile Islands, *341*
Kurusu, Saburu, Japanese diplomat, *292-293*
Kwajalein, *311*
Ky, Nguyen Kao, *467*

Labor, policies:
  in early twentieth century, *8, 65*
  in World War I, *128-129, 153*
  in 1920's, *167, 217*
  in New Deal, *249-250, 269*
  1945-1970, *357-358, 408*
Labor Department (U.S.), *155-156*
Labor legislation, Progressive era, *55-56, 70*
Laconia, 121
La Follette, Robert M., progressive leader, *34, 43, 44, 52, 69, 70, 122, 161, 172*
La Follette Seamen's Act of 1913, *77*
La Follette-Costigan Bill, *219*
Laissez faire, *22*
Lake Nicaragua, *98*
Language training in World War II, *335*
Lansing, Robert, Secretary of State, *124, 140*
Lansing-Ishii Agreement, 1917, *109*
Laos, *451*
Latin America, U.S. policy:
  in early twentieth century, *96, 104, 108, 112*
  in 1920's, *199-201*
  in 1930's, *275, 278, 281-282, 285-286*
  in World War II, *306*
  1945-1970, *412, 416, 426, 430-432, 433, 447-449, 452, 460, 463, 470*
Laval, Pierre, French diplomat, *222, 279*
Lawson, Thomas J., muckraker, *35*
League to Enforce the Peace, *137*
League of Nations, *138, 142, 145, 146, 148-149, 150, 162, 197, 200, 276, 280, 281, 340*
Lebanon, *430*
Left-wing groups, in New Deal, *258-262*

499

500

501

National Credit Corporation, *217*
National Defense Act of 1938, *288*
National Farmer's Holiday Association, *224*
National Farmer's Union, *238*
National Grange, *238*
National Guard, *154, 457, 479*
National health insurance, 424
National Housing Act of 1949, *410*
National Housing Conference, *219*
National income, *206*
National Industrial Recovery Act, *236* and labor, *239, 249*
National Labor Board, *239*
National Labor Relations Board, *249-250*
National Labor Union, *8*
National League, *372*
National Monetary Commission, *67, 75*
National Origins Act of 1924, *169, 181, 196, 197*
National Packing Company, *62*
National Recovery Administration, *236-237, 240, 256, 269-270*
National reform, in Progressive era, *58-78*
National security, *98, 276, 286, 413*
National Security Act of 1947, *404*
National Security Council, *473*
National Security Resources Board, *404*
National Union for Social Justice, *260*
National Urban League, *42, 367*
National War Labor Board, World War I, *128, 152*
National War Labor Policies Board, *128*
National Youth Administration (NYA), *244, 255, 270, 454*
Nationalism:
  U.S., in 1898, *82*
  Europe, in 1914, *112-113, 143*
  cultural, in U.S. of 1930's, *265-268, 273*
Nationalists, *148*
Nativism, *178, 181-183*
NATO, *415-416, 422, 428, 429, 450, 460-462, 470*
Naturalism, *26*
Naval disarmament, *198, 223, 280*
Naval War College, *85*
Nazis, *297, 324*
Nebraska, *167, 224, 246*
Negroes (*see* Black Americans)
Nelson, Donald, in World War II, *325*
Netherlands, *288*
Neutrality:
  U.S., in World War I, *113-123*
  1937-1941, *288, 298*
Neutrality Acts of 1936 and 1937, *282, 283, 284, 288*
Neutrality Proclamation, *117*

Neutrals, in World War II, *321-322*
Nevins, Allan, historian, *267*
New America, *3-32*
New Caledonia, Ohio, *162*
New Deal, *231-274, 406, 407, 408, 423, 424, 454*
  World War I precedents, *124, 226*
  Relief, *235-240*
  Recovery, *241-244*
  Reform, *244-254*
  economic policies, *236-239, 241-250*
  political policies, *253-254*
  social policies, *239-240, 250-253*
  and black Americans, *254-257*
  and protest groups, *257-264*
  impact of, *269-271*
New Deal coalition, *272*
New Diplomacy, in early twentieth century, *94, 100, 102*
New England, *206*
New Freedom, *71-72, 75*
  in New Deal, *245*
New Frontiers, *436, 481*
  John F. Kennedy and, *438-454*
  domestic policies, *440-446*
  foreign policies, *446-454*
New Grenada, *97*
New Guinea, *306, 312*
New Hampshire, *52, 422, 471*
New History, *194*
New Immigration, *16*
New Jersey, *43, 74*
New Left, *379-380, 468, 472*
New Masses, magazine, *265*
New Mexico, *52, 68, 121*
New Nationalism, *58, 71-72, 78, 130*
  in New Deal, *245*
New Order, *277*
New Orleans, Louisiana, *47, 192*
New Panama Canal Company, *98-99*
New York Armory Show (1913), *193*
New York *Call,* 156
New York Central Railroad, *6, 12, 13*
New York City, *12, 17, 37, 42, 46, 47, 56, 59, 186, 187, 192, 223, 332, 373, 379, 384, 386, 392*
New York *Journal, 82, 87*
New York medical licenses, *56*
New York Philharmonic Orchestra, *192*
New York Society for the Prevention of Crime, *47*
New York State, *43, 182, 232, 233, 251*
New York Stock Exchange, *6, 177, 205, 206, 211*
New York *Tribune, 90*
New York *World, 82, 87, 88*
New Zealand, *312, 467*
Newark, New Jersey, *457*
Newfoundland, *289, 290*
Newlands Act of 1902, *63*
Newspapers, and Treaty of Versailles, *148*

Population growth—cont'd
376-377, 381
Populists, 24, 52
Port Colombo, 95
Porter, William J., condemns the
Charleston, 179
Portland (Oregon), 47, 221, 333
Portsmouth (N.H.) Conference (1905),
101
Portugal, 198
Postal Savings Banks, 67
Postwar domestic problems, after
World War I, 151-157
Potsdam Conference (1945), 412-413
Pound, Ezra, poet, 191
Pound, Roscoe, legal reformer, 38
Poverty, 15, 16, 18, 26, 27, 35, 203,
205, 213-215, 216, 219, 220, 221,
261, 264, 359-364, 385, 437, 441,
455, 479
Power, public, in New Deal, 246-247
Power companies, 246
Power projects, 423
Powers, Gary, U.S. pilot, 428
Pragmatism:
and progressivism, 34, 38, 39
in 1920's, 193-194
Prague, 342, 347
Preferential presidential ballots, 52
Preparedness controversy in World
War I, 124, 131
Presidency, 22
in World War II, 322, 323-324, 422-
423
Presidential succession, 401, 404-405
Presidential Succession Act of 1947,
404-405
President's Committee on Civil Rights,
372, 410
President's Committee on Social
Trends, 219
President's Committee for Unem-
ployment Relief, 218
President's Council of Economic
Advisers, 408
Price-fixing:
in World War I, 125
in World War II, 327-328
Prices, after World War I, 153
Profiles in Courage, by John F.
Kennedy, 440
Progressive era, 33-79, 193, 254, 259,
286
Progressive Party:
of 1912, 53, 70
of 1924, 172
Progressive reform, 167, 245
Progressives, 249, 253, 409
Progressivism, 159-160, 163, 164, 248
Prohibition, 178, 183-185, 204
Prohibition Bureau, 185
Proletariat, 19
Prosperity, 1945-1970, 356-359

Prostitution, 46
Protest, 1945-1970, 377-380
Protest groups, and New Deal, 257-
264
Protest marches in Great Depression,
223-224
Protestant ethic, 178
Protestants, 16, 29-30, 38, 178, 182,
186
Protocols of the Elders of Zion, 182
Provincetown (Mass.) Players, 191
Psychology, 40, 194-195
Public education, 366, 367
Public health, 35, 56, 65
Public libraries, 30-31
Public opinion, in World War I, 129-
130
Public power, 423
Public schools, 391-392, 458-459
Public utilities, 53, 245
in New Deal, 245
regulation, 54
Public utility commissions, 54
Public Works, 204, 218, 233, 261, 423
Public Works Administration, 43, 256,
270
Pueblo, Colorado, scene of Woodrow
Wilson's collapse in 1919, 149
Puerto Plata, 95
Puerto Ricans, 383
Puerto Rico, 89, 90, 92, 383
Pulitzer, Joseph, publisher, 82
Pullman, George, 13
Pullman cars, 62
Pump priming in World War II, 327-
328
Punta del Este (Uruguay), 448, 463
Pure Food and Drug Act, 1906, 64
Puritan ethic, 33, 355, 425-426
and Calvin Coolidge, 168
Puritanism, 183, 184
Pyle, Ernie, journalist, 337

Quaker doctrine, 279
Quakers, 216, 219
Quarantine speech (1937), 287
Quemoy Island, 432

Race problems in World War II, 332-
334
Race riots,
1919, 155
in World War II, 333, 373, 457
Racial discrimination, 35, 366, 367,
372
Racial equality, 169, 332-333, 364-
374, 410
Racial integration, 369
Racial prejudice, 19
Racial pride, 364, 366, 370, 372-373
Racial segregation, 77, 131

506

508

514

Weyl, Walter, publicist, *34*
Weyler, Valeriano, Spanish commander, *87*
Wheat:
1919, *153*
in New Deal, *238*
White, Walter, black leader, *188, 189, 333*
White, William L., journalist, *337*
White Man's Burden, *81, 83*
Wilbur, Curtis D., progressive reformer, *48*
Wiley, Harvey, chemist, *64*
Wilkins, Roy, racial reformer, *367, 370*
Williams, Tennessee, playwright, *393*
Williams, William Appleman, revisionist, *420*
Willkie, Wendell, Republican presidential candidate, *324, 336*
Wilson, Edith Bolling, *113*
Wilson, Henry, diplomat, *140*
Wilson, M.L., agricultural expert, *234, 237-238*
Wilson, Woodrow, *43, 44, 161, 164, 166, 232, 235, 245, 250, 316, 324, 340, 345, 401, 425, 426*
as governor of New Jersey, *70, 74*
as president, *72-78*
personality, *74*
life, *72-74*
domestic policies, *75-78, 87*
foreign policies, 1913-1914, *97, 103-110*
World War I diplomacy, *117-123*
Wartime domestic policies, *124-130*
military policies, *130-135*
peacemaking and Versailles, *135-147*
and crisis of 1919, *147-158*
Wisconsin, *43, 52, 56, 182, 251, 406*
With the Marines at Tarawa, *338*
Witte, E. E., social welfare expert, *251*
Wolfe, Thomas, writer, *191, 266*
Women:
in 1920's, *179, 219*
in World War II, *332*
Women's Christian Temperance Union (WCTU), *183-184*
Women's suffrage, *53, 70, 77*
Wood, Leonard, Republican leader, *148, 160-161*
Woods, Arthur, philanthropist, *218*

Working class, *19*
Workmen's Compensation, *56*
Works Progress Administration, *243-244, 254, 270, 273*
Work-study program, *456*
World Court, *196-197*
World Island, *85*
World organization, *142, 149, 412*
World War I:
U.S. in, *33, 112-158, 189, 195, 196, 215*
and New Deal, *235-240, 246, 247, 278, 279, 282-284, 305, 320, 325*
World War II, *352, 364, 365, 375, 376, 420, 429, 436, 438*
U.S. in, *124, 248, 249, 270, 276, 284, 288, 294, 303-350*
Allied defense, *305-308*
Allied offense, *305, 308-313*
Allied victory, *305, 314-316*
domestic life, *322-339*
final phase, *339-349*
WPA Writer's Project, *267*
Wright, Richard, writer, *334*
Wyeth, Andrew, artist, *393*
Wyoming, *53*

Yalta Conference, *340-341, 406, 420*
Yardstick and TVA, *247*
Yellow journalism, *35, 81*
Yerkes, Charles T., streetcar magnate, *12*
Yippies, *380, 472*
Yorktown, *306*
Young, Whitney, and Urban League, *367, 370, 376-377*
Young Commission, *196*
Young Men's Christian Association, *38-39*
Young People's Socialist League, *259*
Youth groups, *236, 259, 359, 364, 376-377, 469*
Yugoslavia, *143, 314, 342*

Zaniecki, Florian, sociologist, *194*
Zelaya, Jose, president of Nicaragua, *102*
Zimmerman, Arthur, German minister to Mexico, *121*
Zimmerman Telegram, *121, 122*